I0235289

Praise for Directing Actors and Judith Weston

"Everything you taught me was more than useful. I am deeply grateful."—**ALEJANDRO GONZÁLEZ IÑÁRRITU**, *The Revenant, Birdman, Biutiful*

"Taking your classes gave me a base, a foundation, a framework to find my own style. To step out on faith."—**AVA DuVERNAY**, *When They See Us, Queen Sugar, A Wrinkle in Time, 13th, Selma, Middle of Nowhere*

"I am eternally grateful for your help."—**TAIKA WAITITI**, *Jojo Rabbit, Thor Ragnarok, Hunt for the Wilderpeople*

"Judith Weston is an extraordinarily gifted teacher. She doesn't so much explain as she changes your consciousness of the creative process and restores your confidence in it, through acting. A kit of concrete, practical tools to make the ineffable reachable, time and time again over many takes or performances."—**DAVID CHASE**, *The Sopranos, Northern Exposure, I'll Fly Away*

"Judith has had a profound effect on my work. I hear her voice often (probably daily) when it comes to my work."—**CAITRIONA BALFE**, *Outlander, Ford V Ferrari*

"Judith's method is wonderful because it is practical. She has given me numerous tools to solve problems on the set and to earn the trust of actors. Her classes and her book are invaluable resources to any director."—**LAWRENCE TRILLING**, *Goliath, Rectify, Parenthood*

"I took a seminar with an acting teacher named Judith Weston. I learned a key insight to character. She believed that all well-drawn characters have a spine, and the idea is that the character has an inner motor, a dominant, unconscious goal that they're striving for, an itch that they can't scratch. I took to this like a duck to water."—**ANDREW STANTON**, *Finding Dory, WALL-E, Toy Story* series, *Better Call Saul, Stranger Things*

"Directing my first movie would have been impossible without Judith's book, *Directing Actors*. Her insights taught me how to audition actors, how to cast intelligently, how to rehearse. When production began, I cribbed a set of Weston reminders on to a 3-by-5 index card, and kept it in my shirt pocket every single day of shooting. She saved me."—**BILLY RAY**, writer-director, *The Comey Rule, The Last Tycoon*; writer, *Captain Phillips, The Hunger Games*

"I love talking to Judith about story and character. She is truly interested in what make people tick and how that is the heart of storytelling."—**RITESH BATRA**, *The Lunchbox, The Sense of an Ending, Our Souls at Night*

"Not only is Judith my single best resource as a director, she's simply one of the best and most generous teachers I've ever had. I wish I could carry her with me every day."—**ANDREW JARECKI**, *The Jinx: The Life and Deaths of Robert Durst, All Good Things, Catfish*

"Judith clarifies the unique relationship between actor and director. She shows you how to promote an atmosphere of safety, allowing creative spontaneity between you and your actors. The value of this cannot be overstated. When you are free to explore ideas without fearing loss of control, great things can happen."—**VICKY JENSON,** *Shark Tale, Shrek*

"Judith Weston taught me how to listen—what she called 'listening with your whole body.' She taught me about the power and the magic of the subconscious world. She showed me doors and windows and portals into creative possibilities I scarcely knew existed. Her wisdom changed the way I write, the way I direct actors—and, with no exaggeration, the way I look at life."—**MARK FERGUS,** *The Expanse* (developed by); writer: *Children of Men, Iron Man;* director: *First Snow*

"I bought a copy of *Directing Actors* right before I directed *Ghost World.* Looking back through it today, the thing that struck me is how dog-eared and tattered it is, which speaks volumes about just how much I referred to it. It's a terrific book—concise, insightful, and practical—and has helped me enormously. Thanks Judith!"—**TERRY ZWIGOFF,** *Bad Santa, Ghost World*

"Judith Weston gave me the greatest gift you can give to a first-time director—she gave me confidence in my ability to work with actors. What my actors didn't know is that most of the brilliant direction I gave them was ripped straight from her book, *Directing Actors.*"—**SHANA FESTE,** *Run Sweetheart Run, Boundaries, Endless Love, Country Strong, The Greatest*

"What Judith shows you in her workshops and her book are simple and effective tools that help you get deeper and deeper into that rich, complex and surprising place."—**DAVID JACOBSON,** *Dahmer*

"Judith taught me to break down the humongous task of directing into smaller, doable steps. She encouraged me to look inside myself for the answers, and to trust my instincts and my passion."—**PATRICIA CARDOSO,** *Real Women Have Curves, Queen Sugar*

"Judith opened the secret door to the magic . . . What I once thought were 'happy accidents' and performance miracles are now the kernels of creativity I relentlessly pursue with an actor finding a performance."—**FRED TOYE,** *The Boys, Snowpiercer* (TV), *Watchmen*

"All the scary, transformative moments I had in Judith's class really paid off. And I can never begin to thank you for all that you've done for me. I'm simply not the same person I was when I started my journey with you."—**ANDREA TOYIAS,** voice director, Blizzard Entertainment, World of Warcraft/Diablo/Starcraft

"Judith Weston has inspired me to be interested in people more than concepts, behavior more than attitudes, process more than results. In her classes I've learned to ask more questions, to trust what is happening, and to always be willing to dig deeper. She is the kind of teacher who makes me excited about taking chances."—**NORMAN BUCKLEY,** *Sweet Magnolias, Pretty Little Liars*

"Thank you for being such a wise classy act."—**ALMA HA'REL,** *Honey Boy, Bombay Beach*

Directing Actors

Creating Memorable Performances *for* Film and Television

25th Anniversary Edition

Judith Weston

MICHAEL WIESE PRODUCTIONS

Published by Michael Wiese Productions
12400 Ventura Blvd. #1111
Studio City, CA 91604
(818) 379-8799, (818) 986-3408 (FAX)
mw@mwp.com
www.mwp.com

Cover design by Johnny Ink. www.johnnyink.com
Copyediting by Ross Plotkin
Interior design by William Morosi

Manufactured in the United States of America

First Printing 2021

Library of Congress Cataloging-in-Publication Data

Names: Weston, Judith, - author.
Title: Directing actors : creating memorable performances for film and television / by Judith Weston.
Description: 25th anniversary edition. | Studio City, CA : Michael Wiese Productions, [2021] | Summary: "Directing film or television is a high-stakes occupation. It captures your full attention at every moment, calling on you to commit every resource and stretch yourself to the limit; it's the white-water rafting of entertainment jobs. But for many directors, the excitement they feel about a new project tightens into anxiety when it comes to working with actors. In the years since the original edition of Directing Actors was published, the technical side of filmmaking has become much more easily accessible. Directors tell me that dealing with actors is the last frontier-the scariest part and the part they long for-the human part, the place where connection happens. Weston's books help directors scale the heights of the actor-director dynamic, learn the joys of collaborating with actors-and become an "actor's director.""-- Provided by publisher.
Identifiers: LCCN 2020041463 | ISBN 9781615933211 (trade paperback) 9781615933358 (casebound)
Subjects: LCSH: Motion pictures--Production and direction. | Television--Production and direction.
Classification: LCC PN1995.9.P7 W45 2021 | DDC 792.02/33--dc23
LC record available at https://lccn.loc.gov/2020041463

Table of Contents

CHAPTER FIVE:

CHAPTER SIX:

Preface to 25th Anniversary Edition

In Spring 1996, just a couple of months before I turned in the manuscript for the original *Directing Actors*, Sidney Lumet's *Making Movies* came out. I raced to my local bookstore. I read it in one sitting, enthralled by its depth, clarity, and loving attention to every aspect of film directing. I was overjoyed that it included an entire chapter on my particular obsession—how a good director works with actors. I revised my book to include quotes from his. I stood in line at a book event to get my already highlighted and dog-eared copy of *Making Movies* signed by Mr. Lumet, wondering whether, when I got to the head of the line, I'd have the courage to whisper to this icon of my field that I, too, was writing a book. I didn't.

At that time, there were very few books of any kind on film directing. Conventional wisdom held that directing actors was a mysterious art that could not be taught, a matter of intuitive talent—you either have it or you don't. I never expected *Directing Actors*, published twenty-five years ago, to become as successful as it has. I feared the concepts might seem extreme, even absurd, to veteran film professionals, at least the ones who thought they already knew everything.

Since 1988, I'd been teaching a workshop of my own design, Acting for Directors, which took directors—gently, one toe at a time—through acting exercises, in order to expose them to tools and principles that actors use to create believable performances, and to let them experience the thrill you can feel while acting.

It's a commonplace to say that the students taught the teacher, but I have lived the truth of that statement every day for thirty-five years. My students constantly challenged me: Why do I need to know this? How can I use this stuff? When Michael Wiese approached me to write a book, I'd been teaching Acting for Directors for six years and was understanding more and more about the barriers to communication between directors and actors.

It was not a given that directors would be interested in a book that was solely concerned with the challenges of directing actors. Michael—a hero and visionary—thought that such a book was worthwhile—and that I should be the one to write it.

As a teacher, I depend on interaction with my students and clients, and the lonely discipline of writing does not come naturally to me. I was motivated to complete the original *Directing Actors* because I was writing it for the people who had taken my workshops. I felt bonded to them. Acting is an experience of public intimacy and they had entrusted themselves to me—even when I was completely unknown as a teacher. I wanted them to carry my voice with them and to know that I respected the risk and tenderness of the workshop experience.

It was bewildering to me when *Directing Actors* entered the mainstream—writing it had felt so personal. I marveled that it became an Amazon bestseller. When I learned it was required reading at film schools, my first reaction, as an old counterculture warrior, was panic—had I somehow become *establishment?* I expected my ideas to appeal to a zealous fringe element—it concerned me that young directors would be encountering my book because they'd been *told* to read it. Would the ideas survive if they entered the brains of fledgling directors in the form of *an assignment?*

I didn't have time to brood. My daily life was the students in my workshops, and the challenge of shepherding them, individually and group by group, through what I sometimes described as a shift in consciousness from "result-orientation" to "process-orientation." An interview with a certain major Hollywood executive always bugged me: When asked what his movies were about, he would reply gleefully, "Asses in seats! That's what my movies are about: asses in seats!" I wanted to offer directors a different path. Of course I want their projects to entertain and succeed at the box office! But I want them to approach filmmaking on an emotional level; to know the joy of storytelling as a search for meaning in the human condition; and to experience artistic *connection* with their collaborators as one of life's great blessings.

In 2003, Michael published my second book, *The Film Director's Intuition*. He said he liked it that *Directing Actors* not only contained actionable advice for filmmakers but also touched on sources of creativity—and he wanted me to go further. I was excited to meet the challenge of taking the concepts of *Directing Actors* to a deeper level. Readers, especially writers, responded to it—I think because it went beyond the mechanics of performance and took the plunge into the topic of *subtext*.

Notwithstanding the good response to *FDI*, my first book, *Directing Actors*, remained my top-performing bestseller, and in 2009 Michael asked me to write a second edition to *DA*. This version was not to be—because, having faced medical challenges, I'd made a pledge to myself not to take on the stress and exhaustion of another writing deadline.

Then came April 2019. Michael and his intrepid second-in-command, Ken Lee, brought me a project I could not refuse: an audiobook version of *Directing Actors*. Readers had asked me for it; I'd always wanted to do it. I am an actor, so I knew I'd want to be the one to voice the words of my text.

I knew that after so many years, updates and rewrites were called for. I had a short deadline for the audiobook so I worked as fast as I could to revise and expand the text of the audiobook from the text of the original 1996 paperback. Once the audiobook was released in September 2019, Michael and Ken proposed this 25th Anniversary print edition. I continued revising and expanding to make this 25th Anniversary edition of *Directing Actors* as comprehensive as I could.

Of course, it's terrifying. Every day, readers of the original *Directing Actors* tell me how meaningful it is to them. I don't want to let them down! I want to lift them up. I want to add to their knowledge, understanding, and confidence.

Although I stopped teaching workshops in 2015, I am still active with one-on-one consultations for individual filmmakers, to assist them in script analysis preparation. But you never know—at some point I may retire. My goal is to make the principles even more accessible for new readers and return readers alike; to describe them in all their richness; to give my clients tools they can make their own, so they can think on their feet when I am not by their side. I've been driven with this 25th Anniversary Edition to give my readers, students, and clients my most complete distillation of everything I know—not so I can make you all mistake-proof—I know I can't do that—but so I can always be with you in spirit, whispering a new question in your ear, suggesting a new idea, challenging you to see any present disaster as an opportunity. Cheering you on.

What's New and Different from the Original

This 25th Anniversary Edition contains revisions that expand and clarify the central concepts of *Directing Actors*. Specific changes include, in Chapter One, for instance, three extra examples of Result Direction. But it would be fair to say that after paying close attention to the feedback and questions of my students, incorporating multiple updated examples from newer films and series, and burrowing further into my own imagination and understanding, I've broadened and deepened the material *on every page*. I hope the foundational concepts familiar to readers of the original edition feel recognizable—and at the same time, totally fresh and new. I have strived to enlarge, tighten, and clarify, until these complex ideas might feel, finally, like common sense.

Chapter Five (*Emotional Event*) is one of the chapters that I revised most extensively. My students have reported to me, over and over, that *emotional event* is a challenging concept. I feel that a sense of emotional event is the central skill that can change you from someone who *wants to be a director* to someone who *thinks like a director*, so I have committed to making this tool simpler, clearer, and more usable.

A big change to Chapter Seven (*Script Analysis*) is that the case-study scene used in the original book and the audiobook has been replaced by a scene from *The Matrix*. Wow. So very lucky and grateful to have gotten that permission! It's enabled me to make the script analysis process both deeper and simpler, and to reorganize my approach, top to bottom, so this chapter can function as a handbook that anyone can follow step-by-step.

My famous Short List of Active Verbs has been expanded and revamped, in Appendix A, with four columns instead of two. The Longer List of Verbs, in Appendix B, is now grouped by emotional category. My clients have been finding these new formats helpful. Appendixes A and B are discussed in Chapters One and Four.

The Script Analysis Guides in Appendixes C, D, and E are discussed in Chapter Seven—these new formats replace the Charts of the original *Directing Actors*.

Chapter Nine (*Rehearsal*) presented a singular challenge. In order to learn how to use rehearsal productively, you must practice—and until 2015 I offered workshops where directors and actors could practice rehearsal techniques under my guidance. When I closed my studio and stopped teaching workshops, I could no longer provide a venue for practice. So I reworked this chapter with great detail and specificity. I want it to be explicitly useful for teachers in film schools and private workshops—or as a guide for individual directors who wish to set up their own rehearsal practice workspaces.

At the request of many readers, I've added two new chapters: Chapter Eleven (*Directing Children*) and Chapter Twelve (*Comedy*). Other topics that readers ask me about—directing for television, working with non-professional actors, or directing scenes with only one character—are woven into existing chapters.

While I was working on this book, the COVID-19 pandemic hit and the entertainment industry began grappling with the potential long-term effects on film and television production. I've added sections to Chapters Eight (*Casting*) and Nine (*Rehearsal*) about directing actors under pandemic conditions. In the early months of pandemic, I was pessimistic about the prospect of directors and actors being consigned to remote communication. But then I decided to follow my own advice and look for the *glass half full*. These are challenging times. But we are artists; we can be pioneers. We can face global trauma and dislocation with a focus on what really matters to our lives and tell the stories that need to be told.

Perhaps we will gain new appreciation for *connection*. Maybe we'll finally understand that connection takes work, even sacrifice. Pre-pandemic, we took connection for granted—we were always around each other, so we believed we were connected. Maybe now we'll do the work. In the twenty-five years since the original edition of *Directing Actors* was published, the technical side of filmmaking has become much more accessible. Directors tell me that dealing with actors is the last frontier—the scariest part and the part they long for—the human part, the place where connection happens.

It is in that spirit that I offer you this 25th Anniversary Edition of *Directing Actors*.

Who Should Read This 25th Anniversary Edition?

Of course a book about directing actors is meant to be read by directors, writer-directors, and actors. But when I look back at the range of students who have taken workshops in my studio and internationally, I recall the faces of editors, screenwriters, cinematographers, animators, producers, and so many more. The truth is that everyone who works in creative industries can benefit from a deeper exploration of character, story, and relationships—which is what this book is intended to be.

The language of the book addresses the needs of directors. My ambitious goal is to present sophisticated concepts in plain language that engages and challenges new directors, but also supports and re-energizes established directors. I have worked to include enough original material that readers of the 1996 paperback will find this new edition enlightening and worthwhile. Still, it's meant to be completely accessible to those who have not read any of my earlier books. This edition is longer than the original, so if that's daunting, there's always the audiobook, which has many of the revisions that are in this 25th Anniversary print Edition.

Let me take a moment to love on my readers who are actors. Actors always got it that a book like mine was needed. Actors—who are way too familiar with "result direction"—shake their heads and say, "Directors need to know all this!" They tell me I'm going to go to heaven. This book is for actors as well as directors—it contains ideas for making acting choices that are bolder, closer to the bone—as well as tools for translating result direction into playable choices. It's meant to be helpful to writers, too—the translation technique is invaluable when writers need to interpret opaque and frustrating notes from producers.

Readers have told me from the get-go that my books benefit them not only professionally, but in their personal lives. Ever since I started taking acting class in a church basement in the early 1970s, I have believed in the study of acting as a laboratory of life. I have seen over and over that acting can expand and enrich daily life—for anyone—in countless ways. Acting has allowed me to look into myself with more honesty and clarity. Acting has lifted me from my own narrow concerns and anxieties. Acting gave me permission to look *inward*—and at the same time invited me to engage my imagination in looking *outward* into the world and the problems and motivations of others. Acting is an exercise in *empathy*—the world needs more of that. Digging deeply into well-written scripts connects us to our humanity. I hope this book will hold interest for any film lover and anyone fascinated by the behavior and inner life of humans.

Acknowledgments

Thank you, first, last, and always, to my readers. Thank you for reading my books, following me on social media, writing me beautiful notes, telling your friends to read my books, and caring about me. Thank you for taking the tools and ideas of my books—and making them your own.

Thank you to my thousands of students and clients around the world—I would not be who I am without you. Being face-to-face and heart-to-heart with you in classes and consultations, watching you do beautiful work in exercises, diving into the subtext of scripts with you, watching the results of our work together manifest in the world—and marveling when your talent and vision take your creations far beyond the humble lessons of my classes . . . You have rejuvenated and inspired me every day.

Thank you to Michael Wiese, Geraldine Overton, and Ken Lee. Michael has been so much more than my publisher—a role model, mentor, business advisor, and a friend. Michael, Geraldine, and their daughter Julia mean the world to John and me.

Ken Lee has been invaluable not just to the writing of this book, but in my life for, well, twenty-five years now—a persistent ally and loving cheerleader. Thank you to the entire MWP community, who, shepherded by Ken and Michael, are warm, generous, and loyal to each other.

Thank you to E. Amato, my editor. If readers like this book, it will have a lot to do with the times she made suggestions as to when a concept needed more detail to explain it properly—and when she pressed me to simplify and tighten. She made me reorganize chapters, clarify ideas, and construct better sentences. I could not have done this without her.

Thank you to the Wachowskis. It was kind of a miracle to receive their gracious permission to include in this book an excerpt from *The Matrix*. Thank you to Mr. Peter Grossman and Mr. David Wirtschafter, who kindly facilitated that permission.

Let me take a moment to acknowledge some sources of quotes and stories included in this book: *The Los Angeles Times, The New York Times, Daily Variety, The Hollywood Reporter, The New Yorker, GQ, Esquire, Vanity Fair, DGA Quarterly, Filmmaker Magazine, IndieWire, Deadline, Salon, Vulture,* and *Collider,* among others, were brilliantly helpful, along with countless DVD commentaries, every episode of *Inside the Actors Studio,* and the interviews and commentaries included in the Criterion Collection.

I've always thought of all my students as the crème de la crème of the film industry—the ones who knew they didn't know everything. There were plenty of dinosaurs who dismissed any new ideas for working with actors as touchy-feely rubbish. So I feel a special gratitude to my celebrity supporters. It never bothered me that some of my directing students and clients feel a bit furtive about my books. I understood their fear that it might not inspire confidence in an actor to catch their director thumbing through, on set, a book with the title *Directing Actors*. Just a few weeks ago, a director client blurted out a worry that if she used verbs awkwardly or too often, her actors might start whispering behind her back, "Oh, she's read the book!"

So it's been all the more poignant that so many celebrities have been generous with their endorsements. David Chase was the first. He took my workshop in 1996. He was already an idol of mine, because of *The Rockford Files, Northern Exposure,* and *I'll Fly Away.* He confided to me the reason he took my workshop: that he had written and was about to direct a pilot he didn't want to mess up—which turned out to be *The Sopranos*. David wrote glowing quotes for me and legitimized my work in the eyes of the world.

Others followed, equally generous and open. Some are referenced in this book. For instance, Billy Ray, who made it his mission to spread the word that hope and comfort awaited directors if they would only read *Directing Actors*. He frequently shares with young filmmakers copies of his famous *Billy Ray 3x5 Card*—and has graciously allowed me to include it in Appendix G.

Thank you to the teachers at film schools and workshops who have placed my books on their lists of required reading. I hope this edition will work even better as a text for your classes. You are welcome to contact me for clarification on anything. I can make myself available for remote Q&A's for groups of your students.

It's been a true honor and joy that I've been invited to teach in countries other than my own—allowed to travel, learn, see beautiful places, make new friends—and to have my book translated into twelve languages other than English. The international organizations that invited me to teach in their facilities began with the Rockport Film & Television Workshops, Télévision Suisse Romande, and the Binger Filmlab—and then all over the world: Directors Guild Canada, Danish Film School, Swedish Film Institute, Screen Ireland, New Zealand Film Commission, Australian Directors Guild, Winnipeg Film Group. There were also individuals who took it upon themselves to organize seminars in Milan, Berlin, Cologne, Toronto, St. John's (Newfoundland), Helsinki, Belgrade, Cornwall, and remotely in Singapore and Beijing. The Binger even brought me to Cape Town, South Africa. There are many to thank, among them: Marten Rabarts, Ido Abram, Frank Beacham, Pico Berkowitch, Bertrand Theubet, Uwe Walter, Stefano Moro, Päivi Hartzell, Jovan Todorovic, Barbara Schock, John Martin, Debbie McGee, Carol Anna McBride, Criona Sexton, Shangwei Liu, Jim Brodie.

Thank you, Wasly Castillo, for initiating and producing the Zoom Q&A workshops I was able to offer during the 2020 pandemic. It was a unique privilege to meet readers and former students online during this vulnerable time, and to hear their questions and stories. These sessions lifted me up and helped me to finish this book. Thank you to the 2020–21 class of the Sony

Diverse Directors Program—whose participants helped me figure out how to make Zoom rehearsals work.

Thank you, Adam Egypt Mortimer, for sharing with me your knowledge and acuity regarding *Alien* and the *Alien/Aliens* franchise. Thank you, Ben Rock, for your support and insight.

Thank you, Maud Simmons, for feedback and advice about the cover art. Thank you, Claudia Luther, for your guidance and editing in my other project. Claudia helped me immeasurably in my constant struggle to learn how to put thoughts into sentences. Thank you, Amy Klitsner, Irene Oppenheim, and Pico Berkowitch for your invaluable editorial assistance in the original *Directing Actors*.

Thank you to my acting teachers. I refer in this book to lessons I learned from Jean Shelton, Gerry Hiken, and Robert Goldsby—but others who influenced me profoundly include Angela Paton, Lillian Loren, Jack Garfein, Wendell Phillips, Paul Richards, Harold Clurman, Stella Adler. I give thanks *every day* to Jean Shelton and Angie Paton, who gave me guidance and inspiration not only in the craft of acting, but also in managing my career and living my life. Both of these glorious dames were not only true teachers and mentors—they were role models and surrogate mothers to me.

Not everyone who writes a book needs to thank their doctors, but I do—medical intervention including osteopathy, oncology, and emotional therapy has kept me alive and productive. Thank you to the sagacity and patience of my health practitioners. Thank you to family and friends who have stood by me in thick and thin.

In the Extended Bio on my website, you can learn almost anything about me. But the most important thing to know is that I have John. My husband, John Hoskins, is the partner of all happiness in my life—he is with me through darkness and light. He is the first reader of every sentence I write, my first champion and my defense from danger and depression. He is the proof that I know how lucky I am.

Introduction

Directors in Jeopardy

For twenty-seven years I taught a seminar I called Acting for Directors. It was limited to twelve participants. On the first morning, I sat in a circle with them and asked each one to say why they had come and what they hoped to get from the workshop, and to speak openly of their problems and concerns. I wrote down what they said, word for word. The following responses are verbatim and representative:

"I thought I was describing my ideas exactly, and the actor said, 'Yes, I understand,' and then he didn't do anything like what we'd talked about. So I just kept repeating the direction and the performance got worse and worse." "How do I get over my insecurities with an established actor?" "How do I analyze a script?" "How can I take off the writer hat and put on the director hat? I tend to rewrite the scripts instead of directing." "How do I get the actors to trust me?" "Sometimes I can tell that something is untruthful or not working, but then I don't know what to do." "How much should I tell them? How much should they tell me?" "Sometimes under the pressure of being on the set, it's hard to see the performance—I can't see what's happening in front of me." "The production and financing problems took up so much of my energy that, once I got to the set, I was exhausted. I had no energy for the moment." "On a television series, the regulars already know their characters, they won't take direction." "How do I keep performance consistent, get them there and keep them there?" "I think I talk too much. It's easy for me to direct someone right out of the role, tell them too much." "How do I give direction when there's no time for rehearsal?" "What do you do when you give a direction that worked in rehearsal

and now that it's time to shoot the scene, the performance doesn't work anymore?" "The actors loved me and I felt very comfortable on the set, but when I got to the editing room it was all crap." "There's never any time!" "I didn't want it to go that way, but I had no choice."

Directors want short answers to these questions, but in order to learn to direct the short way, you need first to learn how to do it the long way. And then, if you practice a lot, you will—gradually—be able to do it faster. Arriving at quick, simple solutions takes a lot of work! This is true in other disciplines—sports, music, science. It's not surprising that it's true in filmmaking as well.

If you did it well the first time, but since then have been struggling, it may mean that in your first attempt you had beginner's luck. In other words, that you are on the roller coaster of the learning curve—which is two steps forward, one step back. You needn't let this frighten you—because the condition of *learning* is a good place to be. This book won't give you a formula for working with actors—because there isn't one. But there are principles; there is a craft. There is a lot of exhilarating, arduous preparation. And then—you get to jump off a cliff without any expectations as to whether it's going to work or not. Ready to be in the moment when you get the actors there, ready to throw out *every scrap* of your preparation if you need to.

Because—there are going to be surprises.

Actors: The Mysterious "Other"

Directing film or television is a high-stakes occupation. It captures your full attention at every moment, calling on you to commit every resource and stretch yourself to the limit; it's the white-water rafting of entertainment jobs. Sadly, for many directors, the excitement they feel about a new project tightens into anxiety when it comes to working with actors.

The entertainment industry is conflicted in its attitude toward actors: actors are both fawned over and looked down upon. Actors are an irrational and baffling "other." Directors who come from a technical background may know little about how actors work. Unlike camera and sound equipment, actors don't come with interchangeable parts you can replace, dials you can adjust. Directors who have come up from the production side of film may even have a prejudice against actors. There can be a feeling on film and television sets that, compared to the expertise and long hours required of crewmembers, what actors do is not really work. After all, anybody who can walk and talk at the same time could do it, right?

Writers who turn to directing may become troubled and anxious when actors fail to speak the lines with the exact intonation the writer imagined they would. Directors of commercials and music videos—highly gifted visually and completely at ease with the camera—are sometimes bored with dialogue and impatient with actors.

It's easy to see how breakdowns in communication can happen when inexperienced directors are paired with experienced, high-profile actors. I heard one story of a major star with a tough-guy image who, every time the director took him aside, would look up and say, loud enough for the crew to hear, "You want me to suck what?" Now maybe the veteran actor was only trying to keep it light—relax the young director by teasing him out of some of his earnestness—perhaps test him with a kind of male-comradery prank to see if the neophyte could take a joke. But it's also entirely possible that the confident celebrity chose to make the hapless rookie feel bad and useless with a crude reference to the stupidity of the direction.

I don't judge this movie star. It's not unusual for actors to lose patience with how little directors know about them. Directors typically put so much attention into assembling the financing and logistics that there's little time left for understanding the characters and supporting the performances. Even well-known actors and directors can be disappointed when they finally work together.

What causes actors to feel let down by their director? Sometimes the director is not emotionally invested in the project and his ideas are superficial. Or sometimes the director has not given attention to the actor's concerns and ideas and not has taken the risk to make a human connection. An actor can hear a director's ideas better if the actor *feels heard.*

If you want audiences to connect with your characters, connect with your actors. Connecting with actors can involve soul-to-soul conversations about the themes of the story—even opening your heart to them about your own emotional wounds. Or it can mean respecting their privacy and allowing them space to navigate the far reaches of their character's inner life on their own. Every actor is different. If you're not sure where a particular actor falls on this spectrum—*ask them.*

An Invitation to Break Habit

The principles and tools in this book are simple, objective, and practical. But they are not a cheat sheet. There is no list of correct answers you can memorize. You've got to let go of doing things "right." I've had students, clients, and readers throughout the world and I've seen that letting go of "doing it right" is hard for many people—in our "normal" world of social interactions, there are so many penalties for making mistakes!

We are mistake-making creatures; we are built that way. You have chosen a profession where mistakes are not always bad. For brain surgeons or airplane pilots, mistakes nearly always have terrible consequences. But for those of us who choose the path of the storyteller, a mistake can be a blessing in disguise. A mistake can jolt our attention away from preconceived ideas and into the present; it can open us to a new creative path. Sometimes a mistake is our subconscious speaking, and we ought to listen to it. If anything, an artist needs to get excited by mistakes—to say, as Robert Altman, Miles Davis, and Pina Bausch always insisted, *there are no mistakes.*

The glass is half full. Negativity is not useful in a director's interactions with actors. When problems come up—if the actor is objecting to a line of dialogue or a piece of staging or the color of a wig or is forgetting his lines or hates his costar—I give you permission to say to yourself, "I'm glad this happened!" And mean it! The reason to be glad is that the actor has given you *information*. Always follow up: "Tell me more"; "What can I do to help?"

Here is a sentence I want you to eliminate from your vocabulary: "I had no choice." We are storytellers—creative choice is what it's all about. If you feel you need a rehearsal period, you *can* carve out the time. You might have to fight for it. You might have to prove you need it and that you have the chops to use it productively. You might have to sacrifice other priorities. *You have choices.* If the producer tells you he can't get the money for the project unless you accept a certain actor in the lead role—perhaps an actor you think is wrong for the part—you must make the *choice* to work with that actor and accept that actor as the best option for the role—or give yourself permission to walk off the project. Before you panic at such a radical suggestion, please understand that I would never encourage anyone to renege on promises or give their word frivolously. My point is that when you persevere *out of choice,* you allow yourself freedom. Freedom builds confidence. Freedom gives you room for creativity.

Some students tell me that the ideas and techniques I put forward seem radical and destabilizing at first. In my early days of teaching, a young writer-director said she found the things I was saying "counterintuitive." At the time I was surprised, because above all, I hope to connect my students and readers with their intuition. The last thing I want to do is dampen your ideas or cause you to distrust yourself. You can't be a good director without faith in your leadership skills and confidence in your ability to act decisively when a quick decision is necessary. But it's easy to mistake opinion for intuition. Everyone's got an opinion. Accessing your intuition is different from adopting an opinion. To open yourself to the rich resources of your intuition, you have to scrape away pop-culture clichés, conventional wisdom, and preconceived ideas.

Wait—did I say you "have to" do these things? No—*you get to!* It's not a decree. It's an *invitation*—to break habit, question conventional wisdom, move beyond your prejudices and assumptions, go below the surface, and awaken your intuition at a deeper level. This takes work, possibly more work than you realized was involved in directing. But I'm going to guide you through it and open the door to a secret world. Once you are on the inside, you will feel liberated.

This secret world where intuition resides is the world of *subtext*. I want to give you faith in the world of subtext—and tools to access it. At times, the tools may sound like rules. Please know that every rule I give you can be broken, and *should* be broken if breaking it makes the movie better. Technique is not an end in itself. It's like sports or music or working for NASA. You wouldn't run a marathon, play a concert at Disney Hall, or send a rover to Mars without a lot of preparation. But once you're prepared—you let go. Even the engineers of NASA JPL had to *let go* during the radio delay (*7 Minutes of Terror*) when they could not control the spacecraft Curiosity in real time.

In other words, learn the rules. Then forget them.

How Actors Work Their Magic

The very best actors make it look easy. Their technique is invisible. You can't see the work. Their feelings well up strong and apparently unbidden. They don't look rehearsed; they appear to be speaking their own words. They "become" the character. To the general public, it looks as though the actor must be improvising—or just happens to have a personality exactly like that of the character.

Even to those knowledgeable about the demands of performing, superior performances are mysterious, a touch of the divine. As much as I know about acting, I can't tell you exactly what actor Song Kang Ho in *Parasite*, or Alfre Woodard in *Clemency*, are doing to create, with nuance and precision, their complex characters—but I know enough to know that they are doing *something*. Rigorous technique and careful detail go into such seamless portrayals. One of the things this book will do is to investigate the actor's world: the tools, resources, and training.

A central requirement of acting that is unimaginably terrifying to most people who are not actors is this: the actor allows herself to be exposed, vulnerable. The success of the actor's contribution depends precisely on her ability and willingness to allow herself to be viewed—without being able to view herself. This means she must surrender completely to feelings, impulses, and choices *without knowing whether or not they are working*! Her responsibility is to prepare—and let go. Like a trapeze artist letting go of the bar and floating in air for those fractions of a moment before the next bar, thrown toward her by an unseen partner, meets her hand.

It's hard for a director who has never taken an acting class to understand the magnitude of an actor's emotional exposure. I hope this book will inspire you to take a beginning acting class. When, in my Acting for Directors workshop, directors stepped into the actor's shoes, they felt transformed. I often heard these words: "I never imagined how vulnerable I'd feel. It's changed me."

The Actor-Director Relationship

Sometimes directors ask me why I want them to know so much about actors. Is the director meant to monitor the actor in each and every choice? Is the director supposed to guide the actor through Method "emotional memory" exercises? If the actor is having problems, should the director give acting lessons on the set? How responsible is the director for the performances?

The director gets to say, "Okay, got it"—or "No, we need another one." When informing an actor that another take is needed, a director is allowed to tell him (*privately*, always) that his performance is not yet where it needs to be—but *not* required to tell the actor exactly what's wrong with his performance or how to fix it. Intrusive micromanaging is rarely welcomed by actors or helpful to them. Directors have magic director tools (camera angles, lighting, blocking, editing—not to mention casting) that give them a huge amount of control over the impact the actors' work finally has on the audience. Controlling and "shaping" an actor's inner life is not the director's job.

But what if you knew enough about characters and story to communicate with an actor on a deep, transformative level of theme and meaning? Or—what if you knew enough about acting to suggest a choice of *intention*, an "as if," or a bit of comedic timing? Wouldn't that be great? You and the actor might resolve the weird co-dependency of this challenging relationship by sharing ideas with each other—by collaborating. For example, blocking (i.e., staging the physical movements of the actors) is the director's job. But it's not unusual for an actor to say, "I have an impulse to move over there on that line." A suggestion like this could give you a new understanding that solves the scene visually in a way you hadn't thought of.

Even with all the power directors have, they sometimes fear the power of actors and even confide to me their fear that an actor will sabotage their vision. But when an actor has a different interpretation from the director's, there's no need for the relationship to degenerate into an ego brawl. The different interpretations can challenge each other, inform each other—*build* on each other. When an actor responds to a director's suggestion by saying, "That gives me an idea for something to work on," this is not a rejection of your idea, but an invitation to creative intimacy—a step into *collaboration*. It's not an occasion for damage control—it's the good stuff. A summons to unlock the subtext of the script, make discoveries, and go places—either together or separately. When an actor surprises you, that's not a bad thing—it's a good thing.

I want you to feel strong in your vision—and at the same time safe to be *emotionally open* in your relationships with actors. A director who makes creative intimacy with actors a priority may achieve a level of communication at which only a word need be spoken; may come up with the insight that turns a competent performance into an indelible one; may be present at the creation of a character who continues to live in the audience's mind long after the movie is over.

Actors on the set of HBO's *When They See Us* have said the attention they received from director Ava DuVernay was like that of a mother. In an interview, Robert De Niro said of his long collaboration with director Martin Scorsese, "Sometimes he's like a priest." Donald Sutherland: "I've often described [the actor-director relationship] as sexual. I'm his concubine."

The director is protector of the story and guardian of the actors playing its characters. It's an emotional engagement, a significant accountability. It can be perilous—it can be restorative. Those who are fearful of intimacy and confrontation should probably not become directors.

What Do Actors Want?

Actors want a director who can tell good acting from bad. That's not as easy as it sounds. In the movie theater or in front of a TV or device, everyone's an expert on good acting, right? Unfortunately, when you're on set in the thick of things, confusion, overload, and brain freeze lie in wait. A director who is unable to recognize emotional truth in an actor is a drag on that actor's creativity and a serious roadblock to successful storytelling. Actors want you to want from them the very best they have to offer.

Communication skills matter, and yet it's less important to actors that the director uses the "correct" language than that the director knows how to *tell a story*. They want you to have *scene-making* skills; to have a feel for blocking and pacing; to have instincts for crafting a scene with a beginning-middle-and-end that is emotionally satisfying and visually involving; to know how to set up and pay off the events of the script so they are both surprising and inevitable. And to know where to put the camera. They want you to be completely prepared and proficient in all the technical aspects of filmmaking. I mean—what will it matter that they do wonderful work if the camera and mic are not in place to capture it?

Actors want you to know what you want—and they want your ideas to be good. They want your ideas to ring true and to be revelatory of human behavior. They want you to know *what the story is,* what the movie is about—and by *what it's about* I mean what it's *really* about, its *meaning,* not just the plot or logline. Actors want a director to care, to be emotionally invested in the project, to love the characters. They respond to a director's passion and personal commitment.

And integrity. Integrity matters. It seriously does. Always be honest.

Here's what actors *don't* want: vague, confusing, contradictory direction (I'll be giving you examples in the next chapter). But whether or not you become adept at giving direction with finesse, actors need time to make a direction their own. A director who knows when to *step back* is fully as wonderful as one who knows when to step in and ask for more.

The thing actors hope against hope for from a director is to be *seen,* as a human being and as an artist. To be challenged, to grow, and to learn. A director with insight beyond the obvious is icing on the cake—actors don't expect it, but they thrill to it. The very highest praise an actor can give a director is to say, "She taught me so much!" Or, "He got me to do things I didn't know I could do."

What's In This Book

I have three ambitious goals. First, to take you on a journey inside the actor's world and introduce you to some ways that actors work, so you can understand that acting is a craft, worthy of respect. And more than that—a rich laboratory of life.

Second: communication tools. I want to help you make your direction briefer, more powerful, and deeper emotionally. "What should I say to actors?" directors often ask me. Or, "They have their own language! I need the vocab!" I promise to give examples of language that may be helpful for communicating with actors—but it's not a question of memorizing jargon or following a list of Dos and Don'ts. Everything I have to say is geared toward making your direction briefer and more loaded—but these techniques and principles mean nothing unless you are committed to deepening your understanding of human behavior. Indeed, the *tools* have as much to do with real life as with movies and television.

Which brings us to the third topic—*script analysis*. Getting underneath the surface of the script and uncovering its real truths. In order to communicate effectively with actors, you need to *prepare* effectively. Directors are so loaded down with logistics, technology, and the stresses of financing that script analysis can feel like an impossible luxury. It's easy to get so exhausted by funding demands and technical minutiae that, even if you have set aside time for studying the script and unlocking its mysteries, you may find yourself staring at the page with nothing coming to you. I can give you simple, practical alternatives to procrastination and despair. My tools can jump-start your understanding, insight, and ideas, and awaken your powers of suggestibility and invention. They can lead you to the storyteller's touchstone—a deep connection to the story on the level of *what it's about*.

There are things you can't learn from this or any book, crucial skills for which there is no substitute for practice and experience—like when a scene is as good as it's going to get and it's time to move on to the next one. You must practice. The path to learning, the journey to expertise is *trial and error*. There will be mistakes. Start making them now. Rehearse scenes and make short films—that you don't even show anyone. Build your chops. Do this for as long as necessary, until the process of disclosing your ideas to actors and listening to theirs becomes second nature. The purpose of this book is not to make you mistake-proof but to offer ideas—food for thought as you create your own path. As you practice and study and make mistakes and develop your skills.

The visual and technical considerations of filmmaking are not dealt with in this book. Most of you reading this book already have knowledge of the technical side of filmmaking—if you don't, you need to get it somewhere. It's very important that you have the technical skills to tell a story visually. But this book should be helpful to you in making your visual choices—because you will be better able to make decisions about blocking and pacing if you understand a script's subtext and the emotional event.

Connection

Scaling the heights of the actor-director relationship, learning to collaborate and challenge each other and grow together—becoming an "actor's director"—can become a lifelong commitment. You can take everything you learn from me and from all your other teachers and from everything you know about life and make it your own. You can choose to give your craft and your actors *everything you've got,* with love, with passion, with humility.

Of course, you need good instincts—what some people call "talent"—and good luck. You don't have a choice about the talent you're born with, or how many lucky breaks will come your way. You do have a choice about whether to do the work of developing and challenging the talent and luck you are given.

CHAPTER ONE

Result Direction and Quick Fixes

Result Direction: What the Hell Is It? (12+ Examples)

The biggest complaint I hear from actors is that directors don't know what they want. This may come as a surprise, because most directors think they have a clear picture in their minds of how they want the movie to look and sound.

While reading a script, most people project a miniature movie version of it on the inside of their foreheads. They fantasize the faces of actors they hope will play the roles, they see the facial expressions, they hear the inflections of the lines. No matter how many times they read the script, they hear and see the same line readings, the same raised eyebrow or frown that they have pictured from the first. They come to think of this as their "vision" of the script.

This is a passive approach to script-reading. It limits your ideas and hobbles your imagination. It denies any life to the characters beyond the four edges of the script's pages. It's like insisting that the earth is as flat and four-cornered as a viewing screen and that people or characters disappear when they walk off the edge. It causes you to look at a line and say to yourself, "How can this be made dramatic?" or "How can this be made funny?" rather than, "What clues does this give me to what the movie is about and what the characters are doing to solve their predicaments?" It may cause you to make artistic choices based on what you know about other movies, rather than on what you know about life.

This mistaken way of reading a script often leads to directors using what is known as "result direction." A director may have labored over financing, three-act structure, storyboards—and still not have done the homework that will help her communicate her ideas to actors. Directors, who tend to feel that their result-oriented ideas are very exact, may be unaware that actors—who want to please the director but need to make *playable choices*—can experience result direction as vague, general, and confusing instead of specific and clear.

Terms like *result direction* and *playable choices* are slippery and may be used differently by different people. What is result-oriented direction? I'm going to take the plunge with thirteen examples:

1) "Can you make it more quirky?"

Describing the *effect* you want actors to have on the audience is a perfect example of directing by asking for a *result*. Instructions of this ilk—such as, "This scene should be funny," or "I need you to be more dangerous," or "Can you give her an epic quality?"—cause an actor's heart to sink. The director wants her to do something different from what she is doing—what can it be? If the actor asks for clarification, the director may go blank and simply repeat himself: "You know, *more quirky*." From this point, the actor-director relationship dissolves into a guessing game, because the direction is vague and general. The actor tries something—is this it? Often, it still isn't. Oftener still, the director really didn't know in the first place what he wanted or how to recognize it. The actor's performance may have deteriorated because she has begun to watch herself, to *get in her head*. It is death to an actor's gifts to put her concentration on the *effect* she is having on the audience.

Describing to the actors the "mood" of a scene—for example, sultry, alienated, electric—can be problematic for similar reasons. Actors who try to *play a mood* can end up evoking exactly the opposite of what the director was hoping for: efforts to "look" serious often produce an unintentionally comic effect; efforts to "be" light and frothy can prove heavy-handed. Their attention has been wrongly placed and thus, their eagerness to produce the desired effect can cause them to concentrate on the effort itself. Consequently, *the effort itself* is the effect that finally reads.

2) **"When you say the line, 'You always do that,' don't put the emphasis on 'always'—instead hit the word 'do.' So, not 'You *always* do that,' but like this: 'You always *do* that.'"**

This is called giving the actor a *line reading*. That is, telling the actor what inflection or cadence to give a line. For instance, if the line is, "Please help me," there are a number of different line readings, each completely reasonable. Like these examples: "*Please* help me," or "Please *help* me," or "Please help *me*." And each different line reading means something different.

What's wrong with giving line readings? Well, worst-case scenario, an inexperienced actor might try to obey you and repeat back the line with the new inflection, but without any life behind it. An experienced actor, of course, will look for a way to give it life—that's her job. But sometimes the line reading makes no sense to the actor. If she asks you what it means, you want to be able to do more to clarify the direction than just repeating the line reading over and over.

If you need an actor to make an adjustment to her performance, it's more helpful to communicate to her the *meaning* or subtext of the line, not the inflection or result. The most dangerous signal conveyed by a director who gives line readings is that he may not even know what the line means, what the *intention* of the character is, or what the scene is about.

3) **"Can you take it down?" Or, "Can you give it more energy?"**

There are directors who seem to have only these two generic directions in their toolkit. When directors rely entirely on these two phrases—"more energy" or "take it down"—over and over in situations that are not at all alike, actors may start to feel that the director does not really know what she is talking about and that the direction has become a string of empty clichés. Worse yet, it may mean that the director is not able to recognize good acting when she sees it. I have seen actors do brave, scary things, and yet afterwards all the director says is that she wants it "bigger."

Of course, sometimes "take it down" or "give it more energy" is a perfectly fine direction. If an experienced actor has overcooked his performance a smidge, maybe pushed a bit and stepped over the line into overacting, he appreciates getting the heads-up to "take it down." If his performance is flat or not making the scene work—in other words, if it needs more energy—he wants to be advised of that; he will respond by making a different *playable subtext choice*. Don't get me wrong: If an actor could do better, he wants to be told!

But less experienced actors can fall into bad traps. An inexperienced actor may interpret "Take it down" as a request to say the line in a monotone. Being asked for "more energy" or to "ramp it up" or "punch it up" can cause them to add emphasis to the uninspired line reading they have already frozen into their performance. Inexperienced actors are vulnerable—don't sabotage them with vague, unhelpful instructions.

4) "You need to get angry on this line."

I've been warming up with a couple of examples of result direction that you may already be familiar with. You probably know it's not cool to give line readings or tell the actor to "be funnier." Now I'm getting to the more complicated stuff—emotions.

Emotions are what it's all about. Storytelling exists to tap into the emotions of the audience, and the way to do that is for the director and actors to access their own emotions. The film *Edward Scissorhands* endures because it goes deep into the pain, sadness, anger, and longing that has been felt by any human being who has ever been isolated, misunderstood, or lonely.

Don't be afraid of feeling.

But. Emotionally investing in your story and all your characters is not the same as deciding what every character feels at a given moment. Telling the actors what their characters should be feeling—angry, disappointed, worried, annoyed, excited, in love, frightened, resentful, disapproving—is a very usual way that direction is given. Here's the problem with it: As soon as an actor *tries* to have a feeling or manufactures a feeling on demand, he looks like an actor, not a real person. People in real life often find our feelings are *obstacles* to what we want; we would prefer *not* to feel nervous at an important meeting, *not* to feel upset when an ex-lover and their new spouse appear unexpectedly at a party, *not* to feel angry when our loved ones disappoint us.

To be playable, a choice must be *choosable*, and *we do not choose our feelings*. This idea can be hard to take in, but I want you to think about it: *we don't get to decide how to feel*. For some reason, we humans don't much like this about our lives. Mediocre actors, as well as much of the general population, go to great lengths to make the world believe they feel something that they don't actually feel. But most of the time no one is fooled. Feelings can be hidden or repressed, but we can't selectively shut down just one feeling. When one feeling is held back, all feeling gets shut down.

Good actors are emotionally free and available to many subtleties of feeling. Emotion and impulse are the center of the actor's world. But feelings are pesky critters, cropping up inconveniently—then disappearing just when you want them. The thing both terrible and wonderful about feelings is that they change. You have seen it in real life—a person can be crying one minute and laughing the next. The truth is, the more you let yourself feel whatever you are actually feeling, the more available you are to a new feeling. For actors, this goes double.

It can have a shrinking effect on actors to tell them their emotions are wrong. When actors are told to have less feeling, they may drop out emotionally—and the scene can then become flat and lifeless. When they are told to have more feeling, they may fall into pushing, or underlining—overacting.

5) "You need to react to her with more shock and anger." An extension of telling the actor what emotion to have is telling him what *reaction* to have. In real life we may *wish* we could plan our reactions—we may wish we could react calmly to bad news; we may wish we could laugh merrily when a client or boss tells an unfunny joke—but it's a fact of life that such disconcerting incidents take us by surprise. In a script, these surprises and reactions are the story's *emotional events*—and the characters don't know they are coming. The actors, having read the script, do know what's going to happen to their characters—and what they are going to do or say when it does. We want the actors' reactions to be not preprogramed but spontaneous and idiosyncratic. That's how their performances give scenes the texture of real life.

6) "When the scene starts, A is worried because B is late. A is relieved when B arrives, but then disappointed because B hasn't got the money, and then B realizes that A has become suspicious that B might be holding out on him."

This is what I call a fully loaded emotional map, outlining all the feelings and reactions you have decided the characters are supposed to have in the scene. It's nothing more than a tedious regurgitation of the dialogue and plot. Sadly, it commonly passes for an explanation of the characters' psychology and understanding of what the script is about.

At first glance, emotional maps look innocuous enough. You may be asking yourself, what could be wrong with this? How else would you describe what happens in a scene? Everybody talks about characters this way, don't they? In fact, people in real life talk about each other like this too. It's called gossip. Like gossip, emotional maps are not only tedious and long-winded but addictive. Director and actors talk a scene to death—going down convoluted rabbit holes, until whatever genuine emotional connection the actors originally responded to has been rendered thoroughly cerebral. It's the surest way to drain a scene or characterization of all its life.

Don't forget, directors need always to look for ways to save time. Endless abstract discussions lead, finally, to *analysis paralysis*. When actors try to follow an emotional map, the performance degenerates into an intellectualized connect-the-dots drawing—contrived and predictable. It can't flow, because it has no *through-line*. It can't advance the story because it has no sense of *emotional event*.

The best direction is simple and to the point. There are more dynamic, briefer, more muscular ways to evoke characterizations than the convolutions of emotional maps. I want you to practice and learn them. Elia Kazan said a director's job is to *turn psychology into behavior*. How to do this? Focus on the *relationships* between the characters: pose questions about their *emotional history*, consider *choices* about their *needs* from each other, create the *emotional events* of scenes—rather than be satisfied with reductive emotional maps.

7) "He's a punk." "She's self-destructive." "He's stupid." "A loser." "A bitch." "A poseur."

These are negative *judgments* on the character. Good actors *never* judge their character. If the actor is not on the character's side, who will be? No one is born bad. Like people, characters become who they are because of their needs, the things that happen to them, and the decisions they make. Neither writer, director, nor actor should judge the character, who, like all of us, has both good and bad sides. The *audience* gets to decide which character is weak or strong, ambitious, lazy, etc.

Audiences love suspense. The craving to know *what happens next* makes them lean into the story. Even if we know that the hero is going to win or the lovers are going to live happily ever after.

Even if it's a "character piece" and all its events are interior, private. When the actor telegraphs to the audience thus: "I'm the good guy," "I'm the loser," or "I'm the villain"—he is playing a caricature. Who can care what happens to him?

It goes without saying that serious drama loses any opportunity for insight or revelation when good and evil are portrayed without ambiguity. Villains portrayed as recognizably human, like Ralph Fiennes's Nazi commandant in *Schindler's List*, are far more frightening than cardboard cutouts. A main character with human flaws, like Sigourney Weaver's Ripley in *Alien*, is more relatable for the audience than a formulaic, perfect hero. If you are directing live-action characters based on the DC or Marvel universes, it's as important to find a central humanity to the character as it is when directing naturalistic drama. Heath Ledger as the Joker in *The Dark Knight* showed us it's possible to meet the demands of genre without caricature. He forever raised the bar.

It's extremely disappointing for a good actor to work with a director who judges the characters. If directors want to have a meaningful conversation with an actor, they need to have unlocked ways not to judge *any* of the characters—this should be a central element of their preparation, their *script analysis*. Instead of judging, the director should approach each character with openness, and—dare I say it—compassion. When the director speaks to each actor, take the side of that character. My personal motto for connecting myself to characters who do things that I believe I would never do in life is this: "This character is me with a little worse luck."

One last, serious warning: If an inexperienced or untrained actor is given direction that is judgmental toward their character—because that actor may not have been trained in techniques with which to translate poor direction into a playable choice—I can just about promise you the results will be disappointing, if not disastrous.

8) "This is how I see the character . . ."

Labeling character traits is something you might recognize from real-life families: one sibling labeled the smart one, one the flaky one, one the responsible one, one the difficult one. While these shorthand descriptions may not be negative—may even be meant as compliments—they are never the whole story.

Narrative filmmakers routinely describe to actors "what the character is like"—haughty, tormented, awkward, fierce. Look, I'm not saying these labels are wrong—tormented people surely exist. I am asking that you *not stop* at such quick branding. The character is not an abstraction that the actor must "become." The character is an active human being with emotional history, with needs—who has free will, who takes chances, who makes mistakes.

9) "Can you play him aggressive, but pleasant?"

Try to avoid describing characters the way that some people describe fine wine. "The character is frightened, but determined." Or, "defensive, yet vulnerable," "cynical, yet caring," "catatonic, yet curious."

Directors mean well—and actors themselves may talk about their characters this way. Both directors and actors may think that a description like this calls attention to the complexity of the character. People *are* complex and it is exactly my goal to allow the characters to have as much complexity as actual people. However, making a long list of contradictory labels does not accomplish complexity.

There isn't only one way of creating complexity in a character—after all, it's complex! Actors who successfully bring to life complex and contradictory characters create rich and detailed *layers*. Just like people, characters may *say* one thing while *doing* the exact *opposite*. Think of a person who says, "I'm sorry" while glaring at you. Or—characters may *alternate* what they are doing—for instance, shifting their *intention* from *punishing* to *apologizing* and back again to *punishing*—with lightning speed. But describing the behavior as "defensive, yet vulnerable" is lazy. And inattentive to the behavior of real human beings.

10) "Let's give [this character] a hostile edge."

I was taught by my teacher Jean Shelton never to *"play attitude."* When you limit your script analysis to a quick psychological sketch of this sort—that the character has a *wary* attitude towards his brother, a *tender* attitude towards his sister, a *hostile* attitude towards his father—you limit your imagination.

Now, describing this hypothetical family the way I did just now would be better than dismissing the family as "dysfunctional." It's okay to note that it sounds like a dysfunctional family—but *don't stop* with that generality. Go deeper. Ask *questions* about the family's *emotional history*: Where is the mother? Is there a history of abuse, neglect, or addiction? What has the father done to lose his son's trust?

Ideas for *objectives* may come out of speculation around these questions. For instance, perhaps our main character is driven by a need *to protect the sister from the brother and father*. A spine so primal can sustain an actor's performance and create relationships of emotional depth and power.

11) "I want more energy, but not hysterical energy." Or, "The character is grossed out, but not *too* grossed out."

Actors are not machines. You cannot dial a performance the way you dial levels on equipment. The *dialing* result direction drives actors to despair and makes them feel that no matter what they do, it will be wrong. Attempts to dial performances are assaults on an actor's connection to the moment. Experienced actors will do their best, but over time will become less interested in what the director has to say. A director who gives *dialing* direction is sending a clear signal to the actors that he is clueless about the character's interior life—and that he has done zero script analysis preparation. I can't help feeling that *dialing* is the very worst result direction.

12) "You need to have a smirk on your face, because the script says so."

Sometimes the script itself seems to be giving an emotional result. Sometimes a character has a line of dialogue declaring his emotional state—such as, "I'm a callous person," or, "I'm frightened." Or another character has a line: "You look so smug." There can be stage directions or parentheticals in the script describing the character's emotions, such as, "disappointed" or "her voice quivering with rage." The actor whose character's emotional state is being described in the text (whether in dialogue or stage direction) may feel obligated to produce that emotion. Many actors ignore—and may literally cross out with a Sharpie—the emotional parentheticals, because creating the emotional subtext is the very province of the actors. (It's a lot like the way directors typically disregard suggestions by the writer for camera angles.)

Don't think of the script as giving emotional instructions. Instead look for the emotional *clues* to the subtext. Actors already torture themselves with worry and stress over whether or not they have the "right" emotion. As soon as they start envisioning the characters in terms of what emotion they "should" be having, their emotional life is dying a little death. Directors can help support them in finding an emotional life that is honest and original by *questioning* the emotional-result stage directions in the script.

13) Bonus example! "Can you split the difference between take 3 and take 5?" "Do it the same but one year younger." "Can you play it more anecdotally?"

These are actual quotes that have been reported to me from actual sets. I call this "ridiculous direction."

Alright. Okay. Who knows? Maybe saying, "Do it the same, but one year younger," will mean something to a particular actor and do just the trick.

But—seriously. It. Might. Not. You need other options.

Quick Fixes

There are powerful tools ready to come to your rescue. I call them *Quick Fixes* because when you know how to use them, they're more efficient than lengthy emotional mapping or facile pop-psychology explanations, and more effective than result-oriented generalities about the characters' character traits or emotional states.

I also call them Quick Fixes because I don't want you to get discouraged about how depressingly familiar you may have found the list of result directions earlier in this chapter. And, okay, let's face it—I wanted you to read this chapter and I knew one titled "Quick Fixes" would be the first thing you'd read, no matter where I placed it in the book, so I figured I might as well put it at the beginning.

These "quick fixes" are not a cheat sheet, but a sophisticated set of *tools* to create believable behavior. To quote directing coach Adrienne Weiss, "An actor shouldn't do something unless something makes him do it. To strengthen a reaction, make what's *pushing* the actor/character stronger." That's what the tools do—address the stimulus, create a *reason* for the character's behavior.

I shouldn't give you the impression that result direction never works, because sometimes it does. When a director has a deep level of trust with an actor, they can probably say just about anything to each other. But how do you get to that trust? I recommend this path: genuine curiosity about what makes actors tick, real concern for emotional honesty from your actors, love for your characters, and an interest in revealing truths about human behavior. Actors pick up on all that.

Along the way, the tools will help and support you. Here they are:

- *verbs* (aka *intention* or *objective* or *need*);
- *facts* (aka *emotional history* or *backstory*);
- *subtext imagery;*
- *emotional event;*
- *obstacle;*

- *metaphor, the "as if"*;
- *physical life*;
- and—*questions*.

These powerful tools are keys to the inner life of the story and its characters. Like result-oriented generalities, the *tools* can stop working unexpectedly—*but they are less likely to*. And if they do stop working, the situation is less hopeless, because *verbs, facts, images, events, metaphor, physical life, and questions*, in addition to being helpful language for direction, are useful *script analysis* tools. They open up your imagination. Once you are alive and active in the subtext of the script, you *will have* new ideas—this I promise you. The tools turn ideas into events and psychology into behavior. They are active and dynamic rather than static, sensory rather than intellectual, specific rather than general, and above all, emotional rather than abstract. Okay. Let's jump in.

Verbs

You may have noticed that many of the examples of result direction involve adjectives—*be quirky, be funny, be dangerous, be sexy, be sad, be angry, be defensive, be suspicious, be awkward, be tormented*. A powerful way to be less result-oriented is to get excited about *verbs* and to incorporate more of them in your communication. Verbs (like *demand, beg, seduce, blame*) describe experience and are more active than adjectives. Some of my directing students tell me that *verbs* have changed their lives.

Here's an invitation that may seem at first burdensome, but I promise you, will be liberating: *get specific*. For example, instead of describing a character by saying he is "being defensive," let's see if we can *translate* that generality into a more specific verb. For now, let's consult the Short List of Verbs, in Appendix A. You might say that the right verb is not on that list. You might want to say that the appropriate verb translation for "being defensive" is *to defend* or *to protect* or *to deflect*.

Totally cool. These are verbs and they might work; I don't rule them out. But I've got to be honest. When I think about the verbs *to defend* or *to protect* or *to deflect*—those verbs feel wimpy to me and I want to keep looking for a *bolder choice*. What about *complain, belittle,* or *warn?* Strong, active verbs.

I found those ideas by thinking about the defensive behaviors I have seen in life (including my own). When people are being defensive, it's often because information is coming at them that they don't like, or don't want to face—information that impairs their self-image. Each "defensive" person has her particular *tactics* to take attention off the information she perceives as an attack. She might *complain* about being picked on unfairly; she might *belittle* the source of the information; she might *warn* the person conveying the information not to persist. She might even *accuse* the other person of something entirely irrelevant, in order to take the conversation off-topic.

I don't claim that the Short List of Verbs (or even the longer list, in Appendix B) comprises all of human behavior—they're examples, to orient you to the world of verbs.

Verbs are a quick fix, but they are also central to the basic understanding of a character—that the behavior of characters (and people) arises from their *needs*. I use the term Verb Family to introduce a constellation of tools: *verb* (or *intention*), *objective* (or *need, through-line*), and *spine*. The Verb Family is valuable for creating a characterization, as well as for structuring a scene. Here are a few examples of how a member of the Verb Family can function as an alternative to common result directions.

Use an active verb instead of an emotion.

A strong, active verb creates an emotional response between characters. That's its job. "To confront" is an example of an active verb. It has an emotional component in that being confronted—for instance, over lying or cheating—has a serious emotional effect on the person being confronted. And—it has a serious emotional effect on the person doing the confronting! I mean, have you ever confronted someone for their deliberate cruelty? Can you imagine how doing such a stressful thing would churn your emotions? (I'm talking about face-to-face, not on Twitter. The anonymity of social media makes confrontation feel easy, but in real life it's not.)

Can you see how "to accuse" or "to punish" is more powerful than "to become angry"? The word "become" is a verb, but it's not active toward another person. Active verbs focus each actor's attention on their scene partner—on the effect they are having on their scene partner—instead of on their own performance. Thus the actors are *engaged* with each other, they are *listening*. When the actors affect each other, *something happens*. If one character is *begging* and the other one is *ridiculing*, something will happen! Someone will get hurt—or won over—or maybe something else no one expected. These are the *emotional events*. Now you've got drama. Or comedy. The verbs work for both.

We cannot decide how to feel; we can decide what to *do*. Verbs are experiential, dynamic, and playable rather than descriptive and result-oriented.

A couple of examples of translations from emotional result to verb:

- Instead of the adjective *vicious*, the verb *to belittle*.
- Instead of adjectives *weak* or *desperate*, the verb *to beg* or *to plead*.

Use a verb instead of an attitude.

Examples of translating *attitudes* to *verbs* or *objectives* kind of make themselves:

- Instead of *an accusatory attitude*, the verb *to accuse*.
- Instead of *a threatening attitude*, the verb *to threaten*.
- Instead of *a mocking tone*, the verb *to mock*.
- Instead of *a friendly attitude*, the objective *to make friends*.
- Instead of *cheerful*, the objective *to cheer the other character up*.

Those are simple ones. Some you have to think about a bit. For example, instead of *hostile,* you might consider the objective *to make her feel unwelcome* or *make her feel uncomfortable.*

Superior actors will not be harmed by your using verbs instead of adjectives and less experienced actors may very well be rescued from disaster. An actor who is floundering may find the right track. A scene may come alive right before your eyes! So instead of asking an actor to "play it sexy" (the result), you might suggest that he "flirt" with her (verb); instead of asking an actor to "be angrier," you might suggest that she "accuse" or "punish" him.

Please do not think of me as the language police! If "a mocking tone" sounds more natural than "to mock," go for it. I want you to become invested in something more important than just using "correct" instead of "incorrect" language. I want you to understand that what is *happening* between characters is more significant than line readings. What matters—however you describe it—is the *intention* underneath, the *need* for each character to have an effect on the other characters.

For the director, the shift from attitude to verb looks like a small one—but really it's a big one. It means thinking of the story as a network of *relationships* instead of a collection of performances. This simple but sophisticated shift to your understanding of storytelling will advance your skills more than you can imagine. Because it helps you determine and recognize *emotional events.* Emotional events tell your story.

It's time for me to mention that when I say *suggest* such and such direction, I really do mean suggest. This is what I like to call the *language of permission.* For instance, "What do you think about this thought I had?" Or, "I was wondering whether this idea might be worth trying . . ." The *language of permission* is not about diplomacy—it's about honesty. If a director has an idea, even one that she is passionately committed to, no one really knows whether it will work until the actors try it.

Use a verb instead of "take it down."

Actors actually hear directors say things like, "Can you take it down by about 90%?" Can you hear how hard it would be to interpret this direction—other than to assume the director hates everything about you? It can sap actors' energy to be constantly told to "take it down" instead of a more specific direction. It can make them feel that you don't care if they commit, that you don't want them to engage.

Verbs can help. You may notice, though, that it will take more thought on your part to articulate precisely what it is you want using verbs. This is why you need to prepare! Yes, I am advocating homework, but the extra mental exertion is good for you! Directing is not supposed to be easy. Asking an actor to *coax* rather than *demand* might be another way of getting them to "take it down." Do you want the actor to punish? To warn? To complain? Each of those verbs would give a different level of intensity to a scene or moment; *punish* might be the most intense and *complain* the least intense. But—you can't be sure until they try it! It's not a chemistry formula, where "X" milliliters of hydrochloric acid combined with "Y" milliliters of bleach will always turn the litmus paper a certain color.

When director Courtney Hunt shot the indie film *Frozen River,* she had already worked with her lead, Melissa Leo, on a short film; she knew that Leo would bring a lot of energy to the set. While shooting *Frozen River,* instead of telling Leo to "take it down," Hunt said in an interview that she would ask Leo to "confess it." This is a brilliant way to adjust a performance! It not only prevents the performance from going over the top, it supports the deep vulnerability of this lost and haunted character.

Use a verb instead of "give it more energy."

Choosing stronger verbs is great for creating more energetic performances. Look at the difference in energy between *to convince* and *to accuse.* In real life, the verb *to convince* is more common than the verb *to accuse*—and for good reason. In the business and social world, *convincing* someone to admit they lied is more diplomatic, and probably more effective, than *accusing* them of lying. But for drama—or comedy—the more heightened verb, *to accuse,* can take the scene to another level. Vivid verbs like *accuse* or *provoke* or *seduce* may be counterproductive in real life—but in narrative fiction, they are more exciting than the socially acceptable verbs like convince.

Use a verb instead of describing "what the character is like" or "how I see the character."

We are what we do. I had an acting teacher who used to roar at us, "If a man is standing on his head in the middle of the road, nobody asks if he's the type!" At the time his statement (which he repeated often, at full volume) was a riddle to me; I pondered it for a long time without understanding. What I know now years later is that actors and directors waste energy and time gossiping about the characters, arguing over whether the character "would do" such and such a thing. *If he does it, he would do it!*

Actors sometimes resist this idea. You'll hear them say: "My character would never manipulate—she's too nice." Or, "My character wouldn't flirt—he's uptight about his sexuality." News flash: Uptight people flirt! Nice people manipulate! Proud people beg! Shy people brag! People are complex! In real life, we do lots of things that are inexplicable to others—and even to ourselves. Actors and directors who get stuck in "what the character is like" miss entirely what a tangle of opposites humans really are. You don't get to the complexity of a character by indulging in *analysis paralysis*—it only piles convolution upon convolution, psychologizing the character to death.

One way to create complexity in characters is to remind yourself that human behavior is often irrational—possibly more often than not. Another way is to understand what makes a character complex is to notice that he does different things at different times. Robert Downey, Jr. is a master at this; he can change intentions (verbs) in the wink of an eye—he is able to charm, challenge, whine, demand, seduce—not all at once (although it may seem like it)—but *one at a time in extremely quick succession.* This makes his characters complex, unpredictable—and quirky.

Don't waste time wrestling over some abstract concept of what the character's personality is. Go for the behavior.

Use a verb instead of a judgment.

Instead of denouncing a character as manipulative, give some thought to the specific behaviors of a manipulative person. For example, the mother, played by Mo'Nique, in the 2009 film *Precious.* I expect that many of us might view Mary as manipulative. But let's go deeper than that negative generality and instead break down—deconstruct—that judgment into specific behaviors or *intentions.* Here are some verbs I thought of: Mary *demands,* she *goads,* she definitely *punishes*—but she also *sweet-talks* and *cajoles;* she even *begs.* Not all at once—different verbs in different situations. She's complicated! More complicated than her luckless daughter, played by Gabourey Sidibe, who has one single need: to make someone, anyone, love her.

Use a verb instead of a line reading.

During your script analysis, you can think up ways to translate the line reading in your head into a verb. The line reading, "*Please* help me" might carry the intention *to beg;* the line reading, "Please *help* me," the intention *to demand;* the line reading, "Please help *me,*" perhaps the intention *to complain.* But when you're out of time, don't beat yourself up. Just remember that when you have the urge to demonstrate a line reading for an actor, what you really want is a particular *intention,* or verb. If you can't think of any other way of communicating what you want than a line reading, it can help if you say something like, "I know it sounds like I'm giving a line reading, but there's an intention I'm looking for and I can't think of the verb."

Use a through-line objective instead of an emotional map.

What do the characters want—or need—from each other? A *through-line objective* implies a verb—because if you *want* something, you will *do* something to get it. It's a more reliable tool than an *emotional map* for uncovering the complicated weave of the characters' shifting reactions to each other's behavior.

Facts

Two kinds of facts are useful to directors and actors: facts that are given in the script and facts that are not in the script, but can be *chosen* to create a character's emotional history. In Debra Granik's film *Winter's Bone*, Ree (Jennifer Lawrence) has a mother who does not speak or interact with her children—that's a fact in the script. The event that triggered the mother's unrelenting silence is not in the script. It could be useful for the actors to make a *choice* as to what that is.

If you encounter a disagreement with an actor about interpretation, go over the *facts* of the scene together. It's a helpful way to understand how the actor arrived at his choice. From there, the two of you may be able to discuss the issue more productively.

Use facts instead of psychologizing.

Facts are often more eloquent than explanations. *He called his mother every day of his honeymoon.* Isn't that fact more vivid and evocative than the psychological analysis, "he is very attached to his mother"?

Many common descriptions of characters strike me as gossipy: for instance, "she can't express her feelings." Even if it is true (and I can't help feeling the phrase is glib and lacks the ring of truth), it seems to me more helpful and accurate to translate this intellectual assessment into a *fact*: "She *doesn't* express her feelings."

Notice when there's no need to explain the facts.

Explanations can dilute the power of facts. Let's take the scene from *When Harry Met Sally* in which Sally (Meg Ryan) and Marie (Carrie Fisher) discuss Marie's married boyfriend. It could be tempting to describe the central fact this way: "Sally's best friend is dating a married man, and she disapproves." But "and she disapproves" is an unnecessary embellishment. Every woman I know, if her best friend is dating a married man, has a reaction. Sally's might be disapproval—or it might be worry; it might be resignation; she might even be hopeful that things will work out better than it looks like they're likely to. Those are possible *choices*. Don't *assume* Sally disapproves—make choices, not assumptions. Let the facts provoke *questions* rather than jumping to conclusions. And, here's a secret, a pro tip: If you start with a run-through or take in which the actress uses her very own personal feelings—in other words, plays the scene *as if it's her own BFF*—it may surprise you how little direction the scene will then need.

Use facts instead of attitudes.

It's not unusual for directors and actors see the line, "I already told you that," and immediately hear in their mind an attitude and tone of exasperation. Don't jump to that conclusion. Instead, take note of the *factual* information in the line: there has been a previous conversation between these two characters. Boom. From that fact, instead of making assumptions, ask questions: How many previous conversations? What was actually said? Did character B, who was told the information and yet is asking about it again, not believe character A? Or did she not listen? Was she distracted by some other secret concern? Facts and questions will begin to suggest an *emotional situation*.

Emotional situation may also be called the *given circumstances* or the *salient emotional facts*. Your curiosity about this emotional situation may lead to insight. It may dawn on you, from your own experience and understanding of life, that people do not always remember conversations accurately; the speaker may think she spoke on this particular subject, but really only skirted the issue, expecting a hint to be understood as a request. The actors can make that choice. Or—the opposite choice: that the topic has been revisited over and over. *Choices* bring a scene alive.

Use facts instead of a judgment.

Instead of labeling a character as a "liar," make a list of all the lies he has told. In other words, make it *specific* instead of *general*. Start with the ones that you know of from the script. Then ask what other lies he may have told that are not in the script. This exercise enriches your connection to the character. Ask yourself, what does he *not* lie about? In other words, what is his *code of ethics?* Even criminals have a code of ethics of some kind. Don't forget to check in with yourself and recall the lies you yourself may have told, and why.

Use facts instead of labeling character traits.

Look for ways to see the character's *situation* instead of labeling his character. Rather than asking an actor to play the character's "awkwardness," call attention to the facts of his situation, perhaps that he has moved to a new school, or has never had a successful date.

Use invented facts to create emotional life.

Backstory facts can be invented. Catherine O'Hara, in an interview for *The New Yorker,* spoke of her wardrobe for Moira in *Schitt's Creek*: "It's strong and it's armor, which is perfect when you've had your life ripped out from under you, like Moira, and you're in this place that's like the town you got out of earlier in life."

Wait, what? I'm a devoted fan of this series—I remember nothing in dialogue or action to inform us that Moira has grown up poor! That backstory was invented! It works perfectly, don't you think?

Imagery

The image recorded in the camera and viewed on the screen—cinematic imagery—is of course central to filmmaking. But I want to talk about *interior imagery,* subtext imagery—an *internal* world of association, memory, dream, wish. By imagery, I don't mean only visuals, but the experiences of all our five senses: what we see, hear, smell, taste, and touch. Imagery is one of the most magical tools of any storyteller. A successful director communicates sensory detail that locates the actors in the immediacy of the characters' experience.

The generalities most people use to describe their experiences are shortcuts, social necessities. Statements like, "it was weird," "it was challenging," "it was cool" are a step removed from primary experience. Primary experience is the experience of our five senses. During an earthquake, we hear very specifically the sounds of breaking glass and car alarms; we feel the bed move under our bodies; our eyes strain in the pitch darkness to pick out shapes; we may suddenly drench in sweat—our sensory life is alive to detail. Later, it becomes socially inappropriate to go into such personal detail; at that point, when asked about the earthquake, we summarized the experience by calling it "scary" or "wild."

Use images instead of asking for emotions.

Sensory memories are powerful evokers of emotion and subtext. The memory of the smell of baking bread can whisk us back to the kitchen of our youth; a phrase from an old song can return us to the delicate yearnings of a long-ago love; reading the news can make us weep or rage.

Imagery can call forth expressive behavior from an actor and make his deep emotions available. Years ago in a workshop, I was directing a scene from the play *Orpheus Descending* by Tennessee Williams (made into the movie *The Fugitive Kind,* with Marlon Brando and Anna Magnani). It starts with Lady, who thinks she is alone, muttering aloud, "I wish I was dead." Val, who has overheard her, steps out of the shadows and says, "No, you don't, ma'am." After a few rehearsals, I was not happy with what the actor was doing with this line; it kept sounding like a line in a play, rather than anything a person might actually say to another person. When I mentioned to him that I thought the moment was not yet fulfilled, he began to speak the line with more emphasis—which only made things worse. He was adding a fake urgency to a moment for which he had not yet found an authentic connection.

What I wanted was that he should *feel moved* by Lady's line "I wish I was dead." I wanted from him a strong emotion that could create in him a compelling need *to help or rescue her*. In the moments while I pondered what to say to deepen his performance, I allowed myself to free-associate to the word "dead." Unexpectedly, from my own memory arose an image of the first time that I saw a dead body of a friend—a person still young—not all made up in a funeral casket, but lying on a gurney in an emergency ward. This experience had happened years ago, yet the image was—and still is—seared in my brain. I pulled the actor aside. I looked him in the eye and asked, "Have you ever seen a dead person?" His eyes shifted, inward it seemed; he said quietly, "Yes." I said, "Let's run the scene." After that, his delivery of the line was honest, direct, and emotionally full.

Use images instead of explanations.

Let's say you are directing a movie with a main character whose backstory is that at the age of four she was left with an unpleasant relative for six months during her mother's hospitalization for a serious illness. Rather than waste time describing and intellectualizing the character's emotional terrain—withdrawn, suspicious, self-destructive—you could instead summon an image. Perhaps that of the door closing on the child's father as he leaves her there, or even the last light of his attempt at a smile.

Such images (memories) live with people and characters the rest of their lives. Calling upon the *imagery* associated with important events approximates more closely the workings of these events on actual human psyches than does *explaining* their effects. Access to such images is one of the actor's most important tools. Directors who can communicate on the level of interior imagery can get actors to do anything.

Metaphor or "As If"

Metaphor, analogy, parallel are also known as the "magic as if" or the "it's like when." After verbs, these are the most powerful tools available to directors.

Use an "as if" instead of instructing actors to produce a mood.

If you wanted a "chilly" atmosphere in a family dinner scene, you might ask the actors to play the scene *as if* the first person who makes a mistake in table manners will be sentenced to death.

Use an "as if" instead of asking for a bigger reaction.

A director told me of directing a scene in which the character wakes up after a night of partying and finds a coworker in her bed. The director wanted the actor to have a reaction of horror—a look of "what have I done?!"—but didn't want to give the result direction, "Be more horrified." So she suggested the adjustment, "as if it's your uncle." This, she reported, really worked.

Use a metaphor instead of dialing a direction.

Instead of the *dialing direction,* "She's mean but not that mean," how about this use of *metaphor:* "It's not as mean as kicking a cat in the head. Maybe as mean as deliberately 'forgetting' to pick up your roommate's dry cleaning."

Instead of "be more cheerful," an adjustment that everything the character opposite her is saying is really good news.

Be like Catherine O'Hara. Use metaphor anytime you want. When Catherine O'Hara describes her wardrobe for Moira Rose as "armor," that's a metaphor.

Events

Emotional event is not the same as plot or incident; it's the underlying human event—like a fight, a negotiation, a trick, a healing, a confession, a seduction. Don't get me wrong—I love a well-plotted story—but what really draws an audience in are the *emotional* events: the moments when the characters are touched, changed. Someone pisses someone off. Someone turns someone on. Someone hurts someone's feelings.

The *events* cause the audience to be involved in the story. Telling the actors that the scene is about a fight between two people who used to love each other just might give them all they need to create the poignancy you are looking for in the scene.

The plot event might be that one galaxy overthrows another galaxy's way of life, but the *emotional event* underlying that plot event might be a betrayal, an act of revenge, or even, as I believe is suggested in the final episode of *Battlestar Galactica,* a gesture of healing.

I'm not claiming that it's easy to tell the difference between plot event and emotional event—*every single one* of my students and clients tells me that the concept of emotional event is the biggest puzzle of directing. It takes work, it takes trial and error, but I can promise you that the "aha" moment when it starts to feel less like something esoteric and more like common sense will be worth it.

How can you spot the difference between *emotional event,* a tool which I believe will change your life as a director, and *emotional map,* which I've repeatedly asked you to avoid? Okay, it's subtle. A red flag is that unhelpful emotional maps often contain the phrase "and then he realizes," or "something makes her . . ."

Don't forget—every director needs to be on the lookout for the fake confrontation, the cliché apology, the "movie" love scene, the pat resolution that is really only a platitude. We don't want to *indicate* the emotional event—we want it to happen in the here and now and let the audience in on it.

What It's About

Sidney Lumet says in his book, *Making Movies,* that *what the movie is about*—its central theme, the sum of its issues, its core, its truth—is the most important thing a director must feel and understand. Lumet insists that *every* decision a director makes about the film should be based on *what the movie is about*—its spiritual truth, if you will. *The Godfather,* a rich and complex story, has many themes and issues—loss; betrayal and the endless cycle of revenge that begins with betrayal; corruption at every level of society; the twentieth-century immigrant experience from Europe to America. Director Francis Ford Coppola chose to make it a story about *family.*

According to Robert Zemeckis, *Forrest Gump* is a movie about grieving. (The interview in which Zemeckis disclosed this so fascinated me that I posted a YouTube video about it, "What Is Subtext?")

My sense of the Lorene Scafaria film *Hustlers* is that it's about loneliness.

Even commercials are *about* something. Car commercials are about one of three things: "protecting your family"; "escaping your family"; or getting laid. When I was growing up in the 1950s and '60s, commercials for beauty products were about women making themselves attractive to men; in today's world, they're about self-empowerment.

Physical Tasks

The simplest thing you can ask of an actor is a physical task.

Use physical life instead of enforcing an attitude or emotion. I heard a story of a director of a major motion picture who was having trouble with a direction to an actor. The actor kept falling into a vaguely seductive manner—even though the scene had nothing to do with seduction. The director felt that, for this actor, seducing was an intention he tended to revert to without thinking—a default. The director asked him to play the scene less seductively; the actor's line readings did not change. She repeated the direction—still no change. The performance was stalled. The scene took place in a kitchen and finally the director said, "Why don't you go to the refrigerator and look for a snack during this conversation. And let's let the refrigerator door be a little stuck." As soon as he had a physical task—the search for a snack—connected to an obstacle—the stuck refrigerator door—the actor was freed from his default setting and the scene played simply and naturally. As it happened, the story was *about* the difficulties families can have communicating during holiday gatherings, so the actor's struggle with the stuck fridge door was revelatory of his emotional predicament—stuck at a family dinner when he would rather be anywhere else.

Use physical life instead of intellectualizing the emotional transitions.

The physical movement (the staging, also called "blocking") of a scene is the director's responsibility. Inventive blocking can expand a director's visual options and add excitement to the storytelling. In real life people's physical movements are manifestations of their inner emotional life. Insightful blocking can reveal the emotional events and help you avoid directing with "emotional maps." A simple way to create the drama of a character's reaction to bad news could be to ask the actor, "Why don't you go ahead and collapse in this chair when you hear this."

Use physical life instead of intellectualizing character traits and succumbing to "fine wine" direction.

Director Tim Burton made sure that Johnny Depp was given the scissorhands prop a whole year before shooting of *Edward Scissorhands* began, so Depp could take them home and practice wearing them. This was such a smart idea! It would have been so easy to fall into intellectualizing the character's psychology, like describing Edward as *vulnerable yet violent*. But *can you imagine* what it would really be like to be doomed to using scissorhands in your daily life? Take a moment to imagine it—imagine it *physically*. The physical scissorhands create deep and complex needs—for human touch, for understanding, and, very possibly, for exacting revenge on the world.

Questions, Questions, Questions

"Do you want it seductive? I can do seductive."

Directors are not the only ones who give actors result direction. Actors do it to themselves! Actors routinely come into casting sessions and immediately ask, "What's this character like?" In rehearsal or on the set, it could easily happen that you use all the tools when you give direction—only to hear the actor respond, "You mean you want it more sarcastic?" Or, "You want me to pump it up?"

Have faith. When an actor asks you for an adjective or emotional result, you are allowed to keep bringing up emotional history, verbs, objective, subtext imagery, obstacles, metaphors, physical tasks—or, especially, what the scene is about. But probably the most helpful thing to do is *ask questions*. Preferably—always—ask questions. And listen to the answers.

Use questions instead of psychological explanations.

The *Winter's Bone* scene where Ree begs her mute mother for help portrays a desolation beyond any abstract explanation of its psychology. You might possibly approach this extreme of loss and isolation by quietly posing the question, "How long has it been since she has spoken to you?" Don't make the actor tell you her choice; there is no wrong answer to this question.

Use questions instead of issuing instructions.

In the earlier example from the *Orpheus Descending* scene, I did not say to the actor, "Use the imagery of a dead body under this line." Instead I asked him a *question*: "Have you ever seen a dead person?" When he said "Yes," I saw something in his eyes—and I stopped talking. I could see he was now ready to come from a truthful place.

Use questions instead of judgments.

The operative question is "Why?" Why did this character pour paint on the windshield of her ex-lover's car? Because she's a bitch? Don't be satisfied with that facile judgment. Let's ask this: What did the ex do that caused her to retaliate?

Use questions instead of frontloading.

By "frontloading," I mean telling the actor all your ideas before they do or say anything. Let them try the scene. Find out what *their* questions are. And when they ask questions—don't feel obligated to think up an answer if you haven't got one.

A good question is better than a bullshit answer.

Use questions all the time.

Directors often think that their job is to explain their ideas, but I think storytelling is more exciting than that. Lawyers and accountants explain things; storytellers are here to suggest, illuminate, juxtapose, and let the audience draw their own conclusions. What would it be like to think of directing not as giving instructions, but as posing questions? What if all the tools I've been discussing—verbs, facts, imagery, events, physical tasks, as ifs—function best in the form of questions to the actor?

- "Do you think these characters have ever pulled off a robbery before?"
- "Do you think he wants to pick a fight? Or is he hoping she will stay calm?"
- "What if the character is lying when she says this line?"
- "What if just before this, she received a disturbing prank phone call?"
- "What are your associations to the imagery of a *totem?*" "A *labyrinth?*" "A *cherry orchard?*" "A *dream extractor?*"
- "What's important about this scene?"
- "Do you have any impulse to turn away from her when she says that?"
- "What is this relationship about?"
- "Do you know what you want?"

Questions are the bomb—with an important caveat. If you ask actors questions, be prepared: the answers they give you may not be the ones you were expecting! If you're not excited about hearing their answers, don't ask the questions.

Translation

When you ask for a *general result,* the worst thing that can happen is that you get what you've asked for: generic characters, clichéd relationships, a stereotyped villain, forced humor, overcooked drama, and no connection.

Good actors won't do this, of course. Good actors will do their very best to decipher result directions and *translate* them into choices that are playable for them—like good writers, who know not to follow producers' notes literally, to instead look for "the note behind the note."

Non-professional actors will have a harder time of it, because they lack the tools of craft with which to make the translation from result direction into playable choices.

It's not a director's job to do the actor's work for them. It's okay to say to an actor: "I know I'm asking for a result here and I'm going to need you to figure out how to make it playable." Allow them time to make the translation.

When actors ask the director what result she is looking for, it may be a trust issue. Directors can easily fall into circumlocution and over-talking. An inexperienced actor may ask for a line reading because he's afraid of being fired if he doesn't decode the director's confusing directives. An experienced actor may have given up on deciphering what the director wants.

An exceptionally seasoned actor probably already knows his character by the time he gets to set. If a director asks for a tweak to the performance, a veteran actor may prefer to get that information via a delivery system likely to be the least inflected with the director's interpretation—like a line reading. If an actor asks you for a line reading, that doesn't mean you should provide it—rather, it might be a good opportunity to assure the actor he can trust his own instincts.

Pro Tips

Tag-team result direction with the tools.

Combining a result direction with one of the tools can turn it into gold. For example, combining a *character label* with *imagery*—as in, "She's an extrovert, like a golden retriever." ("Extrovert" is the character label; the golden retriever is the image.) Or combining an *emotional result* with a *verb*: "His anger makes him punish the world."

Flipping

You can *flip* a result idea to a verb or objective by understanding, for example, that genuinely sexy people *make the people around them feel sexy*. People who are "fun to be with" make others feel like *they* are fun to be with. "Argumentative" people pick fights by making the other person argue with them.

Reframing

If you have an idea about a character's *emotional condition* ("She is worried"), you can reframe it into an *emotional need* ("She needs reassurance"). Instead of telling the actor to *be more confused and embarrassed*, you might say, "I'm thinking this might be a moment of confusion and embarrassment."

Building

Whenever you can, *build on* the actor's idea. The exchange of ideas is not a zero-sum game—ideas can feed and spark each other.

Deconstruction

Break down a simplistic label into its component behaviors. A "quirky" character might change moods—from bright and cheerful to fully sorrowful—with rapid fire flashes. (Of course, I'd prefer to translate those moods into verbs—say moving with rapid fire immediacy back and forth between *celebrating* and *mourning*.) Characters with an "epic quality," such as the royal family in *Black Panther*, have a certain posture; they speak slowly, in the expectation that others will be willing to wait as long as it takes to hear their words.

Recognize a sense of intention when you see it.

You're not expected to come up with the perfect verb every single time. If you're able to recognize a *sense of intention* in actors, you'll be ahead of the game. A sense of intention arises organically when the actors have *objectives* toward each other. When in doubt, ask the actors, "Do you know what you want in this scene?" and let them find their own verbs.

Use the language of permission.

You don't want to be a micromanager who instructs an actor to play a certain verb on a certain line or orders the actor to apply a certain "as if" adjustment to a particular moment. The *language of permission* gives you conversation openers like, "I had an idea that I was thinking might be worth trying," or "What do you think of *punishing* on this line, instead of *begging?*" If an actor's performance could be better, let the actor know—indeed, they want you to! But micromanaging every adjustment and transition is a horror show. So, instead of telling the actor, "Switch from anger to fear on this line," consider suggesting, "I'm wondering whether there might be a transition that could happen around here." Or even be completely direct: "I think we're missing a transition. Do you want to figure it out for yourself or shall we talk about it?"

You don't do this to be nice or make the actors like you. The *language of permission* helps you empower the actors and call upon them to fully participate, to bring all their talent and resources to the role. So, in a way, really, it's selfish on the part of the director—because when the actors are contributing their full energy, the story wins and the director wins. The best thing about the language of permission is that it helps you be more truthful and direct. If you say to an actor, "I think this adjustment is worth trying," instead of, "This is how you should do it," you are actually being more honest—because, until they try it, *you don't really know whether or not it will work.*

Be inventive.

Instead of saying, "Be more insecure," you could say, "Let's find some places where your character's insecurities might show through."

The Privacy Rule

Have I made it clear yet that any of these adjustments—and all conversations of any substance with actors—should happen in privacy? Without the crew or producers listening. Make time for this. Connect with the actors. Trust them. The way to get actors to trust you is to trust them. The tools I am offering are not tricks to manipulate the actors—the goal is honest interactions and honest performances.

The "Same Page"

Sometimes a director complains to me that their movie was ruined because an actor was not "on the same page." Then, when I question the director further, it turns out that what he meant by "not on the same page" was that the actor did not deliver the line reading the director expected. Don't go down that road.

I began this chapter with a description of the most common complaint I hear from actors about directors. But now I offer you the biggest compliment that an actor can give a director: "They knew exactly what they wanted—and gave me complete freedom." That sounds totally impossible, doesn't it? That a director could do both those things at once? It's not impossible—it just takes a lot of work. Mike Nichols, in his *Inside the Actors Studio* interview, was asked what he would do when an actor was not playing "in the same key" as he envisioned the story. Nichols's reply: "I figure it's my job to find the key in which we both can play." In other words, don't play the blame game. You're the director, the leader. Look for ways to take responsibility.

CHAPTER TWO

Moment By Moment

"As a director, it's important to understand the actor's process."—**Chadwick Boseman**

I want to take a stab at bringing you inside the actor's world, into a feeling for some of the challenges of acting. Perhaps you'll think I'm telling you more than a director needs to know. Okay, I'll cop—I'm a believer in knowing more than you strictly need to know. Creativity is bountiful. If you restrict yourself to learning only the things you are sure you will use, you are resisting the very first principle of creativity, which is bounty.

Fear And Control

"I send the actors out to suffer for me every day."
—**Jean Renoir**

Actors are in an unrelenting existential spin. A good performance is an unguarded one. It feels like flying, like letting go and floating free. It's a high like no other. Once an actor feels the euphoria of an unguarded performance, they can't help but want to feel it over and over again. This can make them anxious—self-conscious. When an actor is self-conscious, her interior mantra has unwittingly become: *How am I doing? Am I saying this right? Does the audience get it? Does everybody like me?*

Many actors don't like to discuss their "process." An actor may be superstitious about exposing such subterranean material to the light of day—afraid that once revealed, a technique that has worked a hundred times won't work anymore—that talking about her choices might put her "in her head."

I want directors to know how wildly frightening acting can be, how vulnerable you are when you're out there on stage or in front of a camera, how painful it is to hear criticism, how easy it is to doubt oneself. The actor's face, body, voice, thoughts, and feelings are exposed. He thirsts for a core, existential reassurance and validation. Praise is as necessary to him as water. So is honest feedback when the work is not yet where it needs to be.

Risk

"It's a risk not to take risks."—**Al Pacino**

When actors can't trust the director for truthful feedback, they will look elsewhere for it—maybe the DP, or a member of their entourage. Or, they may critique themselves; they may watch and monitor their performance—in other words, they may become cautious. Cautious acting is not very good acting, because in real life people incautiously make a lot of mistakes—laugh too loud, invest unwisely, marry the wrong person. In movies, they make even bigger mistakes—bring the wrong car to a robbery, walk into a room where the killer lurks, make a foolish wish that magically comes true. High stakes, unpredictability, risk, serendipity, surprise, mistakes, danger give a performance the texture of real life—and the sense of "heightened" reality needed for entertainment. Honest, risk-taking acting makes drama more moving, comedy more startling, adventure more thrilling, mystery more suspenseful.

Being watched is in the job description for an actor. Actors at the top of their game love to give, love to be watched. Like elite athletes, they live to compete, they are hungry to perform. A great actor allows the world into his deepest, most private self, transformed by the created reality of the script. But sometimes actors hide. They make a safe choice instead of a risk-taking one. The "safe" choice can seduce them into formula or cliché—that's what Pacino means when he says, "It's a risk not to take risks."

Even excellent actors can panic and hide. Darren Aronofsky said in an interview for *The Wrestler*, "If there's any accomplishment that's my greatest accomplishment in this movie, it's the fact Mickey Rourke never wears sunglasses in this film. I fought him every day about the sunglasses, because he wants to hide."

It's one of life's little unfairnesses. If an actor takes a big risk and it works, it is much better acting than cautious acting. But if an actor takes a big risk and it doesn't work, it looks much worse than cautious acting—it's called *overacting*. It is so acutely embarrassing to be caught overacting that some actors would rather give a cautious performance than a risk-taking one.

Amy Adams has said in interviews that while making *Junebug*, she was terrified of overacting her exuberant character Ashley; she was afraid that it would come across as a judgment or comment on the character if she accidentally crossed the line into caricature; she loved Ashley's enthusiastic embrace of life and wanted her every moment to be human and recognizable. Her director Phil Morrison had her back. He saw the truth Adams kept bringing to the set every day and *gave her permission* to keep taking risks, to keep going further. She relied on that permission and trusted it—it enabled her to let go and create the moving, indelible performance that launched her career. She depended on Morrison's watchful eye. He was watching her, so she didn't have to watch herself.

Many directors are afraid to tell actors when they are pushing or forcing or getting overcooked (less pejorative terms for overacting). But—and you can trust me on this—good actors are not offended when a director catches a false note and informs the actor. They are grateful. Actors would rather be told the truth than be allowed to continue and ultimately be cut out of the film or—far worse—live to see their overacted or fake performance in the final cut. They need the director to tell them these things. Always take them aside and speak to them *in absolute privacy,* but do tell them. If the director doesn't tell them, they may feel they must watch the performance themselves, and become cautious.

Unlikeable Characters

Actors can make choices they know are wrong out of fear that an unlikeable character will lose the sympathy of the audience. Sentimentalizing a character is as dangerous as judging a character. Fear of hurting her self-image with the audience or reluctance to find disagreeable behavior truthfully in herself—or plain squeamishness—may cause her to resist the role if the character is unlikeable. Shelley Winters, in her interview on *Inside the Actors Studio,* spoke of the distress she felt on the set of *A Patch of Blue* when she—in her own life a civil rights advocate who joined the march from Selma to Montgomery—had to play a racist and say a line using the N-word.

"It was physically impossible . . . I just got to that scene and I would vomit. And I would come in every day and I would have some story [to justify] why this woman got so biased, how she turned out like this, what could have happened . . ." At a certain point, according to Winters, director Guy Green saw that what the actor thought were attempts to humanize her character were really resistances to the truth of the script. The director joined forces with the film's star, Sidney Poitier. Together they convinced Winters that the way to honor the story, which was anti-racist, was to take the bigger risk of facing and finding truthfully the behavior of a person without shame for her racist behavior—with the hollow moral center of a bigot. Her work in the role was brave and revelatory, well deserving of the Oscar she won for it.

In a *Salon* interview, John Turturro said that when Spike Lee asked him to join the cast of *Do the Right Thing,* Lee asked him, "Who do you want to play?" Turturro replied, "I want to play the racist. Because that's what the movie's about."

Honesty

"I have a theory—our job isn't to lie to the audience, our job is to find the truth in the character. If we lie, we're giving the audience a little pinch of poison."—**Bryan Cranston**

"I just try to be as honest as I can."—**Kate Winslet**

"If a scene isn't honest, it stands out like a sore thumb."—**David Lynch**

Contrary to popular belief, acting is not pretending or faking. It is exposing oneself in a very intimate way. Actors in their work must be more deeply truthful than what passes for honest behavior in the regular world. Did I say "must be" more deeply truthful than in the regular world? I absolutely meant "get to be"! It's such a supreme relief to be honest, to be released from the obligations of the social mask.

My first acting teacher Jean Shelton taught me that acting is a noble profession, exactly because it's more honest than the social contract and because a great actor allows the world to witness his private, foolish, vulnerable self. A great director permits and challenges actors to bring their entire knowledge of life and their whole, flawed, idiosyncratic being to every role.

Simple, honest presence, like Brad Pitt in *Once Upon a Time . . . in Hollywood,* is the biggest risk—and the biggest reward. When a director asks an actor for more intensity, the actor may find that what he really needs to do is get simpler, more primal. To strip away the distraction of trying to do it "right," in order to get out of the way of his deeper resources. In other words, when the director asks him for *more,* the actor might very well allow himself to do *less.* This is one of the many reasons why a director should not try to tell a professional actor how to play his role.

Gregory Peck is said to have make a notation next to each line in his script: either "AR" or "NAR"—NAR meant *no acting required,* whereas AR reminded him that for this line, there was *acting required.* If an actor has the line, "I admire you without reservation," and she happens to be working opposite, say for instance, John Lithgow or Meryl Streep, that would be a "no acting required" line.

But plenty of lines are a struggle to say honestly. In a play I directed with a cast of non-actors, one young man had to say the line "I love you" to another character. This kid had a raw talent that I believed in. He always worked with scrupulous honesty and seemed incapable of lying in the regular world as well. He confided to me that I would have to cut the line, because he knew it would make him too self-conscious to say it in front of an audience. I asked him to come early to the next rehearsal. I had him stand on the stage, with me in the audience, and I asked him to tell me how he felt about me. He said, "I respect you. I think you're a good teacher and a good director." Then I said, "Now, I want you to say the words of the script, 'I love you,' but the only thing I want you to have in your mind is to let yourself mean exactly what you just said to me. Don't try to make it mean any more than that." When we opened, his performance in that scene was the most beautiful thing in the show. I had given him permission, you see, to feel that whatever he could bring *in his very own person* was adequate to the role, even if he had never said "I love you" in real life. From that point of honest connection, his imagination was engaged and his performance became a creative thing.

Many actors have a bag of tricks allowing them to achieve a towering rage, zero to sixty, in ten seconds—or to snap off witty lines in the brisk cadence of sit-com. These are marvelous skills to have! But an actor's ability to stay simple and unpredictable—to be a person, not a character—is the foundation of good acting.

In The Moment

"Just because they say 'Action' doesn't mean you have to do anything."—**Marlon Brando**

The legendary acting teacher Sanford Meisner had an exercise he used to do with a new group of students. He would ask them to sit and listen for a whole minute to the traffic outside the building. At the end of the minute, he would ask them, "Did you listen to the traffic in character, or as yourself?" The point of this simple exercise was to teach the young students to be *present in their bodies.* The actor starts with himself, he hears with his own ears, sees with his own eyes, touches with his skin, feels with his feelings. Then, as he does research into the clues in the script, he asks questions; he allows associations, impulses, and understandings to bubble up from deep inside him. He makes the character his own. During a superior performance, the actor may indeed feel that he inhabits the character's skin, that he has "become" the character. The audience may feel that too. What this really means is that he has allowed his imagination to become permeated with associations to the character of the script—while he inhabits his very own skin "in the moment."

The expression *in the moment* is a term of art that actors use and which you may have heard before—it's used not only in connection with acting but also athletics, spiritual disciplines, and life coaching. In everyday life, few of us live moment by moment all the time. When we watch ourselves, calculating the effect of our behavior on others; when we censor ourselves and choose our words and actions to meet social rules and expectations; when something painful or upsetting happens and we don't feel sad or angry until later—we are not in the moment. When we are "in our heads" instead of in our bodies, intellectualizing our feelings and sensations; when, while involved in one activity, our concentration is on the anxiety or anticipation we feel toward an activity in the future—we are not in the moment.

Come to think of it, being in the moment in real life is pretty rare. But it is available on a regular basis if you are an actor. An artist lives in two worlds: the regular, social world, and the imagined world. The knowledge of life we have from observing the everyday concerns of people in the real world is completely relevant to the choices that actors make about their characters. But the *obligations* of the social realm are *not* relevant to the artistic demands of the imagined realm. In the imagined realm, one is allowed to be uncensored, in the moment, free of social demands, unconcerned with result, following impulses, obeying only the deepest and most private truths. Actors have even invented a word for this: *disobligated.*

When an actor is "in the moment," he is relaxed, confident, and alert. He is responsive to the physical world around him; to his own interior world of impulse, feeling, and imaginative choices; to the words and subtext of the script; and to the behavior of the other actors. He is available. He is present. He speaks with a real voice, not an "actor voice." He inhabits his own skin. There is "somebody home" when you look in his eyes. Another term for being in the moment is *being present*—so it is literally the thing that gives an actor screen presence or charisma.

Actors have many jobs—preparing choices, learning lines, hitting marks, committing to the script, and making the direction work—but "moment-by-moment work" makes whatever else the actor is doing come alive. A skilled, experienced actor may reject direction that interferes with her moment-by-moment reality. Inexperienced actors may try to follow direction even if it means faking or indicating the result the director has asked for—once you get to the editing room, however, these clumsy efforts will need to be cut around, if not taken out altogether.

"Moment-by-moment" presence makes an actor seem lifelike and natural even in an extreme plot situation—Javier Bardem in *No Country for Old Men* comes to mind. An actor's commitment to the moment creates the tiny flickers of expression that make his face seem alive in between the words. When the actor deliberately *tries* for such flickers of expression, deliberately tries to hesitate, stutter, wink or grimace, the acting becomes mannered. When such flickers occur "in the moment," they make screen magic, they confer star quality.

"In the moment" for an actor has to do with freedom and fearlessness; it has to do with trust. It has to do with the actor not watching himself. It means that whatever preparation an actor does for a role is done ahead of time. Once the camera starts to roll or the curtain goes up, the actor lets go of the preparation and *allows* it to be there.

Or not! You see, there's a risk that the preparation won't work and the actor will be out there alone, drawing a blank, just saying words, with no inner life, with nothing happening. This is where the fearlessness comes in! Good actors, even after the harrowing experience of a mid-performance loss of concentration, continue to work properly, reworking their preparation and then jumping into the abyss of moment-by-moment presence. They continue to trust the process.

Many directors are in the dark as to the importance of moment-by-moment work and what it looks like. Take an acting class, get up there yourself, feel its terrors and its magic. Talk to actors. Make friends with them. Ask them how they feel about their craft.

The Character Has Free Will

Characters are people. They speak because they have something to say, move because they have somewhere to go. It's not a philosophical argument—it's an observation about good acting. Characters with free will are more believable and interesting than characters whose fates are predictable. The characters don't know what will happen next. Characters, *because they are people,* do things not because it is in the script, but because of the needs and circumstances of their life. In order for characters to have the same agency as a real person and respond freshly to events of the story each time the camera rolls—the character *borrows free will* from the actor.

In a *Los Angeles Times* interview, Leslie Odom Jr. described how this radical idea might operate for an actor. He said that when he played Aaron Burr in *Hamilton,* he imagined Burr in a kind of purgatory, where he has to work through this terrible mistake—the duel in which he killed Alexander Hamilton—and learn whatever he's meant to learn. So every night at the top of the show, he said to himself: "Maybe I can make it turn out differently tonight; if I make some different choices, if I'm kind enough in the right places, it doesn't have to end that way."

The Character Has A Subconscious Mind

> ***"What you have to remember in film is that the camera can read your mind."*—Sydney Pollack**

Geologists say that what we see of an iceberg is only ten percent; the other ninety percent is below water. People are like that, too; the words they say and things they do represent about ten percent of what is going on with them, what they're feeling, thinking, wishing for. The other ninety percent is *subconscious.* In life, people change subjects, make Freudian slips, and forget what they were saying, often without any reason they are aware of. Rather, the association they make is subconscious. Characters are more lifelike and three-dimensional if there are completely unplanned thoughts going on in their subconscious minds. It shows up in the actor's eyes—that sense of "somebody home."

It is the very nature of the subconscious mind that it's not subject to conscious control. That means that the actor must allow the character to borrow her own subconscious. In everyday life, we are all terrified that our subconscious thoughts and feelings will show—it might actually be one of our worst fears. For an actor, being in the moment means trusting her subconscious. This is the bravery of acting.

Permission To Fail

"Our feeling is that the most important thing on a set is that actors have enough confidence to try different things. If there's stress or tension, they won't go out on a limb because they won't want to embarrass themselves if they don't feel completely comfortable."—**Peter Farrelly**

"Permission to fail" means giving the actors unconditional love and freedom to make mistakes. It sounds idealistic, but I assure you it is a very practical thing to do. When I give an actor a direction, if I see a flicker of doubt, I add these magic words: "This might not work." Or a variation like, "I don't know if this will work or not, but I think it's worth a try." When I say the magic words, I perceive a shift in their face and body—more relaxed—and then they almost always do something wonderful.

But—this is important—I'm not trying to trick them! I'm only being honest. No matter how great my idea is, I don't know if it will work until the actor tries it.

The Social Mask

"If people act because they want to hide something of themselves, then I'm not interested. Acting has nothing to do with personal comfort."—**Jeanne Moreau**

What is risk but freedom to make mistakes? A mistake is a moment when we see the abyss open beneath our feet. But—forgive me for getting a little existential here—the abyss really *is* just beneath our feet, ready to open and swallow us. At any given moment each and every one of us is *this close* to letting the social mask slip, putting us daily on the brink of our worst fear—that if the world knew our secrets, we would be revealed as *lacking*—more foolish, lonely, mean-spirited, and boring than we could ever bear to admit. Actors let these moments show. Great actors let these moments show reliably. Great actors and all great artists know this secret: *There are no mistakes.*

When I say "great actors," I don't mean just the ones whose names you know. There are great actors plying their craft without the recognition of major awards—I'm thinking, for example, of Betty Gabriel (Georgina in *Get Out*). All the greats, known or unknown, perform a kind of stripping of the social veneer. It's an emotional, psychological, even spiritual exercise—absolutely unique to each actor—that allows them to work from below the social mask. *Stripping the social mask* allows a character's activities to read and come alive on the screen—even the most ordinary ones, like serving a dinner or walking down a hallway. Even if a *character* habitually and reflexively submits to the demands of the social world (like the title character in 2019's *Diane* or Warden Bernadine Williams in *Clemency*), the actor playing her (in *Diane*, that's Mary Kay Place; in *Clemency*, Alfre Woodard) drops her own personal social veneer. This is how the audience is allowed to engage with the painful vulnerability of a character who is driven, to the point of self-danger, by what others think of her.

Inventive directors can help give the permission and support to go below the social mask. According to the DVD commentary, while shooting the famous orgasm scene from *When Harry Met Sally*, director Rob Reiner felt, after the first take, that Meg Ryan's fake orgasm was not noisy enough to make the scene work. He said to her, "You know, it's only going to be funny if you go for it full force." But on the second take Ryan was still holding back. Reiner said, "Let me show you what I mean." He performed the wildest, most ridiculous fake orgasm he could muster. He did this not to demonstrate how she should play her role, but to break the ice, to let her know he was willing to look as foolish as he was asking her to be. And, in a way, to *prove to her that no matter how foolish she felt, this was a scene that she could not do wrong.*

It may have helped that Rob Reiner was an actor himself. But other directors without an acting background have been able to give this level of permission. Johnny Depp has said of Tim Burton, "He provides an atmosphere that you can try anything. It's so liberating. To have that possibility where you might make an absolute ass of yourself and, you know that, if I fall flat on my face, there's something to cushion that, there's safety there."

Director Michael Mann felt that an important part of preparing to shoot *Collateral* was stripping his two lead actors of their recognizability as movie stars, and he talked to both of them—Jamie Foxx and Tom Cruise—about this challenge. Mann asked Tom Cruise to spend weeks working as a FedEx delivery man, "scanning numbers, getting signatures, being polite in a certain way"—until nobody recognized him.

When Khandi Alexander got her role in *The Corner*, her acting coach told her she needed to lose her "dancer's walk" (she had been a star of Broadway musicals)—so Alexander took a job working as a grocery store clerk in order to help her shift her physical center.

Without stripping down to essentials, the actor will not have screen presence. What is screen presence? Glenn Close calls it giving herself permission to "disturb the molecules" of the atmosphere. Actors may have their own highly private routines to get themselves below the social mask and ready to perform, ready to put out, ready to disturb molecules. James Franco says that for months before shooting his breakout role as James Dean, he didn't speak to the people he was closest to. Does that sound extreme? Actors need to do whatever it takes to get connected to what is basic, essential about life—undistracted by gadgets, meetings, etc.—maybe even indifferent to the needs of family and friends.

Screen presence is a process of overcoming one's automatic pilot. Sally Field has described it as "rawing myself up." Director

Pedro Almodóvar calls it "starting from zero." Actors sometimes use this phrase: "I'm feeling pretty close to the bone here." It means openness to the deeper, more difficult emotions. It means allowing oneself to cross the threshold beyond the socially acceptable sentiments that are useful in ordinary life—like being friendly, helpful, pleasant—into the socially unacceptable emotions: *rage, fear, pain.*

Glenn Close once said in an interview that if she's having trouble in a role, she goes back to her acting coach to "make a total asshole of myself and give myself permission to let go." What I understand her to mean is that, in order to work past her fears of looking foolish, she has to find a safe space to do exactly that—look foolish.

Below the social mask is the scary place in the regular, day-to-day world, but the safe space in the creative world. A director who can meet the actor below the social mask—by being present as a human being, stripped of ego concerns—can feel free to say to an actor, "I think you can go deeper here," or "I think you can get closer to the bone." A director who has "gone deep" herself is best equipped to support an actor who is working "close to the bone." After the best takes, the ones in which the actor is the most unguarded, the actor may feel destabilized and raw. This is a moment of truth for the director, a time when an insensitive response can harm your chances for trust and collaboration. If, at these moments, you are able to acknowledge the actor's emotional nakedness, if you are able to look them in the eye and speak to them from your heart, you may forge an unshakable connection. There is no one thing I can tell you that is the right thing to say at these times. "Thank you," is a good start. But these are the times when the director, too, takes a risk.

Stop Doing It "Right"

"Whatever I said before the take, if you get an impulse, fuck what I said."—**Alan Pakula**

The film industry is notoriously risk-averse. The fear of making a mistake rules—and jeopardizes—so many creative decisions! Actors are expected, and expect themselves, to "nail it." When actors put their concentration on "doing it right," rather than on a truthful, creative choice, that's the real mistake.

When I was taking classes from Gerald Hiken, and the work was bad, he would say, "Do it wrong! Whatever you do, for God's sake, stop doing it right! It's better to do it wrong than to do it right!" He would then get an actor to play, for instance, Lady Macbeth loving and playful. This is a completely "wrong" interpretation—everybody knows that the "right" way to play Lady Macbeth is bitter and mean, right? But damned if it wouldn't come out better! Not just a little bit better, but a thousand percent better. It would have revelation and magic *just because* the actor gave herself permission to *do it wrong*. This is the power of an *opposite*, or even entirely wrong, choice—the power of disobligation to "doing it right"—it can make even a sweet Lady Macbeth believable.

I owe Gerry a great debt. Besides teaching us the magic of opposites, he gave us something else precious beyond rubies. Permission to look foolish. He would constantly egg us on: "Go ahead! Think your most private, embarrassing thoughts *right in front of them!*" (He meant the audience.) He wanted us to be free and uncensored; he wanted us to *lose interest* in whether or not the audience "gets it." The miracle was that when we were free and uncensored, the audience would believe anything!

Here's an idea. If you've given a direction but the actor is still struggling after many takes and it's not only not getting better, it's getting worse, you could try saying something like this: "Let's do it again—but forget everything I told you and just connect to each other." You could even take Gerry's—and Alan Pakula's—advice and say, "You know what? Fuck the right choice. Fuck what I told you to do. Let's do another take and this time—do it wrong."

Disobligation

On a movie set everyone is controlling the variables—except the actors, who must welcome a kind of permanent unpredictability just below their surface. Actors are required to make precise moves so they stay in frame and the camera can follow and photograph them—strict logistical parameters that make an actor's *interior* freedom all the more important. *Obligation,* the pressure to do things "right," is so unfortunate to acting that it may be better for an actor to place a full, relaxed concentration on the "wrong" thing than a tense, strained concentration on the "right" thing.

Gerry would say to an actor struggling through a Hamlet soliloquy, "Stop trying to think Hamlet's thoughts! You don't know what Hamlet was thinking about! It would be better to think about your own to-do list than to try to think the character's thoughts!"

He tended to teach with exclamation marks. I think because he wanted us to understand that he was asking for something very radical. Something that would feel weird and wrong at first but, finally, liberating, subversive, and truthful.

Use It!

Actors have a magic mantra for finding their energy even in the most difficult shooting circumstances: *Use it.* Less than three weeks after breaking his collarbone, actor Josh Brolin was on set in Texas, shooting his scenes for *No Country for Old Men,* playing a character who gets shot, attacked by pit bulls, and falls off a cliff. In an interview, Brolin said that his collarbone pain "worked for me in a funny, bizarre way that can only happen in a Coen Brothers film."

Here's what I say: It doesn't have to be a Coen Brothers film. It can work for any film. For Brolin, the collarbone not only lent a reality to his character's injuries, but even in the scenes before his character is injured, when he seems to carry an inner weight. It reads as a kind of disappointment in his life that makes the desperate choices that get him into so much trouble feel believable. If Brolin had tried to pretend he was in no physical pain from his collarbone, those early scenes might have played flatter, even false. Instead, he seems to have allowed himself to be fully present with all of his real physical pain and by doing so, his physical pain transformed into a mysterious inner, emotional pain that made him compelling from his first moment on screen.

Director Judd Apatow reported in his commentary for *The 40-Year Old Virgin* that Steve Carell *used* for his performance the anxiety he, as an actor, felt in the presence of the superior acting chops of co-star Catherine Keener. Since Carell's character feels inferior toward Keener's character, it worked perfectly.

It's even a joke among actors. In the midst of terrible personal tragedy, the actor brightens up: "I can use this—as soon as someone casts me in *King Lear*!" The socially unacceptable emotions—deep-seated pain, anger, and fear—are gold for an actor.

Commitment To Authenticity

Quentin Tarantino and John Travolta have both described publicly their first meeting, the one that led to Travolta's *Pulp Fiction* role. Travolta had riveted the acting world with his performance in 1977's *Saturday Night Fever*, and then, according to Tarantino, had become lazy. Here is Travolta's report, in a *New Yorker* interview: "Quentin let me have it. He said, 'What did you *do*? Don't you remember what Pauline Kael said about you? What Truffaut said about you? Don't you know what you *mean* to the American cinema? John, what did you *do?*'" Travolta then made this disclosure: "I was hurt—but moved. He was telling me I'd had a promise like no one else's."

This level of transparency between a director and an actor conveys a respect for an actor's work that goes much deeper than regular Hollywood bullshit. It calls for a director to care about *connection* above all else—and to communicate that priority to the actor. When an actor is *connected up to his deepest resources,* there is a deep confidence and the freedom to create something the world will not forget.

The Notorious Insecurity of Actors

Actors are so exposed. It's so easy for them to feel judged and rejected—insecure. Technicians on a set can be ruthless in their condemnation of actors who don't meet social norms, who are standoffish or moody or loud or engage in preparatory rituals that seem bizarre to non-actors. This is terribly unfair. A director should never permit abusive behavior by actors—or anyone else—but as long as an actor's behavior is not abusive, it's okay to indulge their non-standard activities.

If an actor does behave badly, the cause of their bad behavior is nearly always insecurity. Don't take it personally. If they cross a line, speak to them privately. Ask them, "What's up? Something seems wrong today. Can I help?"

Exchange the Promise

What if a high-energy, powerful actor chooses to rant or melt down publicly, in front of the crew? It's very hard to recover from that. But you can take steps to prevent it. At a private meeting early in the process, say to them something like this: "I want us to make a mutual promise to each other. For my part, I will listen to any complaint you have about any aspect of the production—problems with the script, with any department, with any of the other actors—and especially any disagreement with decisions of mine. I will always listen, and I will always do something about it, whatever is in my power. I will keep your concerns confidential. But I need to ask of you in return that you always tell me these things in private." Then look them in the eye and ask them, "Can we agree to that?"

Unrepeatable Moments

"What I try to do before I hear the director say 'Action' is go to what I call, personally, absolute zero. In other words, I do not psych myself up, I psych myself down. I do not pump up my adrenaline, my ego, my passion to win the scene—whatever that means. I try to be as open, as empty as possible, so that whatever there is, is there at that moment."—**Sir Ben Kingsley**

Sometimes when actors create spectacular, magical moments that no one expects—when they "nail" perfectly a particular smile, glance, hesitation, snort, or sob—directors are not pleased, but frightened. Their first response is panic: "What if it can't be repeated?" They often ask me how to get actors to do something again that was so unexpected that it seems unrepeatable.

There are tools to help make performances repeatable enough to cut together—through-line objective, metaphor, emotional event, and of course, good blocking. Directors should absolutely study and practice until they develop those skills. But I invite you to embrace the existential truth that certain unrepeatable moments are just that—unrepeatable. Adopt the first rule of creativity, that creativity is self-replenishing, inexhaustible—the more you use it, the more you will have. If the shot needs another take, stay positive. Instead of fearing it won't be repeated, tell yourself that since you have witnessed a wonderful, unrepeatable moment, there will be another one. Maybe not the same one. Something different.

Maybe something better! The glass is half-full! In order to tolerate and even celebrate unrepeatable moments, a director needs to be in the moment herself. It's not an intellectual understanding. It's an experience of intimacy and risk-taking. Moment-by-moment acting is not just a necessity for a well-directed movie; witnessing it is also a sweet privilege for the director.

Directors Get to Be in the Moment, Too

Any of the suggestions and tools that I make in this book can totally backfire if the director attempts them only because he thinks he should. Direction is most effective—maybe only effective—when the director himself is in the moment. If you're not relaxed, you can't see the actors' performances, you can't hear their questions, you can't come up with ideas—you can't think. Stay present, breathe, make eye contact. Release your shoulders, chest, the muscles around your eyes. Talk less, listen more.

Some directing teachers tell directors they should pretend to be confident on the set even if they aren't. That may be true for maintaining authority with the crew and producers, but with actors, there's no need to keep up a front. Actors understand vulnerability. If you're working with actors who are more experienced than you, it's okay to say, "I'm relying on you to tell me when my ideas are not clear," or even, "If I seem a little nervous, it's because I've been looking forward to working with you for a long time." Don't say these things when the crew or producers can overhear you—the Privacy Rule is there to protect you, as well as the actors. But naming your feelings with the actors creates a safe space for you both, and can help you stay calm and centered.

I understood this the first night I taught an acting class, in 1985. I had behind me 10,000 hours of studying and performing as an actor. I had prepared exercises. But I had never actually taught a class before and had no idea what it would feel like to stand before this group of strangers. When the moment came,

I looked at their faces and I felt their humanity wash over me. I opened my mouth and started talking. It turned out I had things to say. After that, whenever I was teaching, I allowed myself to trust that I had something to give. I prepared—and then turned myself over to the moment.

Disengaging the automatic pilot of social imperatives—trusting instead an internal voice and the humans in front of you—can be harder than it sounds. It's not the same as simply chattering on with no filter—which can be more a way of hiding than truth-telling. You could say I was lucky. I was socially awkward and had an easier time being myself—being real in the moment—when I was teaching than when I was in ordinary social situations. If you find yourself struggling to be present in the moment when you're with actors—try talking less and listening more.

CHAPTER THREE

LISTENING AND TALKING

THE WHAT AND WHY OF LISTENING

> ***"It's really important that you put your attention to the other person. If that happens, then you're not thinking about yourself as much."*—John Turturro**

Sometimes an actor who has lost her bearings falls into this self-defeating interior mantra: "Be in the moment, you idiot!" This won't help. Because when you're in the moment, you don't know you are. You're not thinking about it. Actors use the term "getting in my head" to describe the ordeal of being unable to stop thinking about whether or not they are in the moment. Once an actor has become self-conscious, her concentration is hopelessly fixed *on herself.* When she demands of herself, "Don't be self-conscious!"—*by definition* she defeats her purpose.

The simple, practical way to overcome self-consciousness would be to concentrate on something other than herself. Actors have this secret weapon: *another actor.* For a baseline of believability and presence, surrendering to a scene partner is the safe and reliable place for actors.

The technique (it is a technique) is this: the actor puts more attention on his acting partner than on his own performance. Sanford Meisner used to say, when he addressed a new crop of young actors, "You're not going to like hearing this, but the other actor is more important than you are."

In student films and first features, if the acting is bad, the most likely reason is that the actors were not *listening* to each other. Unless the actor is more involved with what's going on with the other actor than with his own performance, there is a tiny hardening in his face, an invisible veil in front of his expression, a preoccupation in his eyes. A not-there-ness. False notes, lapses in energy, actors who are flat, fake, stiff, "walking through it," "phoning it in," or who seem to be "in different movies"—all these are examples of issues that probably involve a failure of listening.

Listening is not only the cure for a flat, stiff performance, but also the cure for overacting. I love acting that is larger than life, heightened, theatrical—like all the actors in *The Big Lebowski, Postcards from the Edge, In Bruges,* or a Yorgos Lanthimos film. Or Daniel Day-Lewis in every movie he's made. These expansive performances work because at their center, there is a purity of artistic intention. They are grounded in the situations and the relationships. It's only overacting when actors go over the top with no connection to their scene partners.

As long as the actors all say their lines in the right order, a director who is not paying attention can easily lull himself into thinking the actors are listening. The actors hear each other's lines and dutifully say theirs when they should—doesn't that mean they are listening? Not necessarily. *Listening* for actors is not like ordinary regular-life listening. Actors' listening is a skill. It's not just waiting for their turn to deliver a line, it's a special attention paid to the other actor. It's a surrender but it's not passive. An actor's listening is active—*responsive.*

Superior listening skills are invisible to the untrained eye. Kate Winslet is a world-class listener, but no one in the audience watches *Titanic, Little Children, The Reader, Eternal Sunshine of the Spotless Mind,* or *Contagion,* and turns with a sigh to their companion, exclaiming, "Oh, she's such a good listener!" When an actor is a superior listener, their technique is invisible.

There's no such thing as a good actor who is not a good listener. While the camera is rolling, a good actor allows her *full, entire attention* to be on the other actor, on him physically—on the expression in his eyes, the little lines around his mouth, his breath, his smell, the movements he makes—and perhaps even more importantly, the movements he almost makes, *but doesn't quite.*

It's not effortful—rather, a relaxed, sensorial attention. The actor's eyes, ears, scalp, skin are open, soft, able to receive. Thus, she *responds,* rather than *performs.* It's a kind of antenna. A response on a granular level that feels unchosen, unbidden. It's different from listening in real life—where we usually pay just enough attention to stay out of trouble. My favorite analogy for actor's listening is how, when holding an infant in our arms, the child's skin, gaze, breathing, smell become all that matters in the world.

***"Listening is everything."*—Matt Damon**

When the actors are actively listening to each other, it not only makes the acting natural and real, it allows the actors to affect each other, and thus to create *moments*—tiny electric connections that happen *in real time* and make the scene work. If you're directing drama, and you want the audience to engage with the characters and their predicaments and adventures, it's essential that the actors listen. Otherwise, a dramatic scene is just "my turn to talk, your turn to talk"—a scene about two actors' performances instead of a scene about a relationship and an event in that relationship.

If you have a funny script to direct and you don't want it ruined, make sure above all that the actors play off each other.

"Listen, listen, listen, really listen. You think you're listening, but you really have to work at it."
—Vanessa Redgrave

Directors should know the term *listening* because it is a standard term that actors use, but it's not quite accurate. It makes it sound like *listening* is something that is done only with the ears when actually, it's a global response by an actor—not just a function of his ears, but a response of his whole being. Eye contact is a powerful springboard to connection. Losing oneself in another person's eyes is perhaps the quickest fix for actors—a simple, dependable escape from the pressures and distractions of the social world—a ticket to the translucent world where impulse matters—the world where subtext is louder than text. A surrender that releases an actor from the painful awareness of self-consciousness. Many actors beg directors to block the scene so they can have eye contact with their scene partner.

What if the blocking of the scene requires actors not to have eye contact? That's not necessarily a problem. A good actor responds to a kinetic awareness of the other actor's body language and intention. Or the sound of their partner's voice. It's sensorial, not intellectual, so the physical sound of their partner's voice matters actually more than what the other character is saying. Even when the character doesn't seem to listen to other characters, for instance, the overbearing boss in *The Devil Wears Prada,* Meryl Streep is still—always—responding in the moment to her co-stars.

Responding, engagement, or *connection* might be more accurate terms to describe the actor's experience of *listening.* More lighthearted terminology like "getting the back and forth of it," "playing off each other," also describes the experience.

How Can a Director Tell If an Actor Is Listening?

Every director develops their eye, finds her own markers. I'll try to describe what I do—I look for the changes, shifts in their eyes and body in response to the movements and tone of voice of the other actor. These shifts may be almost imperceptible, so I really need to surrender—to sink into the actors, to connect with them until it feels almost like I am sharing their breath. If they are *listening, responding,* there's an aliveness in the muscles underneath the skin of the actor's face. Particularly the tiny muscles around the eyes—which seem to relax and open. Their actual eyeballs may seem to soften, awaken. The best way I have to describe the feeling I get from the actor, from his eyes, from his skin, is a thrilling awareness that *movement is possible and could happen at any moment.*

Now. *Why* should a director be able to tell the difference? A director working with a good casting director might get by without being an expert—because a casting director worth their salt will weed out the bad listeners for you—and because any actor working regularly is a good listener. But what if, while you are getting started in your career, you need to cast from a pool of less trained actors? What if you've cast a stand-up comedian or YouTube personality—or are "street-casting" non-actors? *Listening* is likely to be their weak spot.

For example, *Seinfeld*. Jerry, the main character and center of the show, with a stand-up background and no acting training, was, during the first season, a bit stiff. I believe that what saved the show (besides the brilliant writing) was Julia Louis-Dreyfus, Jason Alexander, and Michael Richards, who were not only fearless and talented but, owing to training and experience, far better listeners than Jerry. Year by year, Jerry relaxed and *responded* more and more to his second bananas—and became a good actor himself because he became a better listener.

I encourage directors to make a *shift* away from assessing and critiquing individual performances, to supporting the *relationships* of the story and the *emotional events* that happen in those relationships. When the actors are playing off each other, the emotional events of the scene come to life—all the director has to do is put the camera in the right place to capture them. Stephen Frears had this to say about directing Chiwetel Ejiofor and Audrey Tautou in *Dirty Pretty Things*: "They started playing well together. That's all you long for in a film. Once they get going together, they're wonderful—and you don't have to do anything!"

If there's no relationship, no engagement, a terrific editor may be able to cut around the footage and patch it into a something that passes for a scene—but *engagement* is an engine that creates pace and flow, and guides you to the edits. Editing becomes more like an organic process and less like damage control.

Chemistry

No matter what the genre—whether it's *The Godfather* or *The Hangover, The Shawshank Redemption, Blue Valentine, Thelma and Louise,* or *Spiderman*—for a movie to be entertaining, it must have central relationships that the audience cares about. So the actors must have what Hollywood calls *chemistry.*

It's a bit shocking to me, but I've noticed that many people think that chemistry is granted by the chemistry gods and that it's either there or it isn't. I've seen the fear in an actor's eyes when he's been called in for a "chemistry read"—a fear that the chemistry gods might decline to appear. If he *tries* to have chemistry with the actor that's put in front of him, guess what—it will look like effort, not at all like magnetism.

I've heard industry professionals refer to chemistry as "the undefinable thing." It's not undefinable at all! It's craft. It's *listening.* Any actor can have chemistry with any other actor if they are good listeners, if they respond to each other, if they are more interested in the other actor than in their own performance. I have read that chemical changes are detected in the brains of people falling in love—but actors can't rely on that! Neither can directors. A magical magnetism can slip away as capriciously as it descends. Romantic leads don't even have to like each other—as long as they *respond* to each other, as long as they *engage,* and *play off* each other. It's really not chemistry—it's craft.

When actors have that connection the entertainment industry calls chemistry, it looks kind of like a ping-pong match. I like the ping-pong analogy because, no matter your level of skill, ping-pong feels like a natural reflex—your impulse to hit the ball back is spontaneous.

Unselfish Actors

> ***"I always try and give as much as I can. You're very lucky if you work with an actor who gives you a lot."***
> **—Kate Winslet**

Actors themselves call a fellow actor who is a good listener *unselfish*. That's what Vera Farmiga meant when, during the 2010 Academy Awards presentation, she described George Clooney, her co-star in *Up in the Air*, this way: "His only objective is to draw from you your best performance, which he cares about more than his own." She is saying that Clooney, a sought-after leading man, is *first and foremost a great listener*—to the point that his concentration is more on making the other actor look good than on looking good himself.

Actor Garret Dillahunt played a James gang member in *The Assassination of Jesse James by the Coward Robert Ford*. In an interview, he said that while they were shooting long days in a freezing cold shack in Alberta, Canada, lead actor Brad Pitt was just as committed to the scene during Dillahunt's close-up as during his own: "He was there every take. We were feeding off each other well, and he would change it up, it was just so much fun." A director should never offer a movie star permission to leave the set after their close-up if there are other close-ups still to be shot. All off-camera actors should be in place for the other actors' close-ups, to give their partner something to play off—to *feed off*, as Dillahunt puts it. Actors call it "generous," but really it's a bare minimum of professionalism. Because, even in close-ups, it's still a two-person scene, it's still a relationship—the off-camera actor is not in the shot, but *is still in the scene*.

Damage Control

Good actors, who give a lot, crave to work with other actors who give a lot. It can be hard for an actor who always surrenders to her scene partner, to play opposite an actor who is not responding, not giving, who is acting up a storm all on his own. It's frustrating and depressing, because the giving actor (that is, the listening, responsive actor) knows that playing opposite a lesser actor makes her job harder. If she tries to "save" her performance by pulling back, retreating from the other actor's wooden performance, that will only make everything worse, including her own performance. It's a downward spiral. In a deteriorating situation like this, you might take the more experienced or better actor aside, and pledge to her that if she continues to stay engaged and work with full commitment, you will make sure that the scene works. And then, you have to do it! You need to do something to change what the other, "problem" actor is doing—or the better actor may start to lose faith in the project.

One of my students told me this story: He had been working in the camera department on a small movie. Morgan Freeman had a scene with a young, very green actor whose performance was impossibly stiff. The director called for take after take. The young, green actor was giving Freeman nothing to work off—and still, Freeman stayed present, stayed connected to her through every torturous iteration of the scene. To the onlookers, it felt like a curse on an endless loop. When—finally—the production moved on to the next scene, my student went up to Freeman and asked him, "How did you do that? How did you stay present for every take, giving her so much when she wasn't giving you anything?" Freeman replied, "I just kept looking into her eyes, trying to figure out what had happened to her in her life, to make her so frightened that she felt she had to hide from me like that."

That's a story of how a superior actor saves his own performance by finding—honestly—a way to surrender to a less competent actor. But if you are the director on this project, and if the more established actor does not save the day for you, you have options. Change the blocking. Or the lines. Take the struggling actor aside and ask, "How are you feeling today? What are you working on? What do you want in this scene?" She may be a trained professional who happens to be nervous on this particular day. Sometimes day players haven't worked in a while; if their scene is opposite the film's lead or a series regular, they may freeze up. A director who gives the day player some friendly attention, rather than a glance of disapproval and exasperation, could work wonders.

If it's one of the lead actors who's become stiff and alienated from his scene partners, it's possible that the interpretation needs to be rethought. It's okay to take an actor aside and ask, "How do you feel things are going?" He might very well say, "It's all shit, isn't it?" Then you can say, "Well, it's not as connected as it could be. Maybe there's a stronger choice we can make. Let's rethink what's needed for the scene." But even if he says he feels fine, it's okay to say, "I'm not sure. I think there's something missing. What are you working on? What's your objective?"

Or—be inventive. Maybe whisper to him something that is not quite true, for instance: "I love what you're doing, but, just for fun, let's change it up, try something else. So-and-so [the other actor] looks bored—let's wake him up!"

It's not okay for directors to lie to actors. Sometimes I tell an actor a performance is going well even though I actually think it isn't—but only because I love actors and trust the process. My subtext if I say such a thing is always this: "I believe in you and I know you can get there." Of course that expression of trust need not be unspoken—you can say it out loud to an actor: "I believe in you and I know you can get there."

Trust is active—it's not something anyone is owed. When I am working with actors, *I trust them*. I trust that, as long as they don't shut down, something good will eventually happen. I think of every actor and director I work with as someone who has come into my care, who has extended generosity toward me.

I believe that a condition of relaxed and vibrant responsiveness is natural, and that if I give permission and confidence to actors, they will open toward the other actor as a flower toward the sun. This allows me to always see actors' resistances and acting problems—or even laziness—as things that are in the way of their true selves, rather than flaws in their personalities. I can be a dog with a bone when it comes to something I need for the scene. I won't give up if it's important. But I don't want actors to be focused on pleasing me—I want them to be focused on their choices, their inner freedom, and most of all, on their partner.

When actors are struggling, I always look for the way to concentrate on what is going right instead of what is going wrong, to see the glass half full instead of half empty, to offer guidance and encouragement instead of criticism and commands. As a last resort, I will say quite directly to the actor who is not connected to his partner, "You're doing too much acting. It's not believable." This, like all direction, must be done in privacy, and for a communication as intense and potentially disturbing as this one, you must take extra care that *no one else* is within earshot.

Special Situations

What about scenes with more than two characters? It's still about relationships. If there are two characters, there is one relationship: A+B. If there are three characters, there are three relationships: A+B, A+C, and B+C. These situations are most easily approached with the tool of *objectives*. Character A may have one objective toward Character B and a different objective toward Character C, etc.

In a scene with only one character, that character still has relationships. If the character is alone getting ready for a meeting, his primary relationship could be with the person he has the meeting with; that person is in the room, not physically, but in his imagination, and thus, still affecting his behavior. Or the character's primary relationship in the scene could be with the objects in the room—if so, he endows these objects with life and agency. Maybe he's gotten into a fight with the buttons on a tuxedo shirt, but the tuxedo shirt started it first. Or maybe a brand-new container of deodorant, hidden in the back of the cabinet, has brilliantly come to his rescue when he feared he had run out.

It's always possible that a character who is alone is carrying on an interior dialogue with himself—his demons, for instance. We all have relationships with our demons. As well as with our better angel. And don't forget there are shows—*The Office* (both UK and US versions) or *Fleabag*—in which characters break the fourth wall and have a relationship with the camera.

If you are directing a script in which one actor plays a clone of his character, I advise you to look for interviews with Tatiana Maslany about creating her clone characters on *Orphan Black*. A *New York Times* article reported that the producers committed to hiring a good actor to play Maslany's body double. Kathryn Alexandre, an actor in her own right, became crucial to the work. She learned the physicality and accent for each clone, "so that Maslany had someone to play off in a multiple-clone scene." The article went on, "Maslany sings Alexandre's praises often, because there's a reciprocity to their craft. Alexandre is often the first to play a clone in a scene, so her dramatic choices often influence Maslany's performance."

While directors are studying at film school, the actors available to them for their scenes are usually acting students from the theater school. Student directors sometimes tell me that the theater school acting seems overly theatrical, stagy, or "too big" for the camera. I happen to love theater, and you can't convince me that *listening* is less important to good theater than it is to good movies. But some theater-trained actors have been taught to prioritize characterization over relationships. In screen acting it's the opposite: moment-by-moment response to an acting partner is the cornerstone of screen acting. I encourage directors to build your comfort level with actors to the point where you could have a dialogue with theater-trained actors about how they work.

Directors often want to know how to work with actors who've been trained in different ways—Meisner Technique vs. Strasberg

Method vs. Stella Adler approach, for instance. Or who come from different acting styles—say, sketch comedy vs. intimate naturalism. The answer is simple: get them to talk and listen to each other; get them to put their concentration on each other; keep each one from acting "all by himself" and screening the other one out. Talk and listen.

Listening Makes the Shots Work

Framing shots is the director's prerogative. But if your set-up is such that there is nowhere for the off-camera actor to stand nearby, you may be making a trade-off—prioritizing your perfect shot at the expense of emotional authenticity. If, when you get to the editing room, you don't see "it"—you don't see the excitement, the revelation, the *emotional event* of the scene—then what? The one thing I don't want you to do at that point is say, "I had no choice."

Making listening a priority may affect your visual directorial choices. David Dobkin, director of *Wedding Crashers,* has said that he likes to shoot "very loose," because he wants to capture the details, the nuances, the awkward moments of real human life, human friendships, human attempts at romance. Lorene Scafaria, the director of *Hustlers,* similarly prioritized the unexpected, the improvisatorial—the details, nuances, and awkward moments of relationships among a group of high-spirited women.

In order to support the actors in their honest and spontaneous reactions, it can be helpful to have more than one camera operating during a take. When shooting the central, heartbreaking courtroom scenes in HBO's *When They See Us,* director Ava DuVernay had four or five cameras going—because, according to the project's editor, Spencer Averick, DuVernay had made it clear that she needed honest, immediate reactions from the parents, the legal team, the kids, the gallery, the judge.

I invite you to study *The Last King of Scotland,* directed by Kevin Macdonald—not only a great movie, but, if you look carefully, a tutorial in prioritizing listening, no matter what the camera frame. Some of the scenes between Forest Whitaker (Idi Amin) and James McAvoy (Nicholas) are shot wide (where you can see each actor head to toe); some are shot in alternating over-the-shoulders; some are shot in tight singles. But in every scene, each character has a powerful effect on the other. The moments when each one's energy *lands* on the other are the moments that tell the story. Even in extreme close-ups, when only one actor is physically in the shot—*both actors are fully emotionally present to each other.*

Language Directors Can Use

You can give praise by saying, "I love the connection you two have," or, "I love how free it's getting, how you're playing off each other." You can give direction in terms of the relationship ("These two have been pushing each other's buttons since they first met when they were seven years old."), rather than micro-managing individual performances ("Can you play that line a little more resentful?").

The director sets the tone on a set. If you, as the director, want to turn a group of actors into an ensemble—ask for it. Say to the actors, early and often, "The listening is important to me." Or, "I'm interested more than anything in the connection." Then—that statement needs to be true! You need to make *connection* your *priority*. Directing with a lighter hand—with less micromanaging, less result-orientation—can help.

More language you might use to encourage listening: "The connection is all I really care about." "I like it when you play off each other." "All I care about is the interaction." "Let's just go for the back-and-forth, the ping-pong of it." "Let yourselves feed off each other." "Let it breathe." "Take care of each other." "Stay with your partner, that's the safe place." "Stay loose, stay alive to each other." "You have everything you need; it's okay to let it go." "Just give the lines to each other." "Keep it simple." "It's okay to relax. Let yourselves connect." "Play off her energy."

Or this: "I think this script will only work if we have ensemble playing."

Here's a bit of advice to the actor who is struggling the way I described at the top of this chapter—whether because she's worried about getting in her head or starting to doubt her choices—"If all else fails, make the other guy look good." It's the quickest, surest way for an actor to improve her own performance.

Directors Should Listen, Too

"Great directors are great communicators, and you can't possibly be a great communicator if you're not a great listener."—**Djimon Hounsou**

Listening is the secret actors have that makes directors feel left out! Now that you know it, you don't have to be excluded! You can train your eye to spot listening. It takes practice. When I first started watching basketball with my husband, my eye could not follow the ball—there was so much going on and it looked to me like all they did was just run in a pack back and forth from one end of the court to the other. But the more I watch, the more I can see specific plays and appreciate the passing game.

In order to tell if the actors are listening, a director needs to be present in the moment. Take a moment to relax your shoulders and the muscles around your eyes. Let yourself breathe without effort. Eventually it will feel good—not even like a job. Surrendering to connection with the actors can feel like a vacation, a restoration—the reward for all the drudgery of getting your project funded and logistically feasible.

It does take some courage, though, because when actors listen, their performances on each take will most likely be slightly different. This can be frightening for directors. That's why the director needs to be prepared, to have done script analysis homework that has taken him below the surface of the script into its subtext, so he can understand and recognize *emotional event* and not just hear line readings.

Listening works in your interactions with actors too. To communicate better, listen more. When you're talking with the actors, pay more attention to their response than to remembering your own ideas. You might be surprised. Your own ideas might get better. We think more clearly when our brains are relaxed—and listening relaxes the brain. So, listen more than you talk. I mean that literally—I can give you a percentage: Of the time you spend with actors, spend less than 50% hearing your own voice. Listen to the actors' words, ideas, and concerns. And don't forget to listen to their subtext—the things they say without words. If the actor sighs or turns away with arms crossed when you say something, ask him if there is a problem; make sure he believes you are interested in his answer.

Inexperienced directors do not realize how important listening is. Even as you are reading this, you may be saying to yourself, "Okay, sure. What's the big deal?" It's one of those things that is simple but not easy. It takes discipline on the part of an actor to surrender their concentration to the other actor, and not be distracted by concerns for making the "right" effect. There's a shift involved for the director as well, a realignment that may feel unnatural at first. It's about letting go of line readings and expressions that you have preprogramed yourself to expect. The reward is entrance to a new level of trust—a trust that honest relationships will carry your story forward.

"Just talk and listen." My own teacher Jean Shelton used to say this to us until we were tired of hearing it. Sidney Lumet uses this expression as well. Talk to a person. Listen to a person. Be a person, not a character. Listening is the thing that makes everything else *actually work*. As one of my students expressed it after taking my Acting for Directors course, "Without listening, all of the other work is like the parts of a car lying unassembled on a factory floor—it's all there, but it ain't goin' nowhere."

CHAPTER FOUR

Actors' Choices/ Directors' Tools

"Most actors' problems, professional or amateur, deal with tension and there are a lot of devices and ways of eliminating it. In a very professional actor, the tension is because they haven't made a vital enough choice—it's not up to a level that will engage their imagination."

—Jack Nicholson

The previous two chapters have focused on the right-brain, improvisatory, unpredictable stuff—in the moment, listening, risk, freedom. I've been making a big deal about giving up preconceived ways of saying a line, but now it's time to talk about structure: the choices that illuminate the material and are the foundation for designing a performance—and double as tools for the director.

Some actors look like they're making a living just being *in the moment.* Think Owen Wilson or Billy Bob Thornton—always natural and fun to watch—alive and responsive without looking like they're trying. But in order to make their imaginations available to moment-by-moment reality, powerful actors find something powerful in the script to connect to.

During their preparation, actors dig through the script for *clues* about the character and story, clues that will lead them to ideas, secrets, revelations that excite them and will function as gateways to their creativity and truth. When good actors get their hands on a great script, they don't think of preparation as a job exactly—more like supercool detective work or a delicious game—or maybe even a spiritual journey of connecting the deepest, freshest meaning of the script to their private understandings and their own inner life.

Ideas lead to choices. Choices generate behavior. Behavior creates the way the lines are spoken. Sanford Meisner put it this way: "The emotional life of the scene is a river and the words are boats that float on the river." I like to think of it as finding ways that *the subtext can be louder than the text.*

Choices can be more or less effective, but not right or wrong. If a choice works and brings the script alive, it's a good one; if it doesn't work, you keep looking. Choices an actor arrives at ahead of time are things to try; they are not a performance until they are activated in the moment, in the presence of the other actors.

Different actors describe this work differently. They may say, "I've made the choice that . . ." Or they may say, "I have some ideas I'm working on." They may have some other private terminology. In any case, a viable choice must be so simple, so primal, so compelling, so immediate that the actor does not need to step out of the moment to locate it. You could say that actors are hoping to get to a point where they feel their character is a secret version of themselves, a point where they achieve a deep, centering connection from which they can fly free, play off the other actor, and follow impulses of the moment. It's a paradox, but when actors' choices are specific, private, and idiosyncratic to their own understanding of life, the audience is more likely to experience the characters' predicaments as universal and relatable.

When directors know more about actors' choices, they can better understand actors and better communicate with them. But these tools have value that goes above and beyond. They can be life and career-changing for directors, because they also function as script analysis techniques—keys to connecting to your own scripts at a deeper, more resonant level.

Recently one of my clients perfectly described what I try to give directors in script analysis consultations. After several sessions, he said to me: "I am realizing that I need to imagine more than what is on the page. I need to imagine the characters' whole lives, not just this sliver contained in the script." This is what the *tools* do for directors.

Following is an investigation of some *tools* actors use to make choices and enrich their characters' inner lives. It's not a list of magic words to be memorized; it's an invitation to make a shift in the way you look at characters' behavior. Some will sound familiar from their brief roll-out in Chapter One's list of Quick Fixes, but now we'll explore them more deeply.

Questions

***"The greatness and ambiguity of art lies in not proving, not explaining, and not answering questions."*—Andrei Tarkovsky**

Al Pacino was in three movies with John Cazale: *The Godfather, Godfather II,* and *Dog Day Afternoon.* In a documentary, *I Knew It Was You,* Pacino speaks about working with Cazale: "He became whoever it was he was playing. And he did that by asking questions. He taught me about asking questions and *not having to answer them.* That's the beauty. What's wonderful about it is you open the door to things. He got so much from the delving into things. I think I learned more about acting from John Cazale than from anybody."

Many actors use questions to open up their characters' inner lives. These artists activate their subtext via suggestion, inference, and mystery, thus creating levels and layers to their characterization. I can't help wondering whether for *The Godfather,* John Cazale, as Fredo, asked himself this question: "What do my brothers say about me behind my back?"

Sometimes directors tell me there are actors who come to the set a "blank slate" and want to be told what to do. I don't believe that anyone in the world is a blank slate. Everyone has experiences, impressions, connections, even if their thoughts have not coalesced to the point that they can confidently assert, "This is my idea." I always want actors to contribute on a level that is meaningful to them, so if they don't volunteer ideas, I ask them questions.

Most actors don't want to be spoon-fed, and even if they ask for it, it may be not good for them. It is a truism of directing that the best way to get an actor to accept your direction is to make them feel it's their own idea. In order to plant an idea that the actor will feel is their own, try questions.

The plot of the film *Inception* uses special effects to dramatize the feat of planting an idea in another person's mind. As I was watching, I thought to myself: This is a magical realism version of something I do every day in my classes and consultations. I don't use the methods employed by the crew of dream extractors: I don't administer drugs and explosions; I don't make my clients drive a bus off a bridge; I don't hypnotize them and then threaten that they'll get stuck in limbo if they wake up. *I ask questions.*

I sometimes ask actors *leading questions,* like, "Do you think he is telling the truth when he says he didn't do it?" It's a leading question because I've *planted* the idea that the character might be lying. I also ask *open-ended questions,* for example, "What do you think is going on in this scene?" I'm still planting an idea—the idea that there is *something* going on in the scene beyond mere plot or exposition.

Posing questions—and paying attention to the responses—can be the most effective way for directors to communicate their ideas. For a director, having good questions is better than having all the answers.

Here's another powerful open-ended question a director can ask an actor: "What questions do *you* have?" Don't be afraid of actors' questions. Even if the answers seem obvious to you. I have seen directors become panicked by an actor's question and conclude that the actor is at a loss. Please try to let go of that idea.

When an actor asks you a question, she might not be looking for an answer—she might be inviting you into her process. She may be keeping her performance fresh by asking questions, by constantly investigating new ideas, opening up new corners of the character's world, adding layers—as a way to keep her work creative, a way to make sure her work keeps moving forward. Some actors like to share these questions with their director; others may do this work privately.

If actors don't volunteer their questions to you, *ask* them if they have any. Listen to them carefully, but—and I know this is a radical suggestion—*don't feel obligated to provide an instant answer*. The simple action of acknowledging a good question releases creativity. Allowing a question to hang in the air instead of anxiously rushing to answer it is not disrespectful—it's stimulating. Naomi Watts has said of working with David Lynch: "When you ask questions, he doesn't give you answers. He wants to maintain the mystery, even for us. I love it." Here are a couple more examples:

In an interview Barry Jenkins discussed shooting the scene in *Moonlight* in which teenagers Kevin and Chiron kiss on the beach. Actor Jharrel Jerome asked Jenkins, "Is this the first time Chiron has kissed another man?" Here's what director Jenkins did next, in his own words: "I didn't say anything. And he looked at me and he said, 'Oh, it's the first time Chiron has kissed anybody.' So—I didn't have to direct a thing!" It's not true that Jenkins was not directing that moment. By not rushing to answer his actor's question, he wasn't abdicating his duties, and he wasn't dismissing or ignoring the actor's question. The director's wordless response was deeply empathetic and empowering, and took the scene in a thrilling direction.

For the *Sopranos* episode in which Tony kills Ralphie because he believes that Ralphie caused the death of his racehorse, actor Joe Pantoliano asked showrunner David Chase, "Did I kill the horse or not?" Pantoliano told an interviewer that Chase refused to tell him! The actor went on to disclose that he then made his own *choice*—that he did not kill the horse. I remember this episode. I remember feeling certain that Ralphie had killed the horse—until that moment in the bathtub when he pleaded for his life. As a viewer, I felt suddenly moved by the hurt and pain behind his eyes. Pantoliano's choice was an *opposite* to what we'd come to expect from Ralphie—he'd done so many horrible things—and it gave the scene pathos and complexity.

The lesson from these stories is that when you empower an actor this way, you need to respect his response. And that if you do, you may get some compelling stuff.

John Cassavetes used to routinely respond to actors' questions by saying, "I don't know." I think that what he meant was, "I may have written the script, but now that you're the character, *you're* the one who knows." Cassavetes knew his characters inside and out, but he wanted actors to find the characters themselves, to make them their own. Actors sometimes got mad at him for not giving them straight answers, but he didn't care—all he cared about was fresh, unguarded, and emotionally honest work.

I think when actors ask a question, very often it is the exact question that they would like *you* to ask *them*. So when a student or client asks me a question, I often respond, "What do you think?" Or, "That's a great question. I have ideas but I'd love to know what your thoughts are." They may know the answer already, but feel insecure. Or, sometimes they know the answer, but don't know they know it.

Let's say the actor asks his director, "Why doesn't my character tell his wife about the letter?" If the director turns the question back—by asking, "What's your thought about that?"—the actor may respond, "I think he wants to protect her. I think he's afraid if she knows about the letter, she'll be in danger." At this point I would be watching his face closely, gauging his emotional commitment to this idea. If he seems to feel strongly, I'll say, "I like that. Let's try it." If he doesn't seem all that invested, I might say, "That's an important question. I like that you're thinking about it." Or I might say, "It's a good question. I have some ideas. Let's brainstorm."

If the actor replies to my question "What do you think?" by saying, "I don't know, I haven't a clue," or "I want to know what you think," then I might say this: "I have some ideas. Maybe he wants to protect her . . . or maybe he has a guilty secret. I lean toward the 'protect her' idea. What are your thoughts?"

What if the actor asks you a question about the letter, and you reply, "What do you think?"—and the actor responds, "I think it's a guilty secret"—and you disagree! Well, the director's least attractive option is to contradict the actor by saying, "No, that's wrong, here is the right answer." My observation is that telling someone their ideas are wrong either makes them shrink inside—or makes them want to argue about it. I prefer to say something more like, "Okay. Tell me more about your thinking." At this point the actor may say, "Do you have a different idea?" In that case I might say, "Yes, I do, and I'm happy to tell it to you. But I'm just as happy to try yours first."

At any point you are free to disclose your idea. It's not a guessing game. It's a back-and-forth in which the director is listening at least as much as she talks.

What if you agree with the actor's choice that the character refrained from telling his spouse about the letter because of a "guilty secret"? There is still another question to ask: "*What* is his guilty secret?" That makes the choice specific. Still—and this may sound strange to you—it may, *or may not,* be important that the director and actor agree on the choice of what the guilty secret is.

When I say the questions are more powerful than the answers, I really mean it. Here's why: because any subtext is better than no subtext; any choice is better than no choice. And because *secrets* are the bomb. The actor doesn't even need to tell the director what choice he is making. I often say this to an actor: "You don't have to tell me what your choice is. You can keep it a secret even from me."

If you ask a question to an actor, and they respond with a blank look, be ready to jump in with an idea of your own. The actor may be embarrassed to reply to a question, afraid to take a risk of looking stupid—this can be just as true of stars as of inexperienced actors. But sometimes when an actor asks a question, they're testing to make sure you have ideas—actors hate it when the director has no ideas. If you're absolutely certain about something you want, don't pussyfoot—tell them your idea clearly and directly. Be ready to tell them why, in case they ask. *Do not pretend to ask a question if you are not interested in the answer!*

Sometimes questions lead you to an idea that unlocks a whole scene. But sometimes the question itself is truly all you need. The character may not know the answer himself! The character may himself be wondering why the hell he didn't tell his spouse about the letter. Characters, like people, most of the time probably don't know why they do what they do. The actor can let the character borrow his own confusion.

But don't let the fact that characters don't know why they do things excuse you from asking *why*. In your script analysis, be like a toddler—always *ask why*. My rule of thumb is: *ask why five times*. Why did he lie? Because the truth would complicate his life. Why would the truth complicate his life? Etc., etc.

Questions work this same way in real life. Say a friend asks you, "What should I do about my teenager's terrible behavior?" Responding with a laundry list of excellent advice could be the least helpful thing you could do. It just might be more supportive to respond with a question, such as, "What do you feel are your options?" You see, with that question, you have *planted* the idea that your friend has options—and that may be the crucial thing he or she needs to hear at this precarious moment.

Opposites

"I'm interested in the flip side, the B-side of people."—**Ralph Fiennes**

Once you take seriously the tool of asking questions, the tool of *opposites* will start to come naturally. One of my students calls opposites "the rescue technique." It's a concrete way to practice "thinking outside the box." During script analysis, as soon as you come up with one idea, consider also its opposite. Whenever you're not sure what to do with a line—find an opposite. If a scene isn't working—do it wrong! An opposite choice can loosen your thinking from unproductive assumptions and pedestrian ideas you may have gotten stuck in without knowing it.

When a character says one thing and means another, the conflict between her words and her inner life makes her automatically complex. It also makes her more like a real person, because people are not especially logical. They don't know who they are or what they want, and they don't do the right thing to get it. They often mean the *opposite* of what they say. We see it in real life: a person who says, "I'm very open to your proposal," with arms and legs crossed, looking at you sideways. His body language is saying he is not open at all.

How many times have you heard someone say, "I'm not angry"? To me, the statement "I'm not angry" is as transparent a clue as a "tell" in a poker game—it's just as likely, or maybe more so, that the person is fuming inside.

Ideas for effective opposites arise from understandings of human behavior, from the artist's lifelong study of the human condition. The idea that a person might insist he is not angry when he actually is comes from my observation that people *in life* seem to think that admitting they are angry makes them look pathetic. Meryl Streep was asked how she came to play her Queen of Mean character in *The Devil Wears Prada* without once raising her voice; she replied that the choice was rooted in her understanding of power: that often the quietest person in the room controls it. Susan Sarandon, in the commentary to *Thelma and Louise*, disclosed that, even though Louise is perceived by audiences as very strong, "I always felt she was on the verge of the abyss. She always felt really fragile to me." Sarandon made the choice that Louise *covers* her fragility with a façade of strength.

A director can also be the one to suggest an opposite. Actor Ethan Hawke told this story about working on *Before the Devil Knows You're Dead*, directed by Sidney Lumet: "There was a line, 'How much time do we have?' and I was playing it really nervous. Sidney came over and said, 'Often when people are nervous, they try to put on an appearance of confidence.'" (Note that this example shows Lumet using the language of suggestion and permission, rather than issuing the result-oriented instruction to "play the line more confident.")

Mysterious Lines

> ***"To me what's most important are the mysterious lines, the things we gloss over, think we understand."***
> **—Andrew Jarecki**

Sometime after she has robbed and killed several men, Aileen Wuornos in *Monster*, played by Charlize Theron, has a line, "I'm not a bad person; I'm a good person." It's a mysterious line, isn't it? Unlocking its subtext is key to making the character believable. Preparing for his role in *The Last King of Scotland*, Forest Whitaker came to his director Kevin MacDonald. He wanted to talk about the scene in which his character, Idi Amin, is preparing to torture Nicholas (James McAvoy). What interested Whitaker about the scene was Amin's line, "I think your death will be the first real thing that happens to you . . . Each time you scream, the evil comes out of you." Pondering this mysterious line gave Whitaker the idea to play the scene like a strict father who believes he is about to do something helpful for a difficult son, rather than as a scene of retribution toward a man who has slept with one of his wives.

Digging into *mysterious lines* can lead you to *questions*, which lead you to ideas for adjustments (*as ifs*) that are *opposite* to the apparent reading of a line, which in turn lead to revelations of the amazing complexities of human behavior.

In the 1995 version of *Cry, the Beloved Country*, one of the characters has a line, "I am a cynical and selfish man. But God put his hand on me." It's a mysterious line! What has happened in the character's past that might cause him to say that? Rather than deciding whether to say this line *piously* or *defiantly* or *sarcastically*, let's start with the question: what specific event occurred to make the character call himself cynical and selfish? There are no further clues in the script as to what this event might be, so the actor goes to his own imagination, as well as his own life and the lives of people he has known. I have worked as an acting coach with incarcerated men convicted of serious crimes—so if I were playing this role, impressions from my powerful and inspiring experience at Pendleton Correctional Facility would surely inform my preparation for this line.

What about the time when I was nineteen and lied to my parents that I couldn't meet them for dinner because I was sick? In fact, I wanted to meet my boyfriend, of whom they disapproved. Then, we were in a bad motorcycle accident. In the emergency room there was a kind nurse. Details of her compassionate face are within easy reach of my memory, even all these years later. The intensity of her intention to help and save me compelled me to croak out a question to her: Do you ride? She said yes. I might go to the memory of her deep brown eyes to create a reality for the line, "I am a cynical and selfish man, but God put his hand on me." I mean, on that terrifying night in the ER of Bellevue Hospital, in spite of my lies and insurrections, *I was still alive.*

The Technique of Three Possible

When you are out of ideas, instead of driving yourself crazy trying to figure out the "right" solution, try the *technique of three possible.* Make a quick list of three possibilities—even if none of them is perfect! Even if at first they all seem crappy! It gets you started. It aerates your brain. It makes you think, makes you imagine. As a bonus, sometimes the "wrong" ideas turn out more interesting than you expected.

The *technique of three possible* is useful for anything mysterious in a script, whether it is a line, an intention, or what the scene is about. No matter how obvious the meaning might seem, I make myself consider alternatives—even when I already have an idea I love. Here's another way to frame the technique of three possible: always have a plan, a back-up plan, and a back-up for your back-up.

Judgment

"One of the first things I was taught as an actor was, 'Don't judge the character.'"—**Chadwick Boseman**

"People in real life aren't good or bad, it's more complicated than that."—**Alexander Skarsgård**

"We're all capable of everything. Very few of us are so secure that the dark side can't take over." —**Richard Gere**

"I have to decide not to give a fuck what people think of me, whether people like me or like this character."—**Kate Winslet**

"I don't believe in bad guys. Everybody has a reason for doing what they're doing."—**Matthew Weiner**

Quick quiz: who said this? "I try to stay on my character's side and bring some kind of humanity. I don't think of him as a horror icon or a 'villain.' I think of him *as a person living his life by his wits.*" The answer is Tobin Bell, an actor who has made his career as the poster child for horror icons, playing Jigsaw in the *Saw* films, as well as Unabomber Ted Kaczynski and other difficult characters. Bell's eloquent statement reveals the central principle behind not judging characters: No matter how wrong a person's actions might be, in their own mind, they are doing the best they can.

Robert De Niro, in a *New York Times* interview, said of his character Frank Sheeran in *The Irishman,* "I never thought of him as being amoral or immoral. He lives in a world where the penalties are harsh if you don't do what you're supposed to do. He says he's going to do something, he does it."

Charlize Theron, Forest Whitaker, Tobin Bell, and Robert De Niro did not judge their murderous characters. Not because their personal ethics are deficient—but because, to really good actors, the imagined world is too fascinating and the opportunity to leap into it too precious, for them to *ever* waste their time minimizing the predicaments of their characters by judging them.

In real life, we are free to think of these individuals—Aileen Wuornos, Idi Amin, Ted Kaczynski, Frank Sheeran—as evil or toxic, and stay as far away from them as we can. But the artists who bring them to life are allowed to embrace, even love them. Glenn Close says that she "falls in love" with every character she plays—and Glenn Close, mind you, has played Cruella De Vil! This does *not* mean that she condones her character's behavior or abandons her own values and ethics. It *does* mean she creates the character's behavior from a belief that every character fights for her dignity and happiness, even if the rest of us—including the actor herself—think in real life that the character's ideas of dignity and happiness are quite mistaken.

A director who negatively judges a character will not be able to have a substantive discussion with the actor playing that character. A good actor will not give his trust to a director who is judgmental toward his character. Vincent Kartheiser said of his character Pete Campbell on *Mad Men*, "I'm protective of Pete. It's still me, you know? That guy is in me. I couldn't do him if he wasn't." You can see how deflating it would be for an inexperienced actor—or infuriating for a successful one—to be approached by a director who makes an off-handed comment about "what an asshole Pete is"—and thinks it's a big joke.

If a character tells lies, instead of calling him "a liar," look at the *specific* reason and purpose for each of his lies. Instead of describing characters as evil or toxic, think of them as "difficult." Guillermo del Toro has said of the Captain in *Pan's Labyrinth* (played by Sergi López) that, "even if he is a sociopath, he needs to really believe he is doing everything he is doing for the good of the community."

Whenever you find yourself thinking that a character is a "perpetual loser," "weak," "vicious," "uptight," or "stupid," you need to keep digging. You need to keep asking *why?* You need to keep looking for reasons that might drive their behavior.

Or *deconstruct* the label that society has given. A selfish person, unconcerned with the feelings and needs of others, is often unfiltered and in the moment—and can be charming company. A narcissist is a person with needs—for adulation, for control—often driven by a deep fear that he is unloved.

I have preferences and principles and even prejudices—just like anyone—so of course when I read a script, there are characters who at first I don't like! One way that I begin the work of resolving my judgments is by *reframing* them. It's unhelpful to beat myself up for judging. Instead, I tell myself, "I have a resistance to the character."

One of my students described to me something that happened when she was directing a film in which a character kidnaps a child. The actor asked the director to take out this plot element, because she didn't want to play such an awful person—a child abductor. The abduction was central to the story—it couldn't be removed—and yet the director stayed calm. Instead of falling into panic that the actor's rebellion would ruin the movie, the director *reframed* the situation with this suggestion: "Your character is in love with the child." From that point, the scenes played beautifully.

I worked with a well-known actor who was anxious about playing a character who he saw as a loser. I offered him this *reframing*: "It's not that you have to turn yourself into a loser. It's only that you invest the other characters with the power to hurt you."

Flaws and Likeability

"The worst piece of advice I was ever given by somebody, a long, long time ago, was 'Clive, it's all about likeability.' . . . I became fearless about that. I don't go into my parts wanting the audience to like me. I'm much more interested that they understand and believe me."

—Clive Owen

"I don't mind people in the bathroom with me. That's my task. To show people when they're at their most unwatched."—**Tilda Swinton**

The insistence among so many studio executives and green-lighters that characters be "likeable" does a great disservice to actors, characters—and the audience, too. Directors as well as actors can love their characters without making excuses for their behavior. Go deeper than "likeability"! Embrace the precious opportunity to face the dark sides of your characters and love them with all their flaws.

In *Little Miss Sunshine,* Greg Kinnear played the role of the father—a difficult man who, in real life, we might judge and dismiss. In the "diner scene," Richard makes his young daughter feel bad about eating ice cream ("If you eat lots of ice cream you're gonna become big and fat"). On the page, it's easy to dislike this father, right? Increasing the challenge for Kinnear was the fact that the film surrounds Richard with male characters (played by Alan Arkin, Paul Dano, and Steve Carell) who are also flawed, but whose flaws are far more charming than those of the misguided father. Co-directors Jonathan Dayton and Valerie Faris described, in their DVD commentary, conversations they had with Kinnear on the road to discovering that, "from Richard's point of view he's trying to teach her something, he thinks he's actually going to help her." They found a *verb,* "to teach." Aha. A *verb* comes to the rescue—making it possible to present this difficult character honestly. And giving us the revelation that a terribly flawed family can still be a loving family. As a bonus, the verb *to teach* (wielded with Kinnear's commitment and skill) is so incongruous (opposite) to the mean-spirited words that it makes this painful scene funny.

The scene in *Michael Clayton* in which Tilda Swinton's character drops her mask (the panic attack in the bathroom when threatened with exposure as a corporate criminal) is probably the scene that won her the Academy Award that year. When actors are afraid of showing this ugly side of humanity, when they pull back and only go half-way—that's when the scene doesn't work and may end up on the cutting room floor. It's terribly important for a fearless actor with zero vanity—like Swinton—to be supported and protected by a director who himself is fearless about letting go.

The Verb Family: Intention, Objective, Spine, Need

"Find the verb."—**Sidney Lumet**

"Verbs are everything, adjectives are for critics."
—**Ethan Hawke**

All living things move toward what they need. Plants grow toward the sun. Babies reach for their mothers. A character's emotional life arises from her *needs*. This principle is at the root of the tool of *verbs* and all branches of the Verb Family: *intention, objective,* and *spine*. These tools originate in an understanding of human need. The term *need* is interchangeable with any one of them.

- The character's *spine,* or script objective, is the need that drives him through the whole story—what the character wants out of life.
- The *objective*—also known as the scene objective or through-line objective—is the *need* or *want* that drives a character throughout an individual scene. The objective is *what the character wants emotionally from the other characters.*
- *Intentions,* aka *active verbs,* are the one-word verbs like those on the lists in Appendices A and B, for instance: demand, persuade, beg, seduce, belittle, accuse. Intentions/verbs are driven by a *need* to have an effect on other characters.

Objective/Need

The character's objective, or *scene objective,* is what he wants or needs from the other character in the scene. He might need rescue; he might need love; he might feel the need to pick a fight—he might even be driven by a need to be punished for his misdeeds.

A director who has no time at all for rehearsal can say to each actor before the first take something like this: "Do you know what you want in the scene?" Or, "Do you know what your character needs?" When Billy Ray directed his first feature, *Shattered Glass,* the rehearsal time he had planned for evaporated at the last moment. He whispered to each actor before each scene, "Do you know what you want?" If they nodded "Yes," he would shoot the scene. Notice he has not asked the actors to tell him *what* their objective is! Secrets are totally cool! If an actor said he wasn't sure, the director took a moment to talk with him quietly or to allow time for the actor to work out his choice for himself. No adjustment was given by the director until after that first take.

Here is the takeaway from this example: *any objective is better than no objective.* It's more important for all the actors to have a *sense of objective,* than for them to have the "right" objective. Different actors may have different terms for the tool I am calling *objective:* They may speak of what the character wants; what the character needs; what the character is fighting for; what drives him; what he cares about; his goal; his focus; his engine; his motivation; his agenda. I use these terms interchangeably. It's not important to have agreement on the terminology—it's important for every character in every scene to need or want something from the other characters.

A character's objective for a scene can be very specific and very simple:

- I want him to leave the room;
- I want him to put his arms around me;
- I want him to laugh;
- I want him to cry;
- I want him to feel sorry for me;
- I want him to kiss me;
- I want him to submit to my will.

The most playable objectives may have both a physical and an emotional component. "Physical component" means that, if you were to achieve your objective, you would know it because of a physical event: the other actor would cry or laugh or put his arms around you or leave the room. That way the actor has a point of concentration that is specific and real, a simple imaginative task. Of course, the physical event I desire might be more nuanced. If I want her to forgive me, my physical task is subtle but still specific—to find forgiveness in her eyes.

The emotional component of this tool is that a character's objective arises out of her needs and feelings, so it's a description of her emotional state, but phrased with a verb. The verb makes it a more dynamic expression than an emotional result. To say that a character "wants to hurt and destroy" another character is more vivid and spirited—a bolder choice—than to describe the character as "pissed off."

Another reason a character's objective is emotional is that if she achieves her objective—*or if she doesn't*—it will *matter* emotionally to her. In simplified terms, if my objective is to get someone to leave the room, when he leaves the room, I win; if he doesn't, I lose. Either way, *I care*—my world is different at the end of the scene from what it was at the beginning.

Choosing an objective for the character is preparation. Once the actor is in front of the camera, he lets go and plays the moment. But if he falters in his concentration, the objective gives him something to fall back on. If his objective is to get her to laugh, he can recover from a failure of concentration—and rescue the scene—by focusing on his partner and replacing the default inner monologue, "Am I funny enough?" with this: "Is that a little smile around her lips? Am I making any headway in getting her to laugh?" His concentration is on her, not on his own performance.

The objective is a communication tool, not a result. A character who wants to calm everyone down may not herself be calm at all! *Objectives are not necessarily rational—in fact they are rarely rational!* This is all too true in real life as well. People can do the wrong thing to get what they want, like when a person *wants respect,* but sabotages herself by *apologizing* for her actions. In the show *Better Call Saul,* everything Jimmy McGill (Bob Odenkirk) wants are good things: he wants his brother to love him and be proud of him; he wants his girlfriend to feel safe and protected; he wants his clients to win their cases. To achieve those worthy goals, he—every single time—does all the wrong things.

It's a safe bet that characters do not know their own objectives. Like people in the real world, the needs and feelings of characters are likely to be so chaotic, and buried so deep, that characters themselves are unaware of them. A character might have the line, "I just want to talk to you," and might, in his own mind, feel certain that that is his objective: *to talk with* the other character. But his deeper *unconscious* need—a secret agenda of which he may be totally unaware—could be something more primal and complex, like a need for intimacy or sex or relief from loneliness. If the character is a predator, we might make the choice that he is driven by a need to release his aggressions upon an innocent person, for wounds he received elsewhere.

Which intent or need—the conscious one (a need to talk with someone) or the unconscious one (for intimacy, apology, relief from rage)—should the actor use in the scene? Whichever one works. You don't know until you try it.

The actor and director *do not need to agree on the objective.* If the actor's idea for his objective is different from yours, it could be a red flag, alerting you that the actor is "not on the same page"—*but not necessarily.* You don't know whether an objective works until the actor tries it. An actor may have an idea that sounds totally discordant to yours, but when he tries it, the performance may look exactly like what you had in mind!

The tool of objective is a great way to open a conversation if you're not happy with the way the scene is playing. You can take the actor aside and ask her, "What are your thoughts about the character's objective?" If you have an idea you think might work better, use the language of permission, for instance: "I was wondering whether perhaps you want him to feel sorry for you."

Some objectives are stronger than others. "Get him to acknowledge you" sounds to me more abstract, and therefore weaker, than "get him to look you in the eye"—because "get him to look you in the eye" is more physical and specific. How about "get her sympathy"? Hmm. "Get her to put her arms around you" could be more playable. But—it would *never* be helpful to argue with an actor about what her objective is! If the actor connects to the objective "get him to acknowledge me," let her try it. If it makes the scene work, great. Whatever you do, *do not* lecture the actor that some other terminology is more correct. When I talk about choosing vivid, strong objectives, my goal is to give you reasons for taking your ideas beyond the obvious, pedestrian choices—not reasons to control the actors' inner life.

Directors and actors may have ideas about what the character *doesn't* want; for example, "She doesn't want to hurt him." Let's give this a little thought to see if we can come up with an objective that is more affirmative—something the character *wants,* rather than something she *doesn't want.* Let's say it's a break-up scene. Perhaps her objective is she "wants him to exit the relationship feeling strong and validated enough to love again." Or—a completely different idea and different kind of person: "She wants him to let her off the hook." Or even, "She wants him to laugh about the absurdity of the fact that they ever got together at all." See, using the *technique of three possible,* I came up with three completely different ideas.

Here's an idea for a question: What is the worst thing that could happen in this conversation? In other words, what event does she wish to avoid at all costs—what's the obstacle? That she might be talked out of her resolve? Or that the other character might get mad or even violent? These are radically different ideas of the relationship—and the scene. I want directors to have *an idea for the scene*—and considering characters' objectives can help.

Humans are complicated and have conflicting needs, right? So it can feel normal to describe a character by saying, "Well, he wants X, but he also wants Y." But I've seen actors struggling to play that formulation—it can easily intellectualize and freeze their emotional reality, almost as though the two choices cancel each other out and flatten the performance. It may be helpful to choose which is his primary need—and call that his *objective*—then think of the other need as his *obstacle*. An elegant solution is to find a *link* between the two needs, as Alexander Skarsgård did when he played Perry in season one of *Big Little Lies*. Skarsgård has told interviewers that he could see that Perry wanted to control and hurt Celeste (Nicole Kidman) and at the same time adored her, even looked up to her. He combined these demons by understanding that Perry wants to control Celeste *because* he fears he is unworthy of her and that, at any moment, she might figure out how inferior he is and leave him.

How about, "He wants X, but knows he can't get it"? A cop-out. Knowing we can't get something does not stop us from wanting it. People want what they want, however irrational. They don't stop wanting something they know they can't have. They don't stop wanting the thing they know won't make them happy if they get it. Hell, they don't stop wanting something even when they do get it! That is the stunning, irrational truth of this tool—and the secret to making it useful.

Intentions/Active Verbs

Someone told me this fact about boxers: They aim their fists not at their opponent's face, but toward the inside of the back of his head—this gives them an *intent to land*. Intention in the world of drama works something like that. Like the boxer's right hook, the actor's intention needs to land on the other actor. If an actor delivers an apathetic approximation of an intention—if instead of *landing* an intention he does what my teacher used to call *playing at* an attitude—the verb will not do its job.

Actors who play with *intention* have a sparkle. The intimate, moment-by-moment response from each actor to the other on a molecular level keeps both actors *alive in their eyes*. Strong intentions activate *listening* and verbs make listening count. Intention is a kind of Listening Plus—listening with a reason. Verbs make performances match in the edit, while still feeling fresh. They add color and vibrancy to a scene.

The character might not know her intention. It's true in real life, too. A character may think she is *apologizing,* but all the while her behavior is clearly *antagonizing.* This would mean she's still mad and, without knowing it, refusing to let her anger go. Or she may think she is standing up for herself, but is actually pleading for recognition. A police officer who holds his knee on the neck of a man for nine minutes may claim—or even believe—that his intent is to restrain, but we who watch the video see in his eyes the intent to murder.

Characters do not choose their intention—it's a truth about their behavior of which they themselves may be unaware. Should an actor play the conscious intention or the unconscious one? Either one may work. The actor doesn't know until he tries it; the director doesn't know until she sees it.

Since the characters' intentions don't need to be conscious, the actors don't need to agree on what each other's intentions are. Character A may feel that he is *teaching* B, and all the while B feels A is *criticizing.*

Verbs are a godsend to actors. When actors get result direction, they can *translate* it into a verb. If an actor is told to *be angrier,* he can make a *translation*—to *punish* the other character, or *tell him off.* If told to "be smug," he can commit to *gloating.* When directed to be "full of self-pity," the verb *to complain* can be a helpful choice. Using verbs supports the actor in placing their full concentration on the other actor—which makes the performance more believable. As a bonus, it gives their character agency. As the best bonus, it gives the story forward movement.

The Short List of Verbs in Appendix A of this 25th Anniversary Edition is expanded from the original publication of *Directing Actors.* It includes additional ways that verbs can be expressed—not only with the one-word verb (like *to convince, to warn, to seduce, to dazzle*), but also in the form of a *subtext* (column two), an *objective* (column three), a metaphor or *"as if"* (column four), or a result formulation (column five). I did this because I want you to be able to see, first, that it's not about exactitude or purity of your terminology; and, second, that *all the tools are all connected.*

There's no need to limit yourself to the verbs on my lists. Here are some perfectly good verbs: to *trivialize*; to *come in gunning*; to *implicate*. The subtext (aka inner monologue) behind the intention *to trivialize* someone might be, "Get over it." The subtext behind *to gloat* might be, "I told you so."

There are nuances to all the verbs—for instance, different kinds of *punishing*. Some people *punish* by withdrawing; others *punish* with verbal abuse.

Verbs are a rescue from result direction. Instead of saying "You feel humiliated," you can speak about a character who is *covering his humiliation*. You don't have to use the exact form of a verb infinitive—instead of *to accuse*, you could say the scene is *about an accusation*. The adjective *menacing* is likely to work better than asking an actor to "be more dangerous"—because *menacing* contains the verb *to menace*.

> ***"I think you have to know what your character wants, and for me, more important than only knowing what your character wants, is how your character is going to get it. That's how you find out who your character is."*—Colin Firth**

When Colin Firth speaks of "what your character wants," he means the *objective*; "how your character is going to get it" is the *verb*. An active verb is something a person *does* to someone else. It's their emotional behavior; it's what they do to get what they need; it's a description of their instinctive reaction to any situation—their emotional tactics or strategies. If my objective is, *I want you to go away*, here are some verbs or *strategies* I might employ: I might *invite* you to leave; I might *demand* that you leave; I might *whine*, or *tease*, or *punish*. I may keep changing tactics (verbs) until I either get what I want—or give up. A single through-line objective can sustain the trajectory of a whole scene. Verbs, on the other hand, can shift within a scene. A complex character can make wide swings from, say, *soothing* to *punishing*, even within one speech.

For many actors, verbs are great quick fixes to add color or variation to a moment. Other actors prefer not to think about individual verbs, but instead, commit to a through-line objective, or need, for the whole scene, and then make shifts from one verb to another strictly in response to their impulses of the moment. Others prefer not to think about objective or intention at all, on the grounds that the character probably doesn't know what he's doing or why he's doing it.

It's completely okay to use the terms verbs, intentions, objectives, wants, or needs interchangeably. Listen for the terms the actors you're working with like to use. Or ask them, "How do you like to work?"

I do not mean directors are never allowed to use adjectives—but—how about maybe not all the time? If you use verbs even 50% of the time, it will help. Even 40%. What's important is not being correct in your language, but making the *shift* in your storytelling approach—from *result* to *relationship*. It takes practice. To be good at it, a director needs to feel it in his bones, not just mechanically apply a verb from the list. If you make that shift, you will have a tool that will help you throughout your career.

At the end of *Slumdog Millionaire*, the character Jamal speaks the line "Latika" twice. This is the only dialogue in a scene that is 90% visual. As played by actor Dev Patel and directed by Danny Boyle, the first time Jamal shouts "Latika!" it seems to me his intention is *to celebrate*—he has found her! Then he spots Salim stalking her with murder on his mind—Jamal again cries out "Latika!" This time his intention is *to warn*. I don't know whether Boyle gave Patel direction in this way, but it makes sense to me.

Use the tool of *building*. If a moment is not being fulfilled with the power it could have, you might take an actor aside and say, "I'm wondering whether there might be a stronger verb here." If the actor says, "Like what?" you might say, "Oh, like goad or provoke maybe." If the actor then says, "Well, I was thinking that I need to *reason* with him," you might say, "Yes, of course. Reason is a good verb. But maybe there's some kind of threat behind it."

Verbs are nothing if not versatile. One verb can describe an entire personality. You could call it a person's—or character's—*dominant verb*. There are people who—no matter what their objective or what the topic under discussion—approach life with the intention to *argue*. For others, the default verb is to *complain*. These behaviors define their natures. I think most of us have come across people who always seem like they're trying to *sell* us something. You probably have friends who fall into a tone of *apology* without being aware of it. Hopefully you have at least a few loved ones whose dominant verb is *to encourage*.

Verbs create the character's *tone of voice*. As Trinity in *The Matrix*, Carrie-Anne Moss has said in interviews that her intention in the club scene, where she first meets Neo (Keanu Reeves) face to face, was *to seduce* him. Trinity's tone of voice toward Neo is *seductive*. Saying that she is seductive toward him sounds like the same thing as saying that she is seducing him—why should it matter to use the term *seduce* instead of telling the actor to *be seductive?* Okay, it might not matter. Or, it might. The verb (*seduce*) puts the actor's concentration on the other actor, so that her inner attention is on *him*, on whether he is getting seduced, rather than on her own performance and whether she is being sufficiently seductive. An actor who is told to "be seductive" may make the translation to the verb "seduce" automatically and almost unconsciously. But it's helpful to everyone if verbs—rather than emotional result—are the currency of communication.

Verbs speak louder than dialogue. Trinity has a line in the club scene: "I brought you here to warn you." So it might be natural to think her intention is *to warn*. And that choice could work. But just because a character says, "I'm here to warn you," doesn't mean the intention must necessarily be *to warn*. The intention is a *subtext*, something that is under the words. Moss's choice—to seduce—creates a magnetic charge to their relationship, catapulting the audience into the story and making us instantly care about the future of this couple. Her subtext choice speaks louder than the words.

Intentions carry a physicality; they are activated by the physical presence of an actor's scene partner. If the intention is *to punish*, then getting the scene partner to *feel punished* is a task, like making a sandwich. That's exactly why an actor, for his close-up, needs the off-camera actor to keep giving him something to play off of—to activate his intention, his psychological task.

The physicality of intention affects the character's body language—and thus the *blocking*. The choice of the Wachowskis, directors of *The Matrix*, to place Trinity in extreme physical proximity to Neo—almost touching *but not quite*—adds to the power and electricity of the scene.

Intentions are emotional as well as physical. If you punish someone, they will feel something—and you will too! Because verbs carry an intent to have an emotional effect on the other person, they stimulate emotion, they put both characters at emotional risk, and thus produce the heightened reality—the raised stakes—of drama.

Or comedy. Jack Black, in *School of Rock*, creates a character with a full and unique commitment to the verb *to party*. Recently, one of my readers notified me on Twitter, with a smiley face, that he was realizing that verbs are a part of daily life: "I did not cook dinner angrily; I accused the frying pan of being unfit for purpose!"

Verbs can create a kind of color palette of emotional range: for instance, these emotional groupings:

- *encourage/lift up/dazzle*;
- *shame/punish/harangue*;
- *beg/apologize/cower*.

In Appendix B, the Longer List of Verbs, I propose some groupings. My goal in creating the verb lists is not to confine you, but rather to offer the rainbow of expression that verbs can give you. I want to expand your emotional range. I'm *not* suggesting that you micromanage an actor with detailed instructions to, for instance, "play *to accuse* on this line. Then play *to seduce* on the next line."

Holly Hunter's character Mel, in an early scene in *Thirteen*, is sitting behind her daughter Tracy (Evan Rachel Wood) and stroking Tracy's hair. The action, of caressing the hair, is both physical and emotional. The words on the page are not inherently emotional (Mel is proposing blonde highlights) but the *intent* is highly emotional—to caress not just with her hands, but with her heart—to envelop with love. Her purpose (objective) is to make her daughter feel safe and protected and cherished. *Thirteen*, directed and co-written by Catherine Hardwicke, observes its characters with great care and honesty. I recognized this mother and this daughter.

When I was a child my mother braided my hair every morning. I resisted her—I wanted unbound, curly hair, I wanted short hair, I wanted anything but my braids. My mother lived her life from a wheelchair from the age of twenty-seven, when she contracted polio and I was five. When I was in my forties, she disclosed to me the reason she had insisted on the braids: to have an excuse to keep me, once a day, as physically near to her as the cumbersome steel contraption would allow.

Sadly, I never felt the caress, I only felt the control. Which gives me the idea that Tracy also experiences her mother's caress as control. The more Mel caresses, the more Tracy pulls away; the more Tracy pulls away, the more desperately Mel holds her close. The stakes grow higher and higher. Tracy pulls away more and more violently until, in later scenes, as Tracy *challenges*, *taunts*, and *goads*, Mel becomes reactive, too—her *caress* mutates to *demand, beg, harangue, reproach*, and *restrain*. This is the weave of *emotional event* that keeps raising the stakes, building dramatic tension—telling the story. Verbs can take you *this far* into the emotional center of storytelling.

The Spine

The *spine* of a character may be called a *script objective, super-objective,* or *overall-objective*. But it's bigger than the character's goal in the story at hand—it's what the character wants out of life. It's her emotional center, her core, her life need, her central drive, or deepest longing. It's what the character is living for, whether they know it or not. As Andrew Stanton says, it's "an itch they can't scratch." A trigger. A hook. A key. Emotional DNA.

It's primal: *the need for parents' approval; the need to protect children; the need to have power over others; the need to matter in the world*. It can be the childhood wound that cries out to be healed. It's like an invisible golden cord tugging at the character from the center of their being. It's deeply rooted in the experiences of early life and is probably in place by the time a character (or person) is eight years old. People never give up. If they didn't get enough approval from their parents, they never stop wanting it.

A *spine* is true about the character before the movie starts and is still true after the movie is over. So it's not the same as the character's arc or narrative drive—also called his transformation—which describes the way a character changes between the beginning of the film and the end. Creating a compelling and believable story arc for your characters is critical to good storytelling. But the spine is something different, a tool that helps the audience feel that the characters are believable human beings. Because everything I'm about to say about characters' spines is true of people, too.

To determine a character's spine, start by listing as many facts as you can that are true about the character when the story starts. Then ask questions. The questions, like the facts, will vary for different stories; one that is almost always useful might be: what is the most important thing that has happened to him?

Next, make a list of possibilities for the character's spine, as many things as you can think of that a person in his situation might want or need out of life. Don't limit yourself to the specifics of the script—look for human needs. If a person grew up poor, he might be driven by a need to have more money than anyone else—in other words, to never be poor again. But not necessarily. A spine affects a person's behavior, but does not predetermine it. We make choices; we have free will. I have known people who grew up poor and devoted their lives to serving the needs of all the poor of the world.

You will start to have ideas; some will seem better than others. Sometimes the spine seems obvious, like Morpheus's need *to find The One*. Well, not to be a pest, but whenever something seems obvious, I like to keep looking. We are told in *The Matrix* script that in the past Morpheus thought he found *The One*, but was mistaken—with disastrous consequences. When you think about it, this *fact* could be overwhelming for anyone. His spine might be *to redeem himself*.

Is it so crucially important to locate one single spine for each character? Not exactly. There might be a constellation of central needs driving a character. It's not a guessing game that you win or lose; it's a tool, a way to communicate emotional information. Since, in drama, *three* is a magic number, we might look for a constellation of *three central needs* for a character. How about this constellation of needs for Trinity:

- *a drive to win her battles;*
- *a longing to find true love;*
- *a deep need to protect and cherish the legacy of a father-figure.*

These are all primal needs that illuminate her actions in the script—and could have been hard-wired in her since childhood.

Some characters are driven by self-hatred, and move like a moth to flame toward their own destruction. A character who's experienced a primal abandonment may be driven by a need for validation. A character who's been hurt or abused may be driven by the need to take their power back. Frank Galvin, played by Paul Newman in *The Verdict*, who lives a life steeped in shame, is driven by a need for redemption.

A spine is usually expressed as a *need*, but it might be interwoven with *metaphor*. In an interview for *Remains of the Day*, Emma Thompson (Miss Kenton) described her central metaphor as a bird beating its wings against Mr. Stevens (Anthony Hopkins). When her wings break against this unyielding man, she accepts marriage to another man who has also never truly joined her in flight. But—she has never stopped wanting to fly. It's her spine.

The spine is an essential tool whenever a film is shot out of sequence, or whenever a big emotional scene is shot over several days, as a way to *track* the character or story, even if the individual scene objectives change. In *The Fighter*, directed by David O. Russell, Dicky (Christian Bale) has different *scene objectives* toward his brother Micky (Mark Wahlberg) in different scenes. Sometimes he *protects and takes care of Micky*, like in the bar scene in which Micky meets Charlene. Sometimes he wants Micky to take care of *him* and protect *him*, as in the scene when the family discovers him at the crack house. At one point, he *sweet-talks and cajoles* Micky into agreeing to a fight that Micky is unlikely to win; in another scene, he *bullies* Micky out of replacing him as his manager.

How can we hold all these conflicting intentions under the umbrella of a script objective—a spine—describing Dicky's central life need? Here's a useful question for any character: Who is the most important person in Dicky's life? Micky's a likely candidate, for sure. So a possible spine for Dicky could be *to stay central to Micky's life*, or even *to keep Micky dependent on him*. The real-life Micky was born when Dicky was eight. Since I believe that a person's spine usually falls into place at the age of eight, that fact feels significant to me.

What about the brothers' forceful and glamorous mother (played by Melissa Leo)? Maybe Dicky's spine is to stay at the center of the lives of *both* his brother and his mother. Or I might take a step further and look for a way to *link* Dicky's conflicting feelings toward these two people, who both hold such power over his psyche. I thought of a complex, but all too human, spine—*to compete with his brother for their mother's love and attention.* I like that one.

Continuing to *ask questions* until you find a *spine* is a great way to keep from judging characters. Instead of labeling a character as selfish, you could say that her spine is her own comfort and convenience—it's the same thing, but subtly more playable. A spine can be an *opposite* to a character's behavior. A character whose behavior is controlling and abusive may be driven by deep feelings of worthlessness.

If you are worried that committing to a spine creates a one-note character—exactly the opposite is true. The tool of spine opens an actor up to human complexity. We are all driven by any number of primal needs: love, success, family, sex, money, independence, respect, power, control, approval and validation, spiritual meaning, comfort, attention, revenge, security, recognition, connection, safety, survival. Some of these needs are contradictory to each other. We want security and at the same time we want adventure. We want recognition, we want control of our lives, we want to have an effect on the world—and we also want love and safety. We all want everything. This is exactly the brilliance of the tool of spine: that there can be a need that drives us, to the point that we sacrifice our other needs, which then gnaw at us inside. A person (or character) can sacrifice his need for love in blind pursuit of a need for power—and still wish for love, too.

Let's say that what an actor likes about her character is that she's strong and independent. If the story calls for this character to have a moment of weakness and self-pity, the actor may ask for changes to the script. But you can reframe: Let go of the character label, that the character *is* independent; instead, think of her as a person who is *fighting* for her independence. Then the moments when she *fails* in that struggle can reveal hidden depths and be poignant, real, and dramatic.

Or funny! Spines work for comedy too! Comedy is ruled by incongruity. Comedic characters have the same serious life needs that all people do, but are frequently doing exactly the wrong thing to get what they want. Take Alan in *The Hangover* (Zach Galifianakis). I would say Alan's spine is that he profoundly craves *to be loved and accepted by the guys*. His foolish *tactic* is to try to make them think he's cooler than he actually is. This behavior does not achieve its objective; it provokes their irritation and pity. Much like the *Bridesmaids* character Helen (Rose Byrne), who pursues her secret, deep *need to be liked* with the wrong-headed tactic of trying *to outdo the others*.

For episodic television, each character's spine needs to be in place from the get-go—the pilot—and be compelling and universal enough to hold the performance together throughout a potential seven-year run. In an *LA Times* interview, Bob Odenkirk was asked why he thought his *Better Call Saul* character, Jimmy McGill, resonated with audiences. Odenkirk said, "The way people relate to it, and I'm just guessing here, is that everybody wants to feel effective in the world." I infer from that statement that "to feel effective in the world" is Odenkirk's understanding of Jimmy's spine.

Actors can choose a spine for their character. But *characters* do not choose their spines. A spine is more like a compulsion—unconscious, most likely. In real life we don't choose our spines—we are compelled by them. My idea for the spine of the Gena Rowlands character in *A Woman Under the Influence* (directed by John Cassavetes) is that she is driven by a need "to get her husband's attention." Mabel loves her children and wants to protect them, but her need to get her husband's attention eclipses her other needs. She doesn't *choose* to abandon her other needs, including her instincts for self-preservation—but this iconic performance is a testament to how powerfully humans can be compelled by irrational needs without their knowledge or volition. Almost as though her spine was pulling her from her gut, against her own will. In a heart-stopping scene, at the dinner table after she returns home from the hospital, she interrupts the family chatter to ask her father, "Dad, will you stand up for me?" This mysterious line opens up for me the idea that Mabel's deep spine, irrevocably hardwired since childhood, is her unfulfilled need for her father's full attention.

A spine can be simple. But watch out for ideas that are merely glib or obvious. Let's take as an example, the character Michael Corleone (Al Pacino) in *The Godfather*. What do you think might be Michael's spine? Power? Control? Family loyalty? To get revenge for the shooting of his father? When I suggest in classes that Michael's spine might be "to make his father proud of him," students sometimes protest that in the beginning of the movie, Michael wants to separate himself from his father and be his own man, and that it is only after Don Vito is shot that Michael decides to meet his father's expectations.

But look at the facts. Don Vito has three sons: the eldest (Santino) is in line to succeed him as godfather; the second (Fredo) is meant to be active in the business, but in a limited way, under careful supervision. The youngest and most talented—the favorite, Michael—is to become a real "American." Not a mafia functionary but a lawyer, perhaps eventually a senator. Michael's independence pleases his father. Having a son in the U.S. Senate is part of Don Vito's plan.

At Connie's wedding, in the first moments that we meet all these characters, Michael says to his date, "That's my family, Kay, it's not me." It's a mysterious line! Actually, he is the same as them, but he doesn't know it yet. All who fill their slots in the mafia hierarchy exist to perpetuate the hierarchy, which means pleasing the Godfather. After Sonny's death, Don Vito's plan changes; Michael accepts his destiny to take his father's place as don. This is his arc, his narrative drive, his transformation—from a typical second-generation American son (ambitious and independent, eager to meet and exceed the aspirations of his immigrant parents) to a single-minded, murderous mafia don. But his spine—his emotional mooring—is his commitment to his father, anchored in a primal need, common to many men, to make his father proud of him.

Now what? Directors reading this may be wondering: Should I tell the actor what his character's spine is? When? Must the actor and director agree on the spine of the character? What if the actor has a different idea? I don't have one-syllable answers to these questions, but I know that *spine* can function as a communication tool. If you feel uneasy about what the actor is doing, you can open a conversation by asking, "What are your thoughts about the spine of this character?"

The spine is a secret, a choice, not something the audience is supposed to track. If what an actor is doing works, why would it matter if the spine he has chosen is different from your idea? I have an anecdote for you that may be more illuminating on this topic than theory or discussion. On the DVD commentary for *Dog Day Afternoon,* actor Al Pacino says of playing Sonny, "I found my key—he wanted to get caught, he wanted his day in the sun." Pacino seems to be using the word "key" to describe what I am calling "spine." At another moment, director Sidney Lumet describes Sonny as "almost suicidally eager to please." So perhaps Lumet thought of Sonny's spine as *to make everyone happy,* whereas for Pacino his character's spine (key) was *to have his day in the sun.* The two of them were participating in the commentary together—I got no sense from their discussion that they thought of their differing views on Sonny's spine as any kind of argument or difficulty. So I persist in my idea that a spine is a choice, a secret, and that, if it works, it's nobody's business.

I think of the spine as heavily influenced by childhood experiences, but of course it may be partly genetic. Anyone can see that infants have distinct personalities: Some seem to have been born with a spine of *needing extra attention,* for example. In a story that aspires to mythical themes, the spines of the characters may be *representational*—that is, determined by fate. (At one point in the *Star Wars* saga, Luke Skywalker tells Rey that it is a Jedi's destiny *to confront fear.*) Even though my script analysis ideas are often based in psychology, if I'm working with an actor or a director who sees character spines as more genetic/instinctual, or representational/

fated, than I do—I don't mind! The tool of *spine* will work either way. It's bigger than intellectualized squabbles about theory or ideology.

A spine is a tool, not an absolute. Its purpose is to give energy to the performance. Emotional charge is what it's all about. If you're stuck, here's a fallback. For film or television, for drama or comedy, the following spines can always work:

- Fighting for love.
- Fighting to win (so that someone else loses).
- A need to be liked and approved of.
- A need to escape one's pain.
- A need to have one's presence count and one's efforts applauded.

These are eternal.

Obstacle (The Stakes)

An actor might win the role of a person who, after many years of hiding her feelings, finally confronts her father about the distance in their relationship. An actor may be thrilled about approaching such a meaty role, and jump in feet first, confronting away, acting up a storm. In real life, of course, confronting one's father is likely to be a painful experience, one that most of us avoid at all costs. To *confront* is a verb. The fact that it's your father you are confronting is the *obstacle*.

Sometimes actors forget that an obstacle is a good thing, not a bad thing. Obstacles strengthen the objective. We know this from real life—if you want something, the problems you must solve to get it make your determination stronger. Actors can get stuck in a comfort zone, and make a choice that enables them not to engage, not to be affected by the other actor—for instance, the verb *to ignore*. Both characters must be affected by each other, even if they struggle to preserve their composure and keep the other guy from knowing they are affected. There has to be something *at stake*.

Obstacles can be external or internal. In Alejandro Iñárritu's *The Revenant,* Hugh Glass (Leonardo DiCaprio) has the need, in the scenes after his son's death, *to avenge the murder;* there are other scenes earlier in the film where his need is *to do his job* (as a scout for fur trappers); in still other scenes, after his attack by the grizzly bear, he is driven by instinct *to endure.* Many of his obstacles are external: the war party that attacks the trappers' camp; the bear; the murderous Fitzgerald; the gravely perilous conditions of survival in the wilderness. He also has internal obstacles: his grief and shame that he was not able to protect his son or save his wife. Obstacles raise the stakes not only for the plot, but also for the character's inner life.

The intersection of *need* and *obstacle* creates a sense of *predicament* or *problem,* and propels the story forward. The simplest way to ensure there is both need and obstacle in a scene is if the characters have competing objectives. If the event of the scene is an argument and both characters have the need *to win against the other*—automatically, the objective of each character becomes the obstacle of the other, right? Or if one character has a need *to win* and the other character a need *to keep the peace.*

Sometimes actors want the director to set up the obstacle for them, perhaps asking, "Would you please tell him to be really mean to me in that scene? That way I'll be able to cry." It's important that directors discourage actors from directing each other—but diplomatically. You could say, "Thank you for telling me your idea. I want you always to feel able to tell me what's on your mind—and I appreciate you speaking to me about it, instead of to him. But I love what you're doing. If you keep connected to him, and keep playing your objective, I think it's going to work fine." If the actor is a star, you may need extra diplomacy. But if an actor, star or no, has complaints about her partner's work in a scene, it's likely a symptom of anxiety over her own performance. A director who listens attentively and supportively can be more helpful than one who springs into knee-jerk "fix-it" mode.

Sometimes an actor wants the director to remove obstacles, for example change out a prop for another that is easier to handle, or adjust the blocking so they can be face-to-face with each other. But actually, physical obstacles can take a performance to the next level. If handling the prop is awkward, it gives the actor something to do. If the character wants the other character to forgive him, but the other actor refuses to look at him, it could add to the dramatic tension—or to the comedy—of the scene.

Actors may object to the writing ("That line is too hard to say," or "My character wouldn't say that"). They may be good ideas, and if you're the writer-director, you can say, "Sure, let's try it." But if you believe in the line and want it spoken as is, you might ask the actor what bothers him about the line, and then tell him what you like about it—in other words, make your case. Please note that in television, any line changes need to be okayed by the writer-producers—but I don't think that situation renders the director powerless. It's still an opportunity to think through what the scene is about and come up with imaginative adjustments to make it work.

If, for whatever reason, the line must be spoken as is, you might ask the actor, "What would you prefer to say?" When he tells you, you might say, "Yes, I agree with you, that's what it means. Do you think you could you speak the line as written, but say your own line silently—as subtext?"

There are accounts from several sources about offscreen conflicts over the writing of the famous taxicab scene in *On the Waterfront*. Apparently, neither Marlon Brando (Terry) nor Rod Steiger (Charley) liked the idea that Steiger's character would pull a gun on his brother. Steiger told the director, Elia Kazan, "Brothers already have plenty of ways to manipulate and control each other—I don't need a gun." Brando said, "I've got all that stuff where I say 'I coulda been a contender' and that my brother and Johnny sold me out, all those dreams of what I could've been—how can I say all that with a gun pointing at me?" They both have a point. It's a big responsibility for the director to make the final decision—will the gun make the scene more dramatic and memorable? Or will it cross the line into silly melodrama?

In an *Esquire* interview, the screenwriter, Budd Schulberg, reported that Kazan said to Brando, "What if you just reach out quietly and push the barrel down a little so it's not pointing at you?" This solution retained the drama of the gun without overplaying it. It also had the virtue of incorporating a graceful response to both actors' complaints. Most importantly, it goes to the question, what is the scene about? It's about two brothers. When Terry gently pushes the gun away, the audience becomes witness to the inarticulate depth and strange tenderness of the relationship; we see that whatever Charley's terrible failures as a brother, Terry knows Charley will not use a gun on him. Pushing away the gun becomes the transforming event of the scene. After it, Terry opens his heart to his brother, and Charley is moved to love and shame—and finally, to sacrifice his own life for his brother.

(One last twist: Brando, in his autobiography, claims to have improvised that whole scene! But the fact that the actor ends up thinking it was all his own idea is a win for everyone. I still think that Brando, Steiger, Kazan, and Schulberg could all be right!)

Imagery

Imagery is the poetry, the resonating sensory subworld of the text. I like to use the terms *subtext imagery* or interior imagery, because I'm not talking about cinematic grammar, or the final images within the four corners of the frame. *Subtext imagery* includes our memories, dreams, longings, fears, fantasies, daydreams, visualizations. It encompasses the entire content of our imaginations, the icons and symbols of our cultural and spiritual lives, our connection to the collective unconscious. It is crucial to our creativity, and even our intelligence, because a central way that we understand and correlate experience and information is with metaphor—like when we describe something by saying, "*This* reminds me of *that*."

It's easy to see how some characters are driven primarily by subtext imagery, like the couple in the film *In the Mood for Love,* who daydream a lot. But what about cerebral characters—like Morpheus in *The Matrix* or Scully in *The X-Files* or the health services workers in *Contagion? Contagion*'s CDC workers, as well as characters in television forensics procedurals, must converse with each other in complex scientific jargon; Morpheus has long speeches explaining the Matrix Construct to Neo. It's terribly important to *endow* these cerebral exchanges with subtext imagery. The actors and director need to do *research* to understand what all the terms mean—and then look for imagery and references *underneath* the jargon. We know this from real life: Some doctors convey images of hope and health under their information; others seem to have a picture of the page from a medical book in their minds when they speak to the patient.

In the TV pilot of *Fringe,* a character has a line, "I feel like I'm living in a Charlotte Brontë novel." It stands to reason that the actor and director need to know something about the novels of Charlotte Brontë. As a better-than-nothing shortcut if time is running out, you can look up Brontë on Wikipedia—but someone who has read *Jane Eyre* will have an advantage in her preparation to play the role or direct the episode.

An actor can play a nuclear physicist without being one. A filmmaker can direct the *Bourne* movies without having been recruited by a CIA black ops program. It's simple: *Do research* into the meaning behind the arcane language. If the actor and director have no reference whatever for Charlotte Brontë or nuclear physics or CIA black ops—the lines and the scene and the whole project become bogus in a way that the audience picks up on without knowing why.

Some films have central images that enter our collective unconscious with layers of deeply evocative emotional and spiritual association:

- *Moonlight* (Barry Jenkins): the image of moonlight on water when Juan cradles Chiron in the ocean;

- *Mad Max: Fury Road* (George Miller): the monumental waterfall of the Citadel gushing extravagantly at the center of vast, uninhabitable desert;
- *Get Out* (Jordan Peele): the Sunken Place.

Imagery pops up everywhere in good writing, giving us, succinctly and vividly, profound emotional information. In a *Pulp Fiction* scene, Vincent (John Travolta) and Jules (Samuel L. Jackson) converse about the Royale with cheese and, later, foot massages. The elaborate specificity of their discussions gives the audience emotional information—that *their relationship is close*—because we know from life that people only discuss such mundane topics with this amount of deep detail if they know each other well. The foot massage *image* awakens separate *associations* for each character. Each character is undoubtedly recalling *specific* personal experiences of giving foot massages—so the actors can too. When actors *fill* or *invest* the writing with specific associations, the characters and story come alive for the audience.

The content of what someone is saying is not the words themselves, but the image those words evoke. Let's say the character has a line, "There was rain today." To give life to the image "rain," the actor invests or endows it with sensory associations. Everybody knows what rain is, but let's adopt a *beginner's mind,* and not take anything for granted. Start with your own memories of rain, all different kinds of rain: hard, needle-like rain; soft, sweet, warm rain; cold rain; rain squishing in your shoes; being indoors in a rainstorm; the sound patterns as the wind brings the rain in gusts; the sight of rain streaming down the window; the condensation on the inside of the pane; mud; the sound of splashing; the taste of rain; the smell of rain; rain on wool; rain running down your collar. Besides memory, there is also the resource of imagination. Even if you have never been inside a tiny mountain cabin during rain, as soon as you give yourself permission to imagine it, it's there. Even if you have never stood naked in the rain, imagining it—really, fully, imagining the sensation of rain against your bare skin—is a transformative experience.

The power of subtext imagery is unleashed by its *associations*. When I free-associate to *rain*, I return to my New England childhood, where summer rain, usually accompanied by electrical storms, might on certain magical afternoons pour down without the danger of thunder and lightning. My brother and I would beg our mother to let us put on swimsuits so we could run and jump in the warm, soaking rain, drenched and staggering around the yard with upturned faces and outstretched arms.

This is all preparation. When it comes time for the actor to deliver the line, "There was rain today" in front of the camera, the word "rain" has emotional weight; there is imagery behind it. The actor is not *trying* to have the image while the camera rolls, he is not stopping the scene to remember his image; he has already done the work and the image will be there.

The imagery behind the text can be imaginative or it can be personal. Personal imagery is sometimes called *substitution*. There are actors who are adamant that they only use imagination; and others who insist that they only use personal material. I mean, in the *Pulp Fiction* scene, are Travolta and Jackson imagining the foot massages that Vincent and Jules have experienced? Or are the two actors remembering foot massages they themselves have given? My own experience is that memory and imagination weave in and out—I could not have a creative life without both, and to me, it makes no sense to get dogmatic over it. But I do find that personal substitution is a powerful engine for my imagination.

When I was acting on stage, one of my favorite roles was the title character in the play *Mrs. Cage*, by Nancy Barr. Mrs. Cage had long monologues on the subject of ironing her husband's shirts. (She was not ironing on stage; she was in a police station, talking about ironing.) Although my mother ironed my father's shirts and taught me how, I had never, as an adult, ironed men's shirts. The writing was so full of specific, highly sensory imagery—the steaming ironing board, the texture and colors of the oxford shirts—that, in my preparation, I focused on the script's expressive imagery, certain it would spark my imagination. But I felt dry. While we were still in rehearsal, I decided to try something: I made a wholesale *substitution* and as I spoke the lines about ironing the shirts, I focused on a sensory experience of wrapping a present for someone I loved. (It was my choice about the character that to her the ironing was a gift, an act of love.) I made my images specific: a specific present, a certain person the gift was for, the sounds of crinkling wrapping paper, the tape snapping off the roll. I quit worrying about getting the *right* image, and instead gave myself completely to my substitution.

Here's the crazy part. Once I let go of *doing it right,* once I surrendered—something miraculous happened. The ironing image kicked in! The hissing from the iron, the crispness of the cotton took hold of me. During many performances, I could feel the steam on my face. I did not try to make the audience believe that I felt the steam, it was just there. This was, for me, a living example of the "magic as if."

Jim Carrey said in an interview for *Eternal Sunshine of the Spotless Mind* that he had poured a lot of his own experience into his role as Joel. Then, at a certain point, spontaneous associations seemed to happen, as though magically, on set. One day the set decorator brought in a green Mustang bicycle for a scene from Joel's childhood memory. Carrey was instantly catapulted to a memory from his own childhood of a green Mustang bike—which, he insisted, the set decorator knew nothing about! When you're working deeply on a creative project, random things don't seem random; when you are focused on the subtext, everything feels like it is part of the plan.

Imagery has a big effect on all of us. If you start thinking about the backyard or stoop of your childhood home, it's going to have an effect on you. Even if actors aren't specifically trained to work with images, it's just true. That's why they are such a useful directing tool. A director who feels at home with subtext imagery becomes an actor whisperer. Here are a few examples:

Gene Hackman has said that just before shooting his death scene in *Bonnie and Clyde,* director Arthur Penn whispered to him this simple phrase: "a bull in a bull ring, wounded." Franco Zeffirelli gave Glenn Close this image for her portrayal of Gertrude in *Hamlet*: "The walls of the castle are filled with her perfume." Kim Hunter disclosed to interviewer James Grissom that on the set of *A Streetcar Named Desire,* Elia Kazan whispered to her and Vivien Leigh that Blanche and Stella were "attached to Stanley by cords as strong and as vital as the umbilical cord that kept us alive in the womb."

According to a producer of *Unfaithful,* director Adrian Lyne ran up to Diane Lane just before the shot of her riding the train home from her first intimacy in her lover's apartment and whispered in her ear, "You're thinking about the lovemaking." Lane made that scene unforgettable with her audacious surrender to this radical permission. An actor can't get to that emotional fearlessness without a total sensory commitment—and the support of her director.

When David Yates directed his first *Harry Potter* film, *Harry Potter and the Order of the Phoenix,* he noted that at the end of the previous installment, a Hogwarts schoolmate had been killed. From this powerful *fact,* he generated a poignant image—that this film begins in "the shadow of bereavement." And he arranged *research*—a meeting between actor Daniel Radcliffe and a bereavement counselor before shooting.

Both director Kenneth Lonergan, on the DVD commentary, and actor Mark Ruffalo, on *Inside the Actors Studio,* have spoken about how together they arrived at a *spine* for Ruffalo's character Terry in *You Can Count on Me.* Ruffalo said, "There's a great image that we talked about: that Terry punches out into the world and his fist goes all the way around the world and hits him in the back of the head." He added, "For a long time as a young actor this was me—so, I know that guy—I have that self-destructive quality in me as well."

Our inner lives are minefields—laced with buried memories, wishes, and fears. A dedicated actor or director will always connect images with associations that are rich in both personal meaning and imaginative breadth. The imagery of Terry punching all around the world is so much more powerful than a simplistic generality like "Terry is self-destructive." The facile explanations of pop psychology do not *stick* the way that imagery does.

Toward the end of *Godfather II*, Fredo is fishing from the dock with Michael's son Anthony, and says to his nephew, "You know, when I was your age, I went out fishing with all my brothers and my father, everybody, and I was the only one that caught a fish. Nobody else could catch one except me. You know how I did it? Every time I put the line in the water, I said a Hail Mary, and every time I said a Hail Mary, I caught a fish." The scene shimmers with deep emotion: the memory of that one perfect day from his childhood, when he caught fish after fish and his father and brothers admired him and even the Blessed Virgin looked upon him with favor. This may be Fredo's most intimate inner image—a vision of his true, pure self, before he was doomed by his bad luck and poor choices. Where did actor John Cazale get his inner imagery? Too private to be any of our business. The more secret, specific, and real his image is to him, the more universal will be the audience's journey via our own imaginations—to the longings and regrets for lost visions of childhood purity and joy—and the more deeply we will care about Fredo and be moved by his terrible fate.

Facts And Clues

The Timeline

The most dire condemnation I've ever heard from an actor about a director? This: "He didn't even know what was going on with the characters in each scene!"

At an absolute minimum, a director needs to know the timeline, and review with the actors, before each scene, where the characters are in the story. For example: *It's the morning after the botched robbery.* The director must know the script backwards and forwards, so he can orient himself emotionally when checking in with the actors. What if you were shooting three scenes in the same location—and shooting them out of sequence? What if you were shooting a script with a plot as complicated as that of *The Prestige*—in which not only time sequence, but identities, are shuffled? You need to have the *facts* of your timeline at the tip of your fingers.

Emotional History

***"Facts are for accountants."*—Werner Herzog**

I include this subversive Werner Herzog quote because the facts that matter are emotional. If you enforce them mechanically, they are dramatically inert. Facts are a character's emotional history, their baggage. We know from our own lives that our emotional history is not dry or conclusive—emotional baggage creates complication, tangent, and obstacle. "I was raised Catholic"—a simple fact, yes? Well, maybe not so much. *I* was raised Catholic, and can trace many confusions of my own nature—acquaintance with guilt and shame, complicated sexual anxiety, identification with the underdog, obsession with the intersection of spirituality and theater—back to that deceptively simple fact.

I like to use the term *emotional history* rather than *backstory*. A person or character who has a history of abandonment has emotional baggage that a person who spent every day of her childhood in a loving family does not. In *Wedding Crashers*, Jeremy (played by Vince Vaughn) has a line of dialogue early in the movie explaining to a friend that he stays overnight with John (Owen Wilson) every year on John's birthday, because John lost his parents in a tragic accident. This line is a literal *exposition* of emotional history for John—the loss of his parents at a young age. It's really more than exposition: It's an *emotionally defining fact* for John. It has everything to do with the differing levels of fragility for these two characters—and with their separate fates at the end of the film.

Question Everything

"*Characters lie!*"—Gerald Hiken

Gerry Hiken—yes, the very teacher who used to demand of me and my comrades that we "Stop doing it right"—had another favorite expression. With a devilish grin, he would stand in front of the classroom, strike a pose, pause theatrically—and in a loud, dramatic whisper, declare: "Characters lie!" I have come to feel that he was imparting to us a central secret of script analysis—that the script is not to be followed literally, like an engineer's drawing, but to be explored as a set of *clues* that can springboard us into our imaginations. He was conveying this crucial insight: *that every character is an unreliable narrator.*

Facts are arid and meaningless unless they lead you to *questions.* And questions, like associations, open up our creativity, get us *imagining.* In *Thirteen,* we see Tracy in the bathroom, cutting her arms with a razor. Question: Has she cut before? In the DVD commentary, director Catherine Hardwicke reports that she and the actor Evan Rachel Wood together made the choice that yes, she has. That *choice* itself leads to more questions: How often? When did she start? Is there a pattern or ritual to these incidents?

I have met young women who have confided to me their experiences with cutting. As I think about the scene from *Thirteen,* I ponder those fragments of conversation. Then I get on the internet and look for blogs. I become more and more emotionally invested with these children, each with a story to tell, and, as I read their words, the imagery of their lives floods me. Some speak of cutting as a way to focus on physical pain and thus avoid emotional pain. Others speak of a condition of numbness in their lives—cutting allows them to at least feel something. I sit quietly and impressions from my research spin into a scaffold of associations. I recall my own teen years. I imagine a young woman I know and love holding a razor to her arm. Soon, I feel love and empathy for Tracy. I have begun to live in the world of the script.

In making the choice that the cutting scene in *Thirteen* was not the first time the character had cut herself, director Hardwicke and actor Wood have created *imagined facts,* that is, the whole series of other times Tracy has cut. They could have made the opposite *choice*—that the scene in the film was the first time that Tracy cuts herself. That different choice would have created a different emotional content to the scene—and perhaps to the whole movie. It's *subtext,* so the audience might not be consciously aware of the difference, but they would *feel* it.

Invented Facts and Off-Camera Scenes

Invented facts are *secrets* that launch actors into a character's reality. They help make ideas playable. Instead of labeling a character trait—*he's a neat freak*—you could imagine details of his life: for instance, that *he irons his underwear.*

If you find yourself "dialing" the performances by describing a brother and sister as "close but not that close"—ask questions to make it specific. How often do they see each other? Call each other? What do they talk about? In other words, what do you mean by "close but not that close"? Do you mean that they see each other once a year, but each time it's like they saw each other yesterday? Or do you mean that they used to be close, but no longer are?

When emotional history is left out of the script, the actor imagines it—as off-camera scenes. Here and there, you find actors and acting coaches who object to imagining anything that is not in the script. But when I suggest imagining off-camera scenes, I'm not staking out a dogmatic position—it just seems sensible to me. Anything that happens between or before the scripted scenes is an off-camera scene. During off-camera scenes, the characters were *somewhere,* doing *something*—even if it is only a ride in an elevator. It makes sense to pose questions about what occurred.

Off-camera scenes can compel the action as effectively as events in the script. According to Al Pacino on the DVD commentary for *Dog Day Afternoon,* he and John Cazale came up with this bold choice: that *Sonny and Sal did not know each other very well before the day of the robbery.* That indeed, they were getting to know each other in the course of this, the most intense day of either of their lives. The lesson of this story is that the two actors *asked the question—how long ago did they meet?* If you don't ask the question, you might make the *assumption* that they know each other well. So—don't make assumptions! Instead, ask questions.

In his commentary for *Alien,* director Ridley Scott says of the Hawaiian shirt worn by Harry Dean Stanton's character, "He probably got it at some intergalactic gift shop where he got cards for the kids, who he's not going to see for four years." Later in the commentary, during the scene in which Stanton's character Brett hesitates to give up his pen, Scott chuckles: "Probably got it at that same gift shop as the Hawaiian shirt!"

The intergalactic gift shops are never mentioned in dialogue. I'm told they're not in stage directions either. Ridley Scott must have *imagined* off-camera scenes in which the crew of the Nostromo made stops at recreation areas established all over the galaxy by the Company. Scott must have communicated this idea to the actors as well as the designers. It's a human detail that brings to life a central element of the story. Because—check it out—*the Company has colonized the galaxy.* And created rest stops with gadgets and impulse-buys to distract the workers from the real fact that their lives are controlled by powers who answer to no one.

The Moment Before

The character's life before the scene starts needs to have a sensory reality. Creating the moment just before the camera rolls may be the most important preparation an actor does. If the scene starts mid-conversation—it needs to feel like that. But even if the scene starts with the characters meeting for the first time, each character has had a life going on before the scene starts. The director can ask each actor privately about their *moment before*—and support them in imagining it. If you have rehearsal, that's a great opportunity to explore the *moment before* by improvising it.

Adjustments: Metaphor; Analogy; "As If"; "What If?"; "It's Like When"

The title character in *Il Postino* has a line, "This is the first letter I've ever received." Acting is all about creating a sense of belief, an experience of seeing the world through the character's eyes, so the actor, who has undoubtedly received letters in his own life, must create a *sense of belief* to justify that line: What would it be like to be a person who has never received a letter? How would it feel, *who would I be,* if I lived in a tiny village all my life, had no education, and had never received a letter?

Or, the actor could find a *metaphor*. In order to deliver believably that line, the actor might say it *as if* he is really saying, "This is the first message I've ever received from a movie star."

Ralph Fiennes has said of his role as Amon Göth in *Schindler's List,* "I tried to put myself in a place where I could imagine what it was like to have a form of prejudice that was so extreme that certain groups of people became equivalent to cockroaches or rats." Here Fiennes used *research*—the metaphor of Jews as comparable to cockroaches was used by Nazis to justify the Holocaust—and created for himself this horrifying *analogy*. It was so effective that after that film came out, he said he met people who seemed to feel that he, the actor, must be as conscienceless as the genocidal SS perpetrators of the Final Solution. Of course, that isn't remotely true. He was using an actor's tool—analogy—and committing to it so fearlessly that it brought the audience to the uncomfortable realization that the face of evil is a human face.

Jennifer Lopez disclosed in a *Los Angeles Times* interview that Lorene Scafaria directed her and the other actresses in *Hustlers* with this powerful *adjustment*: that the women were not sex objects—rather, they were athletes. This is how the movie succeeded as a banner for female empowerment and escaped the confinements of the "male gaze."

Metaphor, analogy, "as if," the "it's like when" (aka *adjustments*) are truly power tools. They pierce through to the heart of the matter in ways that endless discussions of "what the character is like" never can. They tap into the actor's secret weapon: surrendering to "let's pretend."

The magic of the "as if" gives us permission to mess around with the facts of a script. A *fact* in the relationship between Fredo and Michael Corleone is that Fredo is older than Michael. Yet by the end of *The Godfather,* Michael has become the older and Fredo the younger—not literally, but emotionally. This adjustment describes their relationship, not their birth certificates. In *You Can Count on Me,* the characters are brother and sister and yet, they behave toward each other almost like disappointed ex-lovers. I am not suggesting any change to the *literal* facts—I am in no way insinuating that they ever had sex together. It's a figurative analogy—a metaphor—to convey the depth of their need for each other and the pain of their failures to connect.

An imaginative adjustment can be a "what if?" In an interview reported in *Daily Variety,* John Travolta spoke about playing Ben in Harold Pinter's *The Dumbwaiter,* directed by Robert Altman: "I had a scene where I was reading a newspaper aloud to someone. I was rattling away. Altman didn't say much at first. Then he came over and whispered in my ear, 'What if your character is really illiterate and can't read a word on the page, is making it all up as he goes along?'" Travolta paused and then went on: "Wow. That changed everything, permeated the whole scenario."

This anecdote blows my mind. I know *The Dumbwaiter* well—I have performed in it and taught it—Pinter is my jam. So I know that Altman's idea is not indicated in the script—but I also know that nothing in the script rules it out. When Travolta says that Altman's idea "changed everything and permeated the whole scenario," I understand him to mean that it oriented the character to a kind of *true north*—a spine. I can't help wondering where this inspired direction came from. Was it an idea that Altman already had—that it was in Ben's personality to pompously pretend to have authority on every subject? In that case, this "what if" would be a way to create that side of the character without making a judgment that he is "pompous." But perhaps Altman was responding *in the moment* to the playing of the scene; maybe Altman felt the scene was playing flat and needed more oomph—and decided on the spot to try an *opposite*.

In the opening scene of *Alien*, the Nostromo crewmembers meet after coming out of eighteen months of hypersleep. There would be no point in trying to figure out what it's like to wake up after hypersleep—even today, forty-plus years since this film was made—no one knows! It makes far more sense to look for a metaphor, an analogy, an "it's like when." For instance, *it's like when* any group of coworkers (such as firefighters or oil-rig laborers) who live and work on the same premises, rise, take breakfast together, and engage in ordinary early morning banter. Indeed, this is the very power of science fiction and fantasy: to be able to tell simple, human stories with fantastical plots—via a central metaphor.

Jason Bourne, in *Bourne Supremacy*, kills again after having gone for two years without killing anyone. You could say he's disappointed in himself, but I like to use an analogy: *it's like when* a person who's been sober for two years falls off the wagon.

One of my Twitter followers told me of an occasion when an "as if" brought his actor's performance to life: during a scene in which the character was defending their use of a piece of recording equipment that had sentimental value, despite tech issues. The scene wasn't working until the director suggested playing it "as if it's a racist grandfather you're apologizing for."

As ifs help you avoid judging the characters. An arrogant person behaves *as if* everyone else is stupid—or *as if* everyone else is arrogant and needs to be set straight. I got those ideas not from a book, but from my observations of arrogant people. When I ask you not to describe a character as "arrogant," I'm not claiming that arrogant people don't exist—they certainly do! Describing their behavior with *metaphors, as ifs,* and *it's like whens* reminds you to embrace the fact that, flawed as they are, they are human.

As ifs help you avoid result direction. If a family is discussing funeral arrangements and the scene is getting overwrought, instead of directing them to "take it down," the director can suggest that they are talking about this emotional topic *as if* they are considering what to have for dinner. The reason this might work is that it happens in real life! I have seen it!

As ifs also work when the director is talking to the crew. For a scene in *Little Miss Sunshine* when the family is pushing the bus, Dayton and Faris directed the camera operator to pretend there's a sniper loose in the parking lot.

Different *as ifs* for each character can create *conflict* in a scene. In *Before the Devil Knows You're Dead,* the two brothers (Philip Seymour Hoffman and Ethan Hawke) have a scene in which they face the terrible consequences of their botched robbery. You could say that one brother is nervous and the other one calm. Or you could describe their conflicting behaviors with "as ifs": One brother behaves as if what has happened can be fixed; the other as if their lives are now over. This can make a scene with hugely heightened circumstances feel real to the audience, because it gives the actors something *playable.* You see, I'm reasonably sure that few if any of us has actual experience with carrying out a robbery that causes our mother's death—but pretty much everyone knows the human frustration of trying to fix something that's gone wrong when the person you need to help you fix it doesn't believe it can be fixed.

Metaphors help if you want to call attention to the intensity of a scene. For instance, "It's not like the rage you would feel if a drunk driver killed your child. It's more like when the cable company won't come out to fix your service until next Thursday and insists that you be there all day."

Certain "quick fix" adjustments can apply to many scenes:

- As if one character functions as parent, the other as child;
- As if it's a business deal (if they are married);
- As if they are married (if it's a business relationship);
- As if the other character has bad breath.

One more example for this "quick fix" list: *as if having just received a cancer diagnosis*. I can guarantee that this adjustment will confer an instant extra layer of inner life, regardless of the plot.

There are some metaphors that go to the thematic heart of a movie. In a *Los Angeles Times* interview for *Harry Potter and the Order of the Phoenix*, Daniel Radcliffe, speaking of Dumbledore's Army, declared, "We're the French Resistance. And Voldemort and the Death Eaters are the Nazis." Later in the interview he used this analogy: "Harry's like a Vietnam veteran. He's seen awful things and come back to a society that's rejected him. That's the main parallel I've been drawing on."

Students often ask me, when I relate an anecdote like that, who came up with those insightful ideas—the actor or the director? In this case, I don't know. It's possible that Radcliffe, then seventeen, was a kid-genius history-geek who came up with these metaphors himself—if so, director David Yates made the intelligent decision to encourage the young actor and his insights. But it's equally possible that Yates is an actor-whisperer who planted these emotionally and spiritually profound concepts so seamlessly that Radcliffe came to think of them as his own ideas.

Subtext (Mantra or Inner Monologue)

***"Subtext is the skeleton under the skin of words . . . a calendar of intentions and feelings and inner events. What appears to be happening is rarely what is happening."*—Elia Kazan**

Subtext is the thing that is not being said. It's an undercurrent, an inner monologue. Subtext is what a line *really* means—the larger, more truthful meaning that underlies the literal meaning.

Mike Nichols once said, "I've always been impressed by the fact that upon entering a room full of people, you find them saying one thing, doing another, and wishing they were doing a third. The words are secondary and the secrets are primary. That's what interests me most." In other words, every scene has subtext. In fact, the subtext of a scene *is* the scene. It may feel like a risk for a director to put her faith in the subtext, but finally it's the safest place to be.

When the script is good, you get to dig below its surface and devour every juicy morsel. But even when the writing features pedestrian, movie-esque lines like, "Are you okay?" or "What happened?" you need to look for subtext—the thing the character is *not saying*.

If the line is, "Please shut the door," there are multiple options for its meaning, that is to say, its *subtext*. For instance:

1) "Please shut the door—*so we can begin our business meeting.*"
2) "Please shut the door—*you stupid ass!*"
3) "Please shut the door—*so we can finally be alone together, darling.*"
4) "Please shut the door—*and keep that maniac out!*"

The line, "Please shut the door," doesn't change, but its meaning does: the different subtexts give it different line readings. In my workshops and in the *Directing Actors* audiobook, I am able to support these examples with my voice inflections, and demonstrate how *subtext speaks louder than the words*. You can try it yourself.

Subtext happens in regular life all the time. If you redecorate your home and a friend walks in and says, "Oh, you changed everything around," you can tell, by her body language and tone of voice, whether or not she likes the result. Subtext can be the opposite of the apparent meaning of the lines. I'm sure we have all heard an "I'm sorry" whose subtext is "I still think it was really your fault."

Another expression for subtext is *inner monologue*. An inner monologue can be the through-line to the whole scene—a kind of *mantra*. The *mantra* or inner monologue of a character who feels awkward might be this: "I can't believe I just said something so stupid!" No matter what the lines of the script, this is what he is thinking—what he is really saying.

In moments without dialogue, there is subtext. In his commentary for *Bourne Supremacy*, Paul Greengrass, referring to the many scenes in which Bourne is alone and silent, spoke of the need to compel attention without dialogue—in other words with subtext.

There is subtext in the behavior of actors, too. When an actor says, "Yes, I like that idea," but her voice is hesitant and her shoulders are stiff, that could mean that she doesn't really understand the idea or that she is afraid she won't be able to execute it—or something else! A director is not expected to be a mind reader. If an actor says something that surprises or mystifies you—follow up, perhaps by saying, "Please tell me what questions you have."

Physical Life

Wardrobe

There is more than a grain of truth in the opening scene of *Wings of Desire*, directed by Wim Wenders: Peter Falk, playing an actor on his way to a location shoot, is brooding because he has no ideas for the character he is about to play. He consoles himself with the possibility that they might have a good costume for him. "That's half the battle," he says.

Props, wardrobe, activity, movement are defining of a character's personality and situation, with tremendous power to generate creative energy for actors. There is an intimacy to physical choices. And this bonus: If an actor is in her body, she can't be in her head. If an actor is playing a doctor in Victorian England, or an improvised explosive device specialist during the 2003 American invasion of Iraq, the costume, props, and set decoration do more than enhance the visuals for the audience. Costume designer Michele Clapton created wardrobe for *Game of Thrones* that duplicated as closely as possible the materials and, importantly, the *weight* of the clothing that might have been worn in the Middle Ages—an invaluable aid to the actors, who were thus able to step into their characters the instant they stepped into their wardrobe.

Objects

> ***"One thing I've learned is to study your prop carefully, because that's 50% of my job right there. So I have to practice at home."*—Liev Schreiber**

Sometimes actors refer to props as *objects*. This is not an affectation; it supports them in thinking of their character as a person. Objects engender *activities* which actors may refer to as *business*—that's a theater word (the original term is *stage business*), but it's used on film sets, too. It's important for actors to think of props not as obligations, but as opportunities to add richness in their portrayals. If a character is playing cards, the actor can create a *relationship* with the cards—really look at them, really make decisions about whether to draw or hold—not turn them over merely because the stage directions tell him to.

If a character works with a certain prop every day, like a scalpel or gun, the actor needs to spend time with that object and create a connection to it. The objects of a person's daily life say a lot about who she is. Giving life to those objects is as important as finding her inner needs and impulses. When an actor is presented with the prop handcuffs she is to wear in a scene, she needs to make a connection to that object, and give it life. If she gives the object life, it gives life back to her, almost like another actor in the scene. It's not the *idea* of being handcuffed, it's the physical experience, the sensation of the plastic zip tie or cold steel that creates the behavior of her performance.

Activities make a scene more natural. Once in my class, two students were working on a father-son confrontation scene. The student playing the father was confronting away, acting up a storm—it was not believable. I gave him a newspaper and told him I wanted him to read it during the scene, not merely use it as a prop. I told him I wanted him to be able to tell me after the scene was over what the article was about. The scene then played beautifully.

Objects can create mystery and shimmer. In *Blade Runner,* Edward James Olmos (Gaff) first appears in the background. Olmos said in an interview, about his choice to play with a piece of paper and create origami, "I was really trying to find a way to blend into the background and not do anything but also not *look* like I wasn't doing anything. You don't want to distract from the action in the scene, but you also don't want to look artificially still. You need to be like a tree in the wind."

Gesture, Activities, Bits, Business

While shooting *American Gangster,* Ruby Dee made it known to director Ridley Scott and lead actor Denzel Washington that it was important to her that Washington's character, drug lord Frank Lucas, not come across as a hero. She told the *LA Times,* "I have always been against the gangster as hero." Just before shooting the scene in which she demands of her son, "Don't lie to me!" Scott said to her, "When you get to that line, why don't you just slap him?" The slap in that scene was not in the script! The director gave her last-minute permission and this powerful physical *gesture* elevated the entire scene to a whole other level of emotion and clarity. This is how a director builds on the instincts of an actor to generate expressive blocking or business, thus creating *emotional events* that tell the story. The slap in the Ruby Dee/Denzel Washington scene is not just a physical event—it's an emotional event—a filmable *moment*.

Many of Edie Falco's scenes in *The Sopranos* took place in Carmela's kitchen. We saw her cooking, loading the dishwasher, folding laundry. All these *activities* were interwoven with her *intentions*: to conduct investigations, issue ultimatums, conclude negotiations. When she pulled a baked ziti out of the oven, it was always with intention—sometimes *to challenge*, sometimes *to complain*—and other times *to welcome* or *comfort*.

More elaborate physical activities may be described by actors as "bits." One of the most famous physical bits in cinema history was created by Marlon Brando in *On the Waterfront*. In Terry's first scene with Edie (Eva Marie Saint), she dropped her glove. He picked the glove up and put it on his own hand. The glove business activates everything we need to know about how he feels about her: it is playful, boy-like; it highlights the disparity in their education and manners; it reveals his intention (to tease her); it is a sexual metaphor. And it gives Eva Marie Saint a strong, playable objective for the rest of the scene—she wants her glove back!

The Physical Is Emotional

> ***"They can put the clothes on you. But then you've gotta wear 'em."*—Chadwick Boseman**

Physical choices trigger internal transformation. Nicole Kidman spoke to *The New York Times* about the importance of the leather jacket her character wore in *Destroyer*. Kidman refused to take it off, even at home, or let them wash it. She said that wearing that jacket was "part of the [character's] depression." Amy Ryan made the backstory choice that Helene, her *Gone Baby Gone* character, was a victim of child abuse; this led her to a posture and gait for Helene—walking and standing with her head low, "because she's expecting another hit."

At the funeral for the family patriarch early in Season One of *Queen Sugar,* the family is dressed in white. It's a visual stylization that highlights a theme of *death as a homegoing into the light.* As I watched it, I had the impression that each actor had envisioned the *off-camera scene* in which they selected their apparel. Series creator Ava DuVernay directed this episode. I haven't spoken to her about this, but since I know the care and emotional depth with which she approaches filmmaking, I can imagine her making suggestions to the actors: Perhaps the wealthy sister already owns her elegant white outfit; maybe the less wealthy sister has had to adjust her budget in order to purchase hers. Their brother, Ralph Angel, is financially strapped; there's a scene when he stands before a mirror in his suit. The suit means something to him. Is it borrowed? Did it belong to his father? Or has the family chipped in to buy it? Imagined off-camera details take an *idea* (*death as a homegoing into the light*) and make it human, thus causing the thematic choice to permeate the audience's subconscious.

When Red, in *The Shawshank Redemption,* is released from prison, wearing a suit for the first time in forty years, he looks odd, uncomfortable. Instead of *demonstrating* to us the character's awkwardness, Morgan Freeman makes his attention to the suit physical. Freeman the actor knows what it feels like to wear a suit jacket, but the character doesn't. Perhaps the actor puts his attention on the sensation of shoulder padding, thus creating for the viewer the illusion that the shoulder pads are unfamiliar to him. Or perhaps he puts his attention on the armholes, tighter than those of prison blues. Or perhaps on the hat, understanding that the character would lack a sense of where a hat would sit properly on his head; wherever it sat would feel unfamiliar. All this while, Red's objective is *to try to be normal.*

Secrets

Directors can have secrets. According to an article in the *Hollywood Reporter*, Bong Joon Ho's *Parasite* cast puzzled over interpretations of the mysterious green rock that appears and reappears—the director declined to share his thoughts with them.

Likewise, powerful actors keep secrets. Actually, all actors' choices are secrets from the audience, but it's very helpful for an actor to have secrets he doesn't share with his scene partner. It's even okay for actors to have secrets from directors. Don't take this personally. In order for the characters to operate from a subconscious, to have free will, the actors are allowed an inner life that is private and independent.

Meryl Streep once told an interviewer that for every role, she gives herself a special secret, something which her character would not want others to know, and which she herself conceals from her co-stars and director. The interviewer asked for an example, and she disclosed that in *Kramer vs. Kramer* her secret was that Joanna had never loved Ted (Dustin Hoffman). The richness of this secret makes me ask questions. Why ever did she marry him? Did he bully her into it? There is a scene in the movie in which Ted tries to browbeat Joanna into not leaving him. It's easy to imagine him, during their courtship, bulldozing her into a hasty marriage—at twenty, I was pressured into a reckless first marriage, so I know this can happen. Or did they marry because she got pregnant? In that case, perhaps their parents did the pressuring.

Alan Rickman achieved his indelible presence in the eight Harry Potter movies in large part because of a *secret*. At the beginning of the series he insisted on speaking to J. K. Rowling, because at that time she had only written three of the books, and he needed to know where Severus Snape was headed. In a 2012 *New York Times* interview, he said she disclosed to him no plot points, but gave him "a small piece of information that let me know there was more to him than met the eye."

That *secret* became the engine for all of Snape's complex and difficult behavior, and it infused the extravagant detail of the performance—the ferocity of his stares, the formidable range of his verb/intentions, the percussion of his consonants—with truth. Rickman held his secret of the history of intense connection between Snape and Harry all his life.

Why So Many Tools?

I love characters. Can you tell? As a child, I was lonely and misunderstood, and felt closer to the characters in the stories I was reading than I did to my family. When I was reading the classic children's literature of the time—*Alice in Wonderland, Heidi, Tom Sawyer, Treasure Island, Mary Poppins*—I felt heard. I trusted the characters to obey an emotional logic that seemed to be missing in real life. In stories, feelings had consequences; in real life not so much. I have first-hand knowledge of how stories can teach, connect, and rescue. I don't want to make you feel anxious about rules that feel arcane and hard to follow. I don't want you to be looking over your shoulder in case the Language Police are bearing down. I offer you these tools because they gave me the keys to the precious, restorative world of imagination.

To me acting is a laboratory of life, and I love to share everything I have learned with anyone who'll listen. That's why I've set out such a lot of ideas and examples in this chapter! But I don't want you to feel overloaded. I want you to feel safe. I don't think that every director should use every one of the tools. I invite you to practice, to find out which ones work the best for you, until using them feels like second nature, until you can feel them in your bones and not just follow a checklist.

I'm not the only one who uses these tools. Martin Scorsese does too. There's a video produced by Netflix (search for *Martin Scorsese Directing—Behind the Scenes/Netflix*). It shows clips of Scorsese on the set *The Irishman*—he is grabbing a minute here, a minute there, to have substantive interaction with the actors. And—he is using just about every tool in the toolkit: *objectives;* the *"as if"*; *subtext; asking questions; building on the actors' ideas.* And—constantly—the *language of permission.* So in case you were wondering: *Yes, the tools work!*

CHAPTER FIVE

Emotional Event

Defining Emotional Event

Emotional event is the director's most powerful tool—the one that transforms a person who dreams of making a movie into someone who *thinks like a director,* who has what Alexander Payne once described as "the compass."

Mike Nichols called it *the event,* and said that "*event* is where a director's camera sense and actor sense merge." Sidney Lumet's terminology is *what the scene is about*—which he declared is the lodestar for every decision of filmmaking. Directing coach Joan Scheckel calls it the "nugget." You could call it the core of the scene, or the hook, the heart—the central, elusive *thing that is to be shot.* I like the term *emotional event*—because an event is *what happens,* something that propels the story to the next thing that happens. And it's emotional. It's a *human event.*

It's different from literal plot events. Emotional events exist underneath the plot as hidden scaffolding—holding the story together, creating its underlying emotional logic. Unlike plot, emotional events are invisible, subconscious. Like movies themselves, they operate on the audience at a subconscious level.

If nothing *happens emotionally* in a scene, that scene does not belong in the movie. To locate the emotional event, ask some questions:

- *What really happens?* Not the plot—underneath the plot, in the subtext.
- How are the relationships different at the end of the scene from at the beginning?

- What shifts occur in the balance of power? In the level of intimacy?
- What is the new energy that changes the characters' lives?

The central emotional event of a scene is what *causes* the event of the next scene, and thus, moves the story forward—that's how you create drama. An event may *trigger*, or set up, an event later in the story. A betrayal *sets up* revenge; the revenge is the *payoff* of the earlier betrayal. The revenge may also *set up* a further act of revenge. (Intricate cycles of betrayal and revenge animate *The Godfather I* and *II*, as well as *Homeland* and *My Brilliant Friend.)*

Within each scene, there are usually several sections, or *beats*, each with its own (smaller) emotional event, setting up the central one or resulting from it; these may be called *transitions*, or *dramatic moments*. The emotional event of the first beat leads to, or triggers, the event of the second beat; the event of the second beat triggers that of the third beat; etc.

In day-to-day human terms, an emotional event means someone affects our emotions. Here are a few simple examples of common, human emotional events:

- Character A makes character B laugh;
- A hurts B's feelings;
- A pisses B off;
- A turns B on.

There can be more complex ideas for emotional event, based of course on the particular script. Some random examples:

- Character A takes her power back from character B.
- No matter what A does to cheer B up, B remains in a bad mood.
- The characters switch places in a hierarchy: for example, the student teaches the master.
- It's a moral battle and both characters have weapons.
- It's a competition for who is the most unselfish.
- Each reveals a vulnerability to the other.
- A reveals a vulnerability to B and B gives no response.
- A's cruelty causes a further deterioration to B's boundaries.

- A supports B through a breakdown. Or, A talks B off the ledge.
- Each seeks reassurance and both fail to get it.
- They discover yet another thing they have in common.
- A sees in B's eyes that her bad behavior has stopped being cute.
- A makes B face his complicity in his own downfall.
- A gets away with a lie.
- They are fighting for love.

In real life, an emotional event is always unexpected and very often unwanted. It can be embarrassing—we usually don't want people to know that they've upset us. We tell ourselves: *Don't let it bother you. Don't give them the satisfaction.* We control our emotions, especially the big ones—pain, fear, anger, and even joy. We try above all to keep our cool, to maintain the social mask. An emotional event can be a moment when we are caught off guard and the social mask slips. It can be something that exposes us to the whole world or it can be something that exposes us to ourselves, in other words, entirely interior.

There's no set length of time that constitutes an "event." It could be an expression of an experience—an argument, negotiation, seduction, confession, assault, break-up, rejection, reconciliation, or a fight to the death—continuing throughout the scene. Or it might be a single specific moment—say, of humiliation, when someone tells a cruel joke on their partner at a party. It's like real life. We've all had such experiences; we've all known life-changing flashes of defeat, triumph, or connection—and we've all had intimacies and miscommunications that took time to grow.

When each character *wants* something and their wants are at odds, one of them may, at some point, get what he wants. So you could call the events of a scene its *wins and losses*. Iconic acting coach Sanford Meisner called it the "pinch-ouch." People (characters) have wants and needs from each other (their *objectives*). They affect each other, they make each other feel something; at certain moments, one wins (pinch) and other loses (ouch). Thus the emotional event may be *a shift in the balance of power*.

The *Chinatown* scene on Catalina Island between Jake Gittes (Jack Nicholson) and Noah Cross (John Huston) was directed by Roman Polanski as a scene about power. *Chinatown* is deeply concerned with the unlimited power of men like Noah Cross. The two actors had the same objective—the pursuit of raw dominance over the other. They committed relentlessly to that goal, using any strategy—lies, threats, seduction, even an ugly truth—in order *to win.*

Scenes in *Lady Bird* between Lady Bird (Saoirse Ronan) and her mother (Laurie Metcalf) involve power struggles. Both characters are driven, over and over, to prove a point, to win against the other. But are these scenes really about power? By the end of the movie, it's clear that these two were fighting as much for love as for autonomy.

Here's a cool way to figure out emotional event: deconstruct the plot facts; boil them down to their simplest, most human, most relatable form. The plot of *Eternal Sunshine of the Spotless Mind* is fantastical: an office in a run-down building, where people can pay to have the memories of a failed relationship erased? Whoa. But—let's *boil down* the facts of the plot and just watch them turn into emotional events! Learning you've been erased from the memory of your former lover is *the worst break-up*; discovering that all your friends have been complicit, *the worst betrayal.* Traveling back obsessively through memories of a relationship that ended badly—omigod, who hasn't done *that?* Isn't that one of the most common events in the history of romance?

Mike Nichols was not only a legendary filmmaker, but also a mentor and teacher to younger directors. So I'm going to quote him a lot in this chapter. Mike said his question for any scene was always: Is it a *fight,* a *seduction,* or a *negotiation?* The radical simplicity of this idea often gives directors a helpful clarity around the concept of emotional event.

I don't think Nichols intended any of us to approach his list as a formula. There are different kinds of fights: A fight between best friends is very different from a showdown between people who have pretended to be friends, but never actually trusted each other.

These are nuances of behavior and meaning that matter in a story. I find Nichols's options provocative—they make me want to consider *opposites*. I give myself permission to think of the fights in *Fight Club*, for instance, not as fights, but seductions. You might think that love scenes fall automatically into the category of seductions, but—even in *Romeo and Juliet*—they may actually be negotiations.

If you find yourself struggling to discern the emotional event for a scene, use the *technique of three possible*: write down three possibilities, even if at first they all seem bad; cross out the ones that are merely reiterations of the plot; keep asking yourself, What might be the emotional transaction that takes place? Some possibilities: *a misunderstanding, a fight to the death,* or *a challenge to the balance of power in the neighborhood.*

If you still feel stumped, ask yourself this question: At the end of the scene, are the characters closer to each other, more intimate? Or are they more emotionally distant—alienated? It has to be one or the other, right?

Emotional Event As a Directing Tool

Emotional event can be a supremely practical directing tool—the simplest, most effective way for describing to the actors what you want—a practically bulletproof way to find out if actors are "on the same page" with you—or make your case for them to join your interpretation if it's different from theirs.

It's particularly useful with established actors who you fear may not take direction readily. Writer-director Jennifer Fox had made many documentaries before *The Tale*, her first narrative feature, premiered on HBO. In an interview for *Filmmaker Magazine*, Fox spoke of a difference in interpretation she had with Laura Dern and Ellen Burstyn while rehearsing. Burstyn and Dern, playing mother and daughter, felt that in a certain scene, their characters should be angry at each other. Fox told them she didn't want the scene to be a *confrontation*, but rather two adult women *coming to terms with each other*. Framing the two different interpretations as emotional events gave clarity to the discussion; these two forceful actresses were then able to *hear* the director's idea and find a way to make it work for them.

Usually emotional event is a director's tool rather than an actor's tool—a way of understanding the scene's purpose and position in the story—but there are actors who need or even demand to have discussions about these issues. George Clooney and James McAvoy, for instance, have said in interviews that they need to know the place of each scene within the arc of the story—what the function of the scene is in setting up or revealing their character's transformations. For instance, does the argument that leads to the retaliation happen in *this* scene or in *this* one? Other actors would rather not know the emotional event of the scene, because their character doesn't; they prefer to focus on their character's own reality rather than on the purpose of the scene in the story.

What if the director views the emotional event of a scene as an *argument*, but an actor feels that her character is not arguing at all, but is *explaining*. Always pick your battles. It can be totally worthwhile to let the actor try her choice "to explain," rather than "to argue"—because really, you never know. Her understanding of "to explain" could end up looking exactly like your idea of "to argue." This is the purpose of rehearsal: to try things, learn things, move forward. If you've had no time for rehearsal, try her way on the first take. Don't dispute her idea before you see what it looks like.

But if the first take or the rehearsal run-through doesn't work—if it plays flat, if the scene is not firing the way you need it to, not catapulting the story into its next event—then maybe you need *higher stakes*. You can ask her to try a stronger verb—say, *provoking* or *punishing* instead of *explaining*. It helps if you validate her idea first, and build on it rather than argue over it. For instance, "I like what you're doing, but I wondered whether maybe you've already tried explaining and reasoning and are running out of patience, and have reached the point of *goading* or *punishing* or *picking a fight.*" Or, you could say, "Yes, I see what you're after—but maybe there could be *higher stakes* behind it?"

Or, you could try an entirely different approach: asking the *other* actor to play the stronger verb (such as provoke, challenge, belittle). Actor B's stronger intention is likely to stimulate a stronger response in actor A. One way or another, the goal is to set things up so the actors *affect* each other. Perhaps it will relax you if I give you this permission: *Any emotional event is better than no emotional event.*

Find a Way In

Mike Nichols advised directors in a 2006 interview for the *DGA Quarterly* to center the tool of *event* in human problems and human reality. He said, "Throw away the conventions and assumptions—when this happens in real life, *what is it really like?*"

What is it like to be the target of betrayal? How does the discovery of betrayal happen—*really*—not as a movie trope, but in the interactions of human beings? What is it like to fall so in love that you feel no one else in the world has ever felt this way before? Trust me: no one needs another rehash of a standard love scene like those from a hundred other movies—so ask yourself, what is it like? *Really.*

To understand what an event is "really," I may use my own experience as a touchstone. If the event is a *break up,* as part of my preparation, I think about the break ups I've been through—including times I've been in favor of ending the relationship, as well as times that it took me by surprise. If it's a *betrayal,* I allow myself to go down that dark tunnel into my own experiences of betrayal.

I've never been called upon to notify a next of kin that their child or spouse has been killed in battle, as the characters played by Ben Foster and Woody Harrelson must in the 2009 film *The Messenger,* but I have no trouble imagining it—I have a nephew in the military so it's on my mind every day. If I didn't have this personal connection, I would do *research*—read and listen to first-hand accounts until I could imagine what it's like—really.

I haven't had to watch a colleague be devoured by a predator in outer space, as the crewmembers of the Nostromo do in *Alien*—and, since it's set in the future, there's no research available. But I have witnessed a friend under attack by brain cancer. So maybe I'll start there. I use whatever I have to *find a way in*.

So-Called Exposition Scenes

I'd really like you to stop thinking that there is any such thing as an "exposition" scene. Attempts to shoehorn information to establish the reason for the story are bound to deteriorate into storytelling fails. Instead, look for the *events* that are the pay-offs of your story—and look for the events that *set up* those *pay-offs*.

Every scene must have an emotional event, including exposition scenes. No scene is "straightforward"—a scene is not about the information in it. It's about what happens emotionally in the scene:

- The emotional event activates the information so the audience can hear it;
- It activates the plot so the audience can feel the suspense;
- It activates the relationships and storyline so the audience can care.

Emotional Event and Genre: It's All About the Relationship

I am staking this claim: *there is no difference between dialogue scenes* and *action scenes*. Characters are people, so it's all—all of it—about *people* with needs and obstacles who are in a situation and who have an effect on each other. A dialogue scene should feel like an action scene. An action scene should feel like a relationship scene. A "character" movie should feel like a thriller.

The Rock is an action movie. The plot, which includes ambushes, explosions, and face-offs, is suspenseful: there are questions over whether hostages will be rescued and rockets disarmed. But the plot suspense is *activated* by the underlying emotional dynamic: an emerging father-son-like relationship between Stanley and Mason (Nicolas Cage and Sean Connery). Without this undercurrent, the plot could turn into a pile of hackneyed elements borrowed from every other action flick. It's the back-and-forth of the relationship—the uncertainty whether these two difficult characters will come to trust each other in time to save each other's lives—that engages audiences at a subconscious emotional level and makes them care "what happens next."

The plot event of the red pill/blue pill scene of *The Matrix* is powerful and meaningful: Neo changes his very destiny. Leaving behind a world of security and predictability, he chooses to become a *human being* with the responsibility of free will and the heartbreak of mortality. It's a compelling metaphor that resonates with the audience—certainly with anyone who's ever faced a life-altering decision. But as powerful as the metaphor is, both intellectually and spiritually, I propose that we take a moment to look for an underlying *personal event* in the relationship between the two characters, Neo and Morpheus. Here are some possibilities:

1) That it's a *seduction* of Neo by Morpheus;
2) That it's a father/son *metaphor*—that, by choosing the red pill, Neo wins the trust of a father figure and proves his maturity—almost like a teenager must prove his maturity to his father before being given the car keys;
3) That it's a scene about the sudden, intense *connection* between two people who've been watching each other from afar for a long time.

These may seem like humbler ideas than the sweeping philosophical visions of the movie. My point here is that simple, recognizably human transactions underpin the big ideas and give them life. A movie of intellectual and spiritual reach, activated by realities of identifiable human behavior, is a treasure.

Let's look at the opening scene of *Lady Bird*. We find Lady Bird and her mother weeping together over *The Grapes of Wrath*. The moment the audiobook concludes, they fall into a quarrel over where Lady Bird will go to college. Soon, Lady Bird throws herself out of the car.

A young woman throwing herself from a moving car—that's a big event in any life! But I propose that we call it the *domestic event*—what *apparently* happens—and keep looking for the *emotional event*. We could choose from Mike Nichols's options and call it an *argument*. But then I have a question—who wins the argument? I think there's a choice to be made. You could say that Lady Bird loses the argument—after all, she breaks her arm, which has to be painful and annoying. But I can't help wanting to say that its underlying truth is this: She has played the ultimate card a child has toward a parent—threatening her own safety. I believe you could just as confidently say that she *wins* the argument against her mother.

Either choice is legitimate, although in the finished film, there are clues to suggest that filmmaker Greta Gerwig believes that Lady Bird wins the argument. A charming detail of later scenes is Lady Bird, back in class, brandishing her arm cast like a trophy—a gesture expressing a win! The film's ending settles the question—she arrives to New York City. Lady Bird has achieved the goal she's pursued with resolute intention. She has *won* the argument over where she will go to college.

What It's About

Every film needs to be *about* something. Every television series, and each episode in the series. Even commercials and definitely video games. The tool of "what it's about" reveals the purpose and meaning of the project.

Sidney Lumet lays it right out in his book *Making Movies*: The most important thing for a filmmaker to know is *what her story is about*. What matters in human terms. Why the audience should care. Lumet insisted that *what the story is about* affects a director's responses to *any* of the myriad questions that will be posed by designers, crew chiefs, actors, producers, or financiers.

What it's about can be another way of describing emotional event—for instance, saying, "This scene is about power" is another way of saying, "The emotional event is a shift in the power balance." It occurs to me that it might be fair to say the *emotional event* is the delivery system for *what it's about.*

But "what it's about" is an elastic tool with many uses. It can apply to an individual scene, or to a beat in a scene, or even to a particular line or moment. It helps directors avoid result direction. Instead of instructing the actors that their characters *feel regretful,* you can say that a scene is *about regret*—a subtle, but meaningful difference. If you fear that using the term *intention* will sound jargon-y, you can say, "This moment is about wanting to *teach* the other character, not humiliate him."

When I ask a director, "What is your story about?" they usually reply with a synopsis of the plot. But what I'm looking for is what it's *really* about—in other words, its *theme* or *vision.* Its *meaning.* Its *moral,* even. Here are a few examples, undoubtedly subjective, of what a film might be *about:* the fragility and the power of the human spirit (*One Flew Over the Cuckoo's Nest,* Miloš Forman); survival (*Mad Max: Fury Road,* George Miller); mortality (*Birdman,* Alejandro Iñárritu); the loneliness of children (*The 400 Blows,* François Truffaut; *Capernaum,* Nadine Labaki).

Many works of narrative fiction are really, finally, about *family.* Francis Ford Coppola has disclosed that *The Godfather* is about family—and as soon as you hear that, you can see it all over the film. *Shoplifters,* by filmmaker Hirokazu Kore-eda, is about family. Other narrative projects as different in tone as *The Big Lebowski, The Fighter,* and the episodic series *The Americans*—I think they're all about family.

Casablanca, which was filmed during wartime, is about *sacrifice.* Mike Myers declared in an interview that he believed *Shrek* was about *class:* "It's my feeling," he said, "that ogres are working class." David Frankel, director of *The Devil Wears Prada,* found his key, his vision, when he acknowledged to himself his own deep belief:

that the movie was *not* about a horrible boss, but rather a *celebration* of people like Miranda Priestley (Meryl Streep), who, whether or not they are "nice," are excellent at what they do. *Wall-E,* directed by Andrew Stanton, may be about *loneliness*—or perhaps *resilience.*

Martin Scorsese, in an *IndieWire* interview, disclosed that his decades-long collaboration with Robert De Niro has been based on a shared obsession with characters who were "the least among us." That's another way of saying that *the least among us* is what all the films they've made together are *about.*

Redemption is a theme in many powerful stories. Successful redemption, against both external and internal obstacles, drives feel-good films like *Rocky* or *Rudy*—but also Phoebe Waller-Bridge's *Fleabag,* which, however bleak and darkly comedic it can get, is profoundly infused with a belief that human beings can learn and change.

The world of *Chinatown,* on the other hand, is genuinely bleak. Characters are desperate for redemption—and, horrifically, fail to find it. By the end of the movie, Evelyn Mulwray has set in motion events that will deliver her daughter to the worst possible fate, and Jake has repeated the same damning failure he made long ago, when he was a cop in Chinatown.

In *Leaving Las Vegas,* directed by Mike Figgis, it appears that Ben (Nicolas Cage) is the one who needs redemption—but there's a twist. It's Sera (Elizabeth Shue) who is redeemed. Her commitment to practice unconditional love toward Ben no matter whether he deserves it or reciprocates or even acknowledges her, transforms Sera from a person *acted upon* by life, into someone who takes the first steps to claim her agency. 1971's *Wanda*—written, directed, and starring Barbara Loden—follows that same thematic trajectory.

When you know *what the script is about,* you have a way to make sure that everyone involved on the project is making the same film. If, for example, the special effects people have not been told that the movie is about, say, redemption, they may assume it is about groovy special effects. If you don't discuss with the costumers what the movie is about, they may take for granted that, for them, it's about perfect costumes. When actors are not connected up to what the script is about, they may start to think it's about the excellence of their performances.

If a director is having trouble getting through to an actor, it's usually because she hasn't communicated with him on the thematic level, the spiritual level, the level of "what it's about." Directors may feel shy about speaking on these deeper levels—but I think you should try it. If you believe that it's about *redemption*—or *family, class, racism, the loneliness of children,* or *grief*—please tell everyone who works on the project.

Unless you're David Lynch. When David Lynch is asked—by anyone, including actors—what his work is about, he replies, "I don't know." Don't be fooled—none of his work is random—it's all *about* something that matters deeply to him. He chooses not to tell—that's his right—but my recommendation to readers of this book is that you take the leap and share with your collaborators your understanding of what the story is about. That way, if at any point there's difficulty, you can engage them as allies in problem-solving with this reminder: "Let's keep in mind *what the story is about.*"

Above all, hold in your own heart your commitment to *what the project is about.* A filmmaker's connection to what their story is about is central to their artistry. It's the truth of the story, so it's *your* truth, your anchor, your hook. Your true north. If you carried an old-fashioned heart-shaped locket around your neck, it's the image you would put in it.

Make a List of Themes

A step-by-step method for allowing yourself to know *what your project is about:*

- Make a list of every possible theme—any you can think of—let's say ten or more. I'm going to call this the *wide net* of thematic material;

- Ask yourself questions and delve into your understandings of life until you can boil the list of ten down to *three main themes.*
- Allow the *central theme,* the primary idea, the core, the central truth, to bubble up from your subconscious. Don't try to intellectually figure out which is the best choice—let it rise up from your subconscious and claim you. Don't think of yourself as choosing it. *Let it choose you.* Maybe it will come to you in your dreams, or when you're taking a walk or a shower, or while riffing with your lead actor or another trusted collaborator or advisor.

You can approach these steps in any order. Here's an example using the movie *Avatar.* I have never had a personal discussion with filmmaker James Cameron about his choices, so this is all speculation. I propose that the *three main themes* are these: racism, ecological disaster caused by human greed, and grief.

Cameron has been criticized for his handling, as a White man, of the theme of racism. I wonder whether perhaps he felt more deeply connected to another theme—the theme of *grief.* Witness the tender attention given to the scenes of the death and resurrection of Dr. Grace Augustine (Sigourney Weaver). In *Avatar,* the theme of *grief* connects profoundly to the theme of ecological disaster—we mourn for the lost species, the lost habitats, of our beautiful blue planet.

These things are so personal! My husband and I saw *Avatar* with a friend who had lost his wife just two years earlier. The idea that there might be a magical place where a departed loved one can be brought back to life was deeply moving to him. My experience of seeing the film with him saturates any analysis I might bring to it.

In Chapter Four, I told a story about my mother and her wheelchair. So it may not come as a surprise that my own response to *Avatar*—not as a film professional, but as a human person—involves the moment when Jake Sully's avatar steps from the transporter, freed of his wheelchair, and jubilantly sprints across the plains and jungle. The path of my entire life would have radically diverged if my mother, in response to the daily prayers and desperate wishes of five-year-old me, could have magically stepped from the confinement of her chair to dance and run.

If we had started with the *wide net* list of thematic material in *Avatar,* the disability theme would surely have been included. It may not have been a central one for the filmmaker, but as an audience member, I responded to it because it was personal to me. Other themes from *Avatar's wide net* include friendship, youthful romance, sacrifice. The presence of a *wide net* of thematic material enables each audience member to feel that the movie was made for them alone.

Transitions and Through-Lines

Many scenes are structured with the wins and losses going back and forth. These small emotional events are *transitions*: the shifts, the surprises. A new thought, a shift of attention, a reversal. A moment of disbelief, of disappointment, resistance, or surrender. A loss of composure, an overreaction. A change in the emotional temperature. A shift in the power balance. A discovery, a mistake, a turning point. A beat change.

If the scene has become one-note, a director or producer may call for more *modulation* to a performance. This means it needs more variety, more transitions, more discoveries, more shifts. I don't care for the term *modulation,* because it sounds like dialing a machine. I prefer terms like *colors, layers, nuance. Colors* implies expansion of an emotional palette; *layers* implies going deeper; *nuance* implies opposites.

Transitions, the changes in the emotional terrain of the role, are the trickiest part of acting, the places where actors worry the most about whether they are going to be able to do what's expected of them, and may feel the most self-conscious. It's a challenge to "be surprised," when you actually know very well what's coming next. Result direction, like pressing actors to hit a particular emotional "note" on schedule, makes it harder.

In real life, transitions, or shifts in thought or feeling, are utterly unconscious. We do not plan to change our minds, have a new feeling, undergo a change of heart, react, realize, or go off on another train of thought. We may ignore, repress, or refrain from acting upon such tiny inner events, but we can't prevent them from arising—or summon them to our will. Such impulses are set in motion by events in our subconscious.

In narrative fiction, the characters are just like us in real life—they don't know what's going to happen to them, so they don't know how they will react. Their wins, losses, discoveries, choices, and mistakes happen *in the moment*, emerging spontaneously from the subconscious. They are *impulses*. Such impulses—or *transitions*—need to count, or read, on the screen. These impulses are the emotional events—they are the story! So they need to be filmable. We want the camera to be able to seek them out and capture them—but we don't want them to be telegraphed or emphatic. We want them spontaneous, vivid, and real.

Actors have tools to make transitions. Perhaps the most reliable is the *through-line objective*. When both actors are committed to their through-line objectives, simply responding to each other will cause their transitions to occur organically in the moment. The moment-by-moment interaction creates the nuances of the performances.

Another tool for transitions is *imagery and association*. I have a favorite anecdote to illustrate the way that imagery can drive transitions. I'm stealing it from Constantin Stanislavsky's book, *An Actor Prepares*. A woman has just been told her husband was killed in an accident at the factory. She stands in place for minutes, not moving, not reacting. Stanislavski proposes that this question may be going through her mind: *What will I do with the dinner I've prepared if he will not be here to eat it?* The image "husband" connects with the image "dinner" and her mind refuses to budge. More often than we like to admit, the human mind is non-rational, idiosyncratic, and free-associative, untethered to the logical responses we expect of ourselves.

Verbs are powerful tools to make transitions—a simple full change of active verb, without even thinking about the why of it. If an actor changes suddenly and completely from begging to accusing, we (the audience) will know that a transition has taken place. This works especially well in comedy. A great example is the abrupt and instantaneous switch, in the scene that opens *Lady Bird,* from deep *communing* over a moving piece of literature, to fully committed *quarrelling*—with no belabored segue.

Verbs, intentions, and *through-line objectives* create a sense of event, because they forge in each actor a commitment to have an effect on the other actor. When characters affect each other, they are in a relationship, and events can't help but take place: character A *teases* B, who then *takes the bait,* perhaps responds by *punishing* A, etc. Small events build on each other, until the relationship has arrived at a completely different place. The tools of intention and objective will succeed in creating emotional event only if the actors are listening and responding to each other. Yes, it all goes back to *listening.* A story is not a collection of individual performances, but rather a weave of relationships—changeable, dynamic, mysterious.

Robert Redford said that he and Dustin Hoffman, when making *All the President's Men,* had a kind of freebie. Both were A-list movie stars who had competed for roles, but had never worked together. During rehearsal and shooting, their own relationship followed a parallel track to that of the two characters they played—wary at the start and ultimately wholly attuned to each other. So in tune, indeed, that the two actors began learning not only their own lines, but each other's. Soon they could overlap or finish each other's sentences without losing the meaning of the dialogue or the event of the scene. If you watch the movie, you'll see that many of their scenes together feel like music.

If you're the director and this kind of serendipity occurs—embrace it and stay out of its way. But don't count on it coming to your rescue. It's the *director's* job to ask for ensemble playing, to make it clear that each scene is about the relationships. It's the director's job to infuse the cast and crew with a passion for the intention and higher purpose of the project.

If you see, in rehearsal or on set, moments that could be heightened by a sharper transition, resist impulses to micromanage. *Questions* and the *language of permission* are more helpful. Perhaps something like, "I wonder if we have missed a transition in here? Why do you think your character says X at this point?" Or, "What do you make of this line?" Or, "It's gotten a bit one-note. I think we can find more colors." Always be ready to step back if you see the actors becoming confused by your interventions. It's okay to ask them, "Am I talking too much?"

Blocking

Arranging movement and activities is the least intrusive and probably most effective way to support actors in their transitions. Swiveling in a chair, kicking a table leg, sprawling on a couch, engaging with one's phone instead of the other person in one's office, turning one's head to look out a window—such activities can create a moment perfectly. A character leaning up on one elbow in response to a line of dialogue from another character can be as big an emotional event in one movie as a character pushing his antagonist out of the airplane in another.

Blocking includes the positions of the characters at the beginning and end of the scene and their movements and activities during the scene—when and how they stand, sit, wash the dishes, or assemble the bomb. The term "blocking" originated in theater, particularly ballet, where rehearsal for the choreography is blocked out on a grid of lines painted or taped on the rehearsal floor. Even though its origin may seem remote from filmmaking, filmmakers need to know the term *blocking,* as well as the terms *staging* and *choreography*—they are all used interchangeably.

Let's look at a couple of principles that can help you with blocking ideas. First, *obstacle*: useful, for instance, in a scene where a character wants to throw a punch at another but, because it's a business meeting, may take out his aggression by playing with his pen. Obstacles can be invented via little "rules": that an actor is not allowed to sit down until he feels he has *won* against the other actor; or, once he moves toward her, he may not step back.

High status/low status is a potent blocking principle to make physical and visual the power balance between characters. In *All the President's Men*, Jason Robards played Ben Bradlee, who, as executive editor, was a high-status figure at the *Washington Post*. Both in real life and in Robards's performance, Bradlee's personal charisma and confidence expressed itself in body language. Robards played most of the newsroom scenes from the high-status posture of planting his feet on a desk or table, while a dozen subordinates leaned forward in their chairs or stood motionless until they received instructions and were acknowledged or dismissed.

Although the dialogue is wall-to-wall arcane newsroom jargon, the simple, strong high status/low status blocking by director Alan Pakula creates a feeling of suspense—will the powerful alpha male deign to recognize the efforts of the young cub reporters? The moments when he does take notice of our eager protagonists (or doesn't) are like bread crumbs dropped by the director to guide the audience on the esoteric pathways of the story. The personal interactions keep the audience engaged in the rapid-fire dialogue and intricate complexities of plot.

Meanwhile Jason Robards is relieved of obligation to *perform* his character's charm and magnetism—he's got his feet on the table and no one is telling him not to—damn it, that's charisma!

The main character, Uxbal, in Alejandro Iñárritu's *Biutiful*, played by Javier Bardem, has two scenes with a friend in which they discuss death. In the first scene, although the topic is communicating with spirits of the dead, the interaction is ordinary, comfortable—the emotional event is a cozy connection between friends around the kitchen table. In the second scene, Uxbal enters his friend's kitchen and drops to his knees before her. His collapse at her feet is an emotional event that tells us everything about the terrible transformation in Uxbal's inner life from hubris to spiritual resignation.

For an iconic example of blocking that is integral to *scene-making*, do a search on YouTube for "I'm smart Fredo" from *Godfather II*. Michael (Al Pacino) enters the scene and sits across from his brother as an equal, open to hearing what Fredo (John Cazale) has to say. Suddenly Michael stands and looks out the window. At this very moment, he makes the decision to expel his brother from the family.

Pacino—a skilled enough actor to portray this major *transition* with a shift in expression alone—could have been shot in close-up. Because Francis Ford Coppola chose a wide-shot, we lose some nuances of Pacino's expression, but we are invited into the inner turbulence of both characters at the same time—via the radical disparity in body language of the two brothers. Michael moves from sitting across from Fredo, reaching out to his older brother—to standing with his attention fixed on whatever is outside the window—physically and emotionally distanced from Fredo's inner torment.

Meanwhile, Fredo—having begun the scene from perhaps the most memorable low-status position in film history—slumped in the swaying, low-slung deckchair—never rises from that terrible hammock. It's a bold choice—like Uxbal kneeling in *Biutiful*, a supremely dramatic gesture that physicalizes the inner life of the character and elevates the event to a spiritual turning point from which there is no return. Michael rises to deliver his edict of expulsion and Fredo remains immobilized. Like an epic event in the tradition of Greek tragedy, the scene foretells the killing of a brother by a brother—a corruption of God's law whose consequences cannot be reversed.

Learning How To Block

It is said that John Cassavetes did not block scenes, but rather required the camera and sound technicians to follow the events created by the actors' impulses. He trusted himself to shoot so freely because he came from theater and knew how to block a scene. His practice in blocking a scene for theater gave him a foundation that, when he moved to cinema, supported his instinct for spotting the *moments*—the events—when, as Mike Nichols said, "a director's camera sense and actor sense merge."

Here's a step-by-step approach to *learning how to block*.

I keep a set of dollhouse furniture and little dolls that I bought on the internet—not expensive. You could use art supply manikins or action figures, or even little pieces of stiff paper, like folded 3x5 cards. You arrange a miniature version of the set on your worktable—if you don't have dollhouse furniture, you can build tiny beds, chairs, desks, tanks, or volcanoes from cardboard or Legos. Choose figures to represent the characters and move them around while you speak out loud the dialogue and try out ideas for physical movement. Next, make an aerial-view floorplan of your ideas for the pattern of movement (a blocking diagram). If you wish, you can even have someone say the lines and move the dolls or figures while you shoot a video with your phone.

Then do it again. And again. Until you have three alternatives. It's another use of *the technique of three possible*—three different ways the action of the scene could be blocked. Choose the best blocking plan—this is the basis for your shot list. The technique of three possible gives you shot-list backup plans.

Taking all these steps will add time to your preparation—but it's time well spent. Imagining the movement and activity of the characters as if they exist as human beings in three-dimensional space will prepare you to make storyboards and shot lists of greater muscularity and intention. Good blocking—needed for composing effective shots—makes emotional events filmable.

Blocking for dialogue scenes is sadly becoming a lost art. Many visually gifted directors don't seem very interested in dialogue scenes. They plop the actors across from each other and shoot everything in two matching singles—almost as though they think dialogue scenes are inherently boring and there is no way to shoot them more imaginatively than alternating over-the-shoulder shots. But effective blocking can turn a scene that looks on the page like exposition—a "connector" scene—into something that feels like an action scene, building suspense and revealing character.

You may need to study up on the classic filmmakers who knew how to block. It's worth your while to look closely at Elia Kazan's *On the Waterfront*, Mike Nichols's *Who's Afraid of Virginia Woolf?*, Sidney Lumet's *The Verdict*. Nichols says that when he started directing movies, he studied, frame by frame, George Stevens's masterpiece *A Place in the Sun*. Steven Spielberg is a good source—Spielberg blocks dialogue scenes inventively and with a sense of emotional event. Hitchcock, of course: There's a video breaking down Alfred Hitchcock's classic blocking of a pivotal scene from *Vertigo* by video essayist Evan Puschak, aka The NerdWriter. You can find this video on his YouTube channel.

Read David Mamet's book, *On Directing*. You can take some of his editorializing with a grain of salt and still benefit from his actionable advice regarding blocking.

Study the classic examples in order to learn their rules—and then make your own. In David Fincher's commentary for *Fight Club*, he said that the film was staged on practical sets, blocked as though for a stage production, and shot in real time while the actors ran behind set walls to make entrances and even costume changes. Director Michel Gondry has said that he addressed blocking for *Eternal Sunshine of the Spotless Mind* with a similar approach.

What about television? Being proficient in classic blocking techniques is critical for directing episodic television. Directors have complained to me that episodic directors are expected to be nothing more than traffic cops. Well, I don't know about that—I think that if you prepare properly, you can make a real contribution. But—you had better be fucking able to direct traffic! If you're directing a procedural, you need to know which side of the fast-moving gurney each series regular should run alongside. Blocking television scenes effectively means having ideas for when the actors might open a door, make a sandwich, or draw their gun. Use the "dollhouse" method to create a blocking plan. Or, get friends to try your ideas in your living room. If you want to change the blocking from what is in the script you've been given, you may need to get permission. Trying things out in a dollhouse or living room may help you crystalize your ideas and give you confidence to propose them to the writers.

There is also television that is not directed "like television" at all. An observer to the set of *Mad Men* watched director Matthew Weiner blocking a scene: telling one actor who was seated to stand; another to place a folder on the table instead of on the floor, etc. Weiner told the reporter, "I want them not to pay too much attention to each other, so it feels real. Not that TV thing." He was looking to create the texture of life. His fixation was the same as Mike Nichols's: that it should feel like a real office.

Does Everyone Have To Agree On the Emotional Event?

In the *Godfather* "I'm smart" scene, both characters know that Michael has won. But sometimes it's more slippery. A character may think she has won when she hasn't. There's an early scene in *The Fighter* between Dicky (Christian Bale) and his mother (Melissa Leo)—you can find it on YouTube by searching for "The Fighter I started a joke." Alice has just caught him falling out of the window of a crack house. Her objective is probably something like *to make him feel bad for disappointing her yet once more*. Dicky's objective is perhaps *to get around his mother* or maybe *to melt her anger* or—the simplest and most playable choice—to make her stop scowling and instead *smile*.

The blocking options are constrained by the fact that the scene takes place in Alice's car. Car scenes can feel static, but this one does not. The dazzling array of *verbs* employed by Dicky to achieve his goal make the action feel vivid and physical. First, he *cajoles* or *placates*. Nothing works. His efforts *to calm her down* backfire and she escalates from *punishing* to *snarling*. He has practice at managing her moods and shifts his tactic to *soothing*. He physicalizes that verb with a gesture: he caresses her shoulder. She rejects him with a shrug. It is only then that he brings out his big gun—the strategy that I imagine he saves for special occasions: he begins softly singing a song. A particular song: *I Started a Joke*.

From the effect of this tactic—Alice, weeping, joins him—I deduce that the singing of this song together is a *primal, shared memory* from Dicky's boyhood. Real-life Dicky Eklund was born in 1957; the Bee Gees tune came out in 1968, when Dicky would have been eleven—approaching puberty and experimenting with the power he has over the most important woman in his life, his mother.

His tactic of singing the song to her *wins*—he succeeds in getting her to make up. *Making up after a fight* is certainly an event that carries emotion—so you could call it the emotional event. Still, I'm tempted to call it the *domestic event*—what *apparently* happens—because there are questions still nagging at me. For instance, could the emotional event be different for each character? The mother may feel that his recalling the song implies a *promise by Dicky to change his ways*. But Dicky may feel that when she joins him in the song, she has given him *permission to continue his behavior without consequences*. On the level of the fiercely emotional stakes they both have in this relationship, each one might believe with confidence that he—or she—wins.

The director still has his own responsibility, which is to determine the event from the film's point of view. The scene is a brilliant portrait of co-dependence. It's up to the actors and director (David O. Russell) to *deconstruct* its dysfunction—the history of misunderstandings and unspoken agreements that cause these two to hold expectations of each other that are in permanent conflict and allow them to stay as obsessed with each other as they ever were. Leo, Bale, and Russell *did the work* to make it feel like something that happens in a real family.

Emotional Events Must Happen In Real Time

In *Taxi Driver,* director Martin Scorsese took the role of a passenger who orders Travis (Robert De Niro) to "pull over and put the flag down." Scorsese has said that while rehearsing the scene, De Niro told him, "When you tell me to put that flag down, *make* me put it down, 'cause I'm not gonna do it unless you make me." Scorsese said that was the most important lesson in screen acting he ever learned.

Emotional events must happen in real time, right in front of us while the camera is rolling. In the scene from *The Fighter,* Melissa Leo must stand her ground, and *not join the song until Christian Bale makes her*—so he can win his goal *in the moment.* That's how the tool of *objective* works. Each character wants something from the other; each fights for what he needs—someone wins. The person who loses may or may not know she has lost; she may live to fight another day; she may get her power back later.

Directors can give actors permission not to do something *until the other actor makes them.* Even if the stage directions indicate exactly where a certain action is to take place, the director can say, "Don't join the song until he makes you," or, "Don't leave the room until she makes you," Experienced, confident actors give themselves this permission anyway—and directors are wise to recognize it.

Mindless Coverage (and Avoiding It)

It's easy to recognize emotional event in the editing suite! If the scene works, there has been an emotional event. If it doesn't, the emotional event is missing. When it's not there, an editor of great skill may be able to piece together a viable snippet. But sometimes, once you get to the edit, it's too late. You do yourself a huge favor if you can locate the emotional events during script analysis, set them up in rehearsal with blocking to support and reveal them—and then turn the actors loose to bring those events into being *in the moment* while the cameras are rolling.

Mike Nichols said, "The shot can't be separated from the event . . . The only question for the camera is, 'Where do I put it to show what that event is really like?'" That's the purpose of coverage—to record emotional events that can be edited together to tell the story.

Once I was consulting with a director who was worried about how to shoot a dinner table scene with eight characters. I told her *Yes!* You're right to be worried—dinner table scenes are hard because there's only one activity (eating) and limited movement (they're all in their seats). I started asking her about the relationships and the emotional events she wanted to frame and photograph. She seemed to draw a blank. I asked her how many camera set-ups she had planned. Her answer was disconcerting: *seventeen*. I stayed calm and said, "That's a lot of camera set-ups; let's boil this scene down to its emotional events so you can focus on shooting those."

This is an exercise I suggest for any director. If you think you need seventeen set-ups to cover a scene, make yourself figure out how you would shoot it if you only could have five. If you think you need seven, how would you shoot it in three? This is an exercise—I mean, it's your choice how many set-ups to plan—but I want to push you to focus on the emotional events instead of mindless coverage. I want you to present your editor with a cuttable scene, rather than a jumbled pile of moments.

Spine and Narrative Drive

Let's take a moment to revisit the tool of a character's *spine*, from Chapter Four. The spines of the characters intersect with the themes and emotional events to produce a narrative drive—also known as the *arc* and *resolution*. This doesn't necessarily happen in a linear, fill-in-the-blanks way. Sydney Pollack, who directed *Tootsie*, has said that the film is about a man who, by dressing up as a woman, becomes a better man. That does not mean that "to become a better man" is Michael Dorsey's spine. Becoming a better man is his arc, his transformation. *But becoming a better man is not his spine.* He has no desire to be a better man, either conscious or unconscious. He feels just fine as he is. My sense of it is that his spine, both as Michael and as Dorothy, is "to rock the boat." This is an expression of his personality—who he is, who he has always been.

Even though the character undergoes transformation, the *spine* doesn't change. Michael Dorsey *transforms* from the self-centered know-it-all he was at the beginning of the movie, to a man who can admit he makes mistakes and doesn't know everything—someone who is starting, at least sometimes, to put the needs of others ahead of his own. The shrewd and generous script sets up his central transformation with two wildly inventive sub-transformations—first, from Michael Dorsey to Dorothy Michaels; then, from Dorothy back to Michael. But he is always a boat-rocker:

- Before his first transformation, when he won't follow direction when asked to play a tomato;
- During his journey as Dorothy Michaels, like when the show goes live and Dorothy changes lines and starts talking about cattle prods;
- And finally, after his second transformation, when Michael, risking a punch from Julie's father (Charles Durning), chooses to return the engagement ring without warning, mischievously sliding it across the bar.

Maintaining the same spine (to rock the boat) through two major transformations makes the audience feel that Michael/Dorothy (both played by Dustin Hoffman) is *the same person* throughout their adventures.

Spine and Narrative Drive In Franchises

Michael Corleone's spine—*to please his father*—doesn't change even after his father's death. It continues into the sequel, *Godfather II*. We know from real life that this can happen, that a person might still be driven by need for a parent's love and respect even after the parent is dead. Perhaps a theme of *II* is exactly this: that persisting in a need to make a parent happy, even when the parent is no longer able to respond to one's efforts, robs one's own life of its zest. It creates a hollow in Michael's heart.

Finding a spine for Ellen Ripley, the central character in both *Alien* and its sequel *Aliens*, is a unique challenge, because the second film takes place after a fifty-seven-year narrative gap while she was "in stasis." In *Aliens*, Ripley is a mature woman, battered by life, drained of the youthful optimism we'd seen in the younger Ripley. The two films manage to function as one complete story—even though each film had a different director (Ridley Scott for *Alien*; James Cameron for *Aliens*). Two different movies, two different directors, yet Ellen Ripley feels like the same woman. How did they do it? Let's try to reverse-engineer a possible spine for Ripley.

A simple, serviceable spine that could connect the two films might be "to survive"—because she does, when others don't. Perhaps she was born with a stronger survival instinct than the average person; perhaps she has sturdier resources than others. If I was thinking of committing to this spine, I'd do some research into the lives of people who have survived impossible odds, like a concentration camp or Gulag; I'd study their sources of power. But I'd like to play around with another idea.

One way to approach spines is to look at the work characters do. In the first film she's a female ship's officer in a male-dominated world. The film is set in the future, but was made in 1979. The role was written for a man; Ridley Scott cast Sigourney Weaver. At the time the film was made, in order to prevail in the business world if you were a woman, you needed a strong drive to succeed. Ripley is aware of, but not distracted by, male chauvinism on the ship. When the officers above her perish, she takes command and performs her mission. A spine like *a drive to succeed at her job*, against the obstacle of sexism, could be an effective engine for the main character of this film.

In the original script for the second film, there was a scene in which it is revealed that Ripley had a daughter, who grew to adulthood and died during Ripley's stasis. The scene was shot, but later deleted. I saw both these films when they came out. I knew nothing of deleted scenes, but just from watching it, I knew that *Aliens* was about *motherhood*. Even though that scene was deleted, its effect on the film is indelible. It provides a spine for Ripley, *to rescue a daughter*. Newt has become a surrogate for Ripley's own lost daughter. Another way to put this might be to say she is driven by guilt and grief, or by *a need for forgiveness*.

It's true that after the horrors she's gone through, Ripley's spine could have shifted—from *succeed at her job* in the first film, to *rescue her daughter* or *be forgiven* in the second. This could happen for any human who has been through extreme loss and deprivation. But I went back and looked more closely at facts in both films. In *Alien*, Ripley is third-in-command. The two men senior to her are among those who go out to investigate the alien ship. When they return infected, in accordance with her understanding of the quarantine protocols, she refuses to let them back on board—with the purpose of keeping safe the rest of the crew. After she is overridden by the Company's representative—a man who is not supposed to have authority—the two senior officers die, and she becomes commander. She then stops following orders from her bad-faith employer.

In the first part of *Aliens*, she does not want to go back and face the horrors. It's only when she realizes that people—families, total strangers to her—are in danger that she understands she has to do it.

What if the spine embedded in her emotional DNA is *to care for and protect others?* This could encompass her heroics of the first film *and* her fierce devotion to Newt in the second. It could suggest that if she hadn't had the cat to save at the end of *Alien*, she might not have summoned the will to save herself.

The spine *to care for and protect others* could be true of her always; it could have been true of her by the time she was eight. It could account for her singular resilience throughout her whole life—that she is committed to a purpose larger than her own survival. Storytellers can have higher purpose. Characters can, too.

Director's Intention

The emotional event of a particular scene is the thing that keeps the audience interested in the story—but it's also the artistic reason for putting the scene up on a movie screen. It expresses something you want to say about life. I urge directors to know their intention as storytellers—and honor it.

In a 2011 speech, Charlie Kaufman spoke of his objection to the aphorism *The road to hell is paved with good intentions*: "It doesn't ring true to me," Kaufman said. "I think intention is at the bottom of everything. My intentions are shifting and complex and often at odds with each other. And if I know what they are, and watch them closely as they slip and slide all over the place, I have a better chance of putting something honest into the world—and this is my goal."

I think he is saying that we all want to do well, to be recognized, but if your only goal in making a movie is to "knock it out of the park" so you get another, bigger-budget job—that won't be enough to see you through. You need to have something to say. You need to have *meaning* in your work. You need a higher purpose. You need to be able to speak to actors from the heart. If all that is in your heart is the desire to be known as a director, then look for more.

Spike Lee, Ava DuVernay, Alejandro Iñárritu, Bong Joon Ho, Chloé Zhao—to name but a few—all radiate intention throughout their work. You might name it differently—your vision, your mission, your idea, your true north—Jennifer Fox, writer-director of *The Tale,* called it her *soul seat.* You don't need to be an auteur—even without writing their own scripts, the creations of Ridley Scott, Sidney Lumet, Sydney Pollack, and William Wyler have been driven by a purity of *intention to tell an honest story.*

Your artistic intention is your whole singular truth and sensibility. Whether your sensibility is essentially hopeful, or resolutely dark and unforgiving—I don't care. But I want you to believe it's worth finding out. Ask yourself, what is the wound in my soul that cries out to be healed? Ask yourself, what is my higher purpose?

When I ask a client what his script is about and he says, it's about a man who learns the value of friendship, I feel compelled to ask him, what do you know about this from life? Has it happened to you? Have you seen it? *What is that really like?* What are the obstacles, what are the costs? Not just the external obstacles provided by the plot, but the internal obstacles. When you investigate such questions on an emotional level, a human level, a personal level, you *earn* your resolution.

Once I was consulting with a writer-director whose script featured the plot element of a character trapped in a cult. When I asked her about her connection to that theme, she said she had none. Thirty minutes later, casually, as though out of the blue, she mentioned that her older brother had been in a cult and she'd spent her entire childhood watching her parents devote all their energy and money to extricate him. I could have been shocked that she had not connected such a central experience to the facts of her story before meeting with me. But I wasn't. Because I have seen it over and over—filmmakers with a story of great personal urgency staring them in the face without them recognizing it. When you have this level and depth of connection to the material, hold it to your heart—and share it with your actors.

Your storytelling intention takes you into primal events—the triumphs, disappointments, and longings that all humans experience—their losses, hurts, awakenings, and second chances. I want you to learn and care about the real forces that, in your knowledge of life, drive people's actions. In a speech at an awards ceremony, Ava DuVernay spoke these words of advice to young filmmakers: "Every morning, on your way to the set, remind yourself why you are telling this story."

Always Do the Right Thing

Mookie throws a trash can through the window of Sal's pizzeria. As Mookie approaches Sal's, holding the emptied trash can, the neighborhood parts to make a path, creating a guard of honor, standing as sentries of protection and hope. Director Spike Lee staged and paced this climactic scene with stark simplicity to create an emotional charge as inexorable as Greek tragedy.

I re-watched *Do the Right Thing* in 2020 and felt it could have been made today. What is this scene about? Throwing a trash can though the window of a pizzeria? No, it's far bigger than vandalism. What Mookie has done is *redress a wrong*—the death of his friend. In a film a tragically timeless as this one, referencing the wounds and wisdom of generations, determining its intention, its "what it's about," is not an intellectual exercise. Mookie has instigated a long-awaited racial reckoning. The balance of power in the neighborhood has been challenged and the audience should understand that the world as we know it has changed, and needs to keep changing.

The Compass

A director-client asked me to critique a short film he had made. When I mentioned a scene that I thought didn't work, he replied that he had never been excited about that scene, because it had nothing visual to shoot. Listen up. Don't shoot a scene until you have found "something to shoot." This director's not finding the shootable thing in the scene—what the scene was about, its emotional event—was not only a failure to do his script analysis homework, but a failure to care about storytelling. Prepare so you can spot it on the set. Don't wait for the editing room to freak out because it's not there.

Younger filmmakers may not know the name William Wyler. He made box office hits that were also artistic triumphs; he died in 1981. Wyler is a legend to filmmakers like Alexander Payne and Kenneth Lonergan. Payne said of Wyler, "he had the compass." Lonergan said Wyler "puts the camera in the only place it must be for each scene." In other words, Wyler always knew *the thing that is to be shot.*

Wyler was famously uncommunicative with actors and known for shooting an infuriatingly large number of takes for every scene—often delivering this sole direction after each take: "Do it again." Wyler is not the only brilliant director who does not use the language of my tools when giving direction to actors—Wong Kar-Wai is said to work this way as well: "Do it again." But what I believe that Payne and Lonergan mean when they describe Wyler as "having the compass" or "putting the camera in the only place it must be" is that Wyler and others—whether or not they use the vocabulary of emotional event—*know what it is.* In their bones. Yes, emotional event can be a great tool for communicating with actors. Even more important, it's central to a filmmaker's eye.

Emotional event is the tool that my students and clients tell me is the hardest to grasp. Making the shift to using the tool of emotional events effectively may be something that requires 10,000 hours of practice. If you keep at it, you will get it. At one time I myself did not understand emotional event—and now I do. It took me years. Once I understood it, there was a *shift in my consciousness* that has not slipped back. I can spot it in a script—or at least ask questions that will get me to some ideas. And during a performance or rehearsal, I can tell when it's there and I can tell when it isn't.

CHAPTER SIX

Actors' Resources and Training

"I build on my own experience, on that of others—on everything I have heard and seen . . . The day Ingmar [Bergman] gives me the manuscript, he also gives me the right to feel that henceforward I understand the part best."—**Liv Ullmann**

There are excellent actors who have never taken acting lessons, having instead developed a private technique of their own. There are other actors who think of their teacher almost as a priest or guru. I think the best actors find teachers in every experience of their lives. Good actors steal and learn from everyone and everything they encounter. They use everything available to them: memory, observation, imagination, research, sensory awareness, the actor in front of them—and something beyond technique that I'll call sensibility, vision, or, maybe, heart.

Memory or Personal Experience

For every human, our memories—the things that have happened to us—infuse all of our present life. People who aren't actors (actors call them "civilians") often believe they have put their past behind them. Unlike civilians, actors allow their personal experiences to surface and become a tool for illuminating the truth of a character. It's not that any actor's particular life and hard times are more important than those of any other human being. The goal of using personal experience as an acting resource is not self-indulgence but honesty. No one can experience another person's life; each individual is essentially unknown to all others. Hence, by using one's own experience, an actor can achieve originality and emotional truthfulness.

Memory is the basis of what became commonly known, during the 1950s, as The Method, an approach to teaching acting pioneered by Lee Strasberg, a founder of the Group Theatre and the Actors Studio. The center of the Strasberg method is the technique of *affective memory,* also called emotional memory.

For an affective memory exercise, the student selects an emotionally charged event from her own life. She recalls not the emotion itself, but her memories of the physical life surrounding that event—sensory memories like the color of the walls, the smells of the kitchen, the sensation of the upholstery against her skin. The idea is that an actor can select an event with an emotional charge and create the sensory life surrounding that event. With sufficient practice, she can return, at will, to the emotion of the event whenever that emotion is relevant to a role or scene.

After the Second World War, the Actors Studio became the public face of a seismic shift in acting styles. I love vintage movies and revere the great stars of the 1930s and '40s, but, in 1951, Marlon Brando arrived on the screen in *A Streetcar Named Desire,* soon followed by Method stars Montgomery Clift, James Dean, and Geraldine Page. Acting has never been the same. Martin Scorsese, interviewed for the 2007 documentary *Brando,* said, "He's a marker. There's before Brando and after Brando." Another interviewee said: "Before Brando, actors acted; after Brando, they behaved. That's the difference."

Brando, as a member of the Actors Studio, had to have been influenced by Strasberg, but in his autobiography he claims Stella Adler, who prioritized imagination over personal experience, as the teacher who most molded him. I was not myself trained with affective memory exercises. My first teacher, Jean Shelton, encouraged us to make our work personal, but by using *substitution,* an approach that uses personal experience as a metaphor for the experiences of the character. As a teacher and actor, I find the technique of *substitution* invaluable in establishing ground-level honesty in my work. (I described an example in Chapter Four, having to do with ironing shirts.) Substitution is an "as if," but a magic one: "as if my own job is in jeopardy"; "as if my own sister has just shot her husband."

Actors can allow their own memories and experiences to permeate a characterization without using exact techniques like affective memory, substitution, or the "magic as if." The ways they inform their work with their own experiences and understandings of life may be entirely private and idiosyncratic. Chadwick Boseman said, "Regardless of whether the character is real or a fantasy, I always start from myself, because you have to know yourself first."

Observation

An actor can't limit himself to his own experience for preparation. Good actors observe other people, their behaviors, their eccentricities—making conjectures about what makes them tick. If an actor is playing a farm laborer, he will look for ways to incorporate gesture and behavior that differ from a person who has always worked at a laptop. Playing a character who ages in the film, like Cecily Tyson in *The Autobiography of Miss Jane Pittman,* an actor uses her observations of elderly people to create a stiffness in the joints that causes them to move more carefully, or balance issues that cause them to walk and stand with their feet farther apart.

Some actors make their choices based primarily on observation; this is often described as "working from the outside in." An extreme of this approach might be an actor who plans gesture, facial expression, and line readings, practicing them in front of a mirror. When I was studying acting in the early 1970s, my fellow acting students—and I—tended to label this "technical acting"; the pejorative ring was intended.

Surely the best actors work from the outside in—letting themselves be affected by makeup and costume and making choices about vocal patterns, gesture, gait—as well as from the inside out, considering deeply the character's needs and emotional history. Brando was known as an actor who worked from the inside out, but his choices "from the outside in" were equally effective—it was he who insisted on prosthetics for his cheeks to play Don Vito in *The Godfather*.

Imagination

Many actors are drawn to the profession because of an overdeveloped access to the imagination. For many of us (I must say "us," of course, since I am one), *imagined reality* is more compelling than regular, so-called "real" life—and the time spent surrendering to that bubble of belief in the life of characters is precious. An actor's sense of belief in an imagined reality gives him solitude in public and allows him to be absorbed in the created realm, reprieved from the duties of the social realm. It makes actors suggestible and even kid-like.

All of us, actors and civilians alike, are sitting on a vast iceberg of submerged resources—memories, impressions, feelings, impulses, images, associations—which we tend to suppress and put away once they have lost their usefulness to our daily lives. Eventually, the precious resources of our memories and daydreams retreat.

If you're an actor, this wealth is not gone for good. I see the resources of imagination awakened powerfully during improvisation exercises. When I have used improv as a classroom or rehearsal technique, the depth and range of my students' unconscious resources are released—and they are vaster, by far, than what is available to our conscious minds. I've seen students go believably to the controls of a spaceship or the jungles of Vietnam in an improv, when only moments earlier they had been struggling to place themselves in a family kitchen and speak with authenticity the lines of a character who is actually very much like them. I'm an enthusiastic advocate for improv as a means to engage an actor's imagination and sense of belief.

Many actors speak of taking time to "dream" about a role. Some coaches teach a specific method for accessing a role by undertaking a series of physical exercises, and then trusting the dreams that come while asleep. My sense of "dreaming" a story or role is that it can also happen while one is awake—in other words, daydreaming, perhaps while soaking in a bath or taking a walk. Sanford Meisner spoke of daydreaming as a powerful resource for actors. Imagination exercises like improv or dream work or physical movement, awaken an actor's imagination at an impulsive, subconscious level rather than an intellectual level. This can feel foreign to some directors.

Sometimes directors tell me they are analytical by nature and don't understand what I mean by daydreaming the life of a character. It can be an idea or association that emerges slowly, after days of puzzling over a mysterious line. Or it can be spontaneous, as when a detail of a character's circumstance jumpstarts an actor with ideas for the spine ("I think he's in love with death!") or for ways to physicalize: "I've been working on a lower register for her voice"; "There's a certain way she holds her teeth"; "I'll grow a mustache for this role"; "Can I knock over the chair on this line?"

It's possible that a director's mind is more left-brained, more linear, and doesn't work quite like an actor's. If this is true for you, I invite you to appreciate right-brained creatures, to enjoy and trust them, to dip into their world of risk and free-association. A director needs to be both—one moment, left-brained, organized, focused like a laser on the logic of the story of which she is the guardian—and the next moment, fearless about dropping all linear thinking so as to stand face-to-face with the raw interiority of actors.

Research

When Forest Whitaker was cast to play Idi Amin in *The Last King of Scotland,* he went all-out. According to director Kevin Macdonald, Whitaker was very concerned to have all the medals worn by his character "exactly correct," and wanted to know which ones Amin actually merited, and which not. At Whitaker's insistence, the props department located the real chair that Amin had used, his real car, his real helicopter. He learned Amin's tribal language and spent a month hanging out with Amin's friends, children, ex-generals; every day he ate the food Amin ate; on set, he kept his accent both on and off camera; he absorbed Amin into every pore. At the end of the shoot, Whitaker said, "I am so relieved to get this man out from inside me. It wasn't possible to turn him on and off; it was all-encompassing." All that was left was to collect every possible accolade—at the Golden Globes, the SAG Awards, BAFTA, and the Oscars.

On the other hand, Ruby Dee was asked whether she had done any research on Mama Lucas, her character in *American Gangster.* "Oh, my dear," she said, "I grew up in the neighborhood. The whole background of this thing was already with me forever. I knew the whole scene. I knew the shootings in Harlem and the riots and the police brutality—that was with my early consciousness from when I was five or six years old. And the way the banks did not lend Black people money . . . [caused] so many people to play numbers and play the horses . . ."

For Ruby Dee, recipient of many awards for this and other roles, there was no need for research—or for techniques such as substitution or affective memory. It was all—all of it—in her bones.

Channeling

What I call channeling is a mixture of observation, imagination, research, and personal experience. An actor may recognize her character in a person she knows—either personally or as a public personality—and be able to channel them, conjuring their physical and emotional behaviors. It has to be someone the actor feels deeply involved with or fascinated by. Michelle Williams said of playing Broadway legend Gwen Verdon in *Fosse/Verdon*, "It's a little like trying to tap into somebody's spirit."

When Michael Mann asked Jamie Foxx if he could play a cab driver for his role in *Collateral*, Foxx said in an interview that he replied, "'Come on Mike, you know I do my thing.' And Mike said, 'Could you *not* do your thing? Can you be simple? Can you be run-of-the-mill?'" Foxx then says that he "linked onto" a man he knew, "a nice guy who worked with some people who were not so nice, and he was able to work with them for five or six years and never had a serious problem because he was able to maneuver." I think what Jamie Foxx describes as *linking onto* is the same thing I am calling *channeling*. Prompted by his director, Jamie Foxx channeled an ordinary "nice guy" whom he'd worked with on the set of one of his long-running TV shows.

Dustin Hoffman says that when he was cast as Ratso Rizzo in *Midnight Cowboy*, he took to the streets of Manhattan: "I went looking for the guy. I found him on 42nd Street." Johnny Depp famously based his performance of Captain Jack Sparrow in *Pirates of the Caribbean* on Rolling Stones' guitarist Keith Richards. Depp is said to have added a little Ray Bolger (the scarecrow in *Wizard of Oz*), plus a dash of Dean Martin—and voilà.

If you ask an actor for her ideas about her character and she tells you, "Oh, I know this woman. She is exactly like my mother!"—I strongly suggest that you hold back on any detailed direction. She's got something going on—see what it is. Affirm it—build on it if you need to—and whatever you do, don't micromanage it.

Meisner Technique

Sanford Meisner invented the "repetition exercise," a teaching technique that promotes moment-by-moment aliveness and engagement with a scene partner. It's described in detail in his book, *Sanford Meisner on Acting.* Two actors sit across from each other, giving each other relaxed attention. When one of them has an impulse, he may say something—either an observation of the other actor or a statement of his own feelings—such as "Your eyes are brown," or "My stomach is tense." The other actor repeats exactly what the first actor has said. The two of them keep repeating the same phrase, until one of them has an impulse to say something else, which then is repeated in the same way . . . until a new impulse arises.

The exercise needs to be supervised by a teacher who knows what they're doing, to make sure the participants are speaking out of true impulse and not because they feel a need to entertain the viewers or think it's time for them to come up with something clever. The value of the exercise is precisely that you don't have to be clever; if you have no impulse, no idea of what to say, you can repeat back what has already been said. Its proper purpose is to get the actors to stop watching themselves, stop "performing"—to get them out of their heads and into the moment. And to support actors in knowing that surrendering to another actor does not deplete you—it enriches you.

I sometimes use a simplified version of Meisner repetition. I ask one participant to say yes and the other to say no. And then go back and forth, responding to each other, not trying to be interesting or entertaining, not trying to vary their tone of voice, but also not deliberately preserving a monotone—and to keep doing this until I ask them to do something else. This exercise is effective in making *listening* feel normal and relaxed, even for beginners and non-actors. It not only centers each participant in the other actor—it gives them confidence in their impulses.

Living the Character's Experience

Some actors create the character's experience as preparation. Rather than imagining the experiences of the character or finding parallels from their own life, they put themselves through some part of the character's experience themselves. You could call this another approach to research. Daniel Day-Lewis spent months in a wheelchair to prepare to play Christy Brown in *My Left Foot*. As did Eric Stoltz, for his role in *The Waterdance*. Steven Spielberg put the actors through boot camp to prepare for *Saving Private Ryan*.

Sometimes these activities are denigrated as "method-y," but to me they are common sense. Said Michael Mann, "I'm a great believer that whatever the central activity the character is supposed to do in his life, that an actor should be able to do it, to really understand the character." In preparation for shooting *Collateral*, Mann designed a program of target practice and close quarter combat to give Tom Cruise a sense of the kind of training he would have had in the U.S. Army Special Forces. This included exercises (under careful supervision by an expert) using live ammunition. Mann said this was important, so that when the actor is on the set firing blanks, behind the blanks is the *sensation* of firing live ammunition. "The real value is what it does to the actor believing in himself," Mann said in his commentary.

Matt Damon has said that for *The Bourne Identity*, he boxed every day for six months, even though the character Jason Bourne is not a boxer, but a covert operations assassin. It was director Doug Limon's idea that Damon should train as a boxer, telling Damon there's "something about the way a boxer walks, a directness, an economy of movement—they're on the front foot."

In *The Lives of Others*, the character Dreyman has been presented, on his birthday, with the sheet music for *Sonata for a Good Man*; the next day, the friend who gave it to him takes his own life. The character Dreyman becomes seized by a compulsion to learn the piece. The actor, Sebastian Koch, as well as director Florian Henckel von Donnersmarck, felt it would be important for Koch to learn the piece himself. Koch did not even know how to play the piano! He took lessons. He practiced four hours every day. It was "a sort of meditation" that connected him to his character.

***"You can really tell in a movie when an actor picks up an empty suitcase."*—Pedro Almodóvar**

In the *Volver* scene in which Raimunda (Penélope Cruz) drags the body of her dead husband to the restaurant freezer, director Pedro Almodóvar made sure it was a heavy load for real. As preparation for *Volver,* Penélope Cruz spent time cleaning her house; she'd gotten "a bit out of training because of living in hotel rooms," and realized that in order to play Raimunda, she had better know "how to move a broom."

David Dobkin, director of *Wedding Crashers,* asked Vince Vaughn and Owen Wilson to take dance training—not to make them look like trained dancers, but so they'd feel confident and the dance sequences could then be free and full of energy.

Concentration

If a director hears an actor agonizing, "I can't get my concentration," it might be helpful to ask her, "What are you concentrating on?" An actor's concentration is not an abstraction. Some people think you can't concentrate unless you are relaxed, but it's really the other way around: having a simple task to concentrate on is relaxing. Susan Sarandon has said, perhaps half in jest, that she did the best acting of her life in the *Thelma and Louise* scenes when she was driving—really doing the actual driving—without a process trailer. Full concentration on the physical and mental demands of staying on the road kept her from any distractions like trying to "do it right."

"Doing it right" is the worst place for an actor to place concentration. A physical task can be a kind of freebie. The other *tools* can provide a focus as clarifying and liberating as a simple physical activity if the choices are bold: a compelling through-line objective, a deep need, a powerful metaphor, or a strong "as if."

Another dangerous point of concentration is trying to recreate an earlier performance. A "re-performance" *will be bad.* This is an existential truth. Every event, every moment in life, once it passes, is over. We cannot have our lives back after we have lived them. When a director tells an actor, "That was perfect. Do it again just like that," he is asking for something that is just not going to happen. An actor who tries to "re-perform" will only be straining, controlling—aiming. It's a blueprint for stasis and defeat. According to the book *Zen in the Art of Archery*, this principle applies to all motor learning, such as sports, as well as to many humanist approaches in psychology.

Sensory Life

Sensory life is the information from your five senses—what you see, hear, smell, taste and touch. A great contribution of Method-oriented classes is the sense-memory exercise: The actor recalls physical sensation and allows the memory to occur physically (in her body) rather than intellectually (in her mind). In a beginning sense-memory exercise, a student may hold in her hands an object, say a cup of coffee, and put her attention on the sensory impressions it makes on her: the weight of the cup, its temperature, its contours; the sensation of steam against her face; that coffee smell. The attention needs to be sensory, not intellectual—that is, she is registering not an intellectual evaluation of the temperature (such as "it's pretty warm," or "very hot"), but rather the pure sensation against her fingers and palms, her cheek, her nostrils. Then the object is taken away, and she creates an imaginary cup of coffee, that is, a sense memory of the real object. She recalls—not mentally but sensorially—the weight, temperature, texture, aroma, etc., with as much detail as she can summon without strain and without concern for whether anyone can figure out what she is holding. It's not mime; the goal of the exercise is building one's sensory concentration.

Not only Method approaches, but all acting techniques work better when grounded in sensory life. For example, substitution: If the actor is substituting, say, the kitchen table of his own childhood for the kitchen table the set decorator has brought in, he touches the on-set table and allows the sensations of his own childhood table—its color, its scratches, the chewing gum his sister left under it—to rise up in his consciousness.

Sensory exercises can be very freeing. They return us to a child's sense of concentration on very simple things, like the sound inside a seashell or the texture of a rose petal or the smell of warm towels just out of the dryer. I have found that when I guided students in a sense memory of an outdoor place from their past where they had experienced beauty, the reprieve it offered them from the distracting stresses of daily life helped them open and surrender in total safety to their deepest creative resources.

In addition, sense memory has very practical uses. When actors need to play a hot summer scene on a cold day, they create a sense memory of the heat. Jeff Bridges insists that no actual marijuana was smoked on the set of *The Big Lebowski*—he claims it was all sense memory. Sophisticated special effects require actors to perform in front of the green screen as if they are on a precipice or airplane wing. The way to make these feats believable is to imagine the sensory life: the wind against your face, the sharp rock or cold metal under your fingertips.

An actor playing an injured person can place her attention on the physical location of the injury and allow whatever feeling she has to magnify. If a character has gone into shock following a trauma, there is an absence of pain and even sometimes a weird clarity. For cancer, there may be generalized pain, but it can be helpful to center the pain in the stomach. For a person addicted to drugs or alcohol, there can be an array of physical effects: a thick head, a dry mouth, a tightness in the stomach. If a character has a mental illness, it matters to know the diagnosis—and then deconstruct its symptoms into physical behavior.

If a character burns himself on a hot stove, and the actor decides upon and *indicates* the physical movement of his reaction, audiences will sense that it is bogus. Instead, the actor playing the role touches a cold stove *as if* it were hot, and then lets his hand *follow its own impulse* in response to this created, imagined stimulus. Does this mean the actor actually feels the pain of a burn? I can't speak for all actors, but for myself I would say—not at all. That's the wonder of all this acting stuff—*concentration* is the operative word; the actor's concentration sparks a created reality. Imagination does the rest.

Shakespeare

There's almost nothing in filmmaking that Shakespeare didn't think of first. Even though there was no green screen technology in those days, the actor playing Macbeth had to be able to see a dagger where there was none. When actors ask me for suggestions of how to practice alone, I tell them, learn a new Shakespeare monologue every week. Shakespeare is such excellent training because making it sound like human communication is hard! First, you must work out the literal meaning of the strange words—and then look beneath to understand what they *really mean*. If you can do that with Shakespeare—or Emily Dickinson, Maya Angelou, Langston Hughes, or Rumi—you can do it with any script.

I say the same to directors and writers. Shakespeare is extraordinarily cinematic. A serious filmmaker has a lot to learn from the study of Shakespeare, even if you have no interest in directing a Shakespeare play. Did you like *Game of Thrones?* It's heavily based on plots and imagery from Shakespeare. The audience doesn't need to have read Shakespeare to enjoy *Game of Thrones,* but the actors and directors sure do.

When I worry about how we entertainers are going to make it through the COVID-19 pandemic, I remind myself that Shakespeare was writing and producing *King Lear* during one of the worst outbreaks of bubonic plague.

Some directors are wary of theater-trained actors for fear they might be stagy, but there is great value to training in the discipline of theater. Certainly for motion-capture actors—mo-cap acting is more like theater acting than film acting. But beyond the practical value of hiring theater actors for mo-cap roles, there is immeasurable worth for any artist in sinking into Tennessee Williams, August Wilson, Arthur Miller, Edward Albee, María Irene Fornés, Eugene O'Neill—and so many others . . . Molière, Synge, Beckett, Lorca—so much psychological insight, depth of feeling, and thematic richness! To a trained actor, a director who has not read any plays seems virtually illiterate. A director who can make theater references has powerful communication shortcuts: "This couple reminds me of George and Martha." Or, "When I was reading this script, I couldn't stop thinking about Willie Loman."

Post-Stanislavsky

When I started teaching in the mid-1980s, there were mighty arguments about which of the actors' resources was the most important: memory (represented by the Strasberg Method); imagination (associated with Stella Adler); observation/research (practiced by the giant of British acting, Laurence Olivier); or *the actor in front of you* (the approach systematized in the Meisner Technique). There were wonderful actors who studied with each of them. These militant delineations—especially between the camps of memory vs imagination—always seemed artificial to me. I can't buy the idea that memory and imagination are anything other than powerfully entwined.

All these titans—Strasberg, Adler, Meisner, Olivier—were elderly when I began teaching in the mid-1980s, so I always thought that the controversies would die when they did. Not so! The imagination vs memory wars burn as fiercely as ever. I hear that some popular Hollywood teachers claim actors should use *only* imagination, *never* memory, while others insist the opposite. This makes no sense to me. My every experience as a teacher, artist, and human being tells me that imagination and memory interweave and inspire each other—in art as in life.

It's finally, always, from the earliest days of cinema through to the present, a matter of engaging a *sense of belief*. All actors' techniques—objectives, "as if's," the "moment before"—are really means to engage the imagination and allow the actors' sense of belief to kick in. If the actor does not surrender to the story, he may be judging the writing, refusing to suspend his disbelief; he may end up walking through the role or, alternately, forcing or pushing it.

Have we arrived at a post-Stanislavsky age? I don't know many young actors who are studying *affective memory* these days. Roy London, an acting teacher beloved by many excellent actors, said the Method was important in the 1950s because the mannerisms and emotional inhibitions of that repressed era were crying out to be broken through. Things are different now. Younger actors have not been restricted emotionally by their parents the way my generation was. They've had video cameras pointed at them since their birth, and are not as self-conscious as the young actors of my time. I never studied with Roy London, but in a lovely documentary about him, he reminded me of nothing so much as my teacher Gerry Hiken begging us to "think your most private, embarrassing thoughts *right in front of them!*" Like Gerry—or Harold Guskin, whose book *How to Stop Acting* is gloriously freeing and enlightening—Roy London wanted actors to strip down their ego defenses until whatever they were doing was something the world had never seen.

Meisner-style classes are still thriving. If the teacher is good, they can provide effective steps to implant, as a learnable and repeatable skill, expertise in listening and responding—central foundations for good acting. From there, for an actor, it's a matter of finding a scene study class to practice tools of script analysis that give the actor permission to make bold choices and take risks. Many actors supplement scene study with improv classes and find them freeing and invigorating.

It's true there are acting teachers who are arrogant, silly, or downright abusive. It's worth the time and effort to search for one who isn't.

One of the many painful consequences of the 2020 pandemic has been that actors don't have class to go to. I have spent the best moments of my life in acting classes, first as student and then as teacher. I think of the church basement in which I took class with Jean Shelton and the warehouse where I performed in small theater with Angie Paton and Bob Goldsby as places of emotional refuge—but also as cradles of civilization.

Working With Stars

Besides the craft of acting, experienced film and television actors learn techniques of hitting marks, finding their light, not blinking. It makes a director's job easier when actors already know how to do these things effortlessly—but over time, technical facility can make their acting slick and less exciting to watch. Actors can also burn out and get sloppy, "general." They may even take roles they aren't particularly interested in, just for something to do. Or they may have developed a bag of tricks, a set of effects they know they can reliably produce. Jean Shelton used to call this "tap dancing." She meant a reliance on showy emotional or comedic shtick for its own sake, at the expense of being present in the moment.

Popular actors may have a certain *bit* or *gesture* that has become an audience-pleasing shorthand, a nonverbal catch phrase, their trademark. Paul Giamatti has jokingly described his signature cocked eyebrow as "my bread and butter." Actors who have perfected a bag of tricks are capable of wonderful, surprising work. Sometimes they just need a director with guts enough to ask for the good stuff. When Paul Schrader asked James Coburn, who had spent most of his career making easy money in a popular, light-hearted franchise, to take the raw and transgressive role of the father in *Affliction*, he told Coburn, "I want you—but I don't want that *Our Man Flint* stuff." Coburn had trained with Stella Adler; he replied, "Oh, you mean you want me to act?" Then he said, "Okay."

Treat actors—and think of them—as artists. Even if you fear that an actor is being lazy, talk to them seriously about the work. Instead of telling them to stop doing this or that mannerism that you find annoying, engage them in *what the film is about*—that it is about *loss* or *second chances* or *denial*.

Heart

> ***"I know that acting doesn't improve just through study. There's some kind of personal growth to make that change."*—Steve Martin**

Chadwick Boseman, on a talk show, said he wanted audiences to take away this from his performances: "Everybody is the hero in their own story. You should be the hero on your own story."

Laura Dern, in an HBO interview, said, "Playing characters that don't know their own value has always interested me; that is a theme I keep inside my head a lot because it can be a very powerful corporate executive or a broken homeless girl, but both of them don't necessarily trust their worth. That's just a really interesting thing to think about for women and as women."

Forest Whitaker said about working on *Last King of Scotland*, "I felt a deep obligation to Ugandans and to the African nation to try to play this character honestly and truly. It changed the way I think, it changed the way I view things, and it opened my eyes. So it changed my life."

No matter what the medium—and no matter how an actor has trained (or not trained—more later regarding the joys and perils of casting non-professional actors)—the tools of verbs, emotional history, subtext imagery, metaphor, and emotional event *work*. They are normal, non-jargon-y terms that describe human behavior. But it's possible that an actor's best tool is if he *cares*, if he has found something in the script that expresses something he wants to say to the world.

I don't believe that actors—or directors—can do anything really good unless they care. There is a spiritual dimension to storytelling. Bringing narrative fiction alive involves a radical empathy that can be transformative and uplifting. It's a privilege to share with an audience what you feel is important about being human, what you understand about life.

Feelings

"I think that to sing the blues you have to feel it."— **Billie Holiday**

When directors are afraid of deep feelings, this can hold them back in their communication with actors. Actors may have chosen the profession for the very reason that it offers the opportunity to go to dark and difficult places—pain and loss, fear, anger, transgressive sexuality, as well as unpredictable playfulness and wild joy. For actors, expressing deep feelings can be cathartic.

Must the director go with the actor to these extreme places? Perhaps not exactly, and yet in a way, of course, yes—in the sense that it's wonderful when the director can be a *partner* and a *witness* rather than a boss. Directors are allowed—indeed, I encourage you—to talk about emotional life. You can *invite* actors to invest more in the images of the scene, in other words, to make the work more personal. You can *share* your own emotional connections to the material. You can *offer* them freedom, give them permission to "let go even more."

It goes without saying but I'll say it anyway: There is never a need for a director to manipulate, bully, shame or abuse an actor. Ever. If you trust an actor's craft, imagination, and heart, you'll gain access to resources more powerful than you know.

CHAPTER SEVEN

Script Analysis

"Clues are beautiful because I believe we're all detectives. We mull things over, and we figure things out. We're always working this way. People's minds hold things and form conclusions with indications. It's like music. That's the beautiful thing, to figure things out as a detective."—**David Lynch**

Every script contains hidden *clues* to a vast, underlying world of behavior, emotion, and event. You look for *clues;* you look for *evidence.* Then follow up with questions, pursue leads, and brainstorm ideas—like a detective. The clues sift through your brain and imagination until you get ideas.

In Chapters One, Four, and Five, I have described *tools* that are useful for script analysis as well as communication. The tools work for every genre. They work for good scripts and mediocre scripts. Good scripts are complex with rich layers of subtext—a treasure chest—you dig in and hunt for every precious gem. Bob Odenkirk spoke to an *LA Times* interviewer about working with Rhea Seehorn on *Better Call Saul,* and he said this: "[Rhea and I] mentally approach this thing with a similar degree of seriousness, appreciation and focus. There's a lot to look for in these scripts. It's worth your effort to take the script apart and explore the subtext of it."

It's more fun to do script analysis on a good script—but once you've taken on a project, stop judging—engage. Mediocre scripts may be over-explained and obvious, so it's important to open up life *behind* the words, bring texture to the lines, and tease out themes that expand their substance. Material of borderline consequence can be made livelier and more entertaining by using the same script analysis tools you use to dig out the layers of a good script. In other words, treat every script like it's a good script.

Later in this chapter I'll use a scene from *The Matrix* to illustrate some tools of script analysis. In the meanwhile, please allow me a *Matrix* metaphor. Much like Morpheus's description of the Matrix as an apparent world and Zion as the real world, the *plot* of a script is the *apparent story* and the *subtext story* is the *real story*. Once you become free and confident in the subtext world—able to believe in it, create in it, and trust it—it won't be hard to think of the subtext world as more real than the apparent world. You won't need to remind yourself to phrase your direction with "correct" vocabulary or jargon—you'll have insight, understanding, and *connection* to communicate.

And here's a bonus: Directors find their best ideas for where to put the camera when they are comfortable operating in the *subtext story*. Script analysis prepares directors for communicating not only with actors and cinematographers, but also production designers, casting directors, and even the people who control the money.

It's easy to see that script analysis is necessary if someone else wrote the script. If you didn't write it yourself, you need to get so steeped in its story and the lives of its characters that you can *feel as if you had written it*. But script analysis is just as valuable if you *did* write the script. Directing a script you have written is not a matter of simply uploading your ideas into the brains of your collaborators—as Constantin Stanislavsky wrote, "An actor is not a turkey to be stuffed."

Good writers have subtext in mind while they write, but deciding to direct your own script is a commitment to take the script *off* the page. This means that even a writer-director allows the subtext of the script to be rewritten. Everyone knows that the subtext of a project may be completely re-envisioned in postproduction. But not everyone understands that *rewriting the subtext* goes on during the entire process of filmmaking, including casting, rehearsal, and shooting. At times this may feel stressful—but it doesn't have to. It can be exciting, revelatory.

Sometimes people call the shift from writing to directing, "taking off your writing hat and putting on your directing hat." That's a metaphor, of course—there are no actual hats involved. What is involved is making yourself investigate, during script analysis, other ideas besides the ones you already know are good. The *technique of three possible* is great for this. Here's another idea, one that may at first sound like impossible mental gymnastics: Temporarily, as an exercise, pretend that someone else wrote it. Or, maybe this: *Pretend that the characters are people who you are meeting for the first time.*

My writer-director clients sometimes tell me that the script analysis sessions they have with me give them ideas for rewrites. I'm happy if that happens—I want you to have the best script possible. I don't see myself as a competitor with any of the many approaches to screenplay structure. If it helps you to think of one character as "hero," and another as "mentor," or "enemy"—I've no objection. What I ask, however, is that, above all, you think of each character as a *human being in a human situation.*

I love characters, no matter how weird, foolish, lonely, angry, petty, vindictive, irrational, and vulnerable they may be. My touchstone for connecting to the loneliness and irrationality of characters is to be honest about these traits in myself. Essentially, I believe that the two most valuable script analysis tools of all are curiosity and an interest in self-knowledge.

Reading the Script

While reading a script for the first time, or as soon as you put it down, make some notes: your *first impressions,* your *questions,* and the *mysterious lines.* Then *edit the stage directions.* Then, read it again—out loud.

I can't tell you how highly I recommend that you read the script out loud. Read slowly in full voice. Don't whisper or mumble. Don't rush. Don't read in a monotone—but don't perform, don't try to "be" the characters. If you wish to read the stage directions, I suggest that, rather than read them verbatim, you improvise a summary of their salient details.

I don't know what effect this exercise will have on you—but that's the point. Reading out loud forces you to be more in the moment with the script—and no one knows what effect that will have on you. It may help give you a sensation of *beginner's mind*. Or it may help you make friends with the script, and begin the process of *owning* the characters. Just as each actor's prep is a process of "owning" his character, a director's prep includes "owning" every one of the characters.

Stage Directions

Raymond Chandler wrote both novels and screenplays. In his novels, he gave us gorgeous description like, "Even on Central Avenue, not the quietest dressed street in the world, he looked about as inconspicuous as a tarantula on a slice of angel food cake." When Chandler came to write screenplays, he economized.

A writer of a scene without dialogue may be tempted to write his narration with beautiful language in order to keep the interest of the people with power to finance and cast the project. But the director needs to deconstruct it. For instance: What does it mean to say that the character in Chandler's narrative is "conspicuous"? Is he wearing inappropriate clothing? Does his gait call attention to itself? Is he openly weeping? Is his secret intention, unknown even to himself, *to beg for someone to notice him?*

At some point, either before or after you read the script out loud, you should strip down the stage directions (also known as narration). Unless the writer is Samuel Beckett—a dramatist who famously knew exactly when a character needed to pause, or take off a boot, or hand over a hat—actors tend to be skeptical of stage directions. The director should be too, even if you've written them yourself. Some are important—needed in order to follow the action of the scene. Some are intriguing, offering juicy clues to playable choices. Others are superfluous to the actors and director and can be crossed out and ignored.

Stage directions that should be crossed out (with a thin, single line, so you can go back and refer to them if you need to) include those that describe the character's expression or line reading—"a withering look," "livid with rage," "longingly." You cross these out for the same reasons that you stay away from result direction. Many of such "parentheticals" do nothing more than underline the obvious meaning of the line, and are thus unnecessary. An exception might be when the parenthetical calls attention to an opposite, like "kindly" when the line is "Shut up!"—if I saw this in a script, I would find it intriguing, and put a question mark next to it.

Parenthetical indications of where to pause, such as "beat," or "she takes a moment," provide a sense of rhythm for readers in production offices and talent agencies—but a director should question them. First, I ask myself whether this is a good place for a pause. If so, why? Is there an emotional event here? What is it?

Whenever the script says, "He cannot look away," or, "She cannot answer," I cross those right out and replace with "He does not look away" and "She does not answer"—because I think that these behaviors carry more power if they are presented factually. Then I ask *why* she does not answer; why he does not look away.

Questioning every stage direction is useful for a person who wishes to start *thinking like a storyteller* instead of like a consumer of stories. If a stage direction introduces a character by declaring, "She is bright and sparkling," of course I'm going to question that! Her bright and sparkling exterior could be a *cover,* how she presents herself. I want to leave myself open to the possibility that she may, underneath, be angry and frightened.

A stage direction can work for some actors, but be wrong for another. The wrist-cutting scene in *Fatal Attraction* contained the stage direction "laughing." This is an intriguing idea, but Glenn Close objected to it and told her director, Adrian Lyne, that she could not make it work with honesty. He validated her stunning emotional nakedness in this role by letting her know that he preferred her to be honest than to follow the stage direction—and she ended up crying in the scene.

"He struggles with his coat" is an example of a stage direction that is better writing than a parenthetical describing the character as "frustrated." It's also an idea for *business* in the scene. It might be a good idea, worth trying in rehearsal. So I would question or circle it. Finding the movement and activities (aka "business") that physicalize the emotional events of the script is the director's job, and there's no reason not to be open to ideas from any source, including the writer. But if you follow stage directions without thinking, you might miss great ideas that the writer didn't put in. If the script does not indicate that a character "drops her head in her hands" at a certain moment—that doesn't mean she can't do that! Directors are allowed to come up with ideas for blocking that are not in the script—indeed, that is precisely the director's job.

Don't forget that actors can also come up with great ideas for business. Did you know that the rubber glove and the nunchucks were actor Brad Pitt's ideas? (Director David Fincher disclosed this in his commentary for *Fight Club*.) Please—do not accidentally shut down the brilliant improvisations of generous, inventive actors.

Make note of stage directions that introduce us to the characters' personal objects. "A silver-framed photo of his wife and two daughters has been lovingly placed on the desk." This is one of the character's personal objects—I would highlight it—but I would cross out the adjective suggesting inner life ("lovingly"). I'd rather *ask questions*: Why does he have the photo on his desk? Because he loves them and needs them close at all times, perhaps cannot quite function without a constant reminder of their presence in his life? Or is he driven by obligation to the family-oriented mores of his workplace? Those would be two different *choices*. I'm sure you can see how sharply they would affect the interpretation of this character.

Stage directions that give us backstory facts can be intriguing and provocative. "The last time a crime occurred in this town was twenty-five years ago"; "He graduated first in his class at Harvard"; "She has been passed over for three promotions."

Okay, again—*questions*. Why was she passed over for the promotions? Does she have a character flaw that stands in the way of her success? Or is it systemic sexism? Or systemic racism? Or—was there a different reason each time?

For a scene with no dialogue, of course you must give conscientious attention to its description in the script and comb it carefully for *clues* and *evidence*. Then deconstruct your findings. Translate the clues and evidence into an emotional event.

The real reason for crossing out superfluous stage directions and questioning optional ones is this: so you can locate and highlight the necessary ones—the ones that reveal something important that is not disclosed by any dialogue. Such as these: "He searches desperately through the desk drawers until he finds the gun"; or, "They kiss." When someone locates the gun he was seeking, or two people kiss for the first time—those events matter. Leave these in. Pay attention to them. If you have a full-cast table read, these may be the only descriptions that need to be included.

But do cross out "desperately." At the very least, *translate* the adjective "desperately" into *questions*: How much time is left until his presence is likely to be discovered? Who does he suspect may have gotten there first and found the gun that was supposed to have been placed there for him?

The Charts and Guides

Ever since I started giving Acting for Directors workshops, in October 1988, teaching script analysis has been a bear. Over the years I created handouts: charts, lists, outlines. And constantly revised them. I thought of myself as an explorer, charting unmapped territory. Alas, script analysis does not lend itself to the linear modalities of workshops, charts, and books. It's not linear; it's free-associative.

Take notes. You can use a pad or notebook of lined or unlined paper—or your laptop, tablet, or phone. You can take notes on a hard copy of your script or an app such as Scriptation. The purpose of the notes is not to create a document that you email to the actors. Note-taking and list-making are useful for jumpstarting your thought process. When human beings have an exciting idea, we can become consumed with a nagging, unconscious, back-of-the-mind sensation that if we don't *hold on tight* to this idea in our brain, we might lose it. Writing your ideas safely down is a way to alleviate a subconscious fear that you might forget them. Then you can *let them go* because you've got them written down to refer to later. This frees you to have new ideas. Notes and lists are most helpful when they are fluid, not set in stone—when they open you to new ideas.

If you have written the script yourself you may feel you don't need to make notes about your ideas. You may already know what the story means to you, what the script is about, and how you connect to the characters. Make notes anyway. Not to set your ideas in stone, but to set yourself on a journey, to embark on a process. The goal finally is to let go, to turn the characters over to the actors.

A while ago, in my own workshops and consultations, I stopped using the charts from the original edition of *Directing Actors*. Since 2002, when I started teaching the Actor-Director Lab, I've been using the Script Analysis Guide in Appendix C.

Appendix D is a list of topics that I used in Script Analysis and Rehearsal Techniques workshops. The participants and I would take a stack of loose-leaf paper and title each one with the headings from the list. As we worked together in a group, we could shuffle around from page to page, thereby approximating the free-associative nature of the work. For example, when we listed facts on the "Facts" page, we'd flip over to the "Questions" page to note the questions that invariably arose.

Appendix E is an Addendum oriented more to the needs of actors.

People have sometimes asked me to create an app for my script analysis process. I considered it, because I want to be of service in the telling of stories in whatever way is needed. But I don't feel confident that a Script Analysis App would be helpful and have not given my permission to the creation of one. Here's why: It's not a matter of checking off selections or filling in boxes—it's a matter of awakening your deeper resources of connection, invention, insight, and intuition.

The Matrix

In Appendix F you'll find scene 74 from *The Matrix: The Shooting Script*, published in 2001. It's a short scene, in a car, with four characters: Neo (Keanu Reeves), Morpheus (Laurence Fishburne), Trinity (Carrie-Anne Moss), and Cypher (Joe Pantoliano). It's called a "shooting script," which suggests that it was shot as written. The released film does not contain the entire text, which makes me think that some lines may have been deleted during the edit.

The following is an exercise, using a well-written script, to illustrate steps in script analysis. I am not claiming that my process is one the Wachowskis used when preparing to direct this film. I am certainly not suggesting that they ought to have used my ideas to direct the scene rather than what they did! (I love the film as is.) Since I expect most of you to be familiar with this movie, I will sometimes refer to action and dialogue from scenes outside of this scene. With reference to blocking, I may refer to the finished film, which hopefully you'll be able to look at—I feel reasonably certain it will be streaming somewhere, forever.

First Impressions: What I Love; My Reservations and Concerns

Ask yourself—early and often—*why* you are doing this project: what it's about, why it matters to you, why you took the job or why you wrote the script. I find these questions (from section 2 of Appendix C) useful for starters:

- *What do I love about the project?*
- *What, if any, are my reservations?*

Get in the habit of returning to these vital connections over and over during all stages of production—including *every morning* on your way to the set. Keep reminding yourself: *This material chose me. It chose me for a reason.* Your reservations may turn out to be just as revelatory as your passion for the project.

When I sought permission to use this scene from *The Matrix,* I confess I didn't really know why I chose it. There are lots of longer, meatier scenes! Why did I ask for this one? It's less than two pages, with four characters, so how will it be possible to discuss any of the characters in depth? It takes place in a car, so how can I use it to address the all-important topic of blocking? Those are my reservations about the exercise I have set for myself, I guess.

In spite of those reservations, I was in love with this scene, helplessly drawn to it. I love the whole script—who doesn't? But I love *this scene* as I might love a child. I wondered why. I started using this scene in workshop exercises—in order to figure out why I love it so much.

What I love about the scene has something to do with a theme of how we change, and how when we change radically, we can hardly remember the person we used to be. It brings to life the contentment that comes with being accepted by new friends. As well as something about what it's like if you (*Cypher!*) feel hurt and alienated by people you once loved and still wish loved you.

Then too, I'm a sucker for a love story if it feels real. The Neo/Trinity love story is much more than a formulaic action-adventure subplot—it stands on its own with honest things to say about the struggles of finding and expressing love.

Plus, it's a movie of ideas! There are other scenes in the film where the metaphysics are scrutinized with greater detail, but this short scene—even though at first glance it looks like a quick "connector" scene—engages provocative concepts.

First Questions

The first questions I'm going to ask myself are: What are three ways I'm like these characters? What are three ways I'm not like them?

Ways I'm not like Neo:

- I'm not a computer hacker.
- I have no interest in learning martial arts.
- I have no belief that guns will ever be useful to achieve my objectives.

Ways I am like Neo:

- I have father issues.
- I have had the experience of falling in love with someone who fell in love with me first.
- I've had the experience of being plunged back into a world I thought I had left behind—as Neo is on this, his first visit back to the Matrix after the transformations he has undergone on the Nebuchadnezzar.

These associations run deep and meaningful for me.

For the other three characters, I'll only mention my most significant connection to each one. My connection to Morpheus is that I'm a teacher. My connection to Trinity is that I've had the experience of feeling blocked and inarticulate at the exact moment that I most wish to express my most serious feelings. My connection to Cypher—the "villain" of the story—is that I know what it's like to feel rejected by friends who I had expected to take the place of family.

"It's Just . . ." and "I Assume"

Whenever one of my students says, *"It's just . . .",* I prompt them gently: "Don't say, *'It's just.'"* They take a beat. They get it. It's a hard habit to break, though.

I call "It's just" and "I assume" the two greatest enemies of an artist. Instead of "It's just a love scene," say, "It's a love scene." Instead of "He's just apologizing to his mother," say, "He's apologizing to his mother." Do you see what a difference that is? "She's just waiting for the doctor's report after her biopsy." "It's just a confrontation between two friends." "He's just being sarcastic to the judge."

These are huge human events, with significant consequences! A good director inspires the actors. You can't inspire anyone when you use the diminishing phrase, "It's just." As artists, our goal is to *illuminate* human events, not minimize them.

The word "obviously" is another red flag for me. Nothing in a good script is obvious. Other uninspiring qualifiers are "basically," "potentially," "sort of," etc. Think of yourself as a person who can *commit,* rather than qualify and hedge your ideas. Be bold. There's no downside to committing because—you can always change your mind!

There's another phrase that directors all too frequently use as the sum total of their script analysis: "I assume." Do not assume anything. Investigate. Imagine. Choose. If needed, change your mind and choose again.

Pro Tip (for the Whole Script): Make Lists. Cut and Paste.

List the themes. As you do your script analysis, keep jotting down possible themes, as I suggested in Chapter Five. Make it as long as you like, maybe ten or more. At some point allow this *wide net* of possible themes to sift itself down to three main themes. Finally, locate your central commitment to *what it's about*—but don't try to figure it out intellectually—allow it to swim up to the surface and choose you.

List the relationships. For the four characters in our *Matrix* scene, that would be:

- Neo and Morpheus
- Neo and Trinity
- Neo and Cypher
- Trinity and Cypher
- Trinity and Morpheus
- Cypher and Morpheus

Then make cut-and-paste versions of all the scenes in the script for each relationship. If you read through the cut-and-pasted version of all the Neo/Trinity scenes, for instance, you may get ideas of choices about their *emotional history,* each one's *spine* toward the other, and the full arc of the relationship. The cut-and-pasted versions will be valuable for rehearsal, because rehearsing relationships is the best use of rehearsal time.

Chronology cut and paste. If your script happens to be written out of chronological order (like *Pulp Fiction,* for instance), cut and paste to create a version of the whole script with the scenes rearranged into the order in which they occur. This will save you confusion, anxiety, and time.

Do the math. Draw maps. Sketch out timelines and logistics. If a character is in Denver in one scene, and Seoul the next, there must have been a travel day? If there's a flashback, figure out everyone's ages and what year it is. If a project is fantasy or science fiction, make sure you know the rules of the world you have created: In other words, *what is the science behind the science fiction?*

Master list of emotional events. Lists of all kinds can help you track your thoughts as you shift between macro ideas (for the whole script) and micro ideas for moments and behaviors in individual scenes. The granular way I crawl through a scene line-by-line may seem overly detailed to some readers, but I always keep my mind on the prize—ideas for each scene's *central emotional event.*

The most helpful list you can compile will be a list of the emotional events of all the scenes in their chronological order. A kind of *master list* of the emotional events that tell your story. You can change and revise your master list any time you want. Its purpose is not to make a rigid structure set in stone—even in the edit, it can all change—but to keep reminding yourself that your story and characters start out somewhere and go somewhere else.

Some emotional events have special significance—they are inflection points in the story—emotional set pieces—they change everything. For example, in *The Godfather*: Connie's wedding; the shooting of Don Vito on the streets of Little Italy; Michael's restaurant scene; the explosion that takes Michael's wife Apollonia; Sonny's death at the tollbooth; Don Vito's fatal heart attack in the garden; the baptism of Connie's baby. Make notations of such scenes on your master list.

Each scene has its own emotional event. Each scene also plays a part in the arc of the whole story. Some scenes are setting up an emotional event that will happen later, and some scenes are paying off an emotional event that has been set up earlier. A scene of *estrangement* sets up a later scene of *reconciliation*. In scripts of complexity and depth, a scene may be paying off an earlier setup at the same time that it is setting up a payoff that is coming. Make notations (provisional, of course—they can always be changed) of which scenes are *setup* scenes and which are *payoff* scenes.

Keep Reading the Script. Read It Aloud.

After you make your chronology cut-and-paste version, read it aloud. When you read your cut-and-paste version of the script with only Neo and Morpheus scenes, read it aloud. At some point, consider reading aloud all the lines of each character. Perhaps it will be helpful to read the script with another person, switching off roles from scene to scene. Here's my favorite: Read the whole script aloud to another person. Don't act it. Choose for your person to whom you read it, someone who is not there expecting to be entertained, not ready to criticize, but present to support you.

For any of these read-aloud sessions, don't try to act the roles or the scenes. Read slowly. Listen for the subtext. Let yourself hear it as though for the first time.

Whether you read aloud or silently, reread the script often throughout script analysis, preproduction, and rehearsal. Every day if you can. Each time, approach it as though it's the first time. Free your mind of the ideas you have already come up with—you have notes so you don't have to remember them. Embrace *beginner's mind* and allow yourself to rethink, deepen, broaden—and simplify—your ideas. You may be surprised at what comes to you.

Mysterious Lines & the Technique of Three Possible

I like lines that are odd! Non-sequiturs and contradictions—even lines that at first are irritating—can be gold. They can hold the key to an insight you've been resisting. That the key was elusive and the insight hard-won will render its truth all the more powerful. I recommend that you find at least *three* mysterious lines in every scene.

If there's a line you don't like—especially if you're working in television, where directors have limited power to get lines changed—call it a mysterious line and look for three possible ways to make it work. If you decide to go to the writers with a request to change the line, it will help if you've first done everything you can to make it work as written. Not only that—it's a great work-out, like going to the gym for your imagination.

The tool of *mysterious lines* works not just for lines that bother you, but also for lines you love. If you are enamored of their wit or poetry and forget to look for the reality behind them, they lose their meaning—and end up sounding trite.

Okay. Go to Appendix F and read our *Matrix* scene out loud. Slowly.

Now, let's pick three mysterious lines and see where they take us.

First mysterious line: "Almost unbelievable, isn't it?"

A wonderful thing to do in rehearsal is to ask actors to create *the moment before*. Morpheus's first line is a mysterious springboard to imagining what the previous moment might have been. Is he responding to something someone has said just before the scene? Or to a wordless event he has observed?

There is narration containing clues to what might impel Morpheus's line. The narration reads: "Neo cannot stop staring as the simple images of the urban street blur past his window like an endless stream of data rushing down a computer screen." I'm going call this narration a mysterious line, too! Stay with me while I take a small tangent to question and deconstruct it.

First, I edit the line "He cannot stop staring . . ." to "He is looking at . . ."—because that makes his activity *factual* rather than a conclusion. *Fact*: he is looking out the window. Now, we have a *question*: What does he see?

The imagery in the rest of the line is our clue to what he's looking at: "simple images of the urban street [that] blur past his window like an endless stream of data rushing down a computer screen." It's not a factual statement. It's an image, or really a metaphor that mashes-up two images: "the urban street" and "an endless stream of data rushing down a computer screen." Which does he actually see? The shops, pedestrians, and vehicles of an urban street? Or—does he see a stream of raw pixels?

Soon he has a line, "I used to eat there . . . Really good noodles." This line is *evidence* that he can see shops and people and cars, like the ordinary denizens of the Matrix. But it's a *fact* that he is no longer an ordinary denizen of the Matrix. He has undergone unplugging and retraining, to become a "human being." He now knows that the Matrix is not real but a *Construct*.

Perhaps for Neo the street scene is semi-transparent, with the pixels visible behind it? Perhaps his view shifts between street scene and pixels? Okay, I promise not to head down the rabbit hole of speculation about the exact physics of existence on the Nebuchadnezzar versus having the muscles, lungs, and hormone regulation that allows our crew to function when they visit the Matrix. If you are directing this script, you do need to figure this out—the science behind the science fiction—but for now, I'll leave that to Reddit.

What I'm attempting right now is to understand Morpheus's line, "Almost unbelievable, isn't it?" In service of that goal, I want to give this mysterious stage direction a more *specific reality* in my imagination.

The *technique of three possible* is my best invention, my gift to you—please use it! Anytime you find a line that bothers you or doesn't make sense, let it be a *mysterious line*—and make a list of three things it might possibly mean. Don't try to find the right answer but rather, without evaluating your ideas, scribble them down. So, availing myself of the *technique of three possible*, I'll jot down three ideas:

1) Morpheus sees the same thing Neo does—and it's different from what the residents of the Matrix see. Perhaps the pixels of the Matrix Construct are visible to Morpheus and, now, to Neo.
2) Morpheus and Neo see the same street scene that residents of the Matrix see, but with the knowledge of the Construct behind it.
3) Morpheus's line may not be a statement, but a question. Perhaps he wishes to make sure that Neo's training has taken effect by verifying that Neo now has the ability to see past the Construct.

I like idea 1 better than idea 2, because idea 1 is physical. Idea 2 is a more mental version of idea 1. I'm not saying idea 2 is a wrong or bad idea, only that idea 1 might be more playable. In any case, the *choice*, or *secret*, takes place in the imagination of the actors playing Neo and Morpheus. The audience is not shown what Morpheus and Neo see—or is it? The audience sees what the residents of the Matrix see, and is not told whether it's the same thing the crew-members see.

Second mysterious line: "I used to eat there . . . Really good noodles."

First, a question: how long has it been since Neo was last in the Matrix? Many of the scenes since his rescue have been presented in collage—brief moments from his trauma, recovery, and instruction—from scene 29 to scene 70. I'm going to call it a *fact* that there are passages of time between each of these slivers of his new life. But how long are these passages of time? Do they add up to a month? A year? More? What is the timeline of Neo's recovery?

The audience doesn't need to have this information, but the storytellers do—both directors and actors. I'm interested in this particular question because I'm searching for a *metaphor* to describe the experience behind Neo's line about the noodles. I'm looking for an "as if" or an "it's like when." Here are three ideas:

1) It's like when you return to the street of your childhood home—which your family moved away from twenty years ago. If you've had this experience, you know it's a powerful one.

2) It's like returning home after military service. I've read about the alienation returning veterans can feel. For some, the military has come to feel more like the "real world" than the world they are returning to.

3) As if he has just learned that he is adopted.

Now I've got three, and I like them all, but my unruly imagination started nagging at me with a fourth, bonus idea:

4) Who was he with when he ate the noodles? In the couple of brief scenes before he meets Trinity and then Morpheus, we don't see Thomas Anderson (Neo's name in his Matrix life) with anyone we would describe as a friend. That doesn't mean he had no friends—might there have been

> one coworker he felt comfortable enough to have lunch with now and then? The memory of that coworker could be the image underneath the line "I used to eat there . . . Really good noodles."

That fourth idea—that Neo is reminded of a friend from his former life—seems pretty removed from the concerns of our scene and the movie as a whole. But I don't care. I was not censoring myself. I was letting my imagination roam, letting it lead me instead of me trying to lead it. Imagination, by its nature, resists the injunction to be useful. If I command my imagination to go only to useful areas, it probably won't do anything; it will sit there like a stick. Instead of staring at the page, unable to get started on your script analysis process—go ahead and *blurt* out an idea, good or bad, if only to get yourself started.

I permit myself to blurt. I permit myself to go down blind alleys. And here's how a seemingly blind alley might pay off: Imagining Thomas Anderson eating lunch with a coworker launches me into imagining the *opposite*—that, in his Matrix life, both as a worker in a cubicle and as a midnight hacker, Thomas Anderson was always alone. This transforms my idea 4 into this far more powerful one: that among the crew of the Nebuchadnezzar, Neo has, *for the first time in his life*, found friends. The memory of the noodle joint, where he was always alone, is an image of isolation and emptiness that powerfully contrasts with his current feeling of camaraderie and purpose.

Now I like all four of my ideas. I got to this place of creative possibility by not concerning myself with finding the right solution—only with making sure that each of the ideas was different from the others. Abandoning the struggle to find the "right" answer: a way to get myself started, to jumpstart from a condition of listlessly staring at the script, to activate my imagination. Embracing contradictions and incongruities will make you a better thinker, a better imaginer—and a better listener when you are talking with the actors.

Wait, though. When I was rereading this chapter and checking my notes, I remembered that the food on the Nebuchadnezzar is really bad! What if you'd prepared these other ideas, and then, when speaking with the actor slated to play the role, it turned out that the contrast between the delicious food at the noodle shop of his memory and the bad food on the Nebuchadnezzar was his strongest association for this line? Well, you'll be ready. Even though you hadn't thought of this particular idea, you've been going to the gym with the *technique of three possible*. You've been recruiting new imagination muscles—which will be ready when you need them, on the set, when nothing is going the way you thought it would.

I spent a lot of time on the noodles because I think it matters, always, to give special attention to characters' memories. Memories can never be accepted as fully factual; they are tinted by wish and imagination—more *imagery* than *fact*. But memories always contain truth, sometimes a deeper truth than fact.

The *Matrix* scene I chose is so beautifully written that for me every single line shimmers with mystery, including the stage directions. But even when, in less carefully crafted scripts, I come across hackneyed movie-sounding phrases—like, "You just don't get it, do you?"; or "You're sorry? All you can say is you're sorry?"; "You'll never get away with this!"; "What are you doing?"; "Are you all right?"—I call them mysterious lines. When such dialogue is delivered without subtext (with no objective beyond, for instance, finding out if the other character is all right), it sounds forced and untrue. At best it's filler; at worst it drags down the story. Just because such lines show up in movies a lot doesn't mean that anyone really knows what they mean. Unless you find some reality *behind* the words, they will be experienced by the audience as lazy clichés.

Always ask: What is the character *not* saying? Whenever a character breaks off a speech or is cut off by another person, that's automatically a mysterious line—you need to ask yourself, what was she going to say?

Open yourself to the idea that any line—or any silence—might have more than one meaning. Then you won't lose your equilibrium when an actor doesn't relate to something in the script that you have found compelling or beautiful or funny, and you won't panic when the actor interprets it differently. You can use the *technique of three possible* with actors who say, "This line doesn't make sense to me." You can reply, "Yes, it's mysterious. I think there are a few things it might mean . . ."

Paraphrasing (Creating Inner Monologue)

Third mysterious line: "I have these memories, from my entire life but . . . none of them really happened."

This time—a twist on the mysterious line exercise. I'll still use the technique of three possible, but with *paraphrasing*. Paraphrasing may bring to the surface ideas that you didn't know you had.

I'm not going to try to do this "right." I'm just going to start—like automatic writing or stream of consciousness. Here are three possible paraphrases for Neo's line:

1) I hate my memories, I am happy with my new friends, I don't like being back here, it feels like being in a zoo.
2) Did I do the right thing by taking the red pill? It's not so bad back here. It's familiar, easy. These new people in my life expect something from me that I'm not sure I can deliver. I'm frightened by their expectations.
3) Morpheus likes and trusts me. Trinity is the most fascinating creature I've ever met. They chose me to join them on a mission that matters and revealed to me things I've never thought of. For the first time in my life, I am important, my thoughts and observations are meaningful. It's the start of a great adventure. What will the Oracle say to me? Will I pass the test? Or be found wanting?

Those were improvisations around possible subtext—ideas for an inner monologue. I feel closer to Neo for having done that exercise. I wasn't trying to be profound; I was only trying to make each idea completely different from the others. I find that I like all these ideas! I have an inclination toward the third one because I like the idea that Neo is filled with a sense of adventure about meeting the Oracle.

I could translate this thought into an idea for an *emotional event* for the scene: that *Neo gains in confidence*—or, *Neo's sense of adventure kicks in*. If I refer to my *master list of emotional events,* either of these ideas works well as a *setup* for the coming scene in which the Oracle will *destroy his newfound confidence*. Either one also works as a *payoff* to the scene when he was Thomas Anderson and his confidence and sense of adventure were so deficient that he failed to jump off the roof when invited by Morpheus, and instead allowed himself to be captured by agents.

But I'm ready if the actor leans more toward idea 1 or 2. Or has some completely different idea. I'll be better able to hear him for having done the exercise. And better able to think on my feet.

Paraphrasing is an introduction to the actors' tool of inner monologue. It's also a way to orient oneself toward asking of a line, "What is its subtext?" rather than "How should it be delivered?" If you decide to try paraphrasing, let it be fun. If it starts to feel boring, that means you're doing it mechanically, so take a break and come back to it later. Allow the paraphrasing exercise to take you out of your head and give yourself access to your subconscious and thus, your intuition.

Facts and Questions

I've mentioned a few facts already (that Neo is looking out the car window; that there has been some passage of time since he was last in the Matrix), but you may have noticed that these *facts* were mostly of interest for the *questions* they generated: What is he looking at? How long has it been since he last was in the Matrix?

Facts are things that are true before the scene starts. Some facts will be clear; others we can deduce—like a detective. We're not going to insist that the writer spell everything out; instead we'll look for *evidence* and follow clues. But we're not going to pretend to have facts we don't actually have. We're not going to make assumptions. We're not going to jump to conclusions or make judgments. If a character has a line saying something is true, we won't automatically call it a fact. We'll ask questions and look for other evidence.

Fact: This is Neo's first trip back to the Matrix since being unplugged.

Fact: The other three have had the experience of being unplugged. *Deduction*: Each of the other three must have already undergone the experience of their first trip back to the Matrix after unplugging. *Questions*: What was each one's separate experience? What is each one's response to Neo's behavior during his first trip back?

Fact: They have taken the trip to the Matrix in order to bring Neo to see the Oracle. (Wait. Is the Oracle a fact? Or an *image?*)

Proposed fact: Neo had no family when he was Thomas Anderson. *Evidence*: His family is never mentioned, not by him, not by anyone else. *Questions*: What is Thomas Anderson's family history? Is he alienated from his family? Is he an orphan? Do the denizens of the Matrix even have families as we know them?

Questions and More Questions

Coming up with good questions is the main purpose of script analysis. Having good questions is better than having all the answers. If character A says, "Why are you shouting?"—instead of *assuming* that character B is shouting, ask questions: *Is* B shouting? Or does A have a low threshold? Could it be that what actually bothers him is the content of what B said?

There are questions you should ask about every character. Here are some examples. There are more in Appendix E.

- What is this person smart about?
- What does this character find funny?
- What is her level of education?
- Where is his pain?
- What does he enjoy?
- What is he good at?
- In what way is she an artist?
- What does she most fear?
- How does she make her living? Did she choose her profession, or fall into it?
- What is her sexual history? Family history? Cultural/religious history?
- What is her position in the world vis-à-vis social class and finances?
- What experience does she have with discrimination?
- Whom does he look up to?
- What is the biggest thing that has ever happened to him?
- Who is the most important person in his world?
- How is the character different at the end of the story than she was at the beginning?

Examples of questions to ask about every scene: What's the emotional history of each of the relationships? What is happening *for the first time?*

Directors and actors sometimes describe characters in terms of what they are not: "She doesn't have much of a sense of humor," or, "He isn't very smart." Instead, ask questions: "What makes her laugh?" "What is he smart about?"

Everybody is smart about something. A character society calls "slow" is not trying to be slow—"slow" is society's conclusion (that is, *judgment*) about him. I've taught acting classes in the developmentally disabled community and have observed that, unless they are overmedicated, people with developmental deficits have two dominant needs or *intentions*: to *keep up* and to *contribute*.

If you have an idea for a character, for instance, that Cypher "isn't sexy," expand on that idea with questions: What sexual experience has he had? What romantic advances has he made to others on the Nebuchadnezzar? Did he, like Neo, encounter Trinity before he took the red pill? Did he fall in love with her instantly and take the red pill in a wild hope that it would bring him close to her?

The more thoroughly you work on a script, the more questions will crop up. This is a good thing, not a bad thing. The stuff that bothers you can bring the most creativity, like the grain of sand that becomes a pearl by irritating the oyster.

One purpose of asking all these questions is to test your ideas. You don't have to worry that questioning your ideas will make you lose faith in yourself. Testing your ideas against other ideas makes them stronger. You have made notes of your original ideas, so you can always go back to them.

Questions bring our story imaginations to life—daydreaming around the facts of the script gives the material an opportunity to tell us what it is about. Questions prepare us to make *choices*. When I advise you to question everything, I don't mean that it's okay to be wishy-washy or that all options are equal. In order to find the choices that work best for your project, you need to investigate the field of possible options from which to choose—otherwise, it's not a choice, it's an assumption.

When you prepare by asking questions and coming up with multiple solutions, you've got a leg up on communicating with actors. Because, before even meeting with the actors, you know that there's more than one way to understand a scene or a character or a moment. You won't be freaked out when the actors' ideas are slightly—or even a lot—different from yours.

Once the technique of asking questions becomes second nature, you'll feel more comfortable using questions when giving direction. You'll be able to *listen more than you talk* when you are with actors.

Research

Find out the meaning of any unfamiliar word or idea. If it's a period piece, discover as much as you can about the era. For a crime or medical procedural, study up! Learn all about forensics and hospitals. I sometimes fear that young people take the Internet for granted. I'm of the generation that had to trudge to the library, *on foot in the snow, uphill both ways*, so I give thanks to the Internet every day. But don't stop with Google and Wikipedia—roam the stacks of brick and mortar libraries; talk to researchers; watch documentaries; interview people who have had experiences you have not; travel to the places referenced in your script. Spend time with your story using old-fashioned shoe leather and face-to-face interaction. Above all, don't restrict your creativity to what you know from other movies and TV shows.

Keep rereading the script. Not in order to reassure yourself that your ideas of how it will look and sound are all perfect already, but rather to stay open and alive to emerging nuances, to become aware of facts you hadn't noticed, imagery you skipped over—to keep coming up with fresh ideas.

Internal Research

Throughout script analysis, keep delving into *internal research*. That is, always connect your script analysis preparation to your personal experiences, observations, and understandings—to what you know about life. Keep reflecting on the primal topics—like family, class, loss. I mean, what else is life about? If you approach all your preproduction homework technically, that's the product you will have—a movie technically proficient, without soul. How can you ask actors for personal investment unless you make a personal investment yourself?

When Bong Joon Ho accepted his Best Director Academy Award for *Parasite*, he said, "The most personal is the most creative."

Bong was quoting Martin Scorsese who was probably quoting John Cassavetes. Cassavetes, whose work is a *true north* for many serious filmmakers, was known for allowing *zero emotional distance* between himself, his characters, and the audience.

Images and Associations

Our *Matrix* scene is rich with imagery. The noodle shop is an image. Neo's memories are images. The Oracle is an image. The Matrix itself is an image.

Trinity's line, "That the Matrix cannot tell you who you are," keeps tugging at my imagination. The image of a "matrix" of restrictions and expectations ruling our lives and attempting to dominate us by *telling us who we are* is so central to the whole film that I want to take a minute to unpack this image by making associations to my own life—of people and entities that have undertaken to tell me "who I am."

Like the Catholic Church. Certain members of my family. A bully who once tormented me. Right-wing pundits who demonize me and others if we don't adhere to their narrow ideology.

If I let my imagination roam free, there are also carefree associations—like social media quizzes or astrological signs that profess to tell me "who I am." These are fun and sweet, not heavy and dangerous like the Matrix is. Allowing myself to free-associate into areas that are probably not intended by the script supports the health of my imagination, so I never forbid myself these fanciful excursions. I never expect every scrap of my script analysis to be useful—maybe a tiny amount of what we come up with, say twenty percent, or even only ten percent, will lead to an actionable choice.

Ideas For Imaginative Backstory

We get ideas for imaginative backstory by asking questions: What else happened during Trinity's visit to the Oracle, other than what she reveals at the climax of the movie? When did Cypher become the chauffeur of the crew? How often does Morpheus come to the Matrix to visit the Oracle? You could make the choice that he comes frequently, like once a week, to engage in small talk with the only other creature who is of his stature. Or has he only come on the five previous occasions when he thought he had found The One? Either choice can be powerful.

What Just Happened

"What just happened" investigates the gap in time between the scene at hand and the scene previous to it. It's also called *the moment before.* Scene 74 is not quite continuous from scene 73, in which the four-person crew exits their drop-off point and Cypher discards a phone into a trash can and opens the car door on the driver's side.

At the beginning of scene 74, the car is already in motion, so there's been a passage of time since scene 73. Very possibly it's a short amount of time, but it's worth asking how much. How long have they been driving through the streets of the Matrix? Have they been riding in silence? Or has there been conversation? The choice of the *moment before* propels the actors into the moment-by-moment reality of the scene.

Actors are well-advised to create the "moment before"—either with their imagination or with sensory life. The *moment before* is also appropriate for the director's investigation into the characters' lives outside the confines of the frame, in order to feel more confident in your story. It's helpful to ask of every scene: What is it in the middle of? Does it begin at the start of a conversation, or in the middle of one?

Offscreen scenes are as important as the on-screen scenes. Like in real life. If a person has been in an argument or near-accident just before arriving to a business meeting, that meeting will go differently than if they've just received a proposal of marriage. Or a cancer diagnosis.

Objectives

An objective should engage other characters, imply obstacles, and be something that the actor can commit to. You may find the coolest idea in the world for an objective, but if the actor doesn't connect to it, they should make a choice they have confidence in. In your preparation, come up with as many candidates for each character's objective as you can think of. It's fine to prefer one of them, but consider others, so you won't panic if yours doesn't work or the actor's idea is different.

If you're not sure what a character's objective is, don't anguish over it. If you don't have good ideas, jot down three bad ideas—quickly—to get you started. *Technique of three possible!* If you are so sure you know what the objective is that you can't think of any others, then at least make a note of what the opposite to your idea might be. Don't let your brain get ossified.

The rule for objectives is: one per scene per character, unless it's a scene with three or more people in it, in which case each character may have a different objective for each of the other characters.

Here are some useful ways to go about choosing objectives.

1) Look at the facts, and then ask, "What might a person want in that situation?" Make a list. Don't confine yourself to what the character would want, or even to what a rational person would want. Do include what *you* would want under the circumstances.
2) Look at behavior. Give more weight to what the character *does* than to what he says he is doing.
3) Look at the things she talks about, that is, her imagery. This will give us some clues as to the concerns of the character's subconscious, the things she wants but may not know she wants.
4) Look at what happens in the scene, how things end up. Is it possible that the character wanted that to happen? Or, that they wanted to prevent it?

5) Look at all the things people want out of life: love, freedom, power, control, adventure, comfort, security, family, sex, money, respect, honor. We all want everything, right? But there are certain things that we will sacrifice other things for. What is important to the character? What is the thing she will sacrifice for? What does she make the greatest effort to avoid? What interests her?

6) Translate judgments into verbs. Instead of saying, "He's a mean person," ask whether perhaps he is "taking out his frustrations," or, "picking a fight."

7) If nothing at all comes to you, consider these:

- I want you to laugh.
- I want you to cry.
- I want you to take care of me and put your arms around me.
- I want you to feel sorry for me.
- I want you to submit to my will.

8) If you are still feeling blank, ask yourself, "Does he want the other character to feel good? Or does he want her to feel bad?"

9) A character's through-line or primary objective is not always with the other person in the scene. The primary engagement may be with an image or memory, another person who is not present, or even an object. For instance, Cypher may be sustained during this scene by the taste of that steak dinner.

10) When characters say explicitly what they want in the dialogue, keep looking. People who make a point of declaring their motivations may be "protesting too much." Look for the issue or ambivalence that may lie behind their protestations.

It's important to remember that objectives don't have to be realistic. People don't always know what they want; what they want is not necessarily something they can have; and they don't always do the right thing to get it. Following are a quick list of possible objectives for the characters, including some opposites:

Examples of possible objective/need for Neo:

- He wants to belong, to be accepted by the crew;
- He wants to prove himself worthy of the trust that's been put in him;
- He has been told he might be The One: He wants to test the others, to see whether he is, in fact, superior to them.

Examples of possible objective/need for Morpheus:

- To test (or challenge) Neo;
- To support and encourage Neo;
- To maintain his authority over his crew.

Examples of possible objective/need for Trinity:

- To test her feelings for Neo: Is he worthy?
- To get permission from Morpheus to tell Neo the secret of what the Oracle told her;
- To push Neo away, in order to see if he will fight for her;
- To push Neo away, in order to protect her own autonomy.

Examples of possible objective/need for Cypher:

- To make Trinity wish she'd been nicer to him;
- To make Morpheus and the crew finally realize how powerful and important he is;
- To win against Neo, who supplanted him in the crew's hierarchy.

What I want you to do is *not* try to figure out intellectually which one of these choices is right (or why they are all wrong). None of them is right unless it works and none is wrong unless it doesn't work. It's likely that one of them appeals to you more than the others, and that's fine, that's a good thing. Just don't stop with what you are already sure of. I am proposing that you have *a plan, a back-up plan, and a back-up for your back-up*. You need to make the same investment in your back-up plans as you do in your favorite plan—otherwise they're useless for back up.

What's At Stake? aka Issues

Another approach to the through-line objective is to ask, *what's at stake?*

What is at stake for Cypher? The risk that his plot will be discovered and thwarted by Morpheus? The risk that Agent Smith has lied to him and once he's back in the Matrix, he'll remember his life on the Nebuchadnezzar with longing, and regret his choice to betray his friends? The risk that, if the crew is all dead, there will be no one to appreciate that he was the one who was powerful enough to destroy Zion?

For Morpheus and Trinity, who are deeply invested in protecting Zion and its promise of liberation, at stake is the possible loss of all they had ever hoped for—like it is for all those in our own imperfect world who stand up for democracy and justice against autocratic regimes.

Let's also ask what's at stake *personally* for Morpheus? In an earlier scene, Cypher told Neo that there had been five previous kids that Morpheus thought were The One, who were killed by agents. Cypher is not a consistent truth-teller, but in the interest of raising the stakes, let's say his statement about the five previous candidates is accurate. That would mean that there's a lot at stake for Morpheus. If he is wrong once more, will he continue to search? Or might a sixth failure do him in? On what information or intuition does he base his hunches of who might or might not be The One? What were the prophecies of the Oracle regarding the previous five?

What's at stake *personally* for Trinity? Perhaps her autonomy. She has been Morpheus's right hand for a long time: If Neo is revealed by the Oracle to be The One, will she lose her place in the crew hierarchy? If Neo is revealed to be The One, will she be limited—or liberated—by her love for him?

The "what's at stake" could just as well be framed as *issues*. You could say Trinity has an issue with the pull of autonomy versus the pull of love. Cypher's issue is the intrusion of Neo into his world.

For Morpheus, it's like a spiritual crisis—at issue is his faith in the predictions of Zion.

Active Verbs

I don't think directors should decide ahead of time exactly which verb should be played on each line. But I like an exercise I've used in classes—coming up with a "right" choice, a "wrong" choice, and an intriguing choice. It can call our attention to off-kilter ideas that may be revelatory or entertaining.

After Neo says, "I have these memories, but . . . none of them really happened," he turns to Trinity and asks, "What does that mean?" Let's try my right/wrong/intriguing verb exercise on his line, "What does that mean?"

Perhaps your first thought is to say that when he asks, "What does that mean?" he wants information. Sorry, I'm not going to be satisfied with that. More helpful than saying Neo "wants information" might be proposing that his objective is *to find out*. What specifically does he need to find out? Perhaps:

1) *To find out* what his strange feelings mean; or,
2) *To find out* what she feels.

Let's pursue each of these two different ideas for Neo's *objective*.

If you're inclined to say that Neo wants to "find out what his strange feelings mean," then perhaps he is *demanding* an answer from Trinity, or maybe, *challenging* her. Or—an *opposite*—might he be *begging* her to help him understand?

Deconstructing the proposal that he wants "to find out what she feels" could take us down an intriguing path, perhaps to an idea that his *deeper need* is *to make connection* with her or *get closer* to her.

Subtext

Subtext can function as a way to flesh out an idea for a verb. If Neo's verb toward Trinity is *to demand*, then his subtext might be, "You know more about any of this than I do. Don't keep me in the dark! Bring me into the loop!" If it's *to challenge*, his subtext might be, "Do you really know as much as you act like you do?" If it's *to beg*, the subtext might be, "My mind is swirling, tumbling; I'm descending into chaos. I can't tell anymore what's real! *Won't you please help me?*"

If his intention springs from the deeper need of wanting *to make connection and get closer* with her, his subtext might be, "You've brought me this far, and it's starting to make sense, it's starting to feel real, but now I want to come further into your world. I want to know what you know. I feel more real when I'm with you. I want to know everything you know and feel everything you feel."

Obstacle

If Neo's deep need is to be closer to Trinity, or perhaps to be worthy of her, there are obstacles to him expressing that need openly:

- The presence of the other two, Morpheus and Cypher, in the car;
- A certainty on his part that she is out of his league;
- His youth! In the "science behind the science fiction" of this film, he's only very recently become a human being. Perhaps he's still too green to recognize in himself adult feelings like desire.

Adjustments

What if Morpheus chose Neo because Neo reminds him of a particular kid—one of the five that he previously tapped to be The One—perhaps one whose death he was forced to personally witness?

Such an adjustment could give Morpheus the drive to save Neo at all costs—but also an internal *obstacle*—a fear that perhaps his judgment of Neo's capabilities might be clouded by emotion.

What if Trinity and Cypher had sex—once?

An adjustment does not have to be agreed to by both actors. The adjustment can be private; it can be a *secret*. The actor playing

Cypher could make the choice that Trinity has had sex with him—once—and ever since pretended it never happened.

The actor playing Trinity could make the choice that it never did happen, that their relationship has always been no more than what is required for the mission, perhaps with moments of brother-sister type camaraderie and bickering, but definitely nothing romantic. The reason this contradiction in their choices can work is that in real life people often remember the same event very differently! They attach different significance to it—in other words, have different adjustments. This is a good reason for directors to confer with each actor separately.

In addition to "as ifs" that adjust the history of a relationship, an "as if" can be a little shift in perception, for instance, an adjustment by Cypher that every word spoken by Morpheus is like fingernails on a blackboard or like a knife through his eardrum.

Beats

The term "beats" can have more than one meaning. It can mean pauses, changes in mood, or something to do with the musicality and pacing of the scene. There's a story that may or may not be true, that came into actor-speak when one of the great directors from the Moscow Art Theatre came to New York in the 1920s to deliver a series of lectures. An eager young actor asked, "How do you work on a scene?" To which the maestro replied, "Beet by beet"—meaning, in his heavily accented English, "bit by bit." Soon, the story goes, the actor community adopted the expression, "working with beats." They're really the *bits*, the little sections of a scene. Sometimes they're called "units." Breaking down beats provides manageable subsections for working in rehearsal, and helps with blocking, because the rule of thumb is that beat changes are brought to life via physical activity and movement.

Let's break the *Matrix* scene into *beats*. Actually, looking at beats—or sections—is so very useful for script analysis that I often do this step much earlier in my script analysis process. I do a first pass as simply as I can—making a note of when the subject changes and who brings up the new topic, then giving the beat a title. In this preliminary exercise, I'm not making deep decisions on where the emotional shifts take place. It's a quick sketch of what topics the scene concerns itself with; it helps me get a handle on the scene. Usually there are three beats in a scene. In our *Matrix* scene:

Beat One starts at the top of the scene and goes through Trinity's line, "That the Matrix cannot tell you who you are." The subject is the Matrix itself and Neo's response to revisiting it. Or you could give the beat this title: "Neo re-encounters the Matrix for the first time since his rescue and unplugging." This topic may actually have started *before* the top of the scene, so we can't be certain who brings it up. Perhaps it's Morpheus who brings it up when he speaks the first line, "Almost unbelievable, isn't it?" Or perhaps it's the look on Neo's face, described in the stage direction, which reveals this topic.

Beat Two starts with Neo's line, "But an Oracle can," and goes to Morpheus's line, "We're here. Neo, come with me." The subject is the Oracle. Neo brings it up. You could title it, "Neo has questions about the Oracle." For now at least, I'm only giving simple-minded titles, with as little interpretational slant as possible. Later we'll take a stab at uncovering the emotional cause-and-effect between the beats.

Beat Three is only one line, Cypher's "Here we go again, eh, Trin?" Perhaps we could title it "Cypher and Trinity's emotional history." I need to mention here that this line does not appear in the finished film; perhaps it was deleted in the edit. If we look at the scene without Cypher's line, we might say there are only two beats. Or we might say that Beat Three is Morpheus's last line, "We're here. Neo, come with me."

Blocking

Blocking options in our *Matrix* scene are limited. Four people in a car. But I shouldn't say "limited" like it's a negative. There are opportunities for movement—they're subtle, that's all. The stage directions offer suggestions—for instance, indications of where Neo is looking: out the car window, then at Trinity, back to the window, and again to her. I would not insist that the actor follow these indications rigidly. Rather, I'd note a question: Could his repeated glances to her be expressions of their growing relationship and dependence on each other?

After Neo's line to Trinity, "What did she tell you?" Trinity replies, "She told me . . ." Followed by this dramatic stage direction: "She looks at him and suddenly she is unable to speak or even breathe."

Trinity's line, "She told me . . ." is automatically a mysterious line, because of the ellipsis—she cuts herself off. What was she going to say? In a later scene in the movie, she discloses to Neo what the Oracle told her. Is she tempted to reveal that intense information in this scene? Is she tempted to blow him off with a lie? Is it possible that it's not her own impulse that keeps her from divulging the information, but the presence of Morpheus in the car? (Here's a big question I have: Back when Trinity met with the Oracle, did she share with Morpheus what the Oracle told her?)

Scene-Making

Such questions allow us to surrender and luxuriate in layers of subtext—deeper and deeper levels of connection that bring these characters and their relationships to life in our imaginations with more and more complexity and higher and higher stakes.

Now let's return to the director's primary role—shooting the filmable events—which we could call elements of *scene-making* or *scene-shaping*. Trinity's line, "She told me . . ." together with the follow-up stage direction, "She looks at him and suddenly she is unable to speak or even breathe," is an *event*. In the film, it is made into a *filmable moment* with simple, subtle blocking: Trinity quietly turns her face away from Neo and toward her car window. If you want to ask me whether this inspired choice arose from the initiative of Carrie-Anne Moss or from direction from the filmmakers—I don't know. It could have come from either, or from the three of them in collaboration.

Make Events Happen With the Blocking

For another example of the intersection of blocking and emotional event, I'm going to continue reverse-engineering from the finished film. During the first half of the scene, Morpheus turns slightly toward Neo—twice. There's no stage direction in the script describing these movements, so I'll take this opportunity to remind you that another good reason not to follow stage directions rigidly is that you might miss an occasion for revelatory physical activities.

Morpheus's second turn toward Neo occurs after Neo's line, "Obviously." What I'm going to do now is adjust my first outline of the beats of the scene. We're looking for a way to understand how Beat One triggers Beat Two. What if Beat One goes longer than I had it earlier? Say, up through Neo's line, "Obviously." Then Morpheus's second glance would form a kind of *punctuation* to Beat One. Up until now, Morpheus has been Neo's teacher and mentor. Perhaps the event of the first beat was a test of how well Neo has absorbed the lesson that the Matrix is a Construct. With this very slight glance, is Morpheus acknowledging that Neo has passed the test?

In this formulation, Beat Two goes like this: *NEO: Did you go to her? TRINITY: Yes. NEO: What did she tell you? TRINITY: She told me . . . (She turns away.) NEO: What?* We might now call Beat Two "an interrogation," or we could title it, "Neo invades Trinity's emotional space." He presses her to share with him. Had she given him the answer he seeks, that would have changed everything, wouldn't it?

Instead, she stops herself, the car arrives at its destination, and Morpheus interrupts their intimacy by calling them back to work: "We're here. Neo, come with me."

Uncovering the beat changes—for instance the tiny emotional event of Beat One that catapults us into Beat Two—can bring us closer to turning something that could have been an ordinary exposition or "connector" scene, into a dramatic scene.

Get Ideas for Pacing

Many filmmakers think that the pacing of a film can be left for the edit. But let's consider pacing earlier, even now, in script analysis, in order to prepare ourselves to generate creative pacing in rehearsal and on the set.

Do you want to imagine the pacing of Beat One in our *Matrix* scene as slower than the pacing of Beat Two? Maybe. Maybe in Beat One, Neo works through his new understandings slowly, as if he is a patient awakening from anesthesia after surgery. Beat Two might carry more urgency, as he insists on pressuring Trinity for answers, for further intimacy. The lines of Beat Two might tumble over each other, interrupting and even almost overlapping.

Or perhaps the scene works best with a constant pulsing, driving, intense—*fast*—delivery, throughout. This is how the scene seems to have been directed—it works great. It's a directorial choice.

Plot Event, Domestic Event, and Emotional Event

The plot event is a literal synopsis of plot: Neo is chauffeured to his meeting with the Oracle. The *domestic event*—what is apparently happening—is also simple, but makes a shift to a framing that is accessible as an ordinary human activity. I propose that the domestic event in our *Matrix* scene is *traveling to an important destination.*

You see, I feel safe saying that few, if any, of us has ever met with an Oracle—but most, if not all, of us have had the experience of travel to an important destination. The domestic event centers the scene in a recognizably human texture of life.

The *emotional event* goes deeper into speculation about how lives are changed and charged emotionally by interactions among the characters. Let's take Beat Two, which could be described as, "Neo pressures Trinity for answers"—or, "Neo insists on further intimacy from Trinity." "Pressing Trinity for answers" is the domestic event of that beat; "pressing her for further intimacy" is the emotional event.

Here are some options for the emotional event of the whole scene:

- Neo achieves approval and validation from Morpheus.
- Neo takes a step toward further intimacy with Trinity.
- Neo unwittingly scores one more win over Cypher.

Perhaps all of these things happen! As short as it is, it's a layered scene.

Cypher: One Last Mysterious Line

Let's take a look at the last line of the scene, Cypher's to Trinity: "Here we go again, eh, Trin?" Because this line was not in the released film, it's fun to look at it for purposes of instruction—readers won't already have a line reading in mind for it, so it's a genuinely *mysterious line*. Thoughts for its possible subtext:

1) He is calling upon their shared history as companions in the magnificent experiment of Zion and making one last attempt to connect with her.

2) Out of his need to justify his decision to destroy Morpheus, Cypher is reminding Trinity of Morpheus's previous failures. I have known people like this—in my own life as well as in my observation of certain public figures—who, because they themselves have never experienced an unselfish impulse,

cannot believe that anyone who professes an altruistic motivation could possibly be genuine. Such deprived individuals are often compelled by an irrational drive to destroy anyone who lays claim to altruistic motivation—in their minds, they believe they are exposing hypocrisy.

3) This is the last time he will ever see Trinity. The subtext of his line, "Here we go again, eh, Trin?" might be an inarticulate, uniquely awkward expression of "Good-bye"—to the only person for whom he has ever felt love.

Finally: The Shape of the Relationships

A scene can have an emotional *shape*. Let's organize our ideas by making a shorthand emotional sketch of the relationships, based on these ideas for what the scene is about:

1) It's a love scene;
2) It's a romantic triangle;
3) It's a scene about being a newbie in an already tightly-knit crew;
4) It's a scene about chosen family;
5) It's a moment when a teacher acknowledges that he has taught his student all he can, and sends him into the world.

In idea 1, the *shape* of the scene is an emotional bubble inhabited by two: Neo and Trinity. This magic bubble of growing intimacy keeps the rest of the world out.

For idea 2, the emotional center includes three: Neo, Trinity, and Cypher, locked in jealous competition.

In idea 3, Morpheus, Trinity, and Cypher, who have been crewmembers together for a long time, are in the bubble—with Neo on the outside, hoping to be accepted.

For idea 4, we notice that Morpheus and Cypher are in the front seat, like parents, with Trinity and Neo—the children—in the back.

For idea 5, the emotional center is the bubble between Morpheus and Neo.

Always, always, we are keeping our directorial eye on *emotional event*. Thus, for instance, if we like idea 3, the emotional event might be that Neo, as the newbie in an already battle-tested crew, *gains acceptance*. Or it might be the opposite—that the others become more worried about him than they were before.

About idea 1: Really, if we're being honest, every scene is a love scene. What I love about the love story of Neo and Trinity is its honesty: The steps they take toward each other are halting, awkward, like in real life. How about this idea: Up until now, Trinity has been pursuing Neo. In this scene, he opens up to her by sharing memories and feelings, and prodding her for personal information. He is pushing for more closeness. The *emotional event* is that they do become closer—*almost*. They are prevented from opening up fully to each other by—what? Trinity's *internal obstacle* of resistance to revealing her feelings to him? Or the *external obstacle* of Morpheus breaking in to remind them there is work to be done?

Idea 2, "romantic triangle," proposes that, in Cypher's mind at least, he and Trinity are a failed love story. And that even though he's agreed to and set in motion the plot with Agent Smith, he could change his mind! Every character has free will. Perhaps he is—still—waiting for some signal from Trinity that would make him feel she cares enough about him that he might, even at the last moment, subvert and scuttle the scheme. Perhaps the reason he does not change his ruinous course is that he's forced to overhear, from the front seat, the growing intimacy of Neo and Trinity. This idea proposes that the emotional event of the scene is the hardening of Cypher's resolve to carry out the betrayal, out of his hurt that Trinity has abandoned and betrayed him.

Idea 4 centers Morpheus, who, as the patriarch, bears responsibility for the welfare and happiness of the family members he has chosen and committed to. He loves all his children, but he has favorites—who are right now sitting in the backseat. He listens to their conversation (which they are allowing him to overhear) with a complicated array of hopes and fears.

Idea 5 centers Morpheus and the special relationship he has as mentor to Neo.

Micro and Macro

I have been making an extremely granular investigation of this small scene, opening up as many mysterious lines as I possibly can. When I do this, I get ideas for the whole script. Typically, I go back and forth from micro to macro.

In the whole film, who is the main character? Neo. In this scene, who is the main character? Neo? Probably. Unless we want to say Morpheus. There can be scenes in which the main character is other than the main character of the whole film.

In the whole film, which is the central relationship? My inclination is to say Neo and Trinity, but I would never argue if you want to say that it's Neo and Morpheus.

An exercise I find very useful is to imagine what the film would be if it was the exact same story, but told with one of the other characters as the main character. It's not that big a shift to imagine Trinity as the main character. A few scenes spotlighting Neo would be left out. Other scenes that focus on Trinity—which in this script are off-camera scenes—would be added. For instance, scenes depicting her unique, special relationship with Morpheus.

It's absolutely possible to imagine Morpheus as the main character. It would be the story of an intellectual and spiritual giant with a quest to find a worthy successor. A bit like imagining *Star Wars (Episode IV)* as a story that centers Obi-Wan Kenobi rather than Luke Skywalker.

I can even do this exercise with Cypher. It would be a film with a whole different tone—a dark, disturbing movie with an antihero at its center. In this scenario, our main character (Cypher) has been triggered by the arrival of the new golden child, Neo. Cypher chooses his destructive path after witnessing the wreck of his dream that Trinity might love him and being forced to acknowledge his banishment from the golden circle of Morpheus's fatherly attention. Neo is a powerful name for a main character—the new creature, the one who is born. But if the story is about an anti-hero, Cypher (zero) is a brilliant name, too.

CHAPTER EIGHT

Casting

Damage-control casting—focusing your every effort on *not making a mistake*—is foolish. Casting is truly, genuinely, about *risk*. I think some directors hope to cast actors who will make them feel that they are not taking a risk. But risk-averse casting makes no sense. Because—it doesn't exist. You *are* taking a risk. Always. It's scary, but finally safer, to face the fact—yes, it's all a risk. You are going to go through the fire together. You are going to learn from each other.

Casting "Name" Actors

Let's begin this chapter with the very real issue of casting the "name" actors that you may have been told you need in order to get financing. Producers often present the filmmaker with a list of "bankable" actors from which the director is allowed to make her own wish-list for the lead role. The actor is then presented with a pay-or-play offer. In the best-case scenario, this offer is made subject to a meeting between the actor and director. Sometimes, however, the actor's agents insist that it be a straight offer, with no contingency for a meeting before the decisions are made. The director may be allowed the opportunity to send an email to the star, in hopes of luring him into the project with lofty language about goals and aspirations, but the truth is that the only issue the agents and the financial people consider worth negotiating is money.

This is, in my view, one of the things wrong with the entertainment industry—and yet it happens all the time. Conventional wisdom maintains that it's perfectly okay for the director and the actors to meet each other for the first time on the first day of shooting.

I could not disagree more. It's absurd to imagine that any project can prosper if the director and the actors speak for the first time on the day of shooting. The agents who make this demand think they are protecting their clients, but how can it possibly serve the actor to meet his director just before the camera rolls? It's preposterous. And deadly to the project—how can one produce something even remotely entertaining, never mind of artistic worth, if the actors and director don't ever meet and connect?

A director should meet the lead actors before the final casting decisions are made—and continue meeting after the contracts are signed. They should form a *relationship*. The purpose of meeting early and often is to forge a creative bond so you can collaborate on making the best movie possible.

If you do get a chance to meet with an actor you are hoping will take the lead role in your film, don't squander that opportunity by trying to *sell* the actor on working with you. Instead, use the time to *engage* with the actor and build a relationship. Check your own intention! Are you *selling*? Or are you *engaging*? I have more suggestions about how to approach these meetings in my book, *The Film Director's Intuition,* but for now I will say this: When the producers give you the list of actors that the financiers will accept for the role, tell them you want them to make an offer *subject to a meeting*. Sure, they may refuse. They may tell you it can't be done. Ask for it anyway. If you ask, you might not get it—but if you don't ask, you definitely won't get it. So—*ask*!

And when you have this meeting, don't think of it as a shot at bagging a famous actor for your project—as if they're a deer you are stalking. That's so negative! Another way to be negative is to think of the meeting in terms of its potential to make you feel judged and rejected. Don't project negativity. Approach the opportunity with open arms—a chance to grow, to connect, with a fellow artist.

Sometimes a first-time director is desperate to get a star to commit to his film because he's been told he won't get financing otherwise. And then—once the star has accepted, the director becomes weirdly terrified—bizarrely convinced that the star will refuse direction or criticize the script or otherwise make the director's life miserable.

You should know, first of all, that such negative thinking can all too easily become a self-fulfilling prophecy. Movie stars have high energy, higher energy than most people, and lots more experience than you do. They can become impatient with a director who seems unprepared—you may need to prove yourself. Don't take it personally. Borrow energy from them instead of fearing their power.

If you feel so overcome with worry that you don't think you'll be able to treat the star like a colleague, like an artist, and like a human being—then adjust your ambitions, scale down your budget, and cast unknowns around whom you feel relaxed. There are actors out there who are talented, disciplined, exciting, but not well-known—yet. Maybe you'll discover a new star and the two of you will make each other famous.

Casting Directors

You won't be able to get to "name" actors without a good casting director. But whether or not you are casting stars, a casting director is worth the money. They know a lot of actors and have creative ideas.

If you can't afford a casting director, you should cast friends. You could literally cast your own friends, even if they haven't acted before, like Kevin Smith for *Clerks* or Wes Anderson for *Bottle Rocket*. Challenge yourself to keep meeting actors and making friends with them. You won't ever be good at casting unless you are genuinely interested in actors. Go to film festivals, plays, acting classes—look for newcomers, talk to them, get to know them. Invite them to audition for you and then stay in touch—if they aren't right for this project, they might be perfect for the next one.

If you hire a casting director (CD), be sure you are on the same wavelength. Have frank, open discussions about your tastes, your concerns, and your ideas about the characters. View the CD's past work. Be sure she has already read the script and is excited about the project. Ask her questions. Listen to her answers—and her questions.

Even if your lead roles are cast without auditions, you will still need to cast supporting roles. Make sure to discuss how much time the CD is planning for each actor to meet and read with you. Often, a session of ten or fifteen minutes per actor has been scheduled. I think you should ask for more. The casting director will have pre-read the actors she thinks you might be interested in, so it's likely that these are good candidates. For the actor you cast, this might be the only get-acquainted time, the only rehearsal you get. That's why I think it matters to ask for enough time to engage with each one. Discuss this frankly with the casting director—if you feel you want twenty or thirty minutes per actor, ask for it. Tell the CD why you think you can use that extra time productively. Again, she may say it's not possible, but—remember, if you ask, you might not get it, but if you don't ask, you definitely won't.

Casting From Auditions: Guidelines

First, let me ask you: what do you look for in casting sessions? Are you making the mistake of looking for the performance that "nails it"—condemning yourself to sit in a stuffy office or pore over self-tapes until your eyes glaze over—waiting for that magical moment when an actor knocks you out and makes you jump up and down with certainty that this is *the one*!? I just spent a whole chapter discussing *The Matrix*, a film that many people think is about finding

The One. But here's what I really believe: that the radical, revelatory message of *The Matrix* is that *anyone* can be The One—even someone as ordinary, unskilled, and bungling as Thomas Anderson. What makes Thomas Anderson *Neo*—The One—is risk. It's all about taking that leap. Neo finally takes that leap. But, even more importantly, Morpheus and Trinity take the risk of investing their trust in him. That's what I think casting is about: engaging, trusting.

Opposite to the risk-taking approach to casting is the "dream lover" fantasy—but the "dream lover" approach to casting can lead to impulsive decisions that are not in the filmmaker's best interest—kind of like getting married in Vegas after a one-night stand.

So how can you be active in the auditioning process? How can you train yourself to trust and risk? If you're not supposed to look for the performance that nails it, if you're not supposed to look for The One, what should you look for?

Here's a list of areas, principles maybe, that are important to casting:

1) The actor's ability. Is he a good listener? Is he present in the moment? Are his emotions transparent? When you look in his eyes, is there somebody home? Is his voice and body language expressive? Does his work convey a *sense of intention?* Does he make bold, specific, insightful choices? Is he alert to the opposite of what is obvious? Does his work have range and variety?

2) Whether she is right for the part. There may be physical requirements for the role. Be clear about this with the casting director, so you don't waste your time and the actors' time. But I do encourage you to think twice—counterintuitive casting (aka *casting against type*) can be very effective. Charlize Theron, one of the most beautiful, poised women in the modern world, played unbeautiful, socially awkward serial killer Aileen Wuornos in *Monster*, directed by Patty

Jenkins. If you haven't already, please watch Robin Williams in *One Hour Photo* (directed by Mark Romanek), Pierce Brosnan in *The Matador* (Richard Shepard), and Nicolas Cage in *The Weather Man* (Gore Verbinski). These filmmakers saw and trusted something deep and raw and free of vanity in the souls of their lead actors.

3) Whether you can work well together. You need actors who can respond to direction from you. By this I do not mean actors who never question your ideas and never counter them with ideas of their own—I mean the opposite. I mean that you spark each other! That you challenge each other's creativity, that when you are in each other's company you get new ideas. That you enjoy performing for each other.

4) I invite you to care about an actor's artistic sensibility: their taste, instincts, sense of humor, sense of proportion. And their heart. By which I mean fearlessness, trust, commitment, emotional and physical stamina—and a love of performing. There are actors who put the work ahead of their egos, who are truly open—open to their feelings, understandings and impulses, open to the material—open to surprises. Open to the contradictions and complexities of the character, open to the actors they work with, open to fresh insights, and willing to move heaven and earth to find a truthful way to make direction work. These are the ones I want you to search for and work with.

5) Make casting the *relationships* a priority over casting the roles. Making the shift to casting relationships instead of individual roles will help your career more than you can imagine.

6) The best way to know an actor's abilities, whether he is right for the part, and whether you work well together is to have worked with him before. Whenever you cast someone you

> haven't worked with before, you are casting with your fingers crossed. Many great directors—Fellini, Bergman, Cassavetes, Scorsese, Wes Anderson, David Lynch, the Coen Brothers, Jane Campion, Greta Gerwig—work with the same actors over and over. It's a brilliant shortcut to good acting. There is trust, because a director learns how to work with these actors, knows what she can get, what pushes their buttons, where they can go, and when they need help.

And here's something you may not know—actors are terrified of being miscast. There can be a fine line between a risky role that offers a thrilling stretch for the actor, and a role that he's just not right for, and in which he is likely to look inept or even ridiculous. He may spend the whole shoot nursing a secret worry about when the director is going to realize her mistake in casting him. If the director has worked with him before, that worry evaporates, because—let's face it, making a movie together is a kind of trial by fire for a relationship. If the director and the actor have gotten through that and still want to work together again, *that* is a liberating validation for them both.

Along the way, you may find your muse, your alter ego—like Scorsese found De Niro, Nicole Holofcener found Catherine Keener, and Steve McQueen found Michael Fassbender. Scorsese says of De Niro that, "I just found that he was able to go into the underworld of the mind and the heart and soul . . . so we were both like an expeditionary force into the underworld."

It's okay to start your career without your cadre of actor-collaborators in place, but why not make building your ensemble your goal? Stop thinking of yourself as a shopper in a supermarket or a hunter in a deer blind. I meet so many directors who have been ordered by the producers and financiers to set their sights on a certain actor and score the hit. Don't succumb to that cynical approach. Rather than think of casting as hunting, think of it as creating new family.

7) Give each actor your full attention. Instead of telling them what you want, find out what makes each one tick. Instead of looking for the right actor for the role, *try figuring out what would be the right role for each actor*. Reframing your approach like this will open your heart and lift your burdens. It will help you put out energy, and putting out energy will give you more energy.

Casting From Auditions: Procedure

Auditioning and performing are two separate skills. There are good actors who don't audition well—you don't want to miss these gems. Don't forget that for the actors you cast, the casting session is your first rehearsal—and may end up being your only rehearsal. So make your casting sessions feel more like work sessions.

Confer with your casting director to pick scenes (also called "sides") to send the actors, so they can prepare for the audition. SAG-AFTRA requires that sides be made available to actors a certain length of time ahead of their audition appointments. Even if you are shooting a non-union project, it's good to get in practice abiding by Guild rules. Scenes with a lot of physical action may not be the most helpful choice, but you want to pick scenes that go somewhere, that have transitions. The CD will have ideas. If the role has no meaty audition scenes, you might choose a scene from another script, even a play, with a character who reminds you of the one you are casting.

Casting sessions should include time for the actors to read the scene opposite a "reader," as well as time for a short conversation. Some actors like to converse first, because it helps them relax—other actors hate that and just want to get started performing the scene they have prepared. It really doesn't matter which comes first, so tell them at the get-go that you would like to do both and let them make the choice of whether they want to read first or chat first.

I have a plan of attack for casting sessions. People who cast intuitively, and who are good at it, may do these things without realizing they are taking these steps. If you've been casting using your intuition and you feel like it works, then you should keep doing that. You are allowed to cast an actor just because you like them. But in case you've been doing that with unsatisfactory results, here's a checklist.

Let the actor read before you give any direction.

Before the actor starts to read, ask if she has any questions. She might ask, for instance, "How angry do you want this?" Your instinct will be to answer her—because you are a nice person and you want to be helpful—but I suggest that you take a deep breath and give yourself permission *not* to supply the answer. Instead say, "That's a great question, I promise to address it after you do your first reading, and I promise to give you another shot. But first I would love to see what you have brought in."

If the actor balks at reading without getting direction from you and wants you to tell her before she reads the role what the character is like, or how you see the role, that probably means that she is accustomed to auditions in which she is expected to "nail it" on one reading, and she doesn't want to waste her shot without knowing what is expected of her. So let her know, before she does her first reading, that after the first time, you will give her direction and she will have the chance to read the scene again.

Announce ahead of time that you're going to do this—otherwise, when you offer a direction after her initial read, she might assume that what she did first was wrong and that what you are asking now is right. Rather than accidentally conveying the idea that there's a "right" way to play the role, make a point of conveying this idea: "You're going to have more than one chance—I plan to work with you. I want to see what you've come up with on your own, because I am interested in your ideas and your responses to the material." You don't have to use those exact words, of course—what I'm suggesting for you is intention: *to connect, to engage, to encourage, to give permission.* To communicate to the actor that what you're looking for is subtext—not line readings.

I think it's important to see the actor's choices before they have been given direction, in order to get a glimpse into their intelligence and creativity—and to get a sense of what they respond to in the text. Intelligence, creativity, and connection are what you are seeking, not a performance. Actors who are willing to take risks. The best thing that can happen in a casting session is that an actor surprises you. Casting director Mary Vernieu put it this way in an *IndieWire* interview: "A perfect performance in the room is not what we are looking for. We are looking for moments of brilliance, those flashes that show where it can go—an essence, something organic, that makes you know that once they have the role, they can go deep, access deep feelings, have layers. You're looking for a person who has more to offer than what they're showing."

Then, even if you hate what he did the first time, you should have him read it again, with some direction—because you said you would. Integrity matters.

Can they make adjustments? Can they play intentions and objectives?

When you give an adjustment after the first reading, honor your promise that you would respond to her questions. If she asked, "How angry do you want this?" then you might say, "Thanks for bringing up the anger issue with your question earlier. Let's try it this time that you are punishing him, because he's promised over and over not to do this anymore." You need to have made a note of how she played the role in the first reading, so you can be sure that what you ask for next is, in fact, different. So, if she was already *punishing* on her first read, then you might suggest, "Let's try it this time that you are *begging* him not to put himself in danger anymore."

The main reason for asking them to try a new adjustment is to see whether the actor's line readings are different than they were on the first reading. Even if you loved their first reading, if you give them a new adjustment, the line readings should come out different. If you ask the actor to do it a few different ways and they read it the same way every time, that's a red flag about their level of skill and flexibility.

Instead of informing them that, "This is how I see the character . . ." or even, "I want you to . . ." try using objectives. And the language of permission—for instance: "What if she wants reassurance from him?" Or adjustments, like, "Maybe you've already heard this excuse a hundred times." It's good to find out whether they respond to objectives and adjustments. If they don't, but you're still interested in them, put attention into finding a language in which to communicate, perhaps by asking them how they work or where they've studied.

You also want to find out whether they respond to your ideas. You need to keep in mind that the search for actors who respond to your ideas is not the same as the expectation that they will produce the exact performance you have pictured. An actor can be talented and skilled—and still make a different choice from what you expected. The term "on the same page"—ubiquitous in filmmaking circles—can easily be misused. An actor can be entirely in harmony with you in their understanding of the character and the story—and yet not execute the exact expressions and line readings you have set in your mind. I want you to detach from the line readings and expressions in the "movie of your mind" and really see and hear what the actor right in front of you is offering. You might find happy surprises.

Make sure the actor is a good listener.

I suggest that you have each auditioning actor read with someone who is not involved in the casting process. Usually, the casting director or an assistant will offer to be the "reader" for the actors.

I recommend bringing in an outside person—an actor—one who is not auditioning for any role, so you can see whether the auditioning actor is responsive to what she is getting from the person reading opposite her. For that you need a helper actor who is agile, energetic, and who is himself responsive—someone who is not assessing or judging the candidates, or trying to impress you with his skills, but who is giving himself to each auditioning actor. You can have one actor read all the roles; it's not important to have the right genders and ages. If you can pay this "helper" actor SAG-AFTRA minimum for a day's work, please do. If you can't, at least give them money for gas or carfare, buy them lunch, thank them profusely, and keep them in your address book. I suggest that you not promise them a role in the project, but here's something interesting that I've noticed: Sometimes after spending the whole day with an actor who has stepped up to the plate for your project, you start to feel excited about their potential and want to work with them again.

If you don't feel confident in your ability to tell whether or not an actor can listen, try this: Give direction not to the auditioning actor, but to the helper actor. If the "helper" actor plays his part differently and the auditioning actor still reads her lines exactly the same no matter what she's getting from the other person, then you have evidence that the auditioning actor has locked into a line reading, that she has low flexibility and poor listening skills. You want to cast actors who are *responsive,* whose performance changes when the actor opposite them changes. Find that out in casting.

More thoughts for casting sessions.

Casting sessions are opportunities for you to practice "making your case." If you have done your script analysis homework, you should have a reason for suggesting a new objective or adjustment. It will be good practice for you to communicate your ideas—with clarity and simplicity, but also with feeling and connection, incorporating verbs and metaphors that are vivid and apt.

Whenever you are "making your case," make eye contact with the actors.

Allowing the actor to improvise around the lines can unlock the actor's access to subconscious resources, and give you great information about what they have to offer to the role. You can ask actors to go off script in auditions—but there's a SAG-AFTRA rule against videotaping improvs during casting sessions. The rule was instituted years ago because it came to the Guild's attention that producers sometimes used the improvisations of actors to improve their script—without paying the actors for their contributions. If you have any questions about this, contact the Guild.

It's customary to call back the actors you are interested in a second time before you make final casting decisions. At callbacks, it's a good idea to pair them up with other auditioning actors, and observe different combinations to see how they respond to each other. You're casting a relationship, not two performances.

Sometimes, once a star is attached to the project, he may offer to read with other actors in line for other roles. This is a golden opportunity—grab it! Because your goal is to cast relationships. If the star does not offer, consider suggesting it.

Talk to them and with them, not at them.

For the part of the audition that is conversation, don't start by saying, "Tell me about yourself." For actors, that's a stress question. Many actors are shy. If you are hoping that conversation will open a connection with the actor, remember that the best way to encourage another person to be open and frank is to be open and frank yourself. Put energy out. Tell them what the project means to you.

Engage them as artists—that means, talk about the work. In the U.S., there are laws against asking for certain personal information in an employment interview. So avoid topics that are invasive on a personal level—but also refrain from superficial chitchat. Talking about the work gives you all the freedom you need to communicate on a deeply emotional level. Ask them their thoughts about the character. Tell them yours. Don't be afraid to disclose ideas that are deeply important to you.

If the actor comes up with ideas that intrigue you, ask them to read the scene again and infuse it with those ideas. The purpose is to get more information about what resources they bring to the character. You can go back and forth, from talking about ideas, to reading, and back to talking, then reading again.

Above all—*be a person*. Relax your eyes and shoulders, so you can really see and hear them. With every actor, whether or not you think there's a chance you'll cast them, *practice* making connection. Back in the days when I was auditioning, a director once asked me to tell him how I identified with the character. I didn't feel put on the spot—as an actor, I always had ideas and connections and loved the opportunity to share them. You may feel bad about not casting actors after you have asked them to put out that much of themselves, so it may surprise you to learn that actors feel less bad about not getting a role if they've had a chance to give their all.

Casting Non-Professional Actors

There are times when you may feel it's important to "street cast"—search for someone who has never acted, but has lived the life of the character. For the 2015 film *Tangerine*, filmmaker Sean Baker discovered his two leads, Kitana Kiki Rodriguez and Mya Taylor, at a Los Angeles LGBTQ Center two years before shooting, and convinced them to play transgender sex workers Sin-Dee and Alexandra. He then developed the script with them in mind.

The HBO series *Euphoria* found non-actors for the roles of transgender teen Jules (Hunter Schafer) and drug dealer Fezco (Angus Cloud). Casting director Mary Vernieu said, "These kids, they're young. They don't have to be doing anything. Like the characters, they're trying to figure out what they're doing."

Sometimes directors refer to non-professional actors they want to cast as "naturals." I think they mean individuals who are free, uninhibited, unafraid of what people think—who have something to offer. That is, they have an experience or understanding of life that fits them for the role. They open up when they are being looked at rather than shut down like most people who are not professional actors. They are spontaneously interested in other people so they instinctively *listen* to other actors.

I advise you to work with a casting director if you want to go this route. If you are thinking of street casting as a shortcut, a way to save time, you may be fooling yourself. I speak as one who has listened to tearful stories of directors who ended up spending most of the shoot consumed with worry about whether or not their non-professional actors were going to show up each day. You stand a better chance of creating an ensemble using non-professional actors if you have the chops and charisma of Sean Baker or Mary Vernieu.

Don't make non-professional actors audition in the usual sense. Meet them and work with them to see what they bring to the characters. Don't "test" their talents. Support them, love them, improvise with them. Have them improvise with other prospective cast members, so you can see if they are natural listeners and if they feel safe with the professional actors you have cast. As always, cast relationships.

Don't ask non-actors to act. In fact, make a point of asking them NOT to act. Look for people who have an unselfconscious connection to the characters. Let them know they are perfect for the role and they don't need to do any acting at all. Find people who continue behaving naturally when the camera is running.

It's not unusual for a name actor to request rewrites once they've been cast or even before they commit to taking the role. Rewriting may also be needed if you cast non-actors, in order to tailor the role to them, because it's so much better if you *don't ask a non-actor to act.*

Casting From Self-Submitted Tapes

More and more, casting sessions are not conducted in offices, but rather via actors' self-taping. I need to be frank with you that the approaches I've been suggesting work best when you are in the same room as the actors. Don't get me wrong—I think it's great that technology now allows an actor to audition even if he is prevented by logistics from getting to the casting office. When I am consulting on a project, if my director-client wants me to comment on taped auditions, I do my best. But I can't help feeling it's unfair to make actors be their own DP, makeup/hair, continuity, sound, lighting, editor, gaffer. Be honest: Do you really learn anything important about another person—I'm talking about real life now—if you just look at their selfies?

I think you should spend as much time as you can with actors. So if you can be in the same room as auditioning actors, do it. The director spends so much time with crew chiefs, designers, technicians—not to mention the "suits" (producers, executives, financiers)—shouldn't you spend as much time as you can with actors?

Pandemic and Connection (2020)

I have always pushed for directors to be in the same room as actors. I feel certain that *connection*—between the director and actor and between the actors playing opposite each other—is a cornerstone of casting decisions. I have always counselled my clients that if their casting director says, "Oh, you don't have to come in, I can send you tapes," a director is allowed to reply, "I'd like to be in the room as much as possible."

The COVID-19 pandemic has set in motion new protocols and, as of this writing, we don't know how long they'll be in effect, or even whether the coming vaccines will release us entirely from them. The problem of an actor being in Los Angeles when you are in Toronto is no longer the only reason you might not get to be in the same room with an actor you want to cast.

You need to cast your major roles with actors who are excited about the project and connected to your ideas—in other words, "on the same page"—and how can you know that unless you are face-to-face? Luckily, a one-on-one Zoom call offers an excellent chance for connection. Each of you can "pin" each other's screen. The person you're talking to then takes up almost the whole screen, and I have found that the resulting eye contact feels real, almost like you're across from each other in the same room. (If you find the tiny screen with your own image distracting, you can choose Hide Myself in your video settings.)

And there's an upside. Virtual meetings are easier to arrange than in-person meetings so maybe directors will actually get more time with the actors who are thinking of taking a role than has been possible in the past—time for asking questions, sharing connections, acknowledging challenges.

During pandemic protocols, self-tapes will become even more of a given. What if the director wants to follow up on an actor's self-tape, to work with actor and see if the actor can take adjustments? One idea is that the director can be the one to feed lines to the actor. Here's the key to making this work: Don't *perform* the role you are reading; don't *evaluate* the actor's performance while you are reading with him; instead—*receive*.

What about callbacks and relationship reads—where the goal is to see if two actors who might be working opposite each other make an organic connection? Zoom meetings with two or more actors and a director (plus maybe a casting director) can be a challenge. If you are all in "gallery mode," eyelines are unreliable. Perhaps the technology of "speaker mode" will eventually improve, but right now "speaker mode" is distracting.

I've been experimenting in group sessions with directors and actors in order to test the potential of Zoom, and I've discovered that Zoom sessions with more than two participants can be productive. The two actors who are participating in the callback or "relationship read" can be asked to pin each other. Then the director (and anyone else who is observing, such as a casting director) can go to Gallery Mode and even, to promote further intimacy between the actors, turn off their cameras.

I've been encouraging my students and clients to practice casting and rehearsing with Zoom. With practice, the director can detect the responsiveness of actors to each other—what producers call *chemistry*—the thing you are looking for in a relationship read. With practice, a director can develop her "compass," her ability to appreciate connection and detect emotional event. With practice, we can embrace every opportunity for connection.

CHAPTER NINE

Rehearsal

Rehearsal: Pros and Cons

Mike Nichols said, "A good day of rehearsal *means* there will be a bad day of rehearsal." It's like the difference between a hot one-night stand and getting married. When you take the risk of a committed relationship, there are going to be bad times as well as good. And that's okay, because it's rehearsal! There are no cameras so nothing that happens can be wrong. Rehearsal is *permission to fail—in action*!

Directors may resist rehearsal or say they don't believe in it. They fear something wonderful may happen the first time the actors say their lines to each other—and the camera won't be there to record it. It's a sad truth—those perfect first impulses are now gone. But that argument *against* rehearsal is equally an argument *for* it.

Like it or not, rehearsal happens. Even if there is no planned rehearsal, *take one* is rehearsal for *take two*. If the actors meet on set on the first day of shooting, rehearsal takes place *with the camera rolling*. Rehearsal with the camera rolling has worked great for directors like William Wyler, Stanley Kubrick, Penny Marshall, and David Fincher—all of whom have been known to shoot forty-plus takes of a scene. (Tom Hanks described Penny Marshall's approach, during the shooting of *Big*, as "filmmaking by attrition.")

I think what many directors mean when they say they don't believe in rehearsal is that they don't know how to rehearse. If you don't know how to rehearse, that's a legitimate reason not to do it. Many actors are reluctant to rehearse because they don't trust that the director will know how to run a rehearsal. They worry that the director will instead use rehearsal to micromanage the performances. They may even dread rehearsal out of a very real fear that the director will spend it judging them and concluding she should have cast someone else.

Most actors arrive on set prepared to direct themselves. If you are an untried director and you want to have substantive rehearsal, you'll need to convince the actors that rehearsal with you will be productive rather than painful. Good actors would rather be left alone than suffer pedestrian, unenlightened, intrusive direction.

The wild truth is that substantive rehearsal, if you're not used to it, may be a bit terrifying. Lovely, instinctual moments from the first encounters of the actors may collapse and need to be reconstructed in some new way—this means the scene may seem to get worse before it gets better. It's a law of creativity, or maybe a law of nature: *two steps forward, one step back.* Unless it's *one step forward, two steps back*—which sounds more frightening, but actually is also okay.

If you don't feel confident in the skills you need to lead a rehearsal or if rehearsal feels like a stressful chore, here's what to do: *Direct the scene, not the performances.* Know what the scene is about and its emotional event. Have ideas about beats, through-lines, and physical activities that can turn your ideas into behavior. Cast good actors and don't tell them how to play their parts; trust them and encourage their connection to each other. Find revelatory camera placement that carries the audience into the events of the story. Give actors room to invite the audience into the interior world of the characters. When you speak with actors, make eye contact with them. Make yourself available for questions—and *listen.* Then say thank you (with eye contact, so they know you mean it).

Director John Korty

I was hired for my first professional acting job by director John Korty. I remember my audition. I was thrilled to be meeting him. It was 1977; I had already seen and loved the two television movies he was known for: *The Autobiography of Miss Jane Pittman* and *Who Are the DeBolts? And Where Did They Get Nineteen Kids?* In the audition, he was relaxed and present—he smiled at me! It would be fair to say that I was smitten.

We were shooting a made-for-TV teen romance movie based on a Judy Blume novel. I had a supporting role as the older sister of the boyfriend, who was bringing his new girlfriend, played by Stephanie Zimbalist, to meet the family. It was shot on location in Lake Tahoe, and the evening I got there, John Korty called the cast together in someone's room to go over the scenes for the next day. He shared his ideas, asked if we had questions, welcomed the new arrivals—me and the actor playing my husband—and made us feel part of the ensemble. I was so excited I couldn't sleep—*my first job!* The next morning, I didn't wait for the second AD to fetch me; I showed up early to the cabin where we'd be shooting. There was a run-through for camera—I was to bring two cups of coffee to the porch, sit on the step next to Stephanie and exchange dialogue with her. Then, my director John Korty said to me, "Thank you! That was great. Let's run it through again. And—it's okay to talk a little slower."

When I recall his voice—on a morning that changed my life—I can't help but chuckle. My jitters must have caused me, on the first run-through, to race manically through my lines! But John Korty never made me feel embarrassed for my rookie mistake. Rather, he made me feel included—loved—by saying, "It's okay to go a little slower." *The language of permission!* After the next run-through, as I began relaxing into the scene, he said to me, "You can sit closer to her, because you want to welcome her into the family."

Later I learned more about moviemaking and realized he probably wanted to put a tighter frame on our two-shot. And yet, instead of asking for that result, he used terms that referred to the characters' relationship and connected me to my scene partner. He fluently incorporated an *intention* ("welcome her into the family") with simple *blocking* ("sit closer"). Furthermore, his direction aligned naturally and organically with *what the scene was about*. It was about *family*.

He *worked in steps*, rather than *frontloading* his direction all at once:

- Step one: He let me play the scene with no direction.
- Step two: He gave one note ("It's okay to go a little slower"), which I now take to have been his way of saying, *It's okay to be present, to be natural, to talk to Stephanie like a person—to make connection the first priority.*
- Step three: When we ran the scene again and he could see that I was relaxed and engaged with my scene partner, he gave the more substantive note: "You can sit closer to her, because you want to welcome her into the family."

John Korty's direction was relevant, seemingly effortless—and, for an actor, about as playable as direction can be. He was utterly natural and unselfconscious when conveying what I now think may have been a fairly complex idea for this small scene: He directed me to "welcome her into the family" even though I had a line—"I don't want my brother to be hurt"—conveying words of warning. Thus, the objective he suggested was an *opposite* to the lines of the script. This created a subtly uneasy response in my scene partner, Stephanie, who was the main character of the show, leading to what our director may have intended as the emotional event of the scene—a note of friction and doubt injected into a heretofore idyllic illusion of pure young love.

Korty didn't know that I have a younger brother I adore and would do anything to protect. And yet, it felt as if he did. When an actor feels as connected to her director as I did to John Korty, nothing he says or does is random. It all feels creative, even destined.

I hung around the set for the scenes I wasn't in, watching everything. I never saw anyone put down a piece of tape for the actors' marks. Imagine that! He set all the positioning by giving direction that related to the characters' situations and relationships. His impeccable sense of how to stage every scene based on the characters' *needs* and *obstacles* relaxed everyone on set. Actors and technicians alike were devoted to him; I never saw a moment of rebellion from the crew against his actor-centric approach. This TV movie was slighter fare than *The Autobiography of Miss Jane Pittman*—but he treated it with respect and humanity. I was proud of it and proud of my work.

John Korty had such an easy command of the *tools,* like *intention* and *blocking based on emotional event,* and was so fully committed to the *language of permission*—that I left that set thinking this must be the way all film and TV directors worked. On my next job, playing a teacher in an ABC Afterschool Special, I bounced up to the director excitedly: "Hi! What shall we do with Miss Palmer?!" He looked at me like I had two heads and said, "Just do what you did in the audition. Don't worry, you were great." At this moment I realized that ignoring actors was the norm and that John Korty's full commitment to *connection* was the exception. I believe that *in this instant* was born the germ of my commitment to support directors in more meaningful connection to actors.

Goals of Rehearsal

A director's every interaction with an actor is direction. Even if a director avoids contact with actors, the actors are at every moment combing the director's words and body language for clues to his ideas and vision, as well as feedback on their performances; actors make guesses about what the director's wishes might be, and adjust or censor themselves accordingly.

There's no need to allow the actor-director relationship to deteriorate into this sad guessing game. Here are more productive goals:

1) ***Connection.*** Make *connection* your priority—that way, rehearsal is worthwhile even if you don't have time to cover

everything you wanted to. Seize whatever moments you can to engage in soft eye contact, to get *connected up*. These areas matter:

- *The director's connection to the actors.* Listen to the actors; learn their concerns, their questions, their quirks, their sources of energy and power.
- *The actors' connection to the material.* This means making space for actors to safely surrender to the circumstances of their character and the emotional events of the story. Give them time to explore and surrender their resistances, their *judgments* of their characters.
- *The actors' connection to the director.* Actors hear a director's ideas better when the director has earned their trust.
- *The actors' connection to each other*: the back-and-forth, the ping-pong, the *listening*. Make *relationships* your focus, not individual performances.

2) ***Exploring structure and choices.*** Rehearsal is a chance to try out choices for spines, intentions, metaphors, as ifs, for beats and transitions, for emotional events.

3) ***Warm-up the relationships.*** The purpose of rehearsal is not to *nail performances,* but to *warm up the relationships.* If the characters are in a family, nothing beats improvising ordinary family situations. Ditto for coworkers, roommates, etc.

4) ***Transform ideas and information into behavior.*** When Don Vito collapses in the garden, the *information* of the scene is that the line of succession has been set in motion and Michael is about to become the new Godfather. But the simple, recognizably human *behavior* between an old man and his grandson brings us to the heart of deeper thematic truths about family and mortality.

5) ***Honoring the subtext.*** When rehearsal is useful, its purpose is not micromanaging performances or second-guessing

casting choices. It's about making it safe for the actors to let the subtext speak louder than the words.

6) ***Blocking.*** Try out ideas for movement and activities. When you arrive on set for the blocking rehearsal with the DP and crew, anything and everything may change, but it will still be good to have given yourself a head start.

7) ***Set up ways to communicate and work together.*** Rehearsal is a warm-up not just for the scene, but for the actor-director communication on set. The director can ask the actors how they like to work, what they need from their director—some actors like to talk about choices with the director; some don't. You can talk about protocols for the set that allow everyone to function at their best. For instance, if you don't want the actors to watch the playback, rehearsal is the time to bring that up.

8) ***Shortcuts.*** It may be possible for you and the actors to develop *shortcuts* that reflect the turning points of the story's arc. This may enable you, once on set, to say quietly before one scene, "This is the scene where everything is going to hell," and before another, "This is the scene where things are looking up."

9) ***Get things out in the open.*** Rehearsal is a chance for director and actors to be transparent with each other. Ask actors what concerns they have. Share with them your directorial concerns. Communicate. *Exchange the promise* that I discussed in Chapter Two, to ensure that you and they can safely be entirely frank with each other, to wit: the director promises to listen to every suggestion and complaint from the actor; the actor promises to make any such complaints or suggestions to the director *privately*.

10) ***Practice taking risks.*** What if rehearsal is *not* about polishing and perfecting performances, but about *practicing taking risks*—with the exact goal of allowing the actors,

when they arrive on set, to feel free to take risk *while the camera is rolling?*

Producers and crew prioritize *risk-aversion* and do everything they can to control the variables. This is needed for staying on time and on budget, and for keeping everyone safe—but it's the director's job to prevent a risk-averse mentality from overtaking the cast. The performances that audiences enjoy are all about *risk-taking*. Risk-taking is central to honest and entertaining storytelling. Without it, we would never have the 1987 classic *The Princess Bride*. I mean, who would have reasonably believed that allowing a depressed boozer to deliver—*six times*—the line, "Hello, my name is Inigo Montoya, you killed my father, prepare to die," would stay cool for thirty years?

A commitment to risk-taking can sustain you through this scary prospect: What if something amazing happens during a rehearsal, with no camera to capture it? Directors can become frozen with anxiety that such moments will not be replicated perfectly on set. But what if rehearsal is *not* a mini-performance but *practice in taking risk?* Do yourself, your actors, and the project a big, big favor: Don't project anxiety over your favorite moments. Let yourself believe that the fact that wonderful moments happened in rehearsal means that wonderful moments *can happen at any time.*

11) ***Think of it as gardening***: turning over the dirt, fertilizing and composting the soil, sowing seeds. Cultivating, tending, creating beauty and bounty. It's not a data transfer—not a process of uploading your ideas into actors' brains. It's a relationship—an interchange of thoughts, feelings, and commitment.

Skills and Tools of Rehearsal

Take—or Create—a Workshop

I encourage you to study rehearsal techniques in a workshop of some kind, to learn old-school methods à la Sidney Lumet, Mike

Nichols, and Martin Scorsese. Lumet and Nichols used to insist that two weeks of rehearsal for each project be included in their contracts. Scorsese gives himself permission to stop production and work a moment with the actors anytime he feels the need for it. Look for interviews with each of them and, if you haven't already, read Lumet's book *Making Movies*.

The reason for learning how to rehearse the long way—the old-school way—is that's how all learning takes place. You learn how to do it the long way, then *practice* until you get better at it. That's when you become able to accomplish more in a briefer time—and that's when it starts to be more like fun. Real learning only takes place when you can afford trial and error and judgment-free engagement—when it's not about status or ego, it's about the work. So train in a safe space, before you get to the set and there are anxious producers peering over your shoulder, pointing at the clock.

If you're in film school and they don't offer a rehearsal workshop, lobby for it. Or look for a private director-actor workshop. When I was teaching workshops, I saw that it was empowering for the directors to practice scenes from their upcoming projects with actors who would not be playing the roles. It gave them freedom to make mistakes.

If you can't afford film school or private workshops, then set up your own. Find actors, write short scenes or grab scripts off the Internet, get together in someone's living room—or a park or backyard. If you've never pointed a camera at an actor, start with a one-page script with one actor. When you feel confident with that step, move to a two-page, two-person scene. Stick with two-person scenes for a while, until rehearsing two-person scenes feels relaxing and invigorating. Then try longer scenes, including scenes with more than two characters.

Keep to a disciplined schedule. Set the clock for one hour, take a break to debrief with your actors, and work an hour more. Maybe shoot the scene on your phone. You don't need to show the results to anybody. And it's not necessary to shoot at all. It's about process.

If you directed narrative in film school, but then got into making commercials and are now returning to narrative—don't assume it's like riding a bicycle. It's a different set of muscles; you need to limber up; you need to set up a workout schedule with actors—and get back in shape. If you're crossing over to narrative film directing from some other discipline, allow yourself time to learn new skills. For instance, directors of commercials need to stop taking commercial jobs while they prepare to direct a feature film. Directing narrative uses different "muscles" of the brain—you need time and practice to make that shift. If you're crossing from theater directing to film directing, you probably lack cinematic chops—so pick up a camera every day and learn how to tell a story with it.

Take chances, make mistakes, get feedback, pick yourself up and try again. I'm a great believer in the value of surviving mistakes—falling down and getting back up. Surviving mistakes keeps you in a learning mode, so you can keep building your skill set; it clears your head so you can focus on your artistic intention.

Don't embark on a feature-length film without first making short films. I don't necessarily mean something you submit to Sundance. Make a mini-movie every week. With actors. Spend no money. Shoot and edit on your smart phone.

Find the right teacher to take a beginning acting class. Don't talk the teacher into accepting you into an advanced class. Take the beginning class and, if you can, audit an advanced scene study class—to better understand how actors work and how they respond to feedback. Or take an improv class.

Earning or revitalizing your chops by trying out old-school rehearsal techniques in a workshop or living room can turn you into a director who *knows how to work*. You won't have to panic when an actor makes a weird choice, challenges your authority, or develops a resistance to the role. You won't have to worry about whether the actors are "peaking" too soon. You won't have to relegate your every decision regarding timing, pace, and dramatic moments to the editing room. Because you will know how to work.

Overview of Necessary Skills

Quick review of directing/rehearsal skills I've already covered:

- Building on actors' impulses and ideas, instead of telling them they are wrong;
- Encouraging actors to engage and respond to each other;
- Enriching your language and making your ideas more vivid—by using verbs, metaphor, and opposites;
- Focusing your direction around questions, first-person stories, and *disclosure* of your ideas and connections;
- Using the language of permission.

Now, introducing more skills that will step up your rehearsal game:

- How to run improvs;
- Making through-line objectives do your work for you;
- Turning *mysterious lines* into a directing tool;
- Building the blocking of the scene around emotional event;
- Restraining the impulse to frontload your ideas;
- Creating layers;
- Scene-making;
- Working beat by beat;
- Making the case for your ideas;
- Slowing down in the beginning, so you can go fast later;
- Letting the actors work: learning when to step in and when to step back;
- How to get the actors not to stop when they make a mistake;
- How to block a dialogue scene;
- How to ask for pacing;
- Trusting the process and tolerating chaos: *two steps forward, one step back.*

I don't know of a quick way to learn all this. No magic wand, no silver bullet. As the old joke goes, the way to get to Carnegie Hall is "*practice, practice, practice.*"

I've seen directors learn these skills in my workshops by dedicating themselves to practicing in sessions of two or three hours until they learn to love the process. The reason you learn how to rehearse a scene in two hours is not because you expect to ever get that amount of time on a professional set, but for the same reason that baseball players take hours and hours of batting practice in the hope of having an effective outing—which may only last a few minutes—during an actual game.

Practicing will help build your chops and inspire you to devise your own approaches. It's great if you can practice with guidance from a good teacher. But if a guided workshop is not available to you, set up one of your own and ask the actors for feedback—let the actors be your teachers!

Ground Rules: Creating a Safe Space

Have rules in place to protect the safety of actors during rehearsal. There should be no alcohol, no drugs, no lit cigarettes. (If characters in the scene are smoking, in rehearsal the cigarettes should not be lighted.) There must be no risk of physical injury. If there is violence in the scene and the stunt coordinator is not present, indicate the violence without physical commitment. Ditto for scenes with disrobing or sexual intimacy. (Later in this chapter I'll say more about intimacy coordinators and rehearsing sex scenes.)

There must be *no unauthorized video-recording*. If you have a reason for recording rehearsal—for instance, as previsualization of a scene in which the choreography is very exact, or to catch improvised lines that you may want to incorporate into the script—make sure the video is kept private. The intention of rehearsal is to provide a place of freedom where actors can take chances and make mistakes without fear of judgment from rubberneckers. So don't invite anyone to rehearsals who might be tempted to surreptitiously record video for some personal purpose. To be safe, I suggest that you collect all phones and return them at the end of rehearsal. Rehearsal is only useful if actors have the safety to do something foolish without any fear that it will wind up on the Internet.

To be totally safe, find a corner *away* from producers and crewmembers. You may want your script supervisor to be there, to take notes. Perhaps it will be valuable to invite the DP or editor. But make sure that anyone present for rehearsal feels a connection to its sacred intent—which is not to judge or ogle but to engage.

Trust

Directors sometimes ask me how to get actors to trust them. You know who has perfected techniques for getting people to trust them? Psychopaths. Most of my readers are not psychopaths, so my suggestion for how to win actors' trust is to *trust the actors*. Director Lenny Abrahamson (2015's *Room*) had this to say about getting actors' trust: "The only way to actually do it is to be trustworthy and open and meet them like one human being meets another."

If you want people to trust you—trust them! Rather than trying to figure out how to manipulate actors to do what you want, approach the task of enlisting actors in your vision by making it safe for them to take the risks needed to meet the thematic significance of the material.

If actors offer you ideas and questions, don't project onto them an intention *to make problems*; welcome them as collaborators who wish *to make contributions*. When they have ideas, that's good. In fact, if they don't offer their ideas, ask. If they demand to know your ideas first, you can say, "Sure. I have a ton of ideas. I'm very interested to hear yours, but I'm happy to start, if you like."

If you disagree with an actor's idea, there's no need to make him wrong; you can build on what he gives you. If he says, "I think this happens all the time in this relationship," you can say, "Yes, I was wondering about that. What have their previous arguments been like? Let's find what's new about this particular argument." If there's time, improvising a previous quarrel could be really helpful.

If an actor rejects your idea, don't take it personally. Don't argue. You've planted a seed. The way actors absorb ideas from their director is not the same as the way technicians execute instructions about sound levels or camera placement.

Don't use rehearsal to reassess your casting. If you decide an actor has been miscast, recast quickly with minimal drama. If you have doubts, but choose not to recast, do not project your anxieties onto the rehearsal room or set. Take responsibility for the casting and proceed as if the actor is *the best person* for the role. You may need to rethink your ideas so they can fit him. Communicate to him that what you want for this role is whatever he can honestly bring to it. Support him as he finds the way to make the role his own. Actors are better than the rest of us at reading subtext. If you are second-guessing your decision to cast them, *they will know* and may shut down—or, out of their hurt and disappointment, create negativity on the set.

Let actors know they are safe. You have magic directing tools: camera angles, lighting, blocking, and editing. Assure the actors that you won't let them look bad. Let them know they can take risks. Let them know you will light and shoot them effectively, and that if there's even a smidgen of overacting, you will move heaven and earth to make sure it doesn't get past the edit.

Some actors work at a level of image and intuition that is more like a child's than an adult's. Don't judge them for that. It's their job to *play*. Encourage actors to be unafraid to look foolish. It's their job to create honest, revelatory behavior—it's not their job to control the effect. *You* are the safety net. *You* are going to be their witness on set. *You* are going to protect them from judgment and gossip on the part of crewmembers. *You* are going to expend every effort to watch over the edit and protect their hard work.

Improvisation

I admit it—I'm addicted to improvisation as a rehearsal technique. I honestly don't know how to keep a rehearsal fresh and inventive without changing it up from time to time with improvised dialogue and activity. There are filmmakers who rely upon improv to create their scripts—the Duplass Brothers, Larry David, Mike Leigh—but in this book, I am interested in improv as a rehearsal technique for a tightly written script.

Improv breaks actors of line inflections they may have inadvertently set. Improv confers a deep permission to center the scene in its relationships and intentions, rather than reducing it to a random assortment of information, line-readings, and stage directions. Rehearsal improv brings to light insights and impulses hidden in the actors' subconscious. Thus, it builds their faith in their instincts. Improv gets the scripts out of the actors' hands—taking risks, trusting each other.

Improvisation creates chemistry. I've seen it over and over: When actors improvise together, they start believing the other actor is smart and intriguing; they become more interested in that other actor than in their own performance.

Two rules for rehearsal improv: *no denial; no obligation. No denial* means the actors are not to refuse each other's reality. The actor is *not* to plan the route she thinks the improv should take; rather, her task is to respond to her partner. The companion rule, *no obligation,* means she can follow any impulse—and is not required to speak at all. The goal is not to invent clever dialogue, but *to connect.* When I was teaching classes and workshops, I used improv all the time. There is nothing like it for breaking through to a student—actor or director—who is blocked. Or digging into a scene on a more visceral level when it doesn't yet feel real. The basic principle of improv is a powerful one—that an actor's subconscious impulse *matters.*

Actors who say they don't like improv have probably had bad experiences with it—perhaps a director who claimed they wanted improvisation but was actually expecting a certain result and not telling the actors what it is. The only way improv can work is if there is total freedom and trust. Improvisation is not a frivolous undertaking; it is a door to the subconscious, and thus a sacred tool. When unconscious material is uncovered during improvisation, it must be respected. *There is no such thing as an improv that is wrong!* If an improv doesn't go the way you expected, don't critique it! Thank and encourage the actors ("Thanks for trying that!"), then move on.

Here are some possible formats for improv:

1) ***Paraphrasing***

Paraphrasing invites actors to put the lines of the scene in their own words. They *speak the subtext* out loud. They gain confidence that the ebb and flow of their subconscious has a better understanding of the scene than their conscious, analytical mind. It gives them a deep permission to make the character their own.

It can help the director! When I am watching actors improvise scenes, I see more clearly the underlying intentions or emotional event—and get new ideas for blocking.

First, ask the actors to improvise the scene *not using any of the actual lines*. This may be a challenge for actors who pride themselves on being word-perfect with their dialogue. If actors default to the lines they have learned instead of improvising, when they reach the end of the scene, the director can quietly say, *Keep going*. Since they have run out of lines, improvisation will come naturally. Be prepared for the improvised scene to be longer than the written scene. Or shorter.

In a second step, you might ask them to use "half and half" improv. In other words, to include some but not all lines from the script. Stay in this second step for as long as it feels productive. The third step is to use the lines from the script—but *continue to improvise their interior life*. It's a practical application of the principle (from Chapter Two) that characters have *free will* and *a free subconscious*.

2) ***Improv to help them learn the lines***

I don't think it's helpful for actors to hold their scripts for longer than the first read-through. You can ask them to come to rehearsal with lines learned (actors call this being "off-book"), but if the actors have not learned their lines, you can use rehearsal time for this. Break the scene down into three parts. Ask the actors to read the lines of the first section, then put the script down and paraphrase it, then read it again, then put it down, and again put the scene in their own words. Little by little, they'll get closer to the written lines without stress and without adopting rigid line readings. That's my experience, anyway. Granted, my absolute trust in this process probably helps.

3) ***The moment before (and other off-camera scenes)***

Improvising the off-camera scene just before the scene began helps the actors feel that when "action" is called, their characters are not *starting a scene*, they are continuing their lives. In *The Graduate*, for instance, we see Mrs. Robinson at the party asking Benjamin for a ride home. In the next scene, they are both at Mrs. Robinson's house. There had to have been an off-camera scene—in the car during the ride home. Good actors, left on their own, will imagine that off-camera scene.

Mike Nichols, director of *The Graduate*, has said that for him, improvising off-camera scenes was the best use of rehearsal.

4) ***Improvisation around the emotional history of the relationships***

In *The Shape of Water*, co-written and directed by Guillermo del Toro, Eliza (Sally Hawkins) has three major relationships: with Zelda (Octavia Spencer), with Giles (Richard Jenkins), and with Amphibian Man (Doug Jones). Amphibian Man is a new bond, but her connections with Zelda and Giles are longstanding. How could it not be helpful to improvise those emotional histories? To improvise other days—not in the script—when Eliza and Zelda gossip together at work; or when she and Giles watch old movies on his couch and work out tap dance steps? I don't know if the actors did that, but those relationships are so rich and deeply felt that it feels like they did.

Practicing improvisation of off-camera scenes will give both actors and director an understanding *in their bones* that the written dialogues are only a tiny sliver of a vast terrain of intimacy and shared experience.

Many directors ask whether it's a good idea to encourage the actors to go out to a café, restaurant, or even nightclub together. My thinking is that improvising an evening out *as the characters*—not in a public place, but in a dedicated rehearsal space—will be more useful.

5) ***A parallel event or relationship***

If a scene on a space ship has character A accidentally pushing the wrong button that cuts off character B's oxygen supply, you could improvise some other terrible mistake—like accidentally putting a car in reverse when you thought you were putting it in drive. Once the actors are engaged with the emotional life of this situation, the director can quietly say, "Let's go into the scene."

6) ***Improvise the intentions and through-line***

If two characters have habitual behaviors toward each other—say, if one chronically complains about her life, and the other persists in trying to cheer her up and point out ways that things are not so bad—the actors can improvise those *through-line intentions* with invented scenes that are not in the script.

7) ***Silent improvs***

Silent improvs can powerfully create relationship, situation, and texture of life simply by having the two characters—without words—fix dinner together. Or sit silently in a waiting room until the doctor comes out of the ER with news about their mother.

8) ***Anything to shake things up and stay loose***

Improvise in gibberish.

Let the actors switch roles and improvise each other's lines.

Switch up the high status/low status relationship.

Or try a "speaking the subtext" exercise: Each actor says a line and then improvises the subtext of the line. The other actor responds, perhaps with their next line from the script, or perhaps with their own subtext line. This exercise is not helpful if actors try to come up with the "right" subtext; it works when actors say whatever comes into their heads in the moment, whether or not they're sure it's "right" or useful.

9) *Trust the actors*

Ask the actors for ideas. I mean, this should probably be Number One. The actors are likely to have more experience with improv than you! If so, take advantage. For instance, if you're not clear how the "speaking the subtext" exercise works, ask them if they have experience with it—many have, and can teach you their version.

Sometimes actors in a rehearsal space slip into spontaneous improvising—without warning! If you're not used to being around actors, you may not realize that's what they're doing. Learn to recognize this when it happens. Don't stop them. Let them continue. Stay present. The reason that actors might do this is because they know that connection to their partner is their anchor.

Being the director of a project while actors are improvising can be nerve-wracking, because you might feel out of control. If you stay present, the experience of surviving that *out-of-control* feeling will help you build your chops and gain confidence in your leadership skills. One specific skill you may gain is how to detect and *report back,* in playable terms, what you saw in the improv. For instance, on set, a director might say, "I'm remembering a rehearsal improv when it seemed that your objective was *to control* him. Let's try the scene that way on the next take."

A reminder: Before trying any of these improv ideas on a professional set, practice in a workshop situation! Stay simple. Maybe stick with putting the lines in their own words or improvising the moment before. Find people to practice with who will give you feedback that is honest and also kind.

Actors sometimes become so excited about their inventions that they want to add lines from improvisations to the script. Some directors allow and encourage that. But if you don't want them to change the lines, you can say, "Yes, definitely, let's add it, but let's add it as subtext!"

The most important thing about improvs is that they are not performances. *They are never wrong.* They should *never* be critiqued. They are investigations, warm-ups—fertilizer.

Through-lines

Making a choice of through-line for each of the characters pulls the scene together because it defines the relationships. Sometimes I bring up through-lines early in rehearsal, but sometimes later in the process, perhaps after investigating beats and mysterious lines.

An objective—what the character wants—is probably the most useful way to express through-line. If one character *wants to party* and the other *wants peace and quiet*, there's gonna be some drama, right? (Or comedy.) If an actor is talking about his character in an intellectualizing or judgmental way, teach yourself how to (gently) interrupt with, "What does he want in the scene?"

The *objective* is not the only tool to describe through-line. A character's *emotional situation* may be powerful enough to center her through-line—for instance, "the mother of a disabled child." Or the emotional history of the relationship—"seeing, for the first time in ten years, an ex-lover who is now married to someone else." These are *emotionally salient facts* that may be all an actor needs to propel their through-line.

A *metaphor* can also create a sense of through-line: "The wheelchair is her throne"; "Their relationship is like that of a parent and child." The through-line can be framed as an *issue* in the relationship: "They have never agreed on the reason why the partnership failed"; "Each brother fears that the other one is their mother's favorite."

Many two-person scenes have an *absent third character*. The through-line of either character—or both—could be their goals and needs in relation to that third character, rather than to the other character in the scene. In the *Chinatown* scene I referred to in Chapter Five, the absent third character is Evelyn (Faye Dunaway). She is the *problem*, if you will, that Jake Gittes and Noah Cross battle over.

If one of the characters is an addict, the addiction may be the absent third character in every scene. The addict's need for the next drink, the next fix, takes precedence over all other relationships and becomes that character's through-line. Another way to express this idea: *as if* the addiction is the addict's secret lover.

Emotional Event

Here's a simple way to understand emotional event: Everybody wants something; it matters whether they get it or not; each relationship is on a different emotional footing at the end of the scene than it was at the beginning. Your script analysis preparation has given you ideas for what the emotional events of the scene might be. Creating emotional event is the most important use of rehearsal.

Sometimes I begin by asking the actors: "What do you think is going on in this scene?" Then I can build on their responses to introduce my ideas. If you have a strong idea of what the emotional event is—for example, *it's an escalating exchange of insults*—or *it's a step toward healing*—please tell the actors. This is your most powerful directing tool. It's still possible that while working the scene in rehearsal, some other idea may emerge. It's more important to have *a sense of emotional event* than to have the "correct" emotional event. *Any* emotional event is better than no emotional event.

Creating *emotional event* is the best place for the director to focus his energies. It's also the best method of damage control. Anytime there's a problem, say to yourself, say to your actors and to all your collaborators: "Let's focus on what this scene is about."

Mysterious Lines

The lines that I affectionately call "mysterious" are often magic keys unlocking a moment, transition, emotional event, or an important secret in the character's history. Bringing up a mysterious line is a great way to introduce an idea you have, perhaps like this: "I think this line is interesting—what do you make of it?"

Three Different Ways

As an exercise while you are learning rehearsal, try acting out the *technique of three possible*—have the actors try playing the scene three entirely different ways, that is, with three entirely different choices. Make sure at least one of the choices is an opposite to the others. You may be surprised at the confidence this exercise brings to the actors, as well as to the director.

I always thought this idea was my own radical idiosyncrasy and something that could only be useful in a workshop situation—until I came across the commentary for *Secretary*, a singular film about emotional fragility and gender power dynamics. The performances by Maggie Gyllenhaal and James Spader are extraordinary. One of director Steven Shainberg's revelations in the commentary is that he shot every scene three different ways: 1) way over-the-top; 2) hyper-real and understated; and 3) somewhere in between. I take Shainberg's testimony as proof that trying a scene *three different ways* could work in a professional situation, if the actors are up for it—actually, Shainberg says it was the actors who made this proposal.

Don't Frontload

By *frontloading*, I mean when a director talks and talks before the actors get a chance to try—or even say—anything. Don't use precious rehearsal time to list every plot detail until the actors' eyes glaze over. If the actors have read the script, they know the plot! Even if actors ask questions that make you think they haven't read the script, don't list the plot details. Instead, *pitch* them the story of the scene, by boiling down the plot to the facts that paint an emotional picture—the juicy facts. Here's a helpful guideline: practice limiting yourself to two facts per scene. That will focus you on the most salient facts—the exciting facts that propel behavior and event.

Don't forget questions. Make this a rule of thumb: for every fact or idea you bring up, ask at least the same number of questions. And listen to the answers! Listen more than you talk. Any discussion of facts should always go back and forth between facts and questions. Whenever it's possible to allow a fact to generate a question—grab it!

Sometimes directors ask me how to give direction if there's no time for rehearsal. Well, you can't. If there's no time for an intimate back-and-forth in which the director listens as much as she talks, then keep your ideas in your back pocket. When you get to the set, let them try the scene without direction. Pay attention to what the actors are bringing. Take one is effectively rehearsal for take two, so if you've been practicing rehearsal techniques, you may be able to build on what the actors are bringing. Coach Joan Darling used to tell directors, "If you have ten things you want to tell an actor, tell them three." I'd go farther—if you have ten things you want to tell an actor, tell them one.

Listen More than You Talk

The title *director* sounds like someone who orders everyone about. Many successful directors say their job is more accurately described as *selector*. This means a director that *listens* to actors.

A client of mine, preparing for his first feature, had no real experience directing actors. Upon my advice, he rented a space and found actors with whom to practice working on scenes. I had noticed that he loved to talk, so I gave him this assignment: that he should, during his rehearsal sessions, *listen more than he talks*. I gave him a literal percentage: that when he was with the actors, he should hear his own voice less than 50% of the time. When we next met, he reported that the actors told him they had loved the experience. Here's what they said: "It was so interesting that you didn't talk a lot! It was such a relief to not be subjected to constant micromanaging!"

Making Your Case

If you have an idea you really want them to try, disclose your reasons why. Learn to *make your case* for why you think it's worth trying, using facts, imagery, mysterious lines, personal connections. You can say, "I'm basing my idea on the fact that [such and such] has taken place in that earlier scene." Or, "I couldn't stop thinking about line X. I can't stop wondering whether it might mean something totally opposite to what it seems to mean." Or, "The image of the noodle shop gives me an idea for how to make this moment work." Or, "This scene reminded me so much of something that happened to a friend of mine, and I'd love to bring in something she told me about it."

Please note: You're making the case for *trying* the idea—you're not arguing over who is right, or pressing the actor to admit that your idea is better than his.

Pick Your Battles

When a thing is important, fight for it. Standing up for the truest truth is always worth doing. But don't argue with actors. No one will win. Keep in mind that an actor may be resisting an idea because you haven't explained it yet in a way he can hear. Finding the way he can hear it may involve listening to him more closely.

In creative "battles" between director and actor, I don't think any director should *always* give in to the actor—and I don't think any director should always win.

Eye Contact

Learn how to ask actors to sit in chairs across from each other and say the lines with full eye contact and *as slowly as possible*. If they need to refer to scripts, that's fine—ask them to look down for their line whenever they need to, but to only speak the lines while they are looking—connecting—to each other. A preliminary first reading whose purpose is not performance, but more something like "getting the words into the air." Not at full emotional tilt, but not a monotone. Slow enough that something can happen between the words. Rehearsal is all about slowing down in the beginning, so we can go fast when we need to.

The director should allow herself to make eye contact with the actors, too. When speaking privately with the actors, allow your eyes to soften and surrender.

Getting Actors to Not Stop for "Mistakes"

The best parts in a scene are genuine, unguarded *moments* when the actors *affect* each other—which may mean catching each other off-guard and may even feel like a *mistake*. Sometimes a moment catches an actor so off-guard that he forgets his lines. Such inner accidents engender great energy. If the actor permits himself to *stay present* in the moment of unguardedness until the line comes back, something amazing may happen. If the camera is running, you want to catch that. But fear of making a mistake is so hard-wired in most of us that if you want the actors to, on set, override the auto-pilot of stopping for "mistakes," you need to practice that extreme "permission to fail" in rehearsal. You can be quite direct with them about this goal.

Let the Actors Work

Director Gina Prince-Bythewood said in an interview with *Filmindependent.org*, "In the first rehearsal I don't give any direction at all. I give the actors their freedom. I say, 'Show me what you've come up with.' Because I'm hoping, honestly, that it's better." For the same blog post, writer-director Rodrigo Garcia said, "Sometimes actors do things and before I say, 'No, that doesn't work,' I'll try to process it. You have to—especially with the good actors—pay a lot of attention." Sally Field told a *Hollywood Reporter* interviewer that for her role in 2012's *Lincoln*, Steven Spielberg didn't try to tell her who Mary Lincoln was or how to play her. He let the actors do their work.

It may be important for director and actors to be *on the same page* with a choice that is central to the story. But often it will be perfectly fine—no damage whatever to the director's vision—for the actor to make a private, personal, idiosyncratic choice, which she may not even disclose to the director. Learning to tell the difference takes an open mind; it takes trust in the world of subtext; it takes practice.

Actors might not make a full emotional investment in rehearsal. They may say, "I'm not going to go all out in rehearsal, I'm saving it for the camera." And that's okay. You can reply with something like, "I understand you're not making a full investment now. We've got plenty of time." The amount of emotional investment needed in rehearsal may depend on the material. When the material is complex and layered, the actors may wish to work full-out emotionally all through rehearsal in order to open their imaginative and emotional gates to the deeper layers. And that's okay, too.

It is not necessary for the director to "fix" everything in rehearsal. It's completely fine to sit and watch—to be a witness. Maybe you'll get ideas for an adjustment to suggest on set. Maybe you'll be able to remind an actor on set that, "In rehearsal, the bad news your partner brought gave you a need to get away from her and got you over to that window." If the real reason you want him to move to the window is so you can get a cool shot of the reflection, there's no need to hide that information. It's perfectly okay to disclose your directorial concerns and ask for the actors' help in achieving your visual objectives. But if you know how to fold your visual ideas into the concerns of the characters . . . Well, I'm sure you can see what a plus that would be.

Learn to say, "Yes, and . . ." instead of "No, but . . ."

I've been trying throughout to offer ways to build on an actor's idea or impulse, rather than contradict or argue with them. I'll continue to suggest examples. Keep in mind this simple principle, though: *Yes, and . . .*

Other Exercises and Warm-Ups

If rehearsal lags, you can suggest to the actors that they go back and forth at will between lines and improv—whenever they have the impulse. You can tell them that if they feel the other actor is not in the moment, they are allowed to tell the other actor, "I don't believe you"—or ask the other actor, "Why did you say that?"

If they are familiar with the Meisner Repeat Exercise, you can invite them to incorporate it into rehearsal. If an actor feels stuck, or feels she is saying lines with no connection, she can say "I feel stuck," or, "I don't feel connected to you." The other actor can reply, "You don't feel connected to me"—or "I don't feel connected to you." You'll be amazed at how quickly this can jolt them into connection.

Or, an actor can make an observation about the other. This can be actor to actor ("You put highlights in your hair") or character to character ("You've been lying to me for years"). The actors repeat back and forth to each other such remarks until one of them has the impulse to go back to the scene. This helps keep the dialogue sounding believable, like a conversation, rather than like actors saying lines.

A variation on the repetition exercise is a *mantra* exercise, using phrases that illuminate something about each character's emotional situation (like, one actor saying, "Why should I trust you?" and the other saying, "Get over it"). The actors can choose their mantras, or the director can make suggestions. The actors repeat these phrases back and forth to each other for as long as they wish and then go into the lines of the scene. If they forget a line—or really, anytime they feel like it—they can throw in their "mantra" line. This helps create engagement and supports a sense of intention.

Physical warm-ups are great. Throw a ball back and forth. Have a pillow fight. Childlike games like pillow fight, tag, air-boxing, or fake karate—with sound effects, but without physical contact—can liberate actors from overthinking and take them "out of their heads." They also function as natural *listening* exercises. Responding to an air-boxing punch *as though* they've been actually hit centers actors in the give and take of the relationship.

Aggressive warm-ups can be liberating—for example, asking two actors to stand across from each other and repeat, back and forth, these mantras: *"Fuck you!"*—*"You're full of shit!"* Or *"Shut up!"*—*"No, you shut up!"* One of my favorite warm-ups is to ask actors to come up on stage two at a time, with the instruction: "Be monsters together"—it seems to liberate them both physically and emotionally. Of course, you can ask the actors to suggest a warm-up—they probably know more exercises than you.

It's strangely helpful in rehearsal to allow—*encourage*—actors to move more than they would on set. They know they must stay within the frame when the camera is running, so rehearsal is a chance to physicalize their inner life without constraint. This rehearsal permission leads to a human reality we have all experienced: *Inside* we might be screaming and gesticulating *and at the same time* composing our faces and covering our feelings.

There are also quieter warm-ups that allow actors to access, together, deep internal resources. Like this one: Ask the actors to sit across from each other, keeping eye contact for ten full minutes without speaking; tell them that although you don't want them to speak, it's completely okay to have any emotion or express any sound including giggling. Or have them ask each other questions—without giving answers. Or ask the actors to describe to each other their childhood bedrooms.

RULES! Make sure it's understood that all warm-ups and improvisations are optional and that no one is forced to disclose information against their will. Make sure no one in the rehearsal space is surreptitiously recording. Don't allow onlookers unless they understand they've been invited to something serious.

Be Inventive. Go the Extra Mile. Think Outside the Box.

Before filming of *Mad Max: Fury Road,* director George Miller recruited Eve Ensler, playwright and gender-violence activist, for feedback on the portions of the script concerning the sex slaves that Furiosa was smuggling to freedom. Then he brought Ensler to the shoot, to run workshops with the young actresses. Zoe Kravitz spoke of the experience in an interview for the *New York Times*: "Even if a lot of the women's history wasn't in the dialogue, it was really important to George that we understood what we were running from. We would do exercises like writing letters to our captor, really interesting stuff that created deep empathy. I'm glad we had that, because it was such a crazy experience—so long and chaotic—that it would be easy to forget what we were doing if we didn't have this really great foundation that we could return to." Added Riley Keough, "I thought it was amazing that George cared so much. It could have just been like, 'This is a big Hollywood movie, now put on your bathing suits and get outside.'"

Ava DuVernay took rehearsal workshops with me while preparing to make her transition from public relations executive to narrative filmmaker. For a scene in which one of the characters confronts her husband over 106 letters she had sent him while he was away in the military, Ava arrived to class with a satchel. After introducing herself to the actors, she dumped the contents on the floor: "This is 106 letters." She had placed, in each of 106 envelopes, a hand-written love letter. It was a dramatic gesture of invention and commitment that put the actors in the palm of her hand. Even for a class, Ava went above and beyond. From that moment, I knew her future as a narrative filmmaker would not be denied.

Resistances

It's normal for actors to have hidden resistances to a role. If you have a rehearsal period, they can have time to work out resistances at their own pace. Organically working out the resistances of the actors is an important purpose of rehearsal. In rehearsal they can meet the challenge to go deeper, take every risk—this work can release a huge amount of creative energy.

Discussion of an actor's resistances can become emotional. An actor may have a resistance to a character that in fact taps into his deepest soul; he may be resisting something in himself that he doesn't want to face. It's okay to give him space to get where he needs to go in his own time. A director can be respectful of actors' privacy and still be *present*. If you have concerns about intruding, ask them, "Do you want me to step in with you, or do you want me to step back?"

When an actor objects to a line, it may be because he is resisting something about it. If there's no rehearsal time, the line the actor is resisting will probably have to be cut or changed. If that happens, don't resent the actor—she is protecting her ability to be present in the moment. But if you do have time—or are working with an actor you have worked with before—perhaps you can join forces to dig into the obstacles and release her energy.

I think of actors' judgments on their characters as resistances. If an actor says to me, "But she [my character] is so annoying!" I tend to reply, "Okay. Hmmm. That's interesting. I never thought of her that way. Tell me why you think that." I push the actor to be specific: "Okay. Let's make a list of the annoying things she does." I keep asking *why*: "Why do you think she did that?" I interpose examples of times when I or someone I care about has made a similar mistake. I keep it up until we come to an understanding about the character's behavior that is honest and unsentimental, instead of condemnatory and dismissive. Or, if I have an easy enough relationship with the actor, all I may need to say, gently, is, "Well, we don't want to judge her, do we?"

There are some actors who question every direction, who, no matter what you suggest, find a reason why it won't work or why they can't do it. The funny thing about actors like this is that, often, once they have complained and argued and threatened over a direction, they go ahead and do it anyway! Don't worry if the actor rejects your idea. *You have planted the seed and it may grow.* There's more reason to worry if the actor says, "Yes, that's a great idea," but then nothing changes in their performance.

Focus on the Work

What if actors judge the director and resist direction because they are wary of his level of expertise? Don't take it personally. *Don't think of anyone as a difficult actor; think of them as an actor who is having difficulty*. Treat all problems with actors as artistic problems; don't get drawn into anyone's neurosis. At the same time—don't retreat from the relationship. Anytime you are having trouble with an actor, increase your commitment to the solution. Ask them, "Can you tell me what you feel the problem is?" You can say, right out loud, "I am committed to solving this." You can even say, "You can tell me anything, as long as you say it to me privately. I'm not worried about getting my feelings hurt. I am committed to the work."

Commit your energy to higher purpose, to telling the story, *to the work*. If an actor is behaving badly, it's coming from insecurity. Don't let the actor's insecurity make you respond defensively, thus entangling you in your own insecurity. If you feel up to it, you can say—*in strict privacy*—to an actor who is resisting, "I can't help feeling there is something you are resisting." Or: "Is there something on your mind?"; "Is something bothering you?"; "Am I doing something that is getting in your way?" Directing coach Adrienne Weiss puts it this way: "If an actor is acting 'difficult' it's because they are feeling vulnerable. Instead of judging them, gently ask, 'What's going on?'"

You can say, "I absolutely believe you can do it. Do you want me to leave you alone to work it out or do you want to bounce your ideas off me?" If you tell an actor that you believe in them, make sure that statement is true.

Actors' Subtext

Characters have subtext—and actors do too. Listen to what actors say to you—and also to what they are telling you without words. When an actor asks questions, it's more important to *hear the questions* than to answer them. What's her subtext? What is really on her mind? You don't need to be a mind reader. It's quite alright to say, "I'm not sure I understand what you just said. Can you tell me more?"

When a writer-director hears an actor say, "I hate this line," she automatically fears the worst: that the actor hates her for writing garbage and wishes he hadn't accepted the role. Hey—take a breath. The actor's statement is a mysterious line! Make yourself come up with something else his statement might mean. Use the technique of three possible! Off the top of my head, here are three different possible things the statement, "I hate this line," when spoken by an actor, might mean:

1) "It feels stagy and unnatural to me. It's only there for the plot. A real human being doesn't talk like this."
2) "I don't understand this line."
3) "I love this line so much that I'm afraid I won't do it justice."

When in doubt, ask. If what they say makes no sense to you, or throws you into turmoil, ask them what they mean. Bring things out into the open. If the two leads are not getting along, talk to each of them about it—separately—with full transparency and compassion. Enlist their help in finding solutions.

Many directors know so little about actors that they think the best thing that can happen is to cast actors with whom there won't be any problems. I think this is a foolish wish. First of all, it's not going to happen, not on this planet anyway. But here's what else: Problems, mistakes, resistances are openings into the subconscious. And the subconscious is not what we want to avoid—it's where we want to be. If an actor keeps forgetting a line, take him aside and ask, "Is something bothering you about this line?" You might be surprised, or even inspired, by his response.

Even actors who are truly open—the kind I want you to work with—have resistances. They may recognize them—for instance the actor who keeps forgetting a certain line may mutter in your presence, "I must be resisting something here." This is not an occasion for alarm! It means she trusts you, letting you in on the process.

Whatever actors do, love them fiercely, the way a mother loves her children, even the difficult ones. Give them unconditional love.

Anytime a problem occurs, let them know that you are ready to reach into your own chest and hold out your heart.

Making Moments Count: Blocking, Pacing, Scene-Making

Blocking and pacing add up to *scene-making*—creating a reality for the director's idea that is both visual and emotional. It's the central responsibility of the director.

Blocking

Fairly early in rehearsal, ask the actors to put the scene "on its feet"—that is, to put down their scripts and begin adding movement. You might bring it up like this: "Let's start to include some sense of the physical environment." Add a chair, an object, a little at a time. Create a sense of the objects' relationships to the story and characters.

In a *Hollywood Reporter* roundtable, Alejandro Iñárritu said, "You can block and block, but the actor has an internal rhythm." Pay attention to actors' impulses. Practice until you learn how to detect an actor's internal rhythm and introduce your ideas in ways that build on it. Give them time to make your ideas their own.

There are times—musical numbers of course, but also certain scenes like the eight-minute opening of Robert Altman's *The Player*—when detailed, complex blocking must be mapped out and practiced with the discipline of dance choreography. Rehearsal for such shots is called "marking it through" or "walking it through." Actors repeat the movements carefully and precisely until they become second nature—in much the same way as they learn their lines—and then "fill it" with emotional life.

For less tightly choreographed scenes, try this: Give each actor a starting position and allow them, during the first "on their feet" run-through, to move whenever and wherever they have an impulse. From there, you can build on their instincts. Perhaps:

"That impulse you had to move on line X felt like it created the moment, let's keep it." Or, if their movement feels stagy or extraneous, you can say, "I see your impulse to cross to the desk on that line, but I think staying seated will give you more power."

If actors are not getting to where you need them to be for your shot list, consider giving direction with the *language of permission*: "Do you think you can get to the weapons cache a little sooner?"

Be prepared with ideas, but be ready to come up with new ones if the ideas you've prepared aren't working. If you give a blocking direction and the actor forgets it three times in a row, it may mean the blocking is not working—in which case, be ready to change it. Or, it may mean there is something the actor doesn't understand about the scene—in that case be ready to discuss with the actor *what the scene is about.*

Practice and learn to block a two-person scene before you try scenes of three or more characters.

Blocking Templates

There can be an activity the character is engaged in throughout the scene. One character's constant motion counterposed against the other character's stillness can create the entire power relationship (high status/low status). For instance, in *Glengarry Glen Ross*, I can imagine director James Foley suggesting to Al Pacino (Roma) that he always sit in stillness, because this high-status character already possesses confidence in his position of strength—and has no need to jockey for power. The low-status character (in *Glengarry*, that's Levene, played by Jack Lemmon) lacks a locus of strength: His constant motion, sometimes fiddling with objects, sometimes outright pacing—*as though* it is a struggle for him to find his bearings—is a physical and emotional counterpoint to the stillness of Roma or Williamson (Kevin Spacey).

Another blocking template is that a character might have a territory, which he guards or occasionally steps beyond. Character

A's territory can be respected by character B—or invaded, circled, approached, etc.

There can be obstacles—objects that separate the characters, or function as allies, or provide a lightning rod for the relationship. For example, instead of punishing the other character, the actor might *punish* the vegetables she is chopping.

Pace: the Last Frontier

In addition to differing patterns of movement, characters can have different tempo-rhythms from each other. Here's a classic example of a great scene made iconic by *pacing*: the Ferris wheel scene in *The Third Man*, with Orson Welles and Joseph Cotten, directed by Carol Reed. Study it. Notice the moments when Welles is silent, allowing the subtext to be *everything* that is going on. Then notice how he barrels through long stretches of dialogue with no pause whatever, to create an entirely other kind of moment. (P.S. You can find the scene on YouTube, but if you've never seen the film—a brilliant mashup of film noir and Cold War thriller—do yourself a favor and watch it all the way through, first.)

Slowly paced cinema, in the hands of masters like David Lynch, Yasujirō Ozu, Andrei Tarkovsky, or Julie Dash, can keep us on the edge of our seats. But many films by inexperienced directors are *too slow*. A sluggish scene can be rescued by ruthless editing to excise the unnecessary pauses. But *live pacing*—pacing that happens while the camera is rolling and has been explored and set in motion during rehearsal—is integral to the fabric of a successful scene. The rhythm of the movement and activities, the slowness or quickness of the dialogue, the length of the pauses—and more importantly, *what happens* during those pauses—*all* are crucial to the art of scene-making.

Pacing interweaves with intention: for example, an intention *to berate* is likely to be faster paced than the intention *to soothe*. Insightful pacing brings the choices alive and allows actors to connect more naturally to their inner life.

In order to be skilled at guiding pacing, a director must be confident in their awareness of *emotional event*. You can see it in the *Third Man* scene: Harry Lime (Welles) begins speaking at an average pace—until something *happens*. He then slows down—until something else happens—Holly Martins (Cotton) delivers a threat that the police have been notified and may be watching. Harry then exits quickly, delivering, as he gracefully dismounts the Ferris wheel, a famous and briskly paced monologue.

Don't forget that actors can move and speak at the same time.

Now let's talk about rehearsal pace. It's very helpful to slow way down in the early stages of rehearsal. In the very first episode of *Inside the Actors Studio*, back in 1994, Paul Newman described what he did if a director told him, after the first take of a scene, to pick up the pace. He would go off by himself and rework the role from scratch: asking questions, finding beats, opposites, adjustments; changing up rhythms; adding new layers of specific emotional detail. After the next take, when the director said, "Great, just what I wanted," Newman checked with the script supervisor on the length of each take. "A hundred times out of a hundred," he claimed, the script supervisor told him that the second take was longer than the first one—even though the director had told him that the first one was too long! This means that in the initial take the actor was *rushing*, not connecting to the subtext of the lines, because he had not fully investigated that subtext. Paradoxically, "rushing" can make a scene feel slow; if the subtext of the scene is not coming alive, the scene is boring and the audience can't help but wish it over. Newman was describing a legitimate need to *slow down* in order to uncover the details of inner life that will make it worth watching.

This story explains why rehearsal rhythm may helpfully begin at a slower pace than performance rhythm. During rehearsal the actors can explore, let themselves live—and be present and responsive—between the lines. They can find colors and transitions and build connection with the other actor. They can take the time to not say the line until they are ready. But if every scene has the same deliberate rhythm, it won't feel lifelike. Pauses and silences are emotional punctuation to a scene and its emotional event. In real-life conversations, thoughts and words tumble over each other, almost overlapping—until they are brought up short by a *pause*. Pauses must be earned.

It's a danger of rehearsal—one of the reasons some directors prefer to skip it—that actors can get stuck in rehearsal rhythm, locked into a commitment to not say the line until they are "ready." This can make them sound like actors. Sanford Meisner used to tell his students, in order to fling them, kicking and screaming, into the here-and-now—"Speak *before* you're ready! Act before you think!"

The courage of a director to ask actors to pick up the pace is invaluable. It's okay to ask them to "go faster," but the correct term is *picking up cues*. Other useful language for pacing: "Let's take out the pauses—all except for the ones that count." Picking up cues feels almost like overlapping. So, you can suggest that: "It's okay to almost overlap"; or, "It's like you're finishing each other's sentences."

"Picking up cues" also applies to what my mentor Bob Goldsby used to call "internal cues." He meant that his actors should not necessarily pause at the periods and commas, even in the middle of our own speeches. "Punctuation makes it easier to read," he insisted, "but it's not the way people talk."

People in real life pause when they need to take a breath or to think of what to say next. If you need proof, eavesdrop on daily conversations of human beings. Or listen one more time to Orson Welles in the Ferris wheel scene. His pauses achieve their dramatic intention because they are idiosyncratic—and almost never taken at the written punctuation.

When I was a young actor, I was instructed to pause after every line because it would help the editor. But I was a young actor nearly fifty years ago! Advances in technology give editors tools to edit around overlapping. Sound technicians still panic when there is overlapping. Find time, ahead of the shoot, to meet with the editor and the sound technician and have a frank conversation about overlapping.

Making Moments Count

Trust the power of an insightful gesture—and learn how to film them. What if a script calls upon a character to raise her hands and gaze at electrical currents emitting from the tips of her fingers? Even though that shot of Justine (Kirsten Dunst) in Lars Von Trier's *Melancholia* is dependent on special effects, the moment—which takes the audience somewhere they have never been before—has been crafted emotionally by the actor and the filmmaker.

Perhaps the script calls for character A to touch character B's face. It's important to know that while this is a small gesture, it's a huge emotional event. It needs to be *earned*—and *it needs to happen in the moment.*

Eye contact is useful during a simple first read of a scene in rehearsal. Yet, for the *blocking* of the scene, the obstacles to meaningful eye contact can create suspense. And a moment when the characters' eyes finally meet can *count* as an emotional event.

It's hard to make an audience believe that a couple is in love unless there's at least one shot in which the two of them are positioned in the same frame, making full, truthful eye contact in real time. Like in *The Matrix,* when Neo and Trinity turn to each other in full body profile before applying their firepower to demolishing their opponents. It's different in style, but similar in emotional content, to the dreamy moments of shared gaze in *Blue Valentine* between Ryan Gosling and Michelle Williams—or in *My Beautiful Launderette,* with Daniel Day-Lewis and Gordon Warnecke. Those moments of simple, genuine eye contact, when fully witnessed by the audience, pull the audience in and allow us to believe the lovers are destined for each other.

Objects, Activities, and Territories

If you have rehearsal off-set, with no propmaster, bring objects with you. Objects are a powerful tool of the actor. If the physical business of the scene is complicated and difficult, the actors need time to practice and make it their own. During preproduction for *The Old Guard,* the fight coordinator gave Charlize Theron a heavy rubber replica of the axe used by her superhero character; he told her to keep it by her side daily, practice handling it and doing tricks with it until it could feel natural in her hands during filming.

An object may have significance to a character's inner life even if it ends up on the cutting room floor. For the scene in *Before the Devil Knows You're Dead* in which Andy (Philip Seymour Hoffman) is soliciting the involvement of his brother (Ethan Hawke) in the robbery, director Sidney Lumet disclosed in his commentary that he gave Hoffman some business—*to draw a sketch of the robbery location.* The scene was shot and edited in such a way that the audience does not see this sketch! But the activity still matters. Even if it doesn't make it into the shot, it creates subtext.

Work in Steps

There doesn't have to be a set order to your steps in rehearsal. Maybe you'll start with telling personal stories that connect to what the scene is about, or maybe you'll start with sketching out blocking. Rehearsal is a craft—and an art—as fully worthy of a director's attention as the artistry of his lighting and framing choices.

Some people use the term "colors" or "layers" for what I am calling *steps,* as in, "Let's see if we can add another color here." Or, "Yes, I agree that you're picking a fight with him, but I can't help wondering whether maybe there's a deeper layer somewhere—perhaps needing his approval?"

Working in Beats/Scene-Making

Working in beats anchors the emotional life—and its shifts and events—to movement, activities, and pacing. It's a chance to focus on a moment: unpack imagery, reveal the secret of a mysterious line, imagine emotional history of the characters. You can ask questions, share research, personal experience, and anecdotes. You can improvise a beat. You can try it three different ways.

It takes practice to develop a sense of when to let the actors run the scene and when to stop and work a moment. Many actors function at a thoroughbred level; they have an antenna for false notes and work them out themselves; the director can be their witness without intervening. But it can happen that actors, running a scene over and over, lapse into false moments—for instance, rushing past moments that aren't working. If you are able to notice these "stuck" places, you can say, "Let's work this beat."

You don't have to work on all the beats of a scene. You don't have to work on the first beat first. You might want to work first on the hardest beat, the meatiest beat, the one containing the central event of the scene. Or—it might be more helpful to work on a "low-stakes" beat, one that creates a base level of texture of life for the relationships.

Beat changes may be punctuated with movement. Turning beat changes into *physical events* helps the audience follow the story. It helps the actors too: for instance, dropping a plate when a character is taken by surprise.

We want always to be aware of the scene's musicality. A director can disrupt the tempo, creating a sense of syncopation, by *going against* the rhythms that seem to be written into the script. *Stillness* can carry a dramatic moment as effectively as movement. It takes experience—practice—to bring your storytelling talent and style to life with the confidence of maestro Gustavo Dudamel conducting the LA Phil, or Martin Scorsese conducting a take of *The Irishman*. (There is YouTube footage of this.)

Nuts and Bolts

Finding Time for Rehearsal

Since directors are always telling me that there is no time on movie sets for rehearsal, I want to point out two ways that John Korty found time for it:

1) On location, at the end of the day, convening the cast to go over the next day's scenes in the easy manner of someone saying, "Hey, let's hang out";
2) During the rehearsal for camera, which Korty managed to make count as a meaningful exploration of the relationship.

Directors refer to the lack of time for rehearsal in movies and TV as a given. But out of a working day of at least ten hours, how much is spent with the camera rolling? An hour per day? The rest of the time is preparation. Why is preparation time so much more heavily weighted toward technical matters than acting issues?

All too often, the only opportunity for directors to work with the actors is during what is commonly called the blocking rehearsal—which is a run-through with key crewmembers present. Principal actors (the first team) are shown where they are to stand. Sometimes the actors participate in working out the positioning, but often they receive instructions while tape marks are placed. Then stand-ins (second team) are brought in for the setting of the lighting. This is not, on most sets, an opportune time for connection between the actors and the director. In fact, during blocking rehearsal, it's not unusual for actors to feel like they're being moved around like furniture.

John Korty knew how to balance the competing needs of actors and crew and make rehearsal for the camera an opportunity for substantive interaction with the actors. An inexperienced director who pauses to shift her attention to the actors while the crew stands around, cooling their heels, may become the target of eye rolls and snide remarks from impatient crewmembers. That's why it's so useful to carve out private time with the actors before you get to the set—away from the crew.

Time may be allowed for actors to practice special abilities needed for the project—dance routines, for instance. On the set of *Galaxy Quest*, there was "alien school" for the actors playing Thermians. Actresses in the TV series *Glow* were trained in wrestling techniques. Along the way, they deepened the relationships among their characters.

Do try to find time for the actors to explore the set. It's an opportunity for them to use imagination to transform the props provided by the set designer into the objects of their characters' lives.

The Matrix had a year of rehearsal. No studio executive would have ever approved a year of rehearsing relationships and situations—it was justified in the budget as a need for combat training. According to Carrie-Anne Moss, Laurence Fishburne managed to slip in substantive rehearsals of the dialogue scenes. For *1917*, Sam Mendes was given six months of rehearsal—again, the reason was the challenging logistics, but along the way, relationships between characters were developed.

How Long Should Rehearsal Be?

The two-week rehearsal periods that Mike Nichols and Sidney Lumet routinely demanded, or the months of workshopping for *Romeo + Juliet* that Baz Luhrmann is said to have asked for, are examples of *substantive rehearsal*. Substantive rehearsal is only worth doing if the script is emotionally demanding and thematically complex. Lengthy rehearsal time catapults you into a process that involves dismantling as much as constructing. Once the gears are engaged, you can't go back to the simple freshness of the first read. You could say that substantive rehearsal is asking for trouble. If you know what you're doing, it can be *good trouble*. It can be "magic playtime rehearsal"—away from producers, whose job is to *judge*. It can allow director and actors time to let go of judging, and instead *engage*—digging into the material as deep as you can go.

It's more usual that rehearsal must be fit into the director's preproduction obligations. If you fight for it, you may be able to have two to four hours a day set aside to meet with groups of two or three actors, to rehearse the relationships. But if you try to schedule rehearsal, you will learn that rehearsal is the ugly stepchild of film production—last scheduled, first cancelled—always presumed to be disposable.

It's terribly helpful to learn how to be productive with stolen minutes on the set. You can always find actors in the early mornings, in the make-up trailer. Or, if you let people know you need it and want it, you *can* scoop up time on the fly during the shooting day. Leave your DP in charge of lighting prep and snag twenty or thirty minutes here and there with the actors. Or ten minutes, if that's all you can get.

Get Organized

In order to have the confidence to ask for rehearsal, you need to know what you want to accomplish and set goals for the available time frame. Perhaps the reason to have rehearsal will be the complexity of the relationships or the challenging nature of the themes or the unique demands of the blocking. Make sure your script analysis has prepared you to speak unselfconsciously about such issues.

Organize the scenes ahead of time. Locate *sequences* of scenes that are continuous action, and therefore, really one experience. For instance, a scene that starts in a restaurant and continues on the street is a *sequence* of two or more numbered scenes. For the crew, it's two different scenes—but for the characters, it's one experience. The two locations may be—indeed are likely to be—shot on different days. Rehearsal time for the actors to live it as one experience is invaluable. It gives the actors a sense of *through-line*. If the second scene in the sequence is not precisely continuous—if there is some passage of time between the scene in the restaurant and the scene on the street—that off-camera scene can be improvised during rehearsal.

Hopefully, if your script is written out of chronological sequence, you will have created a cut-and-pasted version in chronological order like I recommended in Chapter Seven. Rehearsal is an excellent opportunity for the actors to experience the emotional events in the order in which they happen to the characters. This helps them connect organically with the arcs of the relationships.

Decide which scenes to rehearse. No matter how much time you have for rehearsal, you don't need to rehearse every scene. It depends on the script. Sometimes it's good to use rehearsal time for the big, emotionally complex scenes. But there is tremendous value in focusing on the texture-of-life scenes (such as the breakfast scene that opens *Alien*) to support your cast in creating a foundational day-to-day reality for their relationships.

Notes to Bring to Rehearsal or the Set

Make them succinct. If you've done a *script analysis* that brings you deeper into the center of the story, I'm hopeful that your ideas will be a part of you and you won't need to carry around long lists and thick notebooks. Still, you may need reminders, because it's easy to lose track of your thoughts in the pressures of preproduction and shooting. Boil them down. I'm a fan of 3x5 cards, because they can fit in a pocket and because it's not as annoying for an actor to see a director glance at a 3x5 card as to hang around while she consults her phone. Here are some topics you might include on your 3x5 card:

- What is the story about? (Loyalty? Family? Grief?)
- Your private emotional or spiritual hook into this project, your *true north*. What personal experience or knowledge of life is central to your compulsion to make this movie? If your main character suffers the effects of abandonment, where does your own understanding of *abandonment* come from? If your theme is justice, what is your own commitment to *justice*?
- The story's central image or metaphor. Like vampires. Vampires can be a metaphor for otherness, or for sexual obsession, or for human predators.

- The main character: for example, in *Moonlight,* Chiron (played, at three stages of his life, by three actors: Alex Hibbert, Ashton Sanders, and Trevante Rhodes).
- The central relationship. Sometimes it's easy to spot: In *Once upon a Time . . . in Hollywood,* the central relationship is Rick and Cliff (Leonardo DiCaprio and Brad Pitt). But sometimes there's more of a question, and the director's choice is an artistic commitment. In *Jojo Rabbit,* is the central relationship Jojo (Roman Griffin Davis) and his imaginary friend, Hitler (Taika Waititi)? Or Jojo and his mother (Scarlet Johansson)? Or Jojo and the girl in hiding (Thomasin McKenzie)? I have not spoken to Taika about this, but my feeling is that it's Jojo and his mother.
- The big questions implied by the script—for example, in *Marriage Story*: Why did they get married in the first place?
- Spines of all the characters in the scenes you are shooting today.
- The emotional events of the scenes to be shot today.
- Ideas for possible intentions and/or objectives for characters in each scene you are shooting today.
- For today's scenes: Beats. Blocking sketches. Shot list.
- Where this scene stands in the arc of the story. Is it one of the big scenes—the emotional inflection points of the story? Does it set up a later scene? Does it pay off an earlier one?
- Reminder: It's about the relationships.
- Reminder: Are the actors listening—responding—to each other? Like ping-pong!
- Reminder: Any emotional event is better than no emotional event.
- Reminder: Stay loose. Breathe. Remind others to stay loose.
- Reminder: Give yourself and everyone you work with permission to fail.
- Reminder: Ask the actors: *Do you know what you want in the scene?*

- Reminder: There is no such thing as an improv that is "wrong."
- Reminder: Listen more than you talk.
- Reminder: Love your actors unconditionally no matter their imperfections.
- Reminder: Why are you making this project? What is its higher purpose?
- Anything else that feels important to keep in your pocket during rehearsal and/or shooting (see Appendix G: Billy Ray's 3x5 Card).

Forms of Rehearsal

Meeting One-on-One with Principals

Spend time one-on-one with each of your main actors. Start early, as soon as they're cast. If you can't be in the same room, then meet via FaceTime, Skype, Zoom, WhatsApp video, or whatever new platform is invented. Find a way to be face-to-face. The disembodied voices of a phone call? Nope. It's just not the same.

Please—do *not* allow email to be your only communication with your actors. Email is useful for setting up logistics or extending messages of welcome ("I am available whenever you have concerns. Here's my email so you can contact me anytime!"), but *not* for giving direction.

Here's what I have to say about giving direction via email: Any email communication that *can* be misinterpreted *will* be misinterpreted! The purpose of meeting one-on-one with principal actors is intimacy, connection. The information actors want from you is of a more emotional nature than the information that crewmembers want from you. Reducing the complexities of characters to a few lines of email is disrespectful not only to the actors, but to the characters.

If you feel more comfortable with crew than with actors, disclose that to the actors! As in life, so in filmmaking: Honesty makes everyone feel safer. Telling actors that you feel confused and uncertain around them might make you feel impossibly vulnerable—and yet, I invite you to do exactly that. I predict you'll be surprised by how empathetically actors respond to this—or any—disclosure from their director. Most actors are generous—their response to vulnerability, expressed in private from their director, is almost always generous and loving.

Listen to the ideas of your principal actors. Many have clear, strong ideas and you can save a lot of time by asking what they are. Don't reject an actor's good idea because you didn't think of it first. But remember that actors can be very different from each other! You might ask an actor what her ideas are and she might reply, "Oh, I don't work that way—I'm not cerebral about it." There's no need to press an actor to talk about how they work. Some actors want a lot of input—even hand-holding—from a director, while others maintain an intense privacy about their process. It's all okay. Sometimes you need to spend a lot of time on a moment or idea—and sometimes it takes only a word or smile. It's not a recipe. Sometimes you need a whole cup of flour, sometimes just a pinch of cinnamon.

The purpose of establishing intimacy and connection with actors is not so you can manipulate them more perfectly—it's to ground the work in connection and collaboration. Be sure to have meaningful conversation with your lead actors over *what the film is about*. Delving into *what the film is about* does these things:

- Helps actors connect to their characters;
- Lets them know their director has something to say and they can trust her as a storyteller;
- Offers them a higher purpose for doing the role other than just the money or a way to pass the time.

When actors ask for script changes, listen carefully and take notes. Later, when you're alone, consider their ideas thoroughly; then continue the discussion at your next meeting. If their ideas take the character in a substantially different direction from what you had in mind, think of their request as an invitation to dig deeply together into the story—an invitation to collaborate—rather than a rejection of you.

By the way, very experienced actors may want to take out lines, believing they can convey the intention more effectively with their eyes—they are often right.

You can ask them what they expect from a director. Lupita Nyong'o has said of Jordan Peele, "When we first met, he asked a question no other director has asked me to date: 'What's your process and what do you need from me?' It revealed how empathetic he was, and that manifested in the way he conducted his set—he was always articulate about what he wanted, but also very adaptable. I feel like we sculpted these characters together. He's passionate about his vision without ever being precious." Lupita Nyong'o is saying that Jordan Peele *knew exactly what he wanted—and gave her complete freedom*—the highest praise an actor can give a director.

Disclose your ideas. Please note my use of the word *disclose*. You wouldn't be reading this book if you didn't want to communicate better with actors. The word *communicate* means both listening and disclosing. Tell them why you chose this project. Tell them why you believe it chose you. Open your heart to them.

In a *Deadline* interview, Martin Scorsese spoke about the way he has worked with Robert De Niro on the eleven films they've made together: "Sometimes it's a lot of talk but not necessarily directly about the scene itself. It's about state of mind, or something personal, and we'd talk about things that remind me of something that happened to myself or somebody that I know. What made he or she behave that way? And we would say, something like that happened to me a while back."

I'm a big fan of using *first-person stories* to communicate your ideas to actors. They don't need to be your own stories; they can be stories you've heard or read about. When you share first-person stories with actors, you convey the idea that the things that happen to the characters are not just plot devices—they are triumphs and calamities that happen to *people*. All emotional events, even in movies with extreme plots, are human events.

Use *questions* as a directing tool (see Chapter Four). Just be ready to back off if you get a signal from actors that your questions are becoming intrusive. My favorite use of questions is to pose one and then say, "You don't have to tell me the answer." When actors, and characters, have *secrets*, that's powerful.

Share research—articles or blogs or paintings or any kind of references you find meaningful. Send them links. Follow up. But—if you decide to send actors a list of movies you want them to watch, please *check your intention*. Why do you want them to watch these films? If you just email a long list of movies to an actor without explanation or follow-up, the actor is likely to feel like they are being given the ultimate result direction: "Please deliver a performance like Meryl Streep's in *The French Lieutenant's Woman*"; or "It would be so awesome if you play your role just like Christian Bale in *The Machinist*."

Engage with each of your principal actors on whatever topics they have an interest or impulse to discuss. You may discover things about the actor that help you communicate. If an actor references the language of physics or theater or the military, ask her about it, look it up. If she mentions Eugene O'Neill—go read some O'Neill!

You can't maintain a safe and creative workplace if anyone is melting down in public or if the production is infected with mean gossip. Set the stage for privacy and transparency by asking your principal actors—early—to exchange the promise described in Chapter Two and under *Goals of Rehearsal* earlier in this chapter. Bring it up as soon as possible once casting is final. With eye contact.

Full Cast Read-Through

Should you have one? You need to know the purpose. If you have limited time with the main actors, it might be better spent in rehearsing relationships—two or three actors at a time. On the other hand, a full cast read-through can generate excitement and optimism about the project. It can make the actors feel connected and centered in the story. I have read that Robert De Niro, for instance, insists upon it.

It's possible at this first reading to create a sacred atmosphere, the sense that this is not just a job. This can happen if there is freedom to explore and permission to fail. I think a circle helps. "Table reading" is a commonly used term for a full-cast reading, but my recommendation is—ditch the table. The table functions as a barrier. Call it a "company read" instead of a "table read," and make an open circle, with extra chairs inserted so the actors can move around if they wish—and perhaps sit near their partner in the current scene.

Beforehand, choose someone to read any narration. Edit it until it's as brief as possible. At the reading, introduce this person: "[So and so] will be reading some description—only what's necessary for clarity. He won't be reading parentheticals that suggest the characters' inner life—and you don't have to supply that yet either. Follow your impulses."

Introduce people (or ask them to introduce themselves) and speak about what the script means to you. Tell them you feel lucky to have this cast! Tell them your priorities. (I hope you're going to say—relationships!) Let them know that you want to hear all their ideas and problems, and you want to hear them directly and personally—*in private.*

Let them know that this reading is not a performance, that they can do anything they want, move around, or not, as they wish. You can say, "This is for you, more than for me. I want you to have fun, meet each other and hear the script read. I'm not looking for performance." Then mean it. Approach the full-cast read-through not as a test of the casting or of the script, but as an adventure.

Relationship Rehearsal

What about thinking of rehearsal as rehearsing the relationships, instead of rehearsing scenes? To prepare, determine the main relationships and schedule time for them. For example, I don't know whether director Ryan Coogler called the cast of *Black Panther* for such rehearsals, but logical pairings for relationship rehearsal could be: T'Challa (Chadwick Boseman) and Killmonger (Michael B. Jordan); T'Challa and his father T'Chaka (John Kani); T'Challa and Nakia (Lupita Nyong'o); T'Challa and Zuri (Forest Whitaker); the brothers T'Chaka and N'Jobu (Sterling K. Brown); T'Challa and M'Baku (Winston Duke); Nakia and Okoye (Danai Gurira).

The director will have already met one-on-one with each of these principal actors. The reason to schedule a whole afternoon with T'Challa and Nakia, and a separate whole afternoon with Nakia and Okoye, is that it's a chance for the actors to explore these relationships creatively—separate from their social relationships.

You could call a rehearsal for T'Challa, Shuri (Letitia Wright), and Ramonda, (Angela Bassett)—not just because they are in scenes together, but because they are a family and family bonds are a powerful theme of the story. Rehearsal time for Killmonger and N'Jobu can be valuable even though their screen time together is brief, because the deep sense of lost connection between this father and son informs the action of the entire film.

Of all these rich and significant relationships, I would say that *T'Challa and Killmonger* is the central one. Their scenes together are emotional inflection points of the story—and each character takes up space in the inner life of the other even during scenes when they are not together.

When the two actors arrive for their first rehearsal together, my favorite thing is to take the time to read all the scenes they have together—in chronological order, no matter where they occur in the script—all the way through, slowly—without stopping to talk. If you have limited time with the two of them, this, in my opinion, would be the most useful thing to do. No table. No blocking.

Minimal narration. The idea is to create an emotional space in which there is only the two of them in the whole world.

After this first read-through of all the scenes in this relationship, the director and actors may have thoughts to share. If it feels right, share questions, stories, research, ideas. For example, T'Challa and Killmonger are cousins who have never met. *What if you discovered you had relatives you didn't know you had?*

For this particular script, it could be interesting to read the scenes with each character's father—with Killmonger reading T'Challa's father, and vice versa—because the burden of male lineage is a powerful theme affecting their relationship.

You can suggest improvising the scenes and off-camera scenes. You can try out through-lines. You can work individual beats. You can experiment with blocking. You will rarely be rehearsing on an actual location or set, because sets are being built or lit. If you plan to try out movement and blocking, measure ahead of time the dimensions of the set and mark those dimensions by putting down tape on the floor of the rehearsal space. Bring in provisional furniture to position where you expect the actual set decoration to be placed during the shoot.

Exploring together matters like blocking, emotional history, event, and theme can save you time on the set. But more than that—time spent *working together* is a time to validate them, their presence, their questions; to connect with them on the level of artistic intention; to be their witness as they limber up their emotional and imaginative "muscles"; to prioritize relationships over individual performances; and to get ready to tell a story together.

Scene Rehearsal for Most Professional Situations

Getting a whole afternoon to surrender to magic playtime rehearsal is probably not realistic. If there has been no substantive rehearsal of the relationships before shooting, look for time on each shooting day to convene actors in someone's trailer. You cannot convince me that this isn't possible. Try for thirty minutes per scene. If you only get ten minutes, use it productively by asking questions rather than trying to frontload them with all your ideas. With practice, you *can* get somewhere in ten minutes—and accomplish a lot in thirty minutes. You might start by asking what questions they have and then return some questions back to them: "What are your thoughts?" You might have a simple, conversational reading of the lines, with eye contact, without obligation to perform, to "get the lines into the air." Or, a reading of the lines whatever way they like.

Or not! You don't need to read the lines. You can tell stories. You can address the themes of the script by making simple, relaxed references to your own connection to the material. For example—"My mom works in a state psychiatric institute like the one in this script"; "The relationship between these characters reminds me of my best friend and her ex"; "Something like this happened to me once."

If there's time, and enough room, get them on their feet. You will have blocking ideas that you have worked into your shot list and discussed with your DP. The blocking doesn't get locked until you're on set, but in a thirty-minute off-set rehearsal period, you can *prepare* for the blocking rehearsal by introducing your staging principles. For instance, that one character will be stationary and the other in motion; or that at some point they're both going to find their way to sitting on the floor.

Ask them if they know what their characters want in the scene. You don't need to make them tell you, but if they want to discuss this central choice, this is a good time.

Episodic Television

Directing episodic television has special challenges. All the episodes of *True Detective*, season one, were directed by Cary Fukunaga; for the whole first season of *Big Little Lies*, the director was Jean-Marc

Vallée; all but one of the *Fleabag* episodes (seasons one and two) were directed by Harry Bradbeer. But this is not the norm. Most episodic directors are "hired guns" who come into an established show and are expected to follow the template and direct traffic.

Sometimes directors preparing to helm a TV episode fret that the actors will think they know their characters better than the director does, and therefore won't take direction. Wait, what? Worried that the actors will claim to know more about their characters than you do? They *do* know their characters better than you do! Why wouldn't they? In the world of episodic television, it's a bare minimum of professionalism that actors maintain their characterizations even though there may be a different director every week. That means that their spines have been set since the pilot. It would be a mistake for a director to barge in and try to change basic characterizations—a disservice to the actors and to the viewing public.

They've been doing this long-term rehearsal without you, the "hired gun" director. So, look at the glass half-full—the relationships are already explored and rehearsed. Good episodic television is proof of the value of rehearsal. They've been creating emotional history and relationships—this *frees* them to be in the moment, to take risks, to play off each other.

Prepare by watching every episode so you can know the characters' backstory. See if you can come up with ideas for each one's spine. Notice which scene partners make each other sparkle. Even a hired-gun director should have an *idea*, an *intention*—what many people call a *vision* and what I think of as knowing *what the episode is about*. The director also needs to locate and get connected to the *what it's about* for the whole series.

The more consistent presence on a series is that of the producers and writers—and yet, DGA rules require producers and writers to convey their ideas for the actors indirectly, via the directors. That liaison function may not feel like what you signed up for when you decided to become a director, especially when the wishes of the actors and the wishes of the writer-producers are at odds.

But I like to transform this potential for stress into a potential for connection. Andrea Toyias, senior casting and voice director at Blizzard Entertainment, is in a similar situation—wedged between the issues of writers and actors. In a podcast, she shared this metaphor: that she thinks of herself as a *translator*—or an even more uplifting image—an *ambassador*. She lifts everyone she works with to their higher purpose. You can too.

Pay attention during tone meetings, not just to the showrunners' instructions, but also to their subtext. Give yourself permission to deconstruct their directives into ideas that are meaningful to you. By that, I mean: allow yourself to think of their briefings as *clues* to themes and secrets that matter to them. Then let yourself *translate* these hints into emotional events that you find recognizably human In other words, attune yourself to *the note behind the note*.

For your particular episode, look for relationships, themes, and emotional events. Speak to every actor every day, even if only to hear their questions. You may be able to offer them suggestions of *intentions* or *as ifs* or *opposites* that might help make the dramatic moments more startling and real, and the comedy sharper and funnier.

Don't forget the guest artists and day players. In order to bring the guest actors into the ensemble, they need attention from the director, and an opportunity to rehearse with the regulars. You can be inventive. An actor friend of mine who, as a guest artist on the original *Roseanne*, was playing a poker buddy of the John Goodman character, told me that the director had the actors in the poker scene, including Goodman, spend a morning playing poker together.

Television directors have reported to me that occasionally they encounter chaotic situations that make it challenging for an incoming director to accomplish a vision. In that case, adjust your strategy. Commit to bringing at least some kind of sanity and humanity to the story and the proceedings. I can't help wanting to advise everyone to always look for some way that your presence in any situation, especially a chaotic one, can make things better, rather than worse.

Working With Stars

Please, if you have a movie star in your project, engage with them! Don't just think of them as a meal ticket—the way that your film got financed. They have expertise. They are artists. Actors at a high level of mastery are very canny about scripts and know a lot about directing. They're good at breaking down scripts, putting their finger on the significant emotional detail and the script's playable components. Embrace them as collaborators. The reason you do script analysis in preparation for working with them is not so you can tell them how to play their roles, but so you can *keep up with them*. They are likely to have ideas you may not have thought of. You want to be prepared for their proposals, so you don't feel like they're throwing you a curve.

Some actors test to see if you have ideas. It can happen that a very busy actor has not had time to think through his role and wants the director to share ideas first, as a springboard for his own instincts. Al Pacino was asked in an interview whether he likes the director to inform him what the blocking is or whether he always knows where his character needs to move. Pacino: "I like the director to tell me where to move, and then I decide whether I want to do that or not." I'm aware that this may sound frustrating to a director. Try not to interpret such a statement as a test of wills, but rather as a commitment to arriving at the best idea for solving the scene.

You may need to prove to stars—and regulars on television series—that you know how to do your job. If you're a first-time director working with a big star, your one-on-one, face-to-face meeting with them is a chance to look them in the eye and say, "I've worked as hard as I can to prepare, because this project means the world to me. If there are times when I seem unclear, please tell me what you need from me. You can say anything you want to me—I'll be available 24/7. I only ask that you say it privately."

Movie stars are surrounded by people who don't tell them the truth, who curry favor by yessing them to death. Stars, like all actors, need a director they can trust—how can they trust you if you don't tell them the truth? Don't be intimidated. Director Betty Thomas, on the first day of shooting an HBO movie with Oscar-winner Kathy Bates, saw that Bates seemed to be holding back. After watching dailies, the producer confirmed that the scene should be reshot. Even though she was nervous, Thomas took charge and on the next day said to Bates, "I never got to say anything to you or give you any direction yesterday, but I know you're a thousand times better than that, so we have to do it again." This is *exactly* the right way to approach the situation of a good actor who is not delivering what you hoped. It's not about shining them on—it is the truth.

Here are two safe, effective ways to give direction to actors whose movie stardom is so daunting that you shrink from asking them to adjust their performances:

1) Via the big emotional and spiritual themes: "The scene is about loss";
2) Via the tool of *emotional event*: "This is not an argument, it's a confession."

Many top actors do their best work when the theme of the story is bigger than they are. They look for such stories and they look for directors to work with who care about compelling ideas and can bring them to life.

Always check in. Don't assume that because they're really good, they don't need reassurance. Be their witness. If a major actor is not getting support and honest feedback from her director, she will look elsewhere for it, to members of her entourage: her publicist, her hairdresser. Don't kid yourself about this—when an actor seems self-sufficient and unneedful of your attention, this is more likely to be a danger signal than an occasion to relax. You are the one that is going to make sure their performances are protected by your magic directing tools—the lighting, camera angles, and above all the editing. Make sure they know that. Make sure you do it.

Working With Non-Actors

Please. *Please.* Don't ask non-actors to act. Be honest with yourself about why you want to cast non-actors instead of actors. If you think that non-actors are superior because actors are liars—that isn't true. When directors tell me they want to work with non-actors because they believe non-actors will be more natural than actors, I warn them that it may not turn out that way—because non-actors do not have craft. An actor's craft allows them to repeat memorized lines over and over, making those lines honest and natural every time, without falling into set line readings.

If you are intimidated by actors—you can change that. Take an acting class; hang out with actors. Ask them what they love about acting; their favorite role; their worst and best experiences with a director. Find the ones who share your sensibility and artistic intention. Practice rehearsing with them until you feel open and confident. Keep practicing until you experience actors as your collaborators.

If you feel certain there is a good reason to cast non-actors, be sure to cast someone who is as close as possible to *exactly* like the character they're going to be portraying. And then tell them that: that they are *exactly right* for the part, that they don't have to do any acting at all. Alfonso Cuarón discovered Yalitza Aparicio, who had never acted before, and cast her at the center of *Roma,* in the role of Cleo. He then cast the role of Cleo's best friend, the family's cook, with Aparicio's actual best friend. In the role of Cleo's love interest he cast a young man that Aparicio, twenty-three at the time, thought was cute. Aparicio knew the world of Indigenous women who work as maids for European-Mexican women—her mother was a maid. She was pursuing her degree in pre-school education, so she already knew how to love and protect children—Cleo's spine. Cuarón supported her natural empathy and emotional intelligence and set her up for success by making sure she did not need to "act" at all.

Chloé Zhao, director of *The Rider* and *Nomadland,* has said, "People ask me how you get [non-actors] to feel comfortable with you. Really, you just listen to their stories."

The most important thing is to convince non-professional actors not to start "acting" when the cameras roll. Make it safe for them to keep being themselves while the camera is rolling. Some directors keep a camera running during rehearsals, so non-professional actors can get used to being recorded and understand that there need be no border between being themselves and acting in front of a camera.

Keep reminding them that *you don't want them to act.* Because after take one of the first shot, they are no longer a person who has never acted before! They are no longer a non-actor, but an *untrained actor*—with, quite possibly, many or all of the weaknesses of poorly trained actors, such as the inclination to set their line readings or a fear of looking foolish.

Keep any direction very simple and close to behavior that is recognizable from daily life. This helps them with *listening*—they can talk to the other actors the way they would to people in real life. You can use simple action verbs and adjustments: "Scold him the way you would scold your own kids"; "Tease her the way you tease your sister when she falls asleep in front of the TV"; "Really look at his face and in your mind decide whether you would take a check from this man"; "Do you want [the other character] to feel bad or do you want them to feel good?"; "This is like when you have asked the clerk where the cereal is and he said Aisle 6 and it turns out to be Aisle 13."

It's not so helpful to ask a non-professional actor to imagine a high stakes backstory different from his own. No matter how many times you urge him to remember that he has just gotten out of prison after an unjust conviction, that reminder is unlikely to land—unless this very circumstance has occurred in his own life.

Don't forget, non-professionals don't know about hitting marks or finding their light. You may need to let go of certain nuances.

Attempting to micromanage non-actors in the transitions and complications of the story is likely to bring stress and disappointment to all. Expecting them to recreate blocking from take to take in order to get coverage from every angle is not realistic. If a non-actor gets stuck in a line reading, you may need to change the line. If he insists he can't say a particular line naturally, believe him—and change it.

The one thing you *must* ask of non-actors is to *respond* to the others in their scenes. It may help that you've already told them not to think of what they're doing as a performance—because it really isn't a performance, it's a relationship. There's a simple beginning exercise I find effective as a *listening* warm-up: Have them stand opposite each other and repeat each other's names back and forth. Then follow up with another repeat exercise with one of them saying "Yes" and the other saying "No."

Mixing professional actors with non-professionals will work, as long as all of them *listen and respond* to each other. Talk and listen, that's always the deal. Director Paul Greengrass used a blend of professional and non-professional actors in the making of the film *United* 93. In the roles of flight attendants, pilots, and air traffic controllers, he cast people who had those jobs in real life. He went further: The air traffic controllers he chose had actually been in the control tower that morning of September 11th—so they had no need whatever to "act," did they? They knew their circumstances, they knew their intentions—all too well. The flight attendants and pilots who took the roles of their fallen counterparts on the actual, doomed Flight 93 made the leap, without effort, to a full identification with the inner life and behavior of the characters they were playing, their very own lost comrades.

More Examples of Rehearsal Language

If a professional actor says, "Well, one thing I know for sure is that these two don't like each other!"—that's the perfect time to say,

"Well, what is their history, anyway? Let's think about this. Maybe there's another layer. You're right, it's a struggle for power, but maybe it's really about the love they have both wanted and never gotten from each other."

If there's a false note, it may be because the actor is trying to follow an unhelpful stage direction. If something seems off, consider asking the actor, "Are you concerned about this stage direction that says, 'Her brow furrows with worry'? You don't need to follow that direction explicitly. Let's take a look at what worries she might have."

If an actor is doing something that feels completely weird and wrong to you, take them aside and ask, "Tell me about your choices."

Notice whether an actor refers to her character as "I." That's automatic permission for the director to use the pronoun "you" when talking to her about her character: "Do you know why you left your diary on the table?" Sometimes directors think it's an affectation when an actor refer to their character as "I"—but it's not. It's a legitimate acting technique, a way to bring themselves into closer identification with their role. When I'm directing, I tend to mix it up, sometimes using "you" and sometimes "he" or "she" when referring to the character—doing so feels to me like I am calling upon all the actor's resources—both their personal connection, and their powers of imagination and observation. If you are not sure, ask the actor.

Some people refer to rehearsal as an opportunity to "get comfortable"—but I prefer to call it "getting connected." "Getting comfortable" sounds dangerously similar to staying in a "comfort zone." Don't let actors retreat behind their social mask. As you expand your experience and deepen your intimacy with actors, I hope you will become fearless about asking them to drop their social mask and give you their truest truth.

Look for a response in the actor's eyes when discussing choices. No matter how invested you were in an idea, if you get a blank look, ask him, "What's your thought about trying that?" It's legitimate to ask, "Is that something you can connect with?"

Notice whether you are repeating the same direction over and over. When an actor says, "Tell me again what we're doing here" or, "I'm trying to take this all in," those are clues that your direction is confusing or overly elaborate. At this point, simplify. You can ask them, "Tell me what you understand so far, and how you feel about trying it." Or even, "Do you mean you want me to talk less? Or do you want me talk more?"

When in doubt, stop talking. Run the scene. Or ask them questions. If your discussions with the actors are becoming "heady"—that is, wordy, over-intellectualized, deteriorating into intellectual arguments over whether or not a character "would do" such and such—*stop*. Just stop. Stop talking. Say, "Let's just try it." Or, "Do you know what you want in the scene?" Or, "What do you think?"

Sometimes an actor becomes cautious in his performance and needs to get freer and let go, take more risk. Okay. Rather than telling them to give it more energy, you can say something like, "This character's high level of energy leads them to take a lot of risk, so you have total permission to take big risks, too."

Use the language of permission, rather than the language of enforcement: "It's okay to slow down," instead of "You're going too fast." When you are excited about an idea, present it gently. I find that if I say, "I have the greatest idea! You're going to love it! I know it will work!" the actors feel pressured to please me by doing it "right"—I can see it in their eyes. The most helpful thing I ever say to an actor is, "This might not work." The language of permission is more effective because it's more honest. One reason "It might not work" always works is because it confers permission to fail. But it also works because it's true. The reason I want to try something is to *see* if it will work. I have an idea in my mind and until the actors make it work, that's all it is—an idea. I don't actually know if it will work until they try it.

Another way to bring an actor into my vision is to introduce it by saying, "Something you did gave me an idea." The reason this works is that I never say it to manipulate. It's always true. When I put full attention on the acting, ideas come to me.

Rehearsal is collaborative—at its best, a crescendo of interaction.

If you want the performance "heightened," try using language that suggests digging deeper, rather than pushing harder. Instead of asking for "more tension" or "more build," ask them to choose a stronger, deeper objective, like "goad him into punishing you" or "beg her to forgive you." Instead of saying, "Bigger!" ask them to make the stakes more truthful.

Rather than saying to actors, "Put stress on this word," look for an image or fact that might be behind it. If an actor asks you how to say a line, you might reply, "You mean, what does it mean? Let's take a look." If an actor suggests an attitude or emotion for his character, you can say, "Let's find the verb for it." If an actor says, "You mean you want it more wounded?" you can reply: "*Wounded* is a powerful image. I don't know what you're going to feel, but you're absolutely right, something deeply wounding has happened to this character."

Regarding blocking: "Do you have an impulse to move on that line? If you do, go with it." Or, if they make a movement and you *don't* want that blocking, you can say, "Your impulse to move on that line is great, but let's stay in your position and keep that impulse inside—a few layers down."

When actors question a writer-director about characters, it takes a lot of courage to turn the question back and ask them, "What do you think?" The actor has asked you—as writer—why you made the character say or do this particular thing. It feels like a legitimate question to which you should know the answer—after all, you wrote it! Asking the actor to answer that question herself can feel like a terrifying admission of vulnerability. But there can be thrilling rewards: witnessing an actor be empowered to make the character her own; seeing a character make choices and transitions not because they've been instructed to, but of their own free will.

When praising actors, it's helpful to say things like, "The work is going well," "We're on the right track," "Let's keep going in this direction," "We're in sync"—rather than, "That was perfect," or "You have nailed it," or "When we shoot, do it just like that!"

Tips for Rehearsal Protocol

Don't let the actors direct each other. If you've told them you're happy to hear their thoughts on any topic as long as they tell you privately, that should help. But it's one of the dangers of rehearsal that actors can get chatty about each other's choices. As soon as you notice an actor coming forth with opinions about how someone else's character could be played, take steps tactfully, but firmly, to discourage it. Don't call them out in front of other actors. You can announce a coffee break and take the actor aside. You can use the language of permission, something like, "You don't need to worry about [actor A's performance]. I can take care of it." Let them know you welcome their input, but that they will be supporting the success of the project if they tell you their ideas privately, one-on-one.

You may wish to talk to the actors separately about their choices. Since actors don't have to agree on each other's imaginative backstory, it can be helpful if they don't even know what the other actor's choices are. When actors maintain privacy about their choices, they can surprise each other during the scene.

If producers or an actor have hired an acting coach to be at rehearsal or on set, don't fear their presence—but also don't abdicate your responsibilities. Meet with the acting coach alone; meet with the actor alone; allow the actor and coach to meet alone; and make sure there is time for all three of you to meet together. Be frank and open with everyone about your goals and concerns.

Don't allow yourself to be spoon-fed by the writers' stage directions; stage directions are clues, not instructions. Don't be distracted by the producers' demands. Some producers have good ideas, but it's the director's job to sift through the producers' input for what will serve the project.

Don't read off your script analysis notes while you are directing rehearsal. Look at the actors—not at the script—and *not* at your notes. Your script analysis was preparation. In rehearsal, work in the moment. If your ideas change during rehearsal, that's not a bad thing—that's a good thing. Sydney Pollack's subversive, brilliant idea that *Tootsie* was the story of a *man who becomes a better man by becoming a woman* only came to him after rehearsal had already begun. Rehearsal is a space for uncovering, with the actors, richness and complexity—or simplicity—that you didn't see when you were cogitating all alone with the script.

You are allowed to ask the actors to go deeper, or to make it more personal. You can do this without asking personal questions. You can lead the way. If *divorce* is a topic of the story, instead of asking, "Have you been divorced?" you can begin, "My own divorce was a relief," or, "My divorce was a nightmare," whichever is true.

Be frank and open. Be present. Share your ideas and feelings about the characters and the story. Speak with passion and commitment about *what the story is about*. Let the actors know what you need from them. Be available to hear their communications. Stay relaxed. Be yourself in your body. Stand and move around, to keep your energy flowing. Listen for the dead spot, the false moment, the line that doesn't work. When a dead spot occurs, there is work to do: an event that is yet to be realized, mysterious lines to unlock and understand, facts behind the lines to justify, images to explore, more specific choices to make, transitions to realize.

Some directors struggle with the idiosyncrasies of strong actors—or with the way actors seem to have a private language and instant intimacy with each other that leaves the director out. Get over it. Enjoy their nimble imaginations and their unguarded moments, their sometimes-brutal frankness. Let yourself be inspired by the permission they give themselves to be inventive and candid. Maybe give yourself that permission!

Take chances. Make choices. You can always change your mind. If something doesn't work, don't think of it as a failure. It's an opportunity to move forward.

Keep your sense of humor. Don't forget that in rehearsal there is nothing wrong with having fun. Don't talk just because you think you're supposed to. If you don't have something useful to say, don't say anything. Listen more than you talk. (Have I repeated this often enough? Listen more than you talk.)

Don't try to get to performance. If you leave rehearsal with ideas, with problems still to figure out, with work to do—that's good. Rehearsal should not be a constant repetition until you get it perfect—but rather a warm-up for taking risks in front of the cameras. It should end with questions, with stuff to work on. If you keep rehearsing until you arrive at performance, the actors will be on edge until the scene is shot, trying to remember and hold on to that performance. This won't help them at all on set, where we want them to be ready to work—which means, to take risks.

Last advice: Love the actors the way you love the best people in your family.

Sex, Violence, Pandemic

Neither violence nor sex should ever be improvised, whether with cameras running or in rehearsal. Scenes of violence and scenes with nudity or sexual interaction should be choreographed and marked through without emotional or physical investment. Once the physical life is set, and the actors' safety assured, the emotional life can be filled in as subtext, the same way actors fill with subtext the lines they have learned. All violence should be supervised by a professional in the field of stunt coordination.

Since the #MeToo movement, there are intimacy coordinators to keep actors safe during sex scenes. As with acting coaches or stunt coordinators, the director should meet with the intimacy coordinator alone and also with the actors alone. Then facilitate meetings between actors and the intimacy coordinator, so they can confer together without the director. Finally, find time for all of you to meet together.

Check with the intimacy coordinator, but here are some thoughts: Talk separately with each actor, ask them their concerns. Ask them what experience they have had shooting scenes that include nudity or sexual content, even kissing. Then speak with both actors together. Walk through the choreography of the movements with clothes on, without emotional commitment. Then consider the emotional content of the relationship. Not all nude scenes are alike. The characters have backstory, problems, intention, a physical environment, etc. A nude scene is finally like all scenes, in that emotional nakedness is always required of the actors.

There is an intimacy exercise I have used in my classes. It's really a *permission exercise*. I ask the two actors to sit side-by-side on a couch and to look at each other, to keep eye contact. Then I ask actor A if they are willing to touch actor B's hand. After they have said yes, I ask B if they give permission for A to touch their hand. Then I say, "Okay. Now, A, you can touch B's hand." I make sure they take every step, and give verbal permission before the next step. And I tell them it's okay to have any emotion, even to dissolve into laughter—but not to speak any words. Then I ask B if they are willing to touch A's upper arm, or shoulder, and go through the rest of the permission-giving steps. Then I ask one of them if they are willing to touch the other one's neck.

The neck is really quite intimate. By the time they are touching each other's neck, they have usually achieved a "privacy in public" and almost forgotten I am there. I then ask A to lean over and whisper to B a secret—perhaps a funny or embarrassing story from their childhood. Then I ask B to share a secret with A. The goal is to make intimacy a tool of artistic expression. This exercise can work for any relationship with a history of skin-to-skin contact—not only lovers, but, for instance, mother and daughter.

Look on the Internet for the "36 Questions That Lead to Love." I have not myself tried out this series of questions in a rehearsal situation, but it looks like something that might serve as an intimacy exercise for actors.

Read every interview you can find with director Adrian Lyne. He's been making movies with memorable sex scenes for a long time and has helpful information.

Intimacy coordinators have become as common as stunt coordinators—and now there is now a new position: COVID-19 safety coordinator.

Zoom Rehearsals

What if you can't use any of the techniques I've been recommending—because there's a pandemic and all work meetings, including rehearsals, must follow elaborate protocols arrived at by the unions and producers? As I began preparing this very chapter, we were swept into a global coronavirus pandemic. Months later, as I make final corrections, film and television production is restarting with strict safety protocols—and vaccines are on the horizon. Will interactions among actors and between actor and director ever return to what used to be considered "normal"? What might be sacrificed in the "new normal"? Was the "old normal" really so great, anyway?

During my thirty-five-plus years of teaching, the concept of *connection* has been my true north. My goal has been to help directors build creative intimacy and collaboration with actors. I've always considered *proximity* to be a major factor in making connection—spending time in the same room, making eye contact. Until the spring of 2020 I would never have imagined myself even contemplating the idea of rehearsals conducted remotely.

Since Zoom is the remote communication platform in general current usage, I'll refer to my experiences with Zoom even though there may be other apps coming along.

Zoom works great for two-person calls. If the director "pins" the actor's screen and the actor "pins" the director's screen, it can feel like the two of you are in the same room. One-on-one Zoom communications between a director and an actor can be as effective as in-person meetings—and maybe even more so, since they are so much easier to arrange. A student of mine who recently directed a television episode under pandemic protocols told me the half-hour Zoom conversations she had with each actor before arrival at the set were invaluable—partly because they were the only chance the actors had to *see her face* without full mask and face shield.

My next question was whether it's possible for remote rehearsals of two-person scenes to be of any real value. My concern was that with three people on the Zoom call (two actors and a director), eyelines would be disjointed and the director would be unable to tell if the actors were listening and responding to each other. Would it be possible in Zoom rehearsals for *intentions* to land? Would *confronting*—or *seducing, comforting, punishing, ridiculing,* or *encouraging*—another person have an effect commensurate to the powerful effect it has when you're in the same room?

I'm happy to report that the answer can be yes. The two actors pin each other's screens and the director doesn't pin anyone and instead goes to Gallery View. I've been experimenting in Zoom workshops and this works. The director can even turn off his camera to avoid distracting the actors during a run-through or improv—and then turn his camera back on to give feedback and build on the work. It's even possible to experiment with blocking ideas on a Zoom rehearsal. You need to be inventive.

What about scenes with more than two characters—or even a full-cast read-through? An odd little piece of the puzzle has been provided by television writers. I've been told that writers' room meetings work *better* over Zoom—that they can see each other and be aware of each other *better* than when seated at the usual oblong table. One of my students told me writers feel freer, more productive, and more connected in the Zoom meetings—and that, for writers' rooms, Zoom meetings may be the future.

There is also evidence that full-cast read-throughs via Zoom can work. Early in the 2020 lockdown, the staff of the animated TV show *Big Mouth* started having full-cast reads via Zoom. Animation, of course, is uniquely positioned to survive a pandemic because so much of animation work is already done remotely.

A *New Yorker* article described the first *Big Mouth* company read. Co-showrunner Mark Levin welcomed the cast: "We are so glad that you are all in this room with us. Our Zoom writers' room has given us incredible solace and company and distraction and laughter. And that's what we're all going to give to each other today, okay?" At the end of the session, the article reported that actors seemed uplifted. Said Richard Kind, "That was actually a blast!" Nick Kroll said he felt good about "the human connection and community" of the event. Even the showrunners sounded more satisfied than they expected. Showrunner Andrew Goldberg reported thus: "Maybe not as clear as an in-person read, but it was actually pretty useful."

My sense of it is that the success of the *Big Mouth* company read had to do with letting go of traditional dependence on eye contact and instead surrendering to each other's *voices*. The actor's technique of *listening* is not really about responding to words but about responding to voices, eye contact, and physical presence—sensory life. If eye contact and physical presence are denied to actors, the actors can, like people who have become suddenly unsighted, focus on sharpening their awareness of the *voices* of their fellow actors.

I have a strong feeling that it also helped that the *Big Mouth* group all thought of it as an *experiment*. Because they accepted the premise that *it might not work*, they automatically conferred upon themselves and each other *permission to fail*. Maybe Zoom rehearsals can be of value if we don't call it rehearsal. *Rehearsal* is a flawed term anyway, left over from theater and ballet. In the film world, the purpose of rehearsal is not constant repetition until we get it perfect, like it is in ballet. It's not about practicing how to say the lines, it's about warming up your powers of *responsiveness.*

Directors who convene a Zoom rehearsal or casting session can welcome the actors with a statement of full, uninhibited, joyful *permission to fail:* "This is *not* a rehearsal. This is *not* an audition. We're going to make whatever connection to each other we can—and that's *all* we're going to do. Our only goal is an open and honest exchange. If we're lucky, it might feel like *quality time* together. If, along the way, we learn something about the characters and the story, that'll be gravy."

Some productions are shooting during pandemic by committing to a 14-day quarantine "bubble," during which the whole cast and crew stay in the same hotel, living, throughout the shoot and for two weeks prior, in a campus-type situation. You could Zoom with actors every day—going over ideas or at least creating camaraderie and shared purpose.

There will still be ways to have in-person rehearsals—perhaps outdoors, with everyone in face coverings and observing social distance? I mean, even with masks, actors can communicate with their eyes. The eyes are, as they ever were, windows of the soul.

And of course, life after vaccine distribution will be another adventure. I've been encouraging my clients and participants in my Zoom Q&A's not to resist Zoom and not to fear the new protocols. Even if the vaccines are so effective that emergency protocols become a thing of the past, the usefulness of Zoom meetings will have become a part of us—because meeting via Zoom is cheaper and quicker than traveling to another city or across town in the LA traffic. So lean into it. Seize any opportunity to learn something new. You'll be safe as long as you hold to your heart a conviction that *connection* is the priority.

Please don't give up on connection. I won't.

CHAPTER TEN

Shooting

> *"Once they're in that starting-gate position and ready to go, it's really a case of nurturing, and trusting, and letting them have a good time. What I mean is being allowed to make mistakes, being allowed to try things. The key is that you all agree that you're making the same film."* —**Martin Scorsese**

If You've Had Rehearsal Before You Get to the Set

If you've been able to have rehearsal sessions, whether over Zoom, in a dedicated rehearsal room, in someone's trailer or hotel room, in the make-up area, or in stolen moments in a corner of the set—now you get to bring that process-oriented approach to the set.

When actors get to the set, we want to support their risk-taking impulses. We want to maintain their faith that, even in front of the cameras, they have *permission to fail.* We don't want them to put their efforts into preserving the flawless performances they have crafted—to start "acting with a capital A."

Shooting should feel just like rehearsal—except that shooting is better! Because there's an audience. Actors love audiences—at least, I hope that you have cast actors who love audiences, who come alive when the camera is running.

If You've Had No Rehearsal Before You Get to the Set

Directors sometimes ask me how they can give direction if there's no time for rehearsal. The answer is—you can't. If you've had zero time for meeting, brainstorming, and trying out ideas with the actors before you get to the set, you should trust your casting, trust the actors to come to set prepared, and let them perform the first take without direction. When a director attempts to frontload all his direction in the moments before the shot, the best thing that can happen is that the actors ignore the direction, commit to the choice they have brought to the set, and surrender to their partner. The worst thing is that they may become confused and self-conscious.

If there's five minutes to speak with the actors before you must call "Action," say this one thing: *Do you know what you want in the scene?* Ask this question quietly to each actor. If an actor says yes, trust them and move on. If an actor says, "I have some questions," take the time to listen; validate whatever idea seems to feel strongest to him. Then, after the first take, huddle with the actors—or speak with them individually—in order to, if necessary, offer direction to build on what they've given you.

Even if you have deliberately skipped rehearsal because you don't believe in it, I hope you read Chapter Nine, since the principles of rehearsal apply to shooting. You'll be rehearsing with the camera rolling, that's all. Whether you like it or not, *rehearsal happens*. Take one is rehearsal for take two. Like rehearsal, shooting is a *process*. If you take two steps forward and then one step back, that's okay. Even if you take one step forward and two steps back, you need not lose heart, as long as you embrace the process.

Guidelines for the Set

How can you connect with actors and maintain a creative atmosphere in the midst of all the technical and financial pressures of shooting? Here are suggestions:

1) ***Say something to each actor before and after every take.*** During shooting, the actors are at their most raw. Everything affects them. Let them feel your attention by making a connection before and after every take. You can talk to actors together or to each actor separately. The value of speaking to actors separately is that you can encourage one to make a choice that conflicts with the other actor's choice. So the actors can surprise each other.

If there is nothing important to say, that's okay. You don't need to give them a new direction every time you approach. It's okay to acknowledge them, with eye contact and an encouraging word—or a nonverbal connection, like a nod or smile or a thumbs-up—to keep things loose, or focused, or in any case, connected. To let the actor know he is supported. You can tell a joke, even, or a secret.

2) ***There's no need to shout.*** Do not shout a direction at actors from behind the monitor or across the set. If there are barriers to creating intimacy with the actors before and after takes—whether because shooting conditions are too cramped, with the crew constantly within earshot of you and the actors, or because on-set conditions are highly regulated by COVID-19 safety rules—then arrange ways to give you time to communicate in privacy with the actors. If the problem is tight space, you can ask the crew, "I know there's not much room, but would you mind doing what you can to step back?" My experience is that if you ask politely, people will do their best to help.

If you don't want others to overhear what you say to actors, you can always whisper. Does whispering rather than shouting sound weird or radical? If our goal is intimacy, then of course whispering will be more effective.

3) ***Secrets matter.***

What should you say when you talk to actors? During a Twitter Q&A, Lulu Wang, director of *The Farewell,* shared this wonderful advice: "I often give actors a secret for their character (without telling the other actors), and ask them to think of what they want—and what they're hoping doesn't happen." This is a brilliant use of *secrets* and another way of inviting actors to commit to a *need* and an *obstacle* (see Chapter Four).

You can let each actor make their own choice—a strong, dangerous, personal choice—and keep it a secret. *Secrets* give an actor privacy and autonomy in her inner life; secrets allow the characters free will. When you ask, "Do you know what you want in this scene?" there's no need to make them tell you their choice.

4) ***Don't ask for a re-performance.***

If you love the take or rehearsal that just happened but need to go again, don't say, "Do it again just like that." Instead, say things like: "I love the connection that's happening here"; or, "We're starting to cook"; or, "It's working well, let's keep going"; or, "You're coming up with new things, it's getting richer." Keep the attention *forward.* It's like the shark in *Annie Hall*: if it doesn't move forward, it dies.

5) ***Don't let them be bad.***

Watch for actors lapsing into set line-readings. Watch for tension in actors' faces. Watch for overacting. Watch for false notes. Protect the actors' moment-by-moment reality. Sidney Lumet said he could stand next to the camera, focused on the actors, and whenever his mind wandered, he'd know that something was off with the performances. He was that tuned to *connection*; he was that willing to *surrender.*

When an actor hits a false note, you can address it. You can gently, privately, ask how he felt about the previous take; his response will have an effect on what you say next. If he says, "I know, I know, that was terrible, wasn't it?" your response will be different than if he says, "I thought it was okay"—or, "I felt great about it!"

If you don't like the actor's performance, begin your communication with her by asking what she is working on. You may be able to build on her idea. If your idea is radically different from hers, you can say, "Actually what I have in mind is almost an opposite."

If the actor is unconnected to his partner, ask him, "What do you want in the scene?" or say, "Let's see if we can find a verb." Or suggest a metaphor that creates a *relationship*: "It's almost like children quarrelling over a broken toy."

If there's overacting, you can say (privately, always): "You've got everything you need; you don't need to underline it or show it to us. I'm happy with what you're doing, but it's okay to hold it about ten layers down. I trust you and I trust that it will be there. Let me do the work. Let the camera find it." Or, "Move as much as you want—but *inside*—keep it about ten layers down."

6) ***Let the actors work.***

Don't be afraid to stay low-key about it all and just say, "Let's do it again," When experienced actors feel trusted by their directors, they can often find the adjustment they need on their own. You can say, "Let's forget about any direction I've given you. All I care about is the back and forth. Just talk and listen." Or, "I trust you to bring your private understanding of the character. It's okay to play the scene more like it's you."

7) ***Use the language of permission.***

"It's okay to pick up that knife a little earlier," rather than "You didn't pick up the knife on the right line." Make your direction and feedback positive. Glass half-full!

Entertain this radical idea—that a commitment to the language of permission is as extreme as telling the actor that your direction is optional.

Imagine yourself in the actors' shoes. Don't be afraid to praise them. If an actor is struggling, offer her time, even if there isn't any. Strain is an enemy of our work. Embrace all problems as creative obstacles. Remember: It's always a good day, if only because we are all getting to make a movie.

8) ***Be honest.***

Actors want to know if it's not good enough. As long as you are speaking to them in privacy, you can say things like "You seemed a little off"; or, "We're not quite there yet"; or, "It's in and out"; or, "Let's try something new, I'm not sure this choice is still working"; or, "It's gotten surface-y, the inner life is missing"; or, "The give-and-take is missing, I need you to play off each other."

Or, "Tell me what I can do to help. Are you stuck? Tell me what's bothering you." Or, "I know you can do better." Or, "Are you holding back? It's okay to take more of a risk. I won't let them use a take that makes you look bad." Sometimes plainly telling an actor, "It's not real enough" is exactly what's needed. By the way, "It's not real enough" is a better direction than "It's not angry enough."

9) ***Don't use result direction.***

If you must use result direction, you can say, "I know I'm asking you for a result," or, "I know this is a line reading and you'll need to translate it into something playable." Result direction can do the trick, but not reliably. It's not the same as *doing the work*.

10) ***If you can, learn to "report back."***

If a take has gone exceptionally well, it's usually because the actor was so totally in the moment that she was not monitoring her performance even a little bit. So afterwards, she may have no idea how she got there. If you want her to do the same thing for coverage, the skill to *report back* to her what she has done, but in playable terms—for instance, an *objective* or an *as if*—can save the day. Instead of saying, "Let's split the difference between take two and take four"—a mystifying and frankly bullshit direction—put attention into learning how to discern the actors' choices. For instance: "The thing I liked about the take before last was that you seemed to be putting your partner at ease. This time it seemed as if you wanted his approval. Can we go back to that *putting him at ease* intention?"

11) *Make sure that the actors receive feedback from one source only.*

Any notes that the writer, producers, editor, director of photography, script supervisor, crew, or other actors have about an actor should be told privately to you. Thank the person for their communication. Then take responsibility for what, if anything, can or should be done about it. For instance, if a studio executive tells you an actor should be doing more of X, it's your job, as director, to interpret that suggestion and connect it to your understanding of the *emotional event* of the moment, or *what the scene is about.* Then you have permission—I give you permission—to whisper to the actor, if you want to: "I love what you're doing. We're going to do one more take. You can keep going in this same direction—or change it up—whatever impulse you have." *A communication of total validation and total permission is actually more likely to produce what the executive wants than trying to micromanage the actor into a literal directive.*

Make sure that you are the one who says "Cut." Explain to actors that even if they make a mistake you want them to keep going until you cut the scene. Don't let the DP or crew cut the scene. Sometimes something wonderful happens after a mistake—the actors may be jolted into the moment in a way that no one expected, but turns out to be gold. If you're shooting digitally, there's no reason to stop a scene for an actor's "mistake." If you're shooting celluloid and can't afford to continue takes that have had technical issues, arrange a signal with the camera crew so they can discreetly let you know, and then you decide whether or not to say "Cut."

12) *Prearrange a signal with your DP.*

A cinematographer who had worked with many first-time directors once told me he always takes the director aside before the shoot to prearrange a signal. If the director needed extra time with the actors, she could give this signal to the DP, who would then announce that he needed extra time to set the lighting. It's kind of pitiful, but sadly true, that while everyone accepts the need for time to fix the lighting, producers and crew become impatient if told that time is needed to support the actors.

13) *Just before the camera rolls . . .*

When you say "Action," try not to have an unconscious subtext of "On your mark, get set . . . GO!" This unintended "starting gun" subtext can give actors a feeling that "now it's time to start acting," which can create a subtle tension unhelpful for honest moment-by-moment work. Say "Action" with a sense of allowing, letting go, permission, and connection—more like an exhale, an out-breath, than an inhale.

A scene should always happen in the middle of something. Be on the lookout for an actor "winding up" to start a scene; it can be as simple to spot as an actor taking a deliberate inhale when he hears "Action." There needs to be something going on before the scene starts: an awareness of the physical life of the scene; a relaxed freedom and presence in his own body; and a connection to the other actors.

Before a close-up, you can say to an individual actor, as a way to center them in sensory, human experience: "Tell me about your childhood room." Even if the character's childhood room has nothing to do with the scene, there is nothing like the image of *your childhood room* to center an actor in a sensory reality.

It helps to ask actors to improvise the moment before or speak out loud the subtext of their intentions (for instance, one actor saying, "I'm just here to help" and the other saying, "Like hell you are," back and forth). Even if the actors just say "hello" to each other before the camera rolls, it helps make the scene feel like people talking, instead of actors saying lines. Director Jane Campion encourages actors to say out loud whatever they are thinking before each scene starts.

I can't emphasize enough how much better such a pre-scene exercise will work if you have practiced it in off-set rehearsal. I seriously invite you to practice off-set rehearsal until you are able to make it useful in a professional situation.

14) ***Stand next to the camera.***

Be their witness, not their judge.

I get flack for advising directors to stay next to the camera instead of next to the monitor, but I am serious about making this a priority. It's not about whether or not to use video assist—I've got no gripe if a director uses a hand-held monitor. My concern is intimacy. When the director is far off in Video Village, her absence is felt on the set. Video Village is where the producers settle themselves to watch over the shoot. No disrespect to producers—God love 'em, a good producer is worth gold—but it's the actors and technicians who are actually making the movie. Why would the director want to hang out with producers in Video Village instead of in the company of the people who are making the movie?

Standing next to the camera may even save time. One of the producers of *Precious* told me that director Lee Daniels liked to stand next to the camera, close to the actors, while the camera was rolling. When he did so, the actors would complete the shot in one or two takes. And get this—whenever Daniels moved away from the camera and watched the shot from Video Village, completing the shot would involve many more takes. His presence next to the camera made the actors feel safe and connected—and that made their work freer, more connected. The freer and more connected they felt, the quicker they could achieve the truth of the scene.

Some directors have told me they are afraid their presence next to the camera would make the actors nervous. From reading multiple interviews with Lee Daniels about the making of *Precious,* it's clear to me that this director had already communicated to the actors his deep emotional investment in the story and his belief that they were all collaborators in telling that story. That's the crucial reason his presence next to the camera relaxed them instead of made them nervous. They went freely to dark and difficult emotional areas with him as their witness and sentry.

15) ***Stay loose. Give actors permission to fail.***
For example: "This won't be the last take. I'll definitely do another, no matter how this goes." Or, "This might not work, but I feel like it's worth trying." Freedom to fail may be the director's most powerful tool.

Keep your attention forward. Stay positive. If there's a problem, get excited about finding the solution, even when minutes and dollars are ticking away. Staying calm under pressure nourishes your resources of intellect and imagination. If needed, find a quiet corner to be alone for five minutes. If you relax your eyes and your brain, a new idea will come, I promise.

When an actor blows a take because he got the lines wrong, tell him you don't care if the lines are right—even if you do. When exactitude is required—like if the actor plays a physicist or a Supreme Court Justice—and the actor is struggling to master the arcane terminology, you can go up to her and whisper something like, "This dialogue is a bitch and I know you've worked hard. I'm not worried. We have all the time in the world." I have seen this tactic work like a charm.

Okay, what if you suspect that the actor has not worked hard on the lines? You might ask quietly, "Do you need some time to go over the lines? We can take a break and I can get someone to run them with you." Then find someone to help them, usually the script supervisor. Even if you suspect that the actor has been lazy, you should always treat him like a professional and find a professional solution.

If you have not gotten what you want from an actor after many takes, you might try saying, "You know, I can put this scene together in the edit. I've got enough to make it work. I'm not worried. But let's do it again anyway. Let's do it different. I don't care what, just something different." Releasing the pressure to *do it right* can work wonders.

You can even say, "This time let's do it wrong." Lulu Wang, in a Twitter Q&A, was asked what to do, "if an actor is still not giving you what you want/need take after take . . ." She declared, "I ask them to *break the scene*—in other words, to do it BADLY. Give me all your bad acting, the worst version of the scene, all of the things they're afraid of: cheesy, melodramatic, etc. Sometimes, doing the thing you're most afraid of sets you free."

The terminology, "one more take for safety," is not particularly helpful to actors. If you want one more for safety, consider the advice of director Robert Townsend. When he has gotten the shot and wants to see where else the actor can go, he asks for "One more for love"—and claims he ends up using that "love take" 99% of the time!

16) ***Make it feel like real life, only better.***

On the set of *Goodfellas,* Scorsese brought his mom in to cook for the dinner scenes, so the actors could feel like they're eating an Italian dinner for real. Illeana Douglas said that Scorsese created an on-set environment, "where you literally did not know the difference between when the camera was on and when the camera was off—this environment where nobody feels embarrassed or like they did something wrong."

17) ***Learn to match energies.***

Pay attention to an actor's energy level. If you feel an actor's energy is low, allow your energy to be a little bit higher than hers; that way she'll be able to hear you; as a bonus, you may be able slowly to coax her energy up. If her energy is unnaturally high, allow yours to be a little bit lower than hers; it may calm her.

18) ***Don't absorb negativity. Don't take anything personally.***

If the actors get upset with anything—a technical issue or problems with a costar, even a disagreement with your direction—don't take it personally. Fix the problem if you can, and if you can't, listen anyway. Sometimes all the actor needs to do is get something off his chest. Make sure he vents to you *privately*—not overheard by others.

19) ***Marks, matching, overlapping.***

The director's priority should be to have the scene go somewhere, to take the audience somewhere, to create that shimmer that gives the sense of *something happening*. The actor's priority is to be real in the moment. The worst thing that can happen to an actor's performance is that she buys into a set way of saying her lines. Actors who stay alive and dynamic on every take and seem not to change the performance are actually becoming freer and freer, moving, with each take, a little deeper into the meaning of the script and into their own resources. Remember the word "emotion" has as its root the word "motion."

When actors prioritize the technical considerations of matching shots and hitting marks, performances can become slick and technical. I think it is possible for directors and technicians to approach hitting marks, matching performances, and overlapping with creative solutions instead of conventional wisdom. When you meet with your DP, script supervisor, editor, and sound technician, include these issues in your discussions. For instance, if you've been approaching scenes with the actors in terms of possible objectives and spines, matching will not be as big a deal as you might fear. And if you've had the conversation with your editor and sound technician about overlapping that I recommended in Chapter Nine, you'll be able to feel confident allowing the actors to pick up cues.

20) *Direct the off-camera actor.*

The best way to move an actor off a choice that isn't working may be to give a direction to the other actor, the off-camera actor. If you want the on-camera actor to get angrier, you can ask the off-camera actor to pick the fight. The reason this works is that the scene is about the relationship.

21) *Know when to move on.*

In the days of celluloid, it used to be called knowing when to call out *Print!* A script supervisor may call it "circling" a take. Sometimes an actor can help you decide whether a take is good enough to move on by letting you know whether it "feels" solid. But you shouldn't count on the actor to monitor his performance—that's the director's job. An actor should not be watching, checking, and controlling his performance. Here's why: Sometimes an actor gives a marvelous, unaffected, unguarded performance and thinks, incorrectly, that the take was bad. You'd be surprised at how often an actor says "I didn't feel it" and it's the best take of the day. When the performance has simplicity and truth, to the actor, it may not feel like anything at all.

A director may make mistakes about whether a scene is as good as it's going to be and it's time to move on, but if you're shooting digitally and have saved everything, don't beat yourself up. It just means that you are still learning—and a condition of "open to learning" is the best place to be. All artists are open to learning throughout their lives.

22) *Concentrate. Care. Do what you need to do.*

During filming of *When They See Us*, the wrenching true story of the five young men who were falsely imprisoned for the 1989 attack on the Central Park jogger, the producers and director Ava DuVernay knew that emotions were likely to run high on the set—the show was a recreation not only of the events following the 1989 case, but of the daily experiences of all too many African-Americans. So they hired a grief counselor to be on set, available to all. Not every actor turned to the grief counselor for support—but it matters that it was offered. That level of commitment matters.

Whether or not there has been formal rehearsal, make an effort on set to find time with actors that isn't focused on social niceties or on the logistics of filmmaking—but instead is magic time, quality time, a circle of concentration that cannot be distracted by technical snafus or fears of losing the light. There's no one way to do this. Some directors are playful and charming; some are nurturing; some are almost military in their concentration and authority. Some are low-key; some are goofy; some are business-like; some are magnetic. Some lead the charge with their passion for the project. Some radiate a deeply intuitive, even spiritual, awareness. You are you.

23) ***Be prepared for the actors to become more interested in each other than in you.***

Actors have always been dependent on writers to give them a good script, cinematographers to light and frame them properly, editors to discard their less-than-stellar takes—and directors to shepherd the emotional logic and visual reach of the story. But the central dependence of actors is on each other. Surrender of the actors to each other is their safe place, their creative place. Don't take it personally if the actors forget you're there because they're so involved with each other. All it means is that the story is taking on a life of its own.

24) ***Make your set a safe place.***

Make everyone on set your collaborator in maintaining safety. Insist that the production be a gossip-free zone. Follow all safety protocols cheerfully—but don't allow safety restrictions to get in the way of *connection*. Make this your mantra: *I am committed to safety and equally committed to connection—and I need your help.*

25) ***Be inventive—at every stage of the process.***

If a director is following his notes mechanically because he is too frazzled and stressed out to make decisions and come up with new ideas in the moment; if he is answering questions just to have something to say, without an idea he really believes in; if he is focused on using the right jargon and not making a mistake—I can just about promise that that this director's movie will not come out the way he hoped.

Even if you are very adept at working with actors, there will still be times when you make mistakes and say the wrong thing. Live in your own skin. Take risks. Rehearsal is not useless even if you don't use anything that came out of it. Preparation is not a waste of time, even if you end up veering off in a new direction. The whole entire process, from preproduction through editing, is one of revision and re-envision of the story, until *the story finally discloses itself to you.*

Stay open. You may see amazing things.

CHAPTER ELEVEN

Directing Children

Do You Like Kids?

Working with children can change and elevate a filmmaker. Miranda July was asked how she felt about working with child actors: "It brings out so much love and tenderness. That's a great way to be feeling all day when you are working."

My best advice on directing children is a series of questions: *Do you like kids? Are there children in your life? Are you relaxed and inspired when you are around children?* And this crucial follow-up: *Do you remember your own childhood?*

All of which is to say: *Can you meet children where they are?*

In a commentary, Richard Linklater said he made it part of his prep for *School of Rock* to visit, in his memory, his ten-year-old self. He remembered that when he was ten, he appreciated adults who treated him like a real person; he said that gave him the metaphor and tone of the movie. It also helped that he had a ten-year-old at home: "If I didn't have a ten-year-old kid, I might have been afraid I wouldn't have a rapport."

Children have high energy. That scares some adults, but a good director of children digs that about kids. The truth is that when kids are listless and bored, it's harder to get them to focus and concentrate than when they are full of unpredictable vitality.

Probably no one has had more success directing kids than Taika Waititi (*Jojo Rabbit, Hunt for the Wilderpeople, Boy*). But for Taika, it's not a learned skill—it's his lifeblood, his emotional

DNA. When Taika was tapped to direct *Thor: Ragnarok,* he consulted with me to prepare, because it would be the first movie he directed that he had not written. I already knew him and his work, so I thought of investigating the theme of *family*—it seemed to me that the conflicts in the *Thor* mythology could be approached as family conflicts, and I knew that themes of *family* echoed throughout Taika's work. But when he asked me what I thought of the script, I blurted out, "It feels like it was written by a seven-year-old!" Later he told me that random statement liberated him and gave him a mantra that sustained him throughout the shoot: "Cool! I get to direct a movie that was written by a seven-year-old!" This framing released him to his sweet spot and gave him the relief of *permission*: He knew he already had access to his inner child—and thus had everything he needed to direct the movie.

Casting Young Roles

Here's a major decision: Will you cast children with training and professional experience or children who have never acted before?

If you want to cast non-actor children, please go about it with care and intention. Directing children requires more patience than directing adults, and working with non-actor children requires even more. To anyone preparing to direct a project with non-professional children I recommend a video you can find on YouTube: "The Making of *Rabbit-Proof Fence* Featurette." With this caveat: before you watch the featurette (or the full commentary, if you can find it), please first watch this wondrous film in its entirety!

The main characters of 2002's *Rabbit-Proof Fence* (based on a true story) are three girls of the Stolen Generations of Australian Aboriginal children who were kidnapped by the White government, but escaped and made the long trip home on foot. The events took place in the early 20th century. Director Phillip Noyce felt he needed children to play Molly, Gracie, and Daisy who lived in remote areas of Australia and for whom White culture was not dominant in their daily lives. He met 1200 children, selected sixteen, and hired a coach to work with them. From those sixteen he cast Everlyn Sampi, eleven; Laura Monaghan, nine; and Tianna Sansbury, seven—they are extraordinary.

Director Niki Caro, in a commentary and featurette that's now available in a 15th Anniversary Blu-Ray edition of 2002's *Whale Rider,* describes a similar process for the casting of the lead role. The casting department spread out far and wide over New Zealand; four girls were chosen to take a one-month workshop with a coach. Keisha Castle-Hughes, chosen to play Paikea, was nominated for an Academy Award.

Lenny Abrahamson generously gave many interviews (*The Wrap, IndieWire, The Guardian, Comingsoon.net*) after *Room* came out. Everyone wanted to know how he got that amazing performance from Jacob Tremblay in the role of Jack. Abrahamson says it was a good thing that Tremblay had experience performing in commercials, because this wasn't something a child could do on instinct alone—the boy had to be a disciplined professional: he had to lie in the wardrobe and turn his head just the right way; he had to roll himself up in a rug. When Abrahamson first saw the audition tapes, Tremblay stood out, but Abrahamson worried that he handled the lines almost too well and was "almost too polished" for a naturalistic film like *Room.* But once they met and spent a day together, Tremblay dropped that "performed" quality and quickly proved able to be natural in front of the camera. After finding that Tremblay had a knack for acting—real acting, not just the "bright and breezy" touch that works for a thirty-second commercial—Abrahamson said, "We have our child."

M. Night Shyamalan said in interviews with the *Los Angeles Times* and *Reel.com* that until he met Haley Joel Osment, he didn't believe in such a thing as a "child actor." "I thought—they're not really acting—you catch them at a certain time in their lives and they're just themselves." He thought he'd have to go outside L.A. to find a child natural and innocent enough to play Cole. But

Osment's level of preparation and emotional intelligence calmed all the director's fears. The ten-year-old, who had been acting since he was six, had read the script twice and had a thorough understanding of the character and the movie. Shyamalan had been concerned about exposing a child to the intense material—"but it never entered my mind with him. I treated him exactly the way I treated all of the other actors."

When Saoirse Ronan was cast by Joe Wright to play Briony in *Atonement,* she'd been acting in television and films since she was nine. Jurnee Smollett was already a seasoned performer in sitcoms when she played the title role in *Eve's Bayou,* directed by Kasi Lemmons. Jodie Foster began acting at the age of three and had racked up an impressive resume in television shows and commercials when Scorsese cast her as Iris in *Taxi Driver.* Theodore Melfi, director of *St. Vincent,* found Jaeden Martell, a ten-year-old veteran of commercials, to play Oliver opposite Bill Murray. He'd been looking for four months—and spotted Jaeden in a commercial. Jaeden was playing the role of a fearless kid with such freedom and commitment that Melfi immediately called casting and said, "You've got to find this guy."

To carry a lead role, you need a kid—whether or not they have acting experience—whose imagination is susceptible, who is emotionally intelligent, and whose face expresses every flicker of emotion. You could call it charisma or star quality or the "it" factor. You could call it, as Phillip Noyce did, that indefinable thing that "makes the whole world want to adopt these children." You should spend whatever time you need to find the right child. Abrahamson met hundreds of boys before he chose Jacob Tremblay to play Jack in *Room.* Richard Linklater met 300–500 children, and included a mixture of professional and non-professional kids for *School of Rock.* When casting the lead role of Hushpuppy in *Beasts of the Southern Wild,* Benh Zeitlin found Quvenzhané Wallis after meeting with 4,000 children over a period of nine months.

4,000! To cast the young people in HBO's *My Brilliant Friend,* creator Saverio Costanzo spent seven months and met *8,000* young people.

Doug Atkinson said in his DVD commentary for *Akeelah and the Bee,* "I knew the movie couldn't be made unless we found the right Akeelah. I wasn't just looking for a kid to whom I could dictate a part; I was looking for somebody who understood it and with whom I could have a collaborative relationship." This was Keke Palmer, already an experienced professional actor.

Some directors, however, are adamant that they want untrained actors. And that's fine if you know what you're looking for, and why. Mark Romanek said in a DVD commentary for *One Hour Photo* that he found that studios tended to err on the side of energy and perkiness. Romanek wanted Dylan Smith, who had never acted before, to play Jake opposite Robin Williams as Seymour. He felt confident the boy could play the role, because Dylan seemed naturally unaware there was a camera—and because he was really *listening,* not pretending to listen.

Dillon Freasier, who played H.W., Daniel Plainview's son in *There Will Be Blood,* had never acted before. Paul Thomas Anderson told interviewers that he'd wanted a kid who'd actually grown up around ranches and horses—"a man in a young boy's body." Casting director Cassandra Kulukundis scoured the schools in rural areas of Texas, asking principals and teachers to recommend boys who "knew outdoor work."

David Gordon Green's first feature was *George Washington,* a poetic, profound film with exquisite performances by mostly first-time actors he hand-picked from churches and YMCA casting calls around North Carolina. In a *Los Angeles Times* interview, he said he wanted to avoid "acting school graduates who have learned how to eliminate their regional accents." Here's how he expressed what he was looking for: "people who are either full-grown or have just been born." By children who are "full-grown," I think he means what many would call an "old soul"—and which I would call *emotional intelligence*. My understanding of someone who has "just been born" is an individual who is naturally *responsive* and *emotionally curious*.

Dan Schneider, for decades a creator and executive producer at Nickelodeon, said in a *Daily Variety* interview that he would routinely eliminate the "kid actors who deliver their lines in a kind of 'look how cute I am' manner." He continued, "I tend to avoid kids who are overly trained and don't seem like real kids anymore." Schneider is careful to create a low-pressure atmosphere in his casting sessions, and asks the youthful participants about their day before jumping right in. He doesn't necessarily expect the young actors to "nail it" the first time.

One of my students told me she looks for natural *presence* in children by watching for their *response*—in other words, paying attention to whether they are involved in the scene, even if they are not speaking.

Benh Zeitlin knew he had found his lead when Quvenzhané Wallis refused his direction to throw a water bottle at another actor—because she believed that it wasn't right to do so. Zeitlin said, "I realized this is Hushpuppy, that that's what this whole movie is about: this moral girl who believes in right and wrong so strongly."

When I consulted with Deniz Gamze Ergüven during her preparation to direct *Mustang*, she knew she was unlikely to find young actresses in Turkey who were professionally trained and was worried about finding non-actor children who could convey the distinct personalities of each of the five lead characters. I assured her that she would be safe if she cast the five girls she felt were the most imaginative, the most available emotionally, the most responsive to their partners. She could then encourage them *not to act at all*, to be their truest selves—*under the circumstances of the script*. That would be the best way to get performances that were different from each other—because every single human being who behaves truthfully is different from every other.

After a certain amount of camera testing, Paula Kaplan, a casting executive for Nickelodeon and mother of two, sits down with each potential hire. She told *Daily Variety,* "I want to be in a room with the kid so I can really engage with them and hear how they answer questions—without the manager or the mother."

Create a relationship with the parents of the children you're considering. Martin Scorsese had cast Jodie Foster in *Alice Doesn't Live Here Anymore,* so her mother trusted him enough to allow Jodie to play the far more intense *Taxi Driver* role.

Parents who know nothing about the craft of acting may coach their children with line readings. I'm not sure there's much use in instructing parents not to coach their children, but if you create a genuine relationship with them, you may be able to get them to at least be honest with you about the coaching they have done.

Still, if the parents are actors themselves, the children will get better quality coaching. Quick list of some young actors who were coached by actor parents for their breakout roles: Freddie Highmore (*Finding Neverland*), Saoirse Ronan (*Atonement*), Keke Palmer (*Akeelah and the Bee*), Noah Jupe (*Honey Boy*), Haley Joel Osment (*The Sixth Sense*). Osment has said he did script analysis with his dad for every role.

A director needs from her young actors not only screen charisma, but also an ability to maintain concentration despite the technical distractions of filmmaking. If a child has no professional experience, it's not fair to expect him to behave like a professional. Consider hiring a coach. Creator and director of *My Brilliant Friend,* Saverio Costanzo, had the genius to hire acting coach Antonio Calone. Calone opened a workshop, a kind of laboratory, guiding these new actors through the process of auditioning as well as shooting.

Phillip Noyce hired Rachael Maza, an experienced Aboriginal actress, to support his new actors. Noyce and Maza spent six weeks guiding the children to invest in their roles in ways that were safe, effective, and expressive. Said Maza, who was present not only for casting and rehearsals, but on every day of shooting, "It's not a matter of teaching them to act. It's more a matter of harnessing the energy that's already there." Along the way, Maza and Noyce introduced the children to the technical demands of filmmaking. Noyce says that during final screen testing for *Rabbit-Proof Fence,* they photographed the children with up to five cameras rolling simultaneously. He also spoke to them one by one, to ask how they thought they would feel with cameras trained on them constantly. Since the children in the story become tired and injured during their long trek across Australia, there was also a tutorial in how to walk with a limp.

If you don't have access to a professional acting coach, there are actors who could be great at this. Look for an adult actor who loves children and is connected up to the subject matter, or perhaps an adult actor who used to be a child actor.

The Age of Eight Is a Game Changer

Children, whether or not they've had acting training or ever acted before, are closer to their simple, primal identity than adults. The whole process of becoming "mature"—leaving childhood behind and undertaking the responsibilities of adulthood—involves intellectualizing our feelings.

Infants express their feelings instantaneously: wailing in pain or frustration; screeching with joy. Little by little, children are taught to suppress those spontaneous expressions, taught not to act out their feelings. It's surely necessary to the survival of civilized society that children learn to give attention to the needs of others. But along the way, they also pick up the directive that certain feelings are unacceptable. That means that when an adult wants to become an actor, they need to *unlearn* their social conditioning. As David Lynch has put it, "We think we understand the rules when we become adults, but what we really experience is a narrowing of the imagination."

Children don't have as well-developed social masks as adults. They have good imaginations and have not yet intellectualized their feelings. If a child is older than eight, you can discuss emotions of the character with them quite directly. You can say, "Can you imagine how worried this little girl must be when her sick mother has run out of medicine?" Adult actors might play the scene *as if* the actor's own mother is sick—but there's no need for that with kids, because their imaginations are so susceptible. And for this exact reason—the susceptibility of their young imaginations—it's not a good plan to insert into their heads the idea that their mother could be sick. You can say quite clearly, "Your mother is fine, but the little girl in the story has a sick mother. Can you imagine how sad and worried that girl would be?"

I found a helpful article in *Scholastic.com* regarding cognitive development in six to seven-year-olds that helped me understand why, if a child is younger than eight, it's best not to even mention the illness of mothers. Through the age of seven, a child believes that what he thinks and feels is felt by everyone else as well. Children of six and seven struggle to distinguish between fantasy and reality.

This is why a child younger than eight may not be able to separate herself from the character she is playing. So if you say anything about illness of mothers to a child who's seven or younger—even if the child's mother is sitting right there on set, perfectly healthy—the worry that her mother might be sick could seep into the child's soul.

Instead, with children younger than eight, be entirely direct about emotions. You can say, "Do you know how to be sad if I ask you?" You can reference other movies: "Do you remember how sad and frightened Simba was when he found Mufasa? How much he wanted Mufasa to wake up and comfort him?"

Seven-year-olds who have given deep, beautiful performances include Aida Mohammadkhani (*The White Balloon*), Justin Henry (*Kramer vs. Kramer*), and Tianna Sansbury (*Rabbit-Proof Fence*). Drew Barrymore was only six during shooting for *E.T. the Extra-Terrestrial,* as was Quvenzhané Wallis when *Beasts of the Southern Wild* was shot. Those castings worked out brilliantly—but in order to relieve yourself of practical as well as ethical burdens, my advice to you, if you're casting a six or seven-year-old character, is to search for an eight-year-old who looks younger.

Let's take *Room*. It's in the script that Jack is five—the very first scene is his fifth birthday "party." But Lenny Abramson knew that a five-year-old would not have the emotional stamina to play the role. Abrahamson met Jacob Tremblay when he was seven. He waited until Tremblay was eight before he started shooting. This was so smart! No one who sees the film has any trouble believing that Jack is five—as audience, we suspend our disbelief because we believe the relationship between Jack and his mother.

Casting director Alexa Fogel has said of the young people she found for roles in HBO's *The Wire* (including Michael B. Jordan): "These were four really special boys. They had incredible instincts and listened well. These aren't your typical kids." Please note that the youngest of them was eight—I looked it up.

Eight is a magic age. When a child is eight, you can ask for emotional intelligence—*as well as* innocent imagination and responsiveness. One summer I taught creative dramatics to classes of eight to ten-year-olds. When I used scenes from Shakespeare's *Midsummer Night's Dream,* I learned that you can still have a serious discussion about fairies with a child of eight or nine. When I gave them a half-hour version of *Oliver,* and asked them how they understood the scene where Bill Sikes hits his lover, Nancy—kids knew: "Sometimes grown-ups stay with other grown-ups that aren't good for them."

Kids and Line Readings

When child actors fall into line readings, it means they've not only memorized the line, they've memorized an inflection, an intonation, a set way of saying the line. Their parents may have coached them in line readings. But there can be another reason: Children learn so quickly! And then get bored and fall into a singsong.

Once you start working, in rehearsal or on set, you've got to get them off their line readings—and into a relationship with the other actors in the scene. Their lines need to be a *response* to the other actors. If all the characters in a scene are children, you, or your coach, might set up games of physical interaction, like throwing a ball while they rehearse lines. Or have them play safe forms of physical conflict games, like pillow fighting, fake karate (no actual hits), or imaginary swordplay—while saying lines—with full commitment to sound effects. This will help create a muscle memory of responding to the other actor, rather than replaying the loop of a memorized line reading.

If the parents have drilled the kids with line readings, you may need to change the lines. You can tell the kids *not* to learn lines word-perfect, but rather encourage them to imagine that they are improvising.

Meet Children Where They Are

Don't be afraid to improvise with kids—the more you make it feel like play, the better. If the scene is a bunch of kids planning to save the town from an alien intruder, you could do a parallel improv of kids setting up a fort or club. Or, if the scene is kids setting up a club, you could improvise planning to save the community from the alien intruder—the famous imaginations of children can leap pretty effortlessly to either one.

Verbs work with kids—like an objective to "make him feel bad for what he's done." Metaphors (*as ifs*) are an invitation to "Let's pretend"—like, "Let's try the scene (or improv) like this is a game your friends used to like playing, except there's this one kid who always cheats." The imagery needs to be from the world of kids. If you suggest, "Play the scene as if the mortgage is due"—that's not a big concern in the world of children and is unlikely to land.

For kids, especially in scenes with each other, "let's pretend" is the sweet spot.

Empower the children on set. Let them hold the camera or clap the slate or call *Action*. Phillip Noyce kept the children's families on set so they wouldn't get homesick, and introduced the children slowly to crew, "who we hoped would become extended family." Every day he was affectionate with the children, joking and playing with them, making it a game, acting the scene out for them.

Meet children in their world by using simple emotional concepts that children know, like not being believed, wanting to help, needing a friend, not wanting to share toys. In an NPR interview, Quvenzhané Wallis said that Hushpuppy was "a little girl who wanted to just follow her father, because her mother wasn't there, and she just wanted to go, kinda just like went after everything that he has done."

Lenny Abrahamson found a portal into each scene through the eyes of a five-year-old. "You're looking for things that unlock the scene in simpler, more emotionally available terms, like really strong memories. It's finding ways of describing what was happening in the story that would make sense to him, that would be appropriate for him, and wouldn't scare him." When Jack had to be frightened, Abrahamson asked the boy to recall his scariest nightmares. "He told me about dreaming he was being chased somewhere," said Abrahamson. "I asked him, 'Do you remember what it felt like?' and 'How were you breathing in the dream?' and he'd start panting and doing it a bit awkwardly, and I'd tell him, 'Oh come on, you can really show me,' and then I'd pant at him and he'd pant at me, and then we'd make it a game."

Abrahamson respected Tremblay as a talented and emotionally deep young actor—but still a little boy. They were shooting a scene where Jack had to get angry with his mother and shout at her. Abrahamson said, "He just didn't want to do it." Abrahamson pressed Jake to say why and Jake eventually said he loved Brie too much to be rude to her. "So we brought the whole crew in and we did this shouting competition, turned it into a game." Soon, Jacob was okay with it.

Let kids play. I had a conversation with a sought-after audition coach for children who told me that out of the hour that was booked for his session, he spent forty-five minutes playing video games with the child. After that, the final fifteen minutes would be stunningly productive. He said that whenever he worked this way, the kid got the job.

Make friends with the kids in your project; get a simple, straightforward, fun communication going; involve them in the story; use their ideas; do improvisations. You can use rehearsal to get to some range: the actor's sweet side, quiet side, cocky side. Try all that, but if none of it works, go ahead and demonstrate for them how to do it.

Tell them they are good, even when they aren't. But be sure it's the truth anyway.

Kids In Scenes With Adult Actors

Take time to enlist the adult actors to help you. In a scene with a mix of adult and child characters, what matters are the relationships—not the individual performances and line readings. The adult actors can help tremendously if they create an off-camera relationship with the child actors.

"When I met Brie Larson [to play Ma in *Room*]," said Lenny Abrahamson, "not only did you have an amazing actor, but you've also got this really warm, really funny, really vibrant person. Jack and Ma have gotta be silly together and they've gotta play. Kids know if you're bullshitting and Brie isn't and Jake knew that. We made sure that the set was built three weeks before we shot, so that Brie and Jake could hang out there together and get routines going and we could get Jake totally familiar with the space. We got them to build a lot of their toys and ornaments that they have. They built them together—we gave them tasks every day. Brie was hanging out with Jake, playing Legos with him, talking *Star Wars* with him."

Said Emma Donoghue, the screenwriter, "Brie went to extraordinary lengths to bond with Jake, and she did a lot of coaching of him, too. Even though he was terribly good, he's a small child, so Brie did friendly reminders."

Abrahamson added, "If you're watching the rushes, you'd hear me talking to him all the way through scenes. Brie could tune that out and still be there, and not only tune it out but sometimes help me—'Come on, Jake, just turn around a little bit. You know how you're supposed to sit back like that?'—and then she'd slip right back into the full emotional intensity of whatever she was doing."

Richard Linklater said Jack Black confided his fear of kids because, "Children can tell if you're a phony." But on the set of *School of Rock*, he turned into a kid himself: "Jack is basically a ten-year-old," says Linklater. Black played kids' games with them, but also loved the sensitive scenes—"He's very moral when it comes to kids."

Gore Verbinski reported that Nicolas Cage, in *The Weather Man*, was tender and supportive during shooting of the scene when David takes his daughter (Gemmenne de la Peña) shopping for a new wardrobe.

Benh Zeitlin included Quvenzhané Wallis in the casting of Hushpuppy's father: Three men were in the running and the director had each of them spend time playing games with her. The young actors of *Rabbit-Proof Fence* felt empowered by working with David Gulpilil—a major Australian actor and icon in the Aboriginal community ever since his first role in Nicolas Roeg's 1971 *Walkabout*.

In a 2010 *Esquire* article about Robert De Niro, Jodie Foster is quoted thus:

"By the time I got the role in *Taxi Driver*, I'd already made more stuff than De Niro or Scorsese. I'd been working from the time I was three years old. So even though I was only twelve, I felt like I was the veteran there. De Niro took me aside before we started filming. He kept picking me up from my hotel and taking me to different diners. The first time he basically didn't say anything. He would just, like, mumble. The second time he started to run lines with me, which was pretty boring because I already knew the lines. The third time, he ran lines with me again and now I was really bored. The fourth time, he ran lines with me, but then he started going off on these completely different ideas within the scene, talking about crazy things and asking me to follow in terms of improvisation.

"So we'd start with the original script and then he'd go off on some tangent and I'd have to follow, and then it was my job to eventually find the space to bring him back to the last three lines of the text we'd already learned. It was a huge revelation for me, because until that moment I thought being an actor was just acting naturally and saying the lines someone else wrote. Nobody had ever asked me to build a character. The only thing they'd ever done to direct me was to say something like 'Say it faster' or 'Say it slower.' So it was a whole new feeling for me, because I realized acting was not a dumb job. You know, I thought it was a dumb job. Somebody else writes something and then you repeat it. Like, how dumb is that? There was this moment, in some diner somewhere, when I realized for the first time that it was *me* who hadn't brought enough to the table. And I felt this excitement where you're all sweaty and you can't eat and you can't sleep. Changed my life."

Treat Young Actors As Equals

> ***"It's the same as an adult actor, only you have to be more patient."*—Kenneth Lonergan, *You Can Count on Me, Manchester by the Sea***

Both Phillip Noyce and Lenny Abrahamson say they direct the kids live while the camera is rolling. Noyce also said that for close-ups, he'd be the one, rather than the other children in the scene, to sit behind the camera reciting the offscreen lines. He said sometimes he would change the way he said a line, to get a different performance.

Most directors agree that under the age of five, you don't "direct" a child. You create an environment where they can be themselves and then capture moments that you cobble together in the edit. Gore Verbinski noted in a *Chud.com* interview that often you have to direct children externally: "You have to talk to them about how to make their face because they're not attuned with their instrument." With Nicholas Hoult and Gemmenne de la Peña (in *The Weather Man*), however, "I could direct them the same way that I direct any other actors."

Said Phillip Noyce, "With most performances, the editor has to carefully construct the performance in each scene, and you usually have to manufacture the performance, sometimes totally, carefully selecting the good moments, stringing it all together. But Everlyn was always totally in the scene, whether it called for her to celebrate or suffer, to look determined or to look weak. She was right there, no editing tricks were necessary. Even though they're children, all the history, the heartache, the struggles, the triumphs of indigenous Australia was in them. Everlyn had all the characteristics of the real Molly. What I had to do was calm her fears and let her realize that her natural instincts were all she needed to carry off the part."

You can hear the respect these celebrated directors, Gore Verbinski and Phillip Noyce, felt toward their young charges. They are recognizing the *emotional intelligence* of these young artists.

Neil Young had to direct a children's choir for his album *Chrome Dreams II*. In the final track, Neil sings, "So many lost highways that used to lead home/But now they seem used up and gone." The children respond, "We know the way." Neil told them: "You have to pretend that you're singing to your parents and you know how to have world peace. They don't. You have to tell them while they're sleeping, so they know when they wake up. But you can't tell them too loud or they'll wake up too soon."

Jafar Panahi, director of *The White Balloon*, described in an interview how he worked with seven-year-old Aida Mohammadkhani: "I knew immediately Aida could play this character, yet I decided to test her. I forbade her to do something and made it impossible for her not to do it; then I scolded her and she started to cry. I said to her, 'See how easy it is for me to make you cry? But I don't want to do it that way because it makes you unhappy, and I want us to have another kind of relationship. I suggest we look into each other's eyes every time you have to cry in the film, and when I start to cry, you cry.' She didn't believe it would work, but the first few times we looked at each other we cried together, and then she cried alone."

How Young Actors Approach Their Craft

Abigail Breslin was described by her mother in a *Daily Variety* interview: "In her own personal life she's a very empathetic person and she feels things very deeply." Abigail told the *LA Times* that while shooting the scene in *Little Miss Sunshine* when Grandpa Ed (Alan Arkin) dies, "I thought about my grandpa. He passed away, so I was thinking about him."

Quvenzhané Wallis said of the set of *Beasts of the Southern Wild*: "You have to be serious, but you also have to have fun. I tell jokes, I laugh with the people on set, I play with the director. Then I try to pay attention and see what I have to do. When I need to cry, I think of very sad things, mostly about animals. My favorite animal is a polar bear. They're going extinct, and I really don't want that to happen."

Drew Barrymore, on *Inside the Actors Studio*, said that when Spielberg needed her to cry, "He told me that E.T. was going to go away and that just did it for me."

These young actors seem to be working "from the inside out," allowing personal connections to drive their performances. On the other hand, *Atonement* director Joe Wright, in a *Daily Variety* interview, said this about Saoirse Ronan's acting method: "There's no sense of her dragging it up from inside—there's no sense of emotional recall in her. It's all the projection of her imagination and an act of empathy . . . She's so unlike Briony in real life, except they both have an extraordinary imagination."

No matter how a young actor works, she benefits from *connection* with her director. Keke Palmer, speaking of director Doug Atkinson during press interviews for *Akeelah and the Bee*: "I really like him because when he's directing he is almost Akeelah, because when he was a boy he played scrabble and he was an excellent speller. It's really good working with him because he tells me a lot of things I wouldn't know. He's very patient and he tells me to make it real."

Atkinson learned to adapt his ideas to Palmer's reality. His description of Palmer, on the DVD commentary: "She is like Akeelah—very, very smart, and feels things deeply." He observed in rehearsal that she was probably more fearless than the character. At one point he said to her, "It's like you're about to get on the scariest roller coaster ride of all time," and she rejoined, "But I like roller coasters!" So he abandoned the roller coaster metaphor and said to her, "When you're walking in, you're really scared. Your heart's beating more and more."

Traumatic Material

Lenny Abrahamson: "Children frequently know and don't know at the same time. They are aware of aspects of the world that are shadowy and they choose not to engage with them." He said Tremblay understood the story of Jack and his mom thus: "Well, I live in this room with my mum and we're kept there by this nasty man." Said Abrahamson, "We just told the story like that to him. Exactly like any number of fairytales." Tremblay was told to be very quiet in the wardrobe so the nasty man would not find him, but there was no need for him to be told anything about rape.

In one of Joseph Gordon-Levitt's early feature films, *Mysterious Skin*, he played one of two teenagers whose traumatic past is depicted in flashbacks to an event when the boys were eight. In an interview for *Radiofree.com,* Gordon-Levitt reported that director Gregg Araki "went to extraordinary lengths to keep the boys [the eight-year-old actors in the flashbacks] absolutely ignorant of what the movie was. He wrote false scripts that told a totally different story that were just for them—contrived situations for them to end up playing the moment that he needed. And then he would cut that up with other stuff that he shot when they weren't there so that it creates an illusion of child abuse."

In every interview for *Hounddog,* director Deborah Kampmeier stressed that the rape of the child played by Dakota Fanning was achieved in the edit, not on the set. "You have a child yelling 'Stop it!' and only when you put that next to an image of a boy unzipping his pants do you see that it's rape."

Kasi Lemmons says Jurnee Smollett was never actually on set of *Eve's Bayou* while they were shooting the disturbing events that Eve witnesses. Smollett was told that Eve sees two people kissing. (Actually they were fucking.) Jenji Kohan, showrunner of HBO's *Weeds,* said in an *LA Times* interview that it was routine to shoot scenes with children separately if they involved adult actors in, for instance, a sex scene. "Once the show is cut together," she said, "it will look pretty bad."

Jennifer Fox has reported in numerous interviews, including for *Collider.com* and NPR's *Fresh Air,* that the "sex scenes" between Jason Ritter and Isabelle Nélisse in HBO's *The Tale* were created entirely with magic directing tools. She said, "Having gone through my own experience, a film that would traumatize another child would not have been worth making." Jennifer was happy to follow every rule of the Screen Actors Guild and the State of Louisiana, where they shot. Even though Nélisse was old enough to understand the story, she was kept protected on set. For the close-ups of Jenny's response to the pain of being entered by the predator, Fox says, "We rehearsed totally non-sexual cues. I'd say, 'Act like a bee is stinging you. What would it be like if a dog was chasing you? What kind of face would you make if you had just licked salt?' And then we cut that with shots of Jason Ritter as Bill with an adult body-double."

It takes patience and commitment to protect the children in your care on set. It may help if you remember that a theme of films with young protagonists is often exactly that: the protection of children.

Young Teens

Young teens are vulnerable and, at the same time, wise. Guillermo del Toro, who originally envisioned Ofelia (*Pan's Labyrinth*) as a girl of eight or nine, rewrote the script when he found Ivana Baquero, who was twelve. He told an interviewer from the *LA Times* that he didn't consider it a sacrifice. It allowed him to add thematic nuances that might have been too challenging for an eight-year-old, about death, birth, and the nature of existence itself.

Older Teens

Adolescents are attuned to any hint of condescension from adults; if you approach them with any kind of fakery, they will bust you. Talk to them as equals, with complete transparency. But remember: They are less defended than adults and still in the grip of a struggle with what feels like life-or-death stakes to set boundaries that will allow them to function in the world. They can become self-conscious and mannered at the drop of a hat. A teen may think it would be cool to be in a movie—until they get to the set and realize their friends might see them in the finished film—and then shut down. Even an experienced adolescent actor can panic when required to kiss a girl or boy on camera, or disrobe, even partially. It's important to give them agency. Rather than browbeating them for reneging on their agreement to play the scene as written, have a contingency plan for shooting it from more protected angles.

Gain their trust and respect on a personal level. You could say, privately, to a young actor who is nervous about a kissing scene, "When I was your age, I had never kissed a girl/boy." Or, "I had kissed [truthful number of girls or boys], but never in front of other people, like we're asking you to do now." And then, perhaps: "I can understand if it feels weird, and if you need me to, I'll change it or shoot around it. But—I was thinking, if you're feeling awkward, maybe the character is feeling awkward too? I know this character seems confident, but maybe inside he's as nervous as you are."

A director is in a position to change the trajectory of a young actor's career, or even inject themselves into the young person's psychological development—for better or worse. Make sure you are coming from a higher purpose, that the story you are telling has genuine emotional and spiritual meaning.

Invite them to find their own higher purpose. When she was eighteen, America Ferrara played Ana in *Real Women Have Curves*. In a climactic scene from the film, directed by Patricia Cardoso and adapted from a play by Josefina López, Ana strips off her blouse and pants, and dances around the factory in underwear. Asked in interviews about this scene, she replied: "When I feel like I've spoken for a lot of voices that never get heard, it's worth the embarrassment, and then it turns into pride."

Commit To Them

Once you have taken a child on an emotional journey with you, you have involved yourself in their emotional development. You are now, forever, in their life. It's important to accept responsibility for that.

Drew Barrymore has said, "Steven [Spielberg] was the first adult I'd ever met who didn't patronize kids, who treated them like adults, with total respect and love. He said, 'You can't act your character, you have to *be* your character'—the most important lesson I've ever learned in all of my years of doing this." When the film was done, he became a mentor and almost godfather, and never deserted her.

What About Older Actors?

Older actors can panic about whether they have the endurance for long days on a film set. Senior actors may have lost their relish for demanding roles. If they tell you they're not sure they have the stamina for a lead role, believe them. A veteran actor, who knows the grueling hours of a normal shooting day, will know whether or not they are up to a workday of twelve or more hours. They may need a shorter workday in order to maintain their vitality and focus. If they struggle with lines, ask them if they'd like to be fed their lines via an earpiece or cue cards.

But there's a crazy upside to working with older actors. They have little use for mannerisms or actor's ego. The fact that they are nearing the veil of mortality may make their reasons for taking a role more raw—primal. In 2006, Peter O'Toole played his last leading role in *Venus,* directed by Roger Michell. O'Toole told Michell that at the age of 74, he wanted to do his own stunts, because afterwards he "felt young again."

Andrew Wagner, director of *Starting Out in the Evening,* disclosed in an *LA Times* interview that Frank Langella was open and willing to "strip himself bare in an effort to link up with the loneliness and longing and the disappointment of the character. He was adamant [in his intention to] give a performance that was more closely aligned to *being* and *existing* rather than acting. He understood that at this moment in his career he could give a performance on skill, virtuosity and mastery alone, but those were the very things he wanted to abandon. He wanted to tap into the humanity of this man." Langella himself put it this way: "The older I get, the more the men I play inhabit me in ways that they didn't as much as when I was younger. I just *become* them."

During an interview for CBS, Candice Bergen said of performing in her 70s, "We've finished the bulk of our lives. We're more able to engage in a kind of more brutal honesty."

Actors are called upon to explore the deepest reaches of human longing and human frailty—often they have more self-awareness than the general population. It can happen that the older they get, the closer they approach the essentials of life. Almost like the unforced, unguarded charisma of children.

CHAPTER TWELVE

Comedy

Humor is deeply important to the human condition—it helps us survive dark and painful moments, as well as the daily drudge of routine. Artistically, a connection to the darker side of human behavior is an asset, not just for directing dramatic material, but also for directing comedy—because comedy arises from our shared humanity, and humanity includes pain. I love comedy: its risk-taking; its truth-telling; its revelation of the absurdity of life. The comedic sensibility is all about surprise, incongruity, and subversion of the socially acceptable.

Everyone has a sense of humor—a connection to the absurdity of life. For far too many of us, it's buried in the drone of the ordinary mundanities of living—or stifled by trauma. How do we encourage "the funny" in ourselves? I learned about making people laugh when I was young, as a survival technique. I refined my understanding of comedy by reading, rereading, studying, teaching, and seeing every production I could find of Samuel Beckett's *Waiting for Godot.*

As a young actor in Berkeley, California in the 1970s, I signed up for a Charlie Chaplin class, because I had never seen a Chaplin movie all the way through. I drove into San Francisco once a week for a film and lecture series. It's not enough to passively watch others be funny—you need to study your comedic heroes. Their skills of timing and invention seem ineffable, but in fact, they can be studied and learned.

When you steal, steal from the best. To create a moment of physical comedy while lifting a water jug in the film *Secretary,* director Steven Shainberg suggested to Maggie Gyllenhaal, "Let's do Buster Keaton here."

If you want to direct comedy, take a comedy improv class. It's hard to feel confident that you understand comedy unless you experience it as a performer in front of live audiences. Enjoy the thrill of getting a laugh—it's fully as addictive as the gasp, in a dramatic moment, of an audience holding their breath.

Faster, Louder, Funnier

All the tools in this book apply to comedy. But there are also special skills and techniques that apply specifically to comedy. As a young actor I was taught these three rules of comedy: *Louder. Faster. Funnier.* They sound like obnoxious commands to produce *result,* so let me deconstruct them to their truth.

Louder. Comedy requires energy. It's not about shouting every line. But comedy does depend on an underlying rhythm of actors "topping" each other—check out Stan Laurel and Oliver Hardy (Samuel Beckett's favorite comic duo)—or Lucy and Ethel. "Topping" can happen with an escalation of intention and volume—or, just as often, with a sudden *drop* in energy. This is sometimes called "coming in under"—also known as a "dry" or "deadpan" delivery of a zinger or punch line. Like Steve Martin or Tina Fey.

Faster refers to timing and pace. *Timing* means knowing when to pause and when to plough through *until it's time to pause.* In other words, sometimes it's funnier to pause; sometimes it's funnier not to pause. Timing involves a relationship to the audience—good instincts for timing are rarely perfected without working in front of live audiences, via experience in theater, sketch comedy, or as a stand-up.

Pace means picking up cues—essential for comedy—for instance, the speed of the dialogue in *The Marvelous Mrs. Maisel* or really any television comedy. It takes skill for an actor to pull off this rat-a-tat-tat pace without losing the meaning of the scene. Focusing on *intention* is always crucial.

Activities can have pace as well. Taking a reeeeally long time to sign your name to a document—or to "address the ball" à la Art Carney as Ed Norton in *The Honeymooners*—will always crack me up.

Funnier demands risk. True comic invention is a dangerous business, requiring headlong, uncensored access to the subconscious. Clowning is a serious and noble profession. Great comedic actors expose the most chaotic reaches of their imaginations. I believe it's fair to say that Robin Williams and Jonathan Winters made the world a little bit safer for the rest of us.

Funnier brings up the principle of *incongruity*. Like how anger can be funny when it makes no sense to be angry. Or how someone who is overly calm can be funny in a situation where it makes no sense to be calm. If a character is carrying on about losing his pack of chewing gum *as if* he has lost an envelope containing a thousand dollars, that might be funny. *Funnier* translates into opposites. Choosing an intention that is *opposite* to the apparent meaning of a line is a comedic technique that rarely fails.

Funnier is when the actor knows that people are irrational—and lets himself take the risk of looking foolish. *Funnier* calls for higher stakes. Comedy is just like drama—only worse. Misplacing a favorite pencil is a bigger disaster in a comedy than a drama—a bigger disaster emotionally, that is. In a drama, the misplaced pencil could be a plot element triggering dire consequences. In comedy, the misplaced pencil is an outsized *emotional* disaster, in that the character's sense of loss or even betrayal may far exceed the actual value of the pencil.

The purpose of rehearsal for comedy is warming up relationships and warming up comedic chops. *Incongruity* feels weird—even wrong—if you're not used to it. So, an actor who hasn't done comedy—or hasn't done it lately—uses rehearsal time to warm up their okay-ness with looking foolish.

More Principles of Comedy

Set up gags. Every gag line needs a straight line—the punchline needs a setup. Comedy used to be dominated by the terms "straight man" and "funny man"—George Burns was the straight man for Gracie Allen, Carl Reiner for Sid Caesar and later Mel Brooks, Dan Aykroyd for John Belushi. Like the language, the concept itself is somewhat old-fashioned, but it can come in handy.

In the *Seinfeld* episode "The Library," Jerry is flat-out the straight man or setup person for Mr. Bookman. Jerry feeds setups, one after another, to Philip Baker Hall so Hall can top Jerry with the payoffs—the jokes, or gags.

LeBron James was cast in his first acting job in *Trainwreck,* directed by Judd Apatow. He played himself—LeBron James. The premise was already charming—that LeBron James was giving relationship advice to his best friend, a prominent orthopedic surgeon played by Bill Hader. In his scenes with James, Hader played meticulously "straight"—setting James up with every line—so James could shine as the naturally funny person he is.

Jokes can be wordless. In Ace Ventura's battle with the bubble wrap, you could say the bubble wrap is the straight man for Jim Carrey's Ace.

Sometimes there's a "straight man/funny man" template for the whole show. As the central character in *30 Rock,* Tina Fey tended to give the setups to all the wackier second bananas. In Liz Lemon's scenes with her boss Jack Donaghy, Fey fed the straight lines for Alec Baldwin's zingers. This format had been established by Mary Tyler Moore some forty years earlier: Mary tirelessly fed the setups to Ed Asner's Mr. Grant.

Schitt's Creek is a madcap show in which every character in the Rose family tops each other with the funny—except one. At the 2020 Emmys, Eugene Levy said, "I guess it's kind of ironic that the straightest role I've ever played lands me an Emmy for a comedy series." He was acknowledging that his character, Johnny Rose, functioned as the "straight man" for Moira (Catherine O'Hara), David (Dan Levy), Alexis (Annie Murphy), and Johnny's nemesis Roland (Chris Elliot). The only times Eugene Levy got to go over the top were his scenes opposite Emily Hampshire as the unflappable Stevie. Stevie gets her laughs not by *topping* but by *coming in under*.

In all the *Seinfeld* scenes containing the four central characters, there is no straight person. They riff off the roles of straight and funny for each other so seamlessly that you can barely tell who is setting up the gag and who is paying it off. This also happens when Tina Fey pairs with Amy Poehler—for instance, on SNL or award-show host appearances—and in *Broad City* scenes with Ilana Glazer and Abbi Jacobson. Or *Key & Peele* sketches with Keegan-Michael Key and Jordan Peele.

Listening. Comedy shines when there is ensemble playing. The actors play off each other—a ping-pong effect. The engaged interactions between Christina Applegate and Linda Cardellini in Netflix's *Dead to Me*—or between either one of them and any of the other characters—creates their impeccable pace and timing, and turns every scene into a jewel.

Always play comedy for real. Annie Murphy has said that *Schitt's Creek* showrunner Dan Levy insisted that at all times the over-the-top behavior of the characters be rooted in realities of pain and confusion embedded in the emotional situations and relationships.

If the character is flipping out over his missing pencil, that outsized expression of loss or betrayal must be every bit as real and truthful at its emotional core as is required for the most realistic drama. At the center of comedy is real pain. In a *Hollywood Reporter* interview, Dean Parisot said of directing *Galaxy Quest*, "I see comedy as tragedy, so I looked at the film as a drama that happened to be funny."

A light touch. You need to make it real, but you also need to give the audience space to breathe—so they can laugh. Let the human situations be serious, but *don't get self-serious.* Allow yourself to expect the audience to get the joke. Meryl Streep brings a subtly playful undertone to her role in *The Devil Wears Prada* by allowing herself to enjoy Miranda's intention to *belittle* everyone.

Authenticity. Taika Waititi is a master at eliciting performances that are comedic and heartbreaking all at once. In a Q&A, he asserted that the minister's sermon in *Hunt for the Wilderpeople* actually happened. Later, in a private conversation, I asked him about it: "I was at that funeral," he told me! As ridiculous as it seemed, it was authentic.

People are essentially foolish and life is essentially absurd. Comedy requires of actors a willingness to look foolish. Comedy requires a director to support and protect actors in that risk-taking. Comedy requires all storytellers to appreciate the absurd in human endeavor—without falling into cynicism. Viewing life through the lens of its absurdities is *not* the same as deciding that life is meaningless.

Judd Apatow and Paul Feig encourage actors to improvise while the camera is running. Rob Reiner has the chops to offer actors specific comedy advice—like whether it's likely that there will be a bigger laugh if the actor holds a microsecond longer before giving the punch line, or when it might work stronger to come in "under" instead of topping. Any director who has *the comedic touch*—who knows when to give permission to take a bigger risk and can detect opportunities for opposites and incongruities—is a blessing to the world. But—the techniques and gadgetry of comedy must always be in service of the storytelling—of which the director is the guardian. Always look for the humor in a dramatic script and the pain that is underneath comedy.

One last piece of advice. Edit. Be ruthless. If it's not funny, cut it.

Epilogue

"To dig deeply into the way things are, through people, is what I like, and what the people who work with me like also. To find out the delicate balance between living and dying. I mean, I think that's the only subject there is."—**John Cassavetes**

A student told me he'd been at a party and had the good fortune to be seated next to one of the Coen brothers; I can't remember now which one. The young director asked Ethan (or Joel) if he would give him just one tip, one secret to help him in his own career. Joel (or Ethan) looked at him and said, "Where were you born? . . . How different is your hometown now from when you lived there? . . . Do you have brothers and sisters? . . . Tell me about your relationship with them . . ."

The young director had politely replied to all these questions, but as he was telling me this story, his voice was thick with misery and resentment: *Why couldn't his hero have given him even one piece of actionable advice?*

I knew my student desperately needed comfort and validation, but I had to tell him the truth: "He answered you perfectly. He gave you something precious, a secret tip that is central to his art and his success. He demonstrated for you the best advice for any storyteller—that you should be interested in everyone you meet."

I don't know if there is a collective unconscious, but I know that if there is one, it is only of use to you if you awaken it—by involving yourself in the world around you. Surrender to all the arts. Don't limit yourselves to films and music. Read novels, poetry; go to museums. Watch documentaries. Immerse yourself in nature.

Study science and history. Look into yourself, your own emotional history; disclose it to others. Interview your friends and find out their life stories. Allow yourself to detect subtext in your daily interactions. *Be interested in everything.*

Study films—but really *study* them—put in the time to deconstruct and examine, shot by shot, the skills and choices of the filmmakers you admire. Don't just peruse films in order to sort them into piles: "I like this"; "I don't like that." Take hold of the films you care about and examine them intimately. Learn from them.

Daydream. Eavesdrop. Do things you've never done before. Figure out how to become a person to whom others tell their secrets. Ask the big questions about the human heart and what makes people tick. Embrace your own past, including its secrets and terrors. Allow characters to take on a life of their own, a life outside the camera frame. Let characters do things you didn't know they were going to do.

Many of the directors who have read my books or studied with me think that my intention is to protect the actors. I do love actors. They are imperfect creatures and their imperfections are dear to me. If you don't feel the same way about actors, but you want to direct movies, you need to do something about that—take an acting class, befriend actors, talk to them, figure them out.

But I'm going to tell you a secret—my true intention has always been to protect the characters. When I was teaching my Acting for Directors workshop, sure, I wanted the directors to walk in the shoes of actors, but secretly I was even more committed to the idea that directors should walk in the shoes of characters. As an actor, as a teacher, as a child, I have been rescued by characters in stories—over and over. I owe them.

All learning is two steps forward, one step back. Get excited about failure. I know I'm taking a big chance when I give you my secrets in a book, where I can't respond to your questions and can't watch and monitor your use of them. Any of these ideas can misfire. Once a student reported to me that her first attempt to use the techniques from my workshops was distressing. She said, "The tools you gave us were power tools; they were like a sharp-edged sword. When we used them incorrectly we cut ourselves." Find a way to practice the use of these tools in a safe situation. Adjust them. Make them your own. Don't operate out of fear. Don't say, "I had no choice."

In his book *Outliers,* Malcolm Gladwell proposes that, in order to feel confident in your field, you need 10,000 hours of practice. Others have pointed out that, preferably, this should be supervised practice. I have found this to be true. Reach out—mentors and teachers surround you. Ask for their help. Listen to them.

I don't mean that you are not allowed to make a movie until you've put in 10,000 hours of practice directing actors—what I want you to understand from the "10,000 hours" trope is this: *You don't learn this stuff just by being exposed to the information.*

The Internet has spoiled us. It's easy to feel that if we've found a site that's engaging and well-written, we now know and understand the information it offers. You may not want to hear this but I need to tell you: You don't learn how to be a director by watching movies. You need to put yourself in the mix. You need to try, fail, learn—get your hands dirty. The good news is that *learning* can become a way of life, a path of joy.

Characters have *objectives;* people do too. On some days a perfectly valid objective for a director might be to get through the morning without collapsing. But directors can unconsciously fall into sterile objectives like "to not make a mistake," or "to protect my ego." Always put the work first. What is your objective toward the audience? If you want them to see how smart you are, how sensitive; if you want them to be a witness to your pain; if you want to indoctrinate them or punish them or ingratiate yourself to them—then you could be headed for trouble.

Take risks. Give your all. Your creativity is not a bowl with a finite amount in it, which can be emptied, but a natural spring from an unseen, unknowable source. When you give of everything you have, you are priming the pump. If you're not sure what you're doing, don't hold back, be expressive anyway. A breakthrough is then possible. If you play it close to the vest, then you might not get into trouble, but you won't get anywhere else either. Don't try to be a good director—or a good actor—or a good writer. Make the story human. Make the story real. It's not about you, it's about the work.

Don't make a movie just to make a movie. Look for what is odd in the world around you. Look for what is important about human experience. Tell stories about those things. Jane Campion disclosed in a documentary, *The Piano—25 Years On*, that her mother had told her of meeting a woman who severed her own ring finger upon learning that her husband had been unfaithful. This first-person story gave Campion the confidence to write—and direct—the scene in which Alisdair (Sam Neill) maims Ada's (Holly Hunter) hand.

Read these books: *Kazan on Directing, Cassavetes on Cassavetes,* and *Kieślowski on Kieślowski.* I don't mean that you are required to use the techniques of Elia Kazan, John Cassavetes, and Krzysztof Kieślowski—or that you should feel like a failure if you don't reach the same artistic heights as each of them. But their collections of journals and interviews can show you something important—that is, *how deeply* a filmmaker is permitted to dip into his own subconscious, and how much freedom a filmmaker can allow to the inner lives of characters. They can help inspire you to search for the truest truth, in every detail of your work.

Challenge yourself. Prepare exhaustively. Concentrate. Then let it go. Have fun. Aim high, because we are human and we are going to fall short. If your goal is to "get by," then you won't. If your purpose is to give your all and hold out for the truest truth, then, with a little luck, you might get by.

APPENDIX A

VERBS
SHORT LIST, EXPANDED

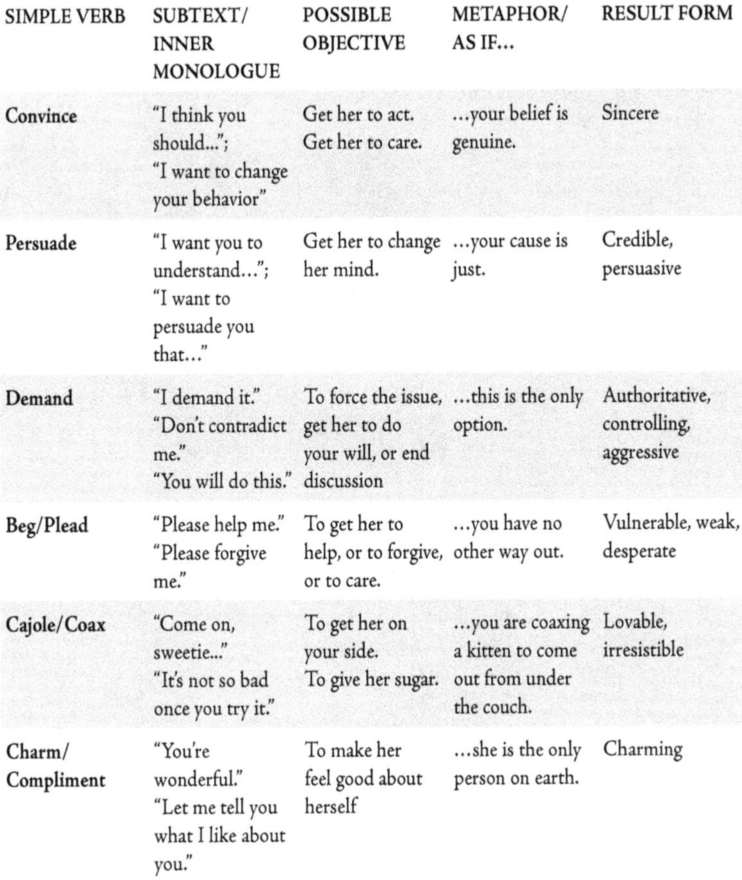

SIMPLE VERB	SUBTEXT/ INNER MONOLOGUE	POSSIBLE OBJECTIVE	METAPHOR/ AS IF...	RESULT FORM
Convince	"I think you should..."; "I want to change your behavior"	Get her to act. Get her to care.	...your belief is genuine.	Sincere
Persuade	"I want you to understand..."; "I want to persuade you that..."	Get her to change her mind.	...your cause is just.	Credible, persuasive
Demand	"I demand it." "Don't contradict me." "You will do this."	To force the issue, get her to do your will, or end discussion	...this is the only option.	Authoritative, controlling, aggressive
Beg/Plead	"Please help me." "Please forgive me."	To get her to help, or to forgive, or to care.	...you have no other way out.	Vulnerable, weak, desperate
Cajole/Coax	"Come on, sweetie..." "It's not so bad once you try it."	To get her on your side. To give her sugar.	...you are coaxing a kitten to come out from under the couch.	Lovable, irresistible
Charm/ Compliment	"You're wonderful." "Let me tell you what I like about you."	To make her feel good about herself	...she is the only person on earth.	Charming

SIMPLE VERB	SUBTEXT/ INNER MONOLOGUE	POSSIBLE OBJECTIVE	METAPHOR/ AS IF...	RESULT FORM
Comfort/Soothe	"Everything will be alright, there's nothing to worry about. I'll take care of you."	To make her feel safe.	...she is surrounded by love.	Protective, warm
Encourage	"You're smart and you're talented and I know you can do it."	To give him faith in himself.	...you have secret knowledge of his potential.	Supportive
Apologize/ Confess	"I'm sorry." "I wronged you."	To get his forgiveness.	...you accept the consequences.	Shame, guilt
Tease/Entertain	"I'm going to have fun with you."	To make him laugh, be silly.	...teasing a child or friend.	Funny, uninhibited
Flirt	"I think you're cute."	To make him blush or smile.	...you can get away with it.	Flirtatious
Seduce	"I need you. I want you. I know you want me."	To make him feel sexy. Get him to make love to you. Get him to buy something.	...you know he wants it.	Sexy
Dazzle	"Wait till you see..!" "You've got to see this!"	To get him as excited about this as you are.	...this is the most wonderful thing in the world.	Excited, animated
Incite/Preach/ Exhort	"Open yourselves to the truth!"	To get him emotionally committed.	...there is nothing more important.	Passionate
Challenge/ Provoke/Goad	"Are you man enough?" "I dare you." "You wanna fight?"	To pick a fight. To get her angry. Get her to hit you.	...she is weak.	Edgy, touchy
Brag	"I deserve recognition for this."	To make her proud of you & your accomplishments.	...it's something you are genuinely proud of.	Self-assured, proud

SIMPLE VERB	SUBTEXT/ INNER MONOLOGUE	POSSIBLE OBJECTIVE	METAPHOR/ AS IF...	RESULT FORM
Complain/ Whine	"It's not fair. Why is it always me? Why doesn't anything ever go right?"	To make her feel sorry for you.	...your problems are worse than anyone else's.	Pathetic
Accuse	"You can't get away with this." "I saw you do it!"	To make her feel ashamed. To get her to apologize.	...she has done wrong.	Righteous, angry
Confront	"I know your game." I see right through you."	To expose her.	...you are in control.	Confrontational
Warn (Nag)	"I'm warning you." "You better not."	To make her worry.	...something awful might happen.	Cautious
Warn (Threaten)	"Watch your step or you'll be sorry"	Get her to back off.	...you have the power to punish.	Threatening
Punish (adult)	"You're a bad person." "I'm through with you."	To make him feel his actions are unforgivable.	...he is beyond redemption.	Harsh, severe
Punish (child)	"You were told not to do this."	Make him see the consequences.	...you are withholding approval.	Disapproving
Ridicule	"You are ridiculous."	To make fun of him, make him feel silly, foolish.	...he is absurd.	Mean
Belittle	as special as you think you are."	To make him feel small.	...he has no value on the planet.	Vicious
Knife	"You hurt me—I will hurt you back."	Make him feel pain.	...you have murderous intent	Rage
Scrutinize	"What is going on behind your social mask?"	Get information you have no right to.	...he is under a microscope	Curious
Pry	"How much money do you make? "How often do you have sex?"	To put him on the spot.	...you have the right to know.	Nosy, invasive

APPENDIX B

Verbs

Longer List, Grouped By Emotional Category

Section I—Common Family/Social/ Business Interactions

REASON AND NEGOTIATION
Inform, explain, speculate, clarify, justify, reason, negotiate, dicker, bargain, haggle, grapple, cut a deal, conspire, brainstorm, hatch a plan, dream up, hammer out thinking together

INFLUENCE
Convince, persuade, sway, give assurance, guide, maneuver, cajole, coax, induce, prevail upon, sweet-talk, hustle

INFLUENCE (STRONGLY)
Plead, beg, entreat, importune, appeal, pray, manipulate

TAKE AUTHORITY
Demand, order, summon, direct, command, compel

GIVE INSTRUCTION
Teach, encourage, instruct, lecture, preach, expound

TAKE ATTENTION
Brag, upstage, bluff, one-up, dramatize, clown, entertain, rant

STAND UP FOR ONESELF
Compete, take charge, set him straight, let him know who's boss, let him have it, show him the door, take him down a peg, fight for yourself

REBELLION
Challenge, defy, rebel, revolt, renounce, reject

CREATE EXCITEMENT, ENTHUSIASM AND RIOT
Incite, exhort, kindle, galvanize, enflame, infuse, thrill, dazzle, electrify, arouse, awaken, engage

GET A RISE OUT OF PEOPLE
Startle, shock, shake up, expose, trigger, disturb, agitate, pester, make waves, rock the boat, barge in, call his bluff

GIVING IN
Accommodate, concede, yield, acquiesce, capitulate, tolerate, apologize, back peddle

EVASION
Hint around, imply, create doubt, make excuses, push away, put up your guard, shut out, dodge, deflect, stonewall, evade, repulse, fake out, string along, beguile, defend against, discourage, turn off

WHINE AND COMPLAIN
Complain, whine, nag, pout, sulk, mope, gripe, wheedle, steer, manipulate

GET INFORMATION THAT MAY NOT BE YOUR BUSINESS
Pry, quiz, interrogate, insinuate, meddle, intrude, invade, encroach, inspect, calculate, diagnose, categorize

Section II—Aggression

Retaliation (for a wrong that has been done)
Accuse, blame, punish, shame, scold, chastise, reproach, reprove, reprimand, condemn, disapprove, point one's finger, retaliate, thrash

CONFRONTATION
Nail, pounce, confront, antagonize, get the jump on, test, invade his space, stare him down, look daggers, one-up, set the record straight, put him in his place

Suppress and Torment (deny another person's freedom and happiness)
Berate, attack, abuse, harass, menace, badger, browbeat, bully, force, intimidate, aggravate, knife, coerce, pressure, persecute, crush, clobber, wallop, violate, rape, castrate, destroy, hammer, suppress, torment, confine, weigh down, poison, subdue, annihilate

Warn and Nag
Warn, admonish, threaten, harangue, remind, nag, find fault, put a damper on

Ridicule and Humiliate
Criticize, ridicule, mock, belittle, discourage, disparage, deflate, dampen, demean, deny, disparage, sneer at, vilify, disrespect, undermine, humiliate, taunt, jeer at, rag on, look down on, make a fool of, talk down to, spit upon

Harassment by unwanted attention
Stalk, hunt, pry, scrutinize

PICK A FIGHT
Goad, bait, prod, provoke, bait, dare, challenge, engage, get his goat, pester, bother, fuss, quibble, contradict, insult, negate, battle, get in the way, interfere

Section III—Affirmation

LIFT UP OTHERS
Encourage, empower, assure, help, foster, nourish, support, boost, bolster, build up, crown, reward, honor, stimulate, enliven, cheer, inspirit, treasure, endorse, champion

GIVE APPROVAL
Affirm, flatter, compliment, reassure, validate, vouch for, salute, applaud, praise, show appreciation, make him feel accepted, make him feel approved of

SHOW FRIENDSHIP AND GOOD WILL
Share, greet, bless, surrender, confide, attend, give attention, entrust, reach out, befriend, cooperate, open up, reminisce

SHOW MERCY AND COMPASSION
Forgive, rescue, heal, comfort, console, care for, take care of, soothe, caress, cherish, hold, touch, defend, grieve

PLACATE AND PACIFY
Placate, pacify, defuse, lull, pamper, indulge, appease, smooth over, enfold, smother, suffocate, overwhelm, kill with kindness

PLAYFUL
Celebrate, tease, tickle, needle, banter, play, please, entertain, clown, amuse, divert, lighten, humor, jolly

SEDUCE AND CHARM
Dote upon, drool over, savor, nuzzle, ogle, hypnotize, lure, tempt, tantalize, seduce, flirt, entice, woo, fondle, charm, flatter, compliment, butter up, spoil, undress, make love

APPENDIX C

Script Analysis Guide For Directors

1) THE PURPOSE OF SCRIPT ANALYSIS

To find your own take on the material, so you can do something original.

To feel relaxed and confident because you are deeply connected to the characters and the story. So that when you get with the actors, you can be present and can see what is in front of you—and build on what the actors are bringing.

Turn psychology into behavior.

Turn attitudes into relationships.

Turn your ideas into moments.

2) QUESTIONS TO START (and REVISIT throughout)

What do you love about the script? What reservations or resistances do you have? What are your concerns? What are the challenges? What could go wrong?

What is the story about? What is it *really* about? What is your *idea?*

Where are you in the script? What is your emotional connection, your "way in"? What is your personal investment, your hook into the story? Why do you care? What do you bring to the table? Why are you the person who should tell it? What is your intention? Why did this project choose you?

Why should the audience care? What is important about the story? Why must it be told?

What is the metaphor? What makes it universal?

Who is the main character? Why are you driven to tell this character's story?

For each character: name three ways you are like this character, and three ways you are not.

What is the tone? What are your visual ideas? What is your sensibility?

What research have you done on the references and topics in the script?

What is your professional goal? What do you want to achieve with this project? What do you want to learn by directing this project? Why do you direct?

3) WHAT'S IN THE SCENE? What CLUES does the script give you, either in dialogue or stage directions?

Imagery

Facts, aka emotional history, circumstances, backstory, biography

Questions

Mysterious Lines

Beats (aka sections, chapters)

Issues

Themes

4) WHAT TO DO NEXT: UNPACKING AND DIGGING

Research. Investigate the references. On the Internet: look up everything, but don't stop there. Find people who know things about the subject matter of the script and meet them, talk to them. Travel, go onsite. Don't limit yourself to the obvious research. Awaken your curiosity.

Unpack the imagery. Investigate the subtext imagery. Free-associate. Make personal associations. Roam around. Allow subconscious associations to surface.

Unpack the emotional history (facts). Make personal associations. Free-associate. Keep doing research. Keep asking questions; let the new facts you uncover lead you to questions.

Embrace questions. Look for what is odd. Don't assume. Ask why. Think of three possible answers for each question. If you can't think of right answers, start with wrong answers.

Mysterious Lines. Find at least three mysterious lines in every scene and perform the "mysterious lines" exercise (three possible meanings) with each of those. If you have more time, keep finding more mysterious lines and perform the exercise with each one. (Note: mysterious lines can be in the stage directions as well as the dialogue.)

Look for clues, not instruction. Reread the script.

The questions and clues are more valuable, more powerful than the answers!

Make a list of themes and issues.

Make a list of the relationships in the story. And the issues in those relationships.

What happens in off-camera scenes?

What are the characters NOT saying?

Keep re-reading the script to find new clues, or to see clues in a different light.

Keep connecting to what you know about life from your own experience and observation.

Keep looking for ways that you may be unconsciously judging any of the characters. Find ways to resolve those judgments.

You need to look for ideas so strong, so real, so true to life that you don't have to consult your notes to remember them, so powerful that *you can't unthink them*. Then, for each powerful, true idea, make yourself consider its opposite. Make yourself come up with another idea that could work just as well—Back-up Plan. Then, a Back-up for your Back-up.

This work can bring you to emotional detail and complexity. It can help you to boil down the scene to its central Emotional Situation, its Emotional Event.

5) CHOICES/TOOLS

The Moment Before

Other Off-Camera Scenes

Through-line Objective. The Need

Intention

Spine

What's at Stake?

A Sense of Obstacle; a Sense of Problem.

Issues. Themes.

Metaphor. The "It's like when . . ." The "As If . . ."

Inner Monologue/mantra/subtext. What does the line mean? What does it *really* mean?

The central Emotional Situation.

The interior imagery—what the character is thinking about/obsessed by—underneath whatever they are saying or doing.

6) SCENE SHAPE and VISION, or IDEA

Beats, also known as sections, or chapters, or scene-lets

Emotional Events, also known as moments, transitions, colors, turning points, power shifts, dramatic moments, comedic moments. Wins and Losses. Conflict.

The Central Emotional Event of the Scene. How is the relationship different at the end of the scene? How does life change irrevocably for the characters in this scene?

What it is about? The core, the central "as if," or metaphor.

Blocking and Physical Activities: the physical life that illuminates emotional events.

What is the shape of the scene?

7) THE WHOLE SCRIPT

What is it about?

Spines of the characters

What is the shape of the story?

8) PERSONAL STORIES

For the three ways you are like or not like each character, find personal stories that illustrate those connections.

Find personal stories that illustrate or illuminate any of the situations and moments of the script.

9) OPPOSITES; THE TECHNIQUE OF THREE POSSIBLE; CURIOSITY

Just a reminder about the power of OPPOSITES and the rescue of the TECHNIQUE OF THREE POSSIBLE. And—the most valuable script analysis tool of all: CURIOSITY.

APPENDIX D

Script Analysis List of Topics

In the Script Analysis and Rehearsal Techniques class that I taught from 1993 to 2015, I would ask the participants to take sheets of paper and title each one with the following headings. Then, we'd make our notes on these pages:

- Facts
- Questions
- Mysterious Lines
- Imagery and Associations
- Inner monologues
- Possible Themes
- Possible Spines
- Central Character and Central Relationships
- Other Possible Choices
    - Backstory ideas
    - Ideas for Through-Line Objectives
    - Verbs
    - Adjustments
    - Subtext
- Research
- Issues
- Physical life / Blocking
- Beats / Transitions
- Events
- Ideas and Insights
- What It's About
- Tone and Style
- Problems / Resistances

Eventually, we'd transfer our notes to a separate page for each character, and a separate page for each scene.

APPENDIX E

Script Analysis Addendum for Actors

Actors can use the same tools and questions as in Appendix D (Script Analysis Guide for Directors). But here are more questions that may be helpful for an actor:

- What are the character's values?
- What are her interests?
- Where is she vulnerable? How can she be hurt? What's at stake for her?
- What is she not saying?
- Whom or what does the character trust?
- Look for ways that the character is facing some unpleasant truth about himself—or refusing to face it.
- Look for ways that he makes mistakes.
- What are his dreams? His hopes? His fears? His longing?
- What is his "soft spot"?
- What has he seen happen to others that he is determined to keep from happening to him?
- What is the character smart about?
- How much self-knowledge does he/she have?
- What is he/she lying about?
- What secrets does he/she have? What is his/her most important secret?
- How does he use his intelligence?
- In what way is this character an artist?
- Is the character protecting himself from pain in his past?
- What hunger drives him? (e.g., hunger for affection, for respect)
- What is he looking for in a mate?
- What makes him laugh?
- What might cause him to lose his sense of humor?
- What is the character's biggest problem? His most immediate problem? Long-term problems? In what ways has he dealt with his problems in the past?

- Whom does he look up to? Does he have a mentor?
- What is the biggest thing that has ever happened to him?
- How is the character different at the end of the script (or scene) than at the beginning?
- What is happening to her for the first time in this scene?
- What is she doing in this scene that she has never done before?
- What is she lying about? To others? To herself?
- How much self-knowledge does she have?
- What are her demons?
- What is her blind spot?
- What is her family history?
- Her educational history?
- His cultural history?
- Financial history?
- Religious history?
- Sexual history?
- Always ask, Why? Why did she tell her sister about the phone call? Why did he leave the door unlocked? There are reasons why characters do things other than the convenience of the plot. Look for things that strike you as odd; embrace them. The questions are more important than the answers.

Don't limit yourself to this list of questions!

Every time you ask one of these or any other questions about the character, ask it also about yourself. And don't forget: The answers to these questions are not a performance! Don't think of your preparation as filling out a form, or crossing tasks off a list. If you can't think of the "right" answer—come up with three wrong answers! If a question doesn't do anything for you, if it doesn't speak to you--skip it and go to the next one. Looking at these questions is a way to aerate your unconscious, to prepare yourself for choices and ideas. And to get you ready so the director and the other actors can have an effect on you. As Meryl Streep has said, the performance does not exist until the other actors are there. The purpose of choices is to get you out of your head, not into your head. For instance, your INNER MONOLOGUE during any given run-through may be different from what you thought it would be when you were preparing—indeed, if you are in the moment, it is *likely* to be different every single time.

APPENDIX F

Text of *The Matrix*, Scene 74

Neo sits beside Trinity in the back. He cannot stop staring as the simple images of the urban street blur past his window like an endless stream of data rushing down a computer screen.

MORPHEUS

Almost unbelievable, isn't it?

Neo nods as the car continues to wind through the crowded city.

NEO

God…

TRINITY

What?

NEO

I used to eat there… Really good noodles.

He is speaking in a whisper, almost as if talking to himself.

NEO

I have these memories, from my entire life but… none of them really happened.

He turns to her.

NEO

What does that mean?

TRINITY

That the Matrix cannot tell you who you are.

NEO

But an Oracle can.

TRINITY

That's different.

NEO

Obviously.

He turns to the window for a moment and then turns back.

NEO

Did you go to her?

TRINITY

Yes.

NEO

What did she tell you?

TRINITY

She told me…

She looks at him and suddenly she is unable to speak or even breathe.

NEO

What?

The car suddenly jerks to a stop.

```
                    MORPHEUS
        We're here. Neo, come with me.

Neo and Morpheus get out of the car. Cypher
looks into the rearview mirror at Trinity.

                    CYPHER
        Here we go again, eh, Trin?

He smiles as she turns to the window.
```

APPENDIX G

Billy Ray's 3x5 Card

1) "Do you know what you WANT with this line?"
2) Make them affect each other, concentrate on each other.
3) Give adjustments to the off-camera actor.
4) Verbs not adjectives. Intentions, not emotions.
5) Put them in the pre-scene world. "Where were you two minutes ago?"
6) Enforce eye contact. Make sure they're listening to each other.
7) "Don't be afraid to do less."
8) *Camera captures subtext*—that which the character does NOT want to reveal.
9) Give them as-ifs and what-ifs, give them physical tasks.
10) Get their concentration OFF the words.
11) Always tell actors the truth.
12) Celebrate mistakes.
13) Admit when you don't know something.
14) Let them try silly accents, wrong choices. Allow them to have FUN.
15) Give them sensory input: sights, sounds, smells . . .
16) Let them know the WRITER IS NOT IN THE ROOM.
17) "If you are not affecting him/her, what else can we try?"
18) Duck the credit for everything that goes well, take the blame for everything that goes badly.

Bonus: Say please and thank you. A lot.

Index of Selected Names and Titles

About the Author

Judith Weston has been teaching directors, actors, and writers for over 35 years. She lives in Los Angeles, where she ran a studio from 1985 to 2015, but her reach is international—having taught in Europe, Canada, Africa, Asia, and Australia/New Zealand.

The original paperback of *Directing Actors* has been a consistent best-seller since it was published in 1996, and has been translated into twelve languages. Her second book, *The Film Director's Intuition,* is precious to many as a deeper dive into script analysis and rehearsal techniques. There's an audiobook version of *Directing Actors,* revised and updated in 2019 from the original paperback, and read by Judith.

This *25th Anniversary Edition* is a long-awaited expansion and update to the original *Directing Actors.* She's put everything she's got into it and hopes it will be helpful to both new and experienced directors.

Judith consults privately with directors and writer-directors, and can be available to give Zoom seminars for schools and organizations. For more information, including links to her social media presence, please visit her website:

www.judithweston.com

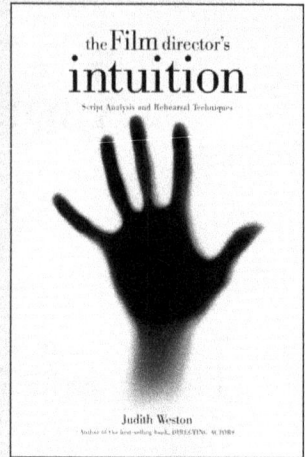

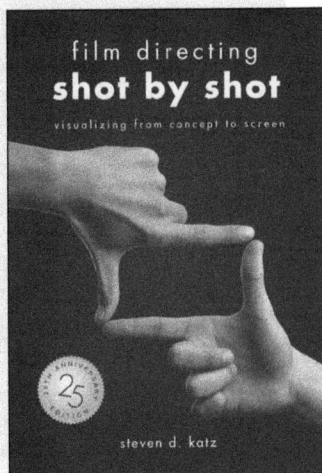

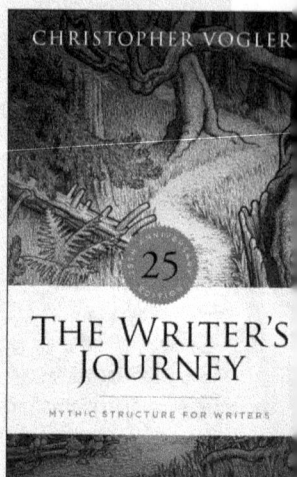

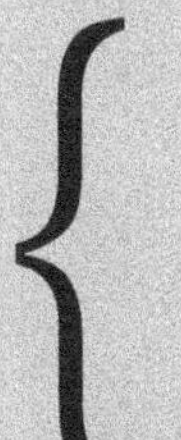

THE MYTH OF MWP

In a dark time, a light bringer came along, leading the curious and the frustrated to clarity and empowerment. It took the well-guarded secrets out of the hands of the few and made them available to all. It spread a spirit of openness and creative freedom, and built a storehouse of knowledge dedicated to the betterment of the arts.

The essence of the Michael Wiese Productions (MWP) is empowering people who have the burning desire to express themselves creatively. We help them realize their dreams by putting the tools in their hands. We demystify the sometimes secretive worlds of screenwriting, directing, acting, producing, film financing, and other media crafts.

By doing so, we hope to bring forth a realization of 'conscious media' which we define as being positively charged, emphasizing hope and affirming positive values like trust, cooperation, self-empowerment, freedom, and love. Grounded in the deep roots of myth, it aims to be healing both for those who make the art and those who encounter it. It hopes to be transformative for people, opening doors to new possibilities and pulling back veils to reveal hidden worlds.

MWP has built a storehouse of knowledge unequaled in the world, for no other publisher has so many titles on the media arts. Please visit www.mwp.com where you will find many free resources and a 25% discount on our books. Sign up and become part of the wider creative community!

Onward and upward,

Michael Wiese
Publisher/Filmmaker

www.ingramcontent.com/pod-product-compliance
Lightning Source LLC
Chambersburg PA
CBHW070405100426
42812CB00005B/1640

* 9 7 8 1 6 1 5 9 3 3 3 5 8 *